Clashing Views
on Controversial
Educational Issues

6th edition

Clashing Views
on Controversial
Educational Issues

6th edition

Edited, Selected, and with Introductions by

James Wm. Noll
University of Maryland

The Dushkin Publishing Group, Inc.

For Stephanie and Sonja

Taking Sides ® is a registered trademark of
The Dushkin Publishing Group, Inc.

Library of Congress Catalog Card Number:
90-84855
Manufactured in the United States of America
Sixth Edition, First Printing
ISBN: 0-87967-932-8

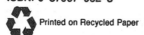 Printed on Recycled Paper

The Dushkin Publishing Group, Inc.
Sluice Dock, Guilford, CT 06437

PREFACE

Controversy is the basis of change and, hopefully, improvement. Its lack signifies the presence of complacency, the authoritarian limitation of viewpoint expression, or the absence of realistic alternatives to the existing circumstances. An articulate presentation of a point of view on a controversial matter breathes new life into abiding human and social concerns. Controversy prompts re-examination and, perhaps, renewal.

Education is controversial. Arguments over the most appropriate aims, the most propitious means, and the most effective control have raged over the centuries. Particularly in the United States, where the systematic effort to provide education has been more democratically dispersed and more varied than elsewhere, educational issues have been contentiously debated. Philosophers, psychologists, sociologists, professional educators, lobbyists, government officials, school boards, local pressure groups, taxpayers, parents, and students have all voiced their views.

This book aims to present opposing or sharply varying viewpoints on issues, both fundamental and of current concern, in the field of education. Those which address fundamental issues, such as the purposes of education, the control of schooling, the moral development of the young, and the establishment of a productive learning atmosphere, are taken from the works of prominent and seminal thinkers whose ideas are much discussed.

With the background provided by the examination of arguments on fundamental issues, the student is better prepared to analyze specific issues currently undergoing heated debate. These include "choice" plans for schools, home schooling, preventing urban dropout, early childhood education, whole-language versus basal readers, cultural literacy, measurement-driven instruction, discipline, tracking, cooperative learning, mainstreaming, bilingual education, sex education, and teacher testing.

I have made every effort to select views from a wide range of thinkers—philosophers, psychologists, sociologists, professional educators, political leaders, historians, researchers, and gadflies.

Each issue is accompanied by an *introduction*, which sets the stage for debate, and each issue concludes with a *postscript* that summarizes the debate, considers other views on the issue, and suggests additional readings. By combining the material in this volume with the informational background provided by a good introductory textbook, the student should be prepared to address the actual problems confronting the schools today.

My hope is that the students will find challenges in the material presented here—provocations that will inspire them to better understand the roots of educational controversy, to attain a greater awareness of possible alternatives in dealing with the various issues, and to stretch their personal powers of creative thinking in the search for more promising resolutions of the problems.

i

Changes to this edition This sixth edition represents a considerable revision. There are six completely new issues: *Should "Choice" Plans Include Private Schools?* (Issue 9); *Is Home Schooling a Viable Alternative?* (Issue 10); *Can Schools Prevent Urban Dropouts?* (Issue 11); *Should Whole-Language Replace Basal Readers?* (Issue 13); *Do Group Rewards Undermine Cooperative Learning?* (Issue 19); and *Are Current Sex Education Programs Lacking in Moral Guidance?* (Issue 21). In addition, the affirming selection for Issue 20 (*Is Bilingual Education Justifiable as a Policy?*) has been replaced in order to update the position.

Supplements An *Instructor's Manual with Test Questions* (multiple-choice and essay) is available through the publisher for the instructor using *Taking Sides* in the classroom. A general guidebook, which discusses methods and techniques for integrating the pro-con approach into any classroom setting, is also available.

Acknowledgments I was greatly assisted in my work by the suggestions from the many users of *Taking Sides* who responded to a questionnaire sent by the publisher. Their comments have enhanced the quality of this edition of the book, and are reflected in the six new issues as well as the issues that have been retained. Special thanks go to those who responded with specific suggestions for the sixth edition:

Fred Abel
Berry College

Pat Bacon
University of Kentucky

Francis Curtiss
University of Scranton

Joanne B. Engel
Willamette University

James Garofalo
Aquinas College

George D. Gates
Idaho State University

Arley Howdsen
California State University, Chico

Lynn Hutchinson
Walsh College

Catherine Jarjisian
Oberlin College

Fintan Kavanagh
Marywood College

Randy Michaelis
Whitworth College

Bernard Miller
Rider College

John Pappandrea
William Rainey Harper College

Roy Pellicano
Brooklyn College

Basil J. Reppas
University of Northern Iowa

Evelyn Sayers
Indiana University/Purdue University, Indianapolis

Donald S. Seckinger
University of Wyoming

James Wm. Noll
College Park, MD

CONTENTS IN BRIEF

CONTENTS

Noted philosopher John Dewey suggests a reconsideration of the traditional approaches to schooling, giving fuller attention to the social development of the learner and the quality of his total experience. Robert M. Hutchins, former chancellor of the University of Chicago, argues for a liberal arts education geared to the development of intellectual powers.

Writer and editor Clifton Fadiman argues for standardized subject matter, which rescues the learner from triviality and capriciousness. Educator John Holt feels that an imposed curriculum damages the individual and usurps a basic human right to select one's own path of development.

Associate editor Richard Rodriguez presents the case that the United States, as a society of immigrants, must be bound together by knowledge of the dominant cultural heritage. Associate professor of secondary education Alba A. Rosenman counters with an antiassimilationist argument for augmenting cultural diversity.

Professor of education Lawrence Kohlberg outlines his theory which, following Dewey and Piaget, links values to cognitive growth. Professor of education Edward A. Wynne feels that the schools, under the influence of Kohlberg and others, have abandoned our educational traditions.

Professor of education R. Freeman Butts warns that current efforts to redefine the relationship between religion and schooling are eroding the Constitution's intent. Professor of political science Robert L. Cord offers a more accomodating interpretation of this intent.

Noted psychologist and proponent of behaviorism B. F. Skinner critiques the concept of "inner freedom" and links learning and motivation to the influence of external forces. Noted psychologist and educator Carl R. Rogers offers the "humanistic" alternative to behaviorism, insisting on the reality of subjective forces in human motivation.

David Guterson, a public school teacher, explains why he and his wife
educate their own children at home. Professor of educational administration
William Konnert and public school principal Josef Wendel raise legal and
logistical issues concerning this option.

Professor of education and former school superintendent Larry Cuban offers
some basic assumptions and specific guidelines for dealing with the urban
dropout problem. Paul Woodring, an emeritus professor of educational
psychology, attacks the conventional wisdom and turns his attention outside
the school.

Siegfried and Therese Engelmann, as advocates of teaching academic skills
to preschoolers, offer a program through which parents can shape the
learning environment of their children. David Elkind, a leading critic of
"superkid" programs, insists that formal instruction does not fit the preschooler's unique modes of learning and may actually cause damage to very
young children.

Author and lecturer Alfie Kohn argues that group rewards decrease individual motivation and performance. Research professor Robert E. Slavin counters that a system of rewards encourages subject matter mastery.

Department of Policy Studies chairman Alberto M. Ochoa and personnel employee Yvonne Caballero-Allen examine the fallacies in recent attacks on bilingual education efforts. Professor of history of education Diane Ravitch feels that research on bilingual education is inconclusive and is often misinterpreted by zealots.

Professor of education Kevin Ryan argues for movement toward a firmer moral grounding of sex education programs. Peter Scales, a leading advocate of sexuality education, feels that current objections to these programs are unwarranted.

Gregory R. Anrig, president of the Educational Testing Service, makes the
case for the National Teacher Examination as a legitimate tool for measuring
qualifications. Linda Darling-Hammond, the director of the RAND Corporation's Education and Human Resources Program, provides examples of what
she feels are serious deficiencies in this type of test.

INTRODUCTION

Ways of Thinking About Educational Issues
James Wm. Noll

CULTURAL AND SOCIAL DYNAMICS

Concern about the quality of education has been expressed by philosophers, politicians, and parents for centuries. There has been a perpetual and unresolved debate regarding the definition of education, the relationship between school and society, the distribution of decision-making power in educational matters, and the means for improving all aspects of the educational enterprise.

In recent decades, the growing influence of thinking drawn from the humanities and the behavioral and social sciences has brought about the development of interpretive, normative, and critical perspectives which have sharpened the focus on educational concerns. These perspectives have allowed scholars and researchers to closely examine the contextual variables, value orientations, and philosophical and political assumptions which shape both the status quo and reform efforts.

The study of education involves the application of many perspectives to the analysis of "what is and how it got that way," and "what can be and how we can get there." Central to such study are the prevailing philosophical assumptions, theories, and visions which find their way into real-life educational situations. The application situation, with its attendant political pressures, sociocultural differences, community expectations, parental influence, and professional problems, provides a testing ground for contending theories and ideals.

This "testing ground" image applies only insofar as the status quo is malleable enough to allow the examination and trial of alternative views. Historically, institutionalized education has been characteristically rigid. As a "testing ground" of ideas it has often lacked an orientation encouraging innovation and futuristic thinking. Its political grounding has usually been conservative.

As social psychologist Allen Wheelis has pointed out in *Quest for Identity*, social institutions by definition tend toward solidification and protectionism. His depiction of the dialectical development of civilizations centers on the tension between the security and authoritarianism of "institutional processes" and the dynamism and change-orientation of "instrumental processes."

Similarly, the "lonely crowd" theory of Riesman, Glazer, and Denny portrays a civilizational drift from a traditional imposed and authoritarian value structure to a socialized and internalized ethic to a contemporary situation of value fragmentation. Having cracked, or at least called into question, many of the institutional rigidities of church, school, and home, people in technologically advanced societies face three basic possibilities: learning to live with diversity and change, sliding into a new form of institutional rigidity, or reverting to traditional authoritarianism.

The current situation in education seems to graphically illustrate these observations. Educational practices are primarily tradition-bound. The twentieth-century reform movement, spurred by the ideas of John Dewey, A. S. Neill, and a host of critics who campaigned for change in the 1960s, challenged the structural rigidity of schooling. The current situation is one of contending forces: those who wish to continue the struggle for true reform, those who demand a return to a more traditional or "basic" model, and those who are shaping a new form of procedural conformity around the tenets of behaviorism and competency-based approaches.

We are left with the abiding questions: What is an "educated" person? What should be the primary purpose of organized education? Who should control the decisions influencing the educational process? Should the schools follow society or lead it toward change? Should schooling be compulsory?

Long-standing forces have molded a wide variety of responses to these fundamental questions. The religious impetus, nationalistic fervor, philosophical ideas, the march of science and technology, varied interpretations of "societal needs," and the desire to use the schools as a means for social reform have been historically influential. In recent times other factors have emerged to contribute to the complexity of the search for answers—social class differences, demographic shifts, increasing bureaucratization, the growth of the textbook industry, the changing financial base for schooling, teacher unionization, and strengthening of parental and community pressure groups.

The struggle to find the most appropriate answers to these questions now involves, as in the past, an interplay of societal aims, educational purposes, and individual intentions. Moral development, the quest for wisdom, citizenship training, socioeconomic improvement, mental discipline, the rational control of life, job preparation, liberation of the individual, freedom of inquiry—these and many others continue to be topics of discourse on education.

A detailed historical perspective on these questions and topics may be gained by reading the several interpretations of noted scholars in the field. R. Freeman Butts has written a brief but effective summary portrayal in "Search for Freedom—The Story of American Education," *NEA Journal* (March 1960). A partial listing of other sources includes: R. Freeman Butts and Lawrence Cremin, *A History of Education in American Culture*; S. E. Frost, Jr., *Historical and Philosophical Foundations of Western Education*; Harry Good and Edwin

Teller, *A History of Education;* Adolphe Meyer, *An Educational History of the American People;* Robert L. Church and Michael W. Sedlak, *Education in the United States: An Interpretive History;* Merle Curti, *The Social Ideas of American Educators;* Henry J. Perkinson, *The Imperfect Panacea: American Faith in Education 1865–1965;* Clarence Karier, *Man, Society, and Education;* V. T. Thayer, *Formative Ideas in American Education;* Frank P. Besag and Jack L. Nelson, *The Foundations of Education: Stasis and Change;* H. Warren Button and Eugene F. Provenzo, Jr., *History of Education and Culture in America;* and David Tyack and Elisabeth Hansot, *Managers of Virtue.*

These and other historical accounts of the development of schooling demonstrate the continuing need to address educational questions in terms of cultural and social dynamics. A careful analysis of contemporary education demands attention not only to the historical interpretation of developmental influences but also to the philosophical forces which define formal education and the social and cultural factors which form the basis of informal education.

EXAMINING VIEWPOINTS

In his book *A New Public Education,* Seymour Itzkoff examines the interplay between informal and formal education, concluding that economic and technological expansion have pulled people away from the informal culture by placing a premium on success in formal education. This has brought about a reactive search for less artificial educational contexts within the informal cultural community, which recognizes, the impact of individual personality in shaping educational experiences.

This search for a reconstructed philosophical base for education has produced a barrage of critical commentary. Those who seek radical change in education characterize the present schools as mindless, manipulative, factory-like, bureaucratic institutions that offer little sense of community, pay scant attention to personal meaning, fail to achieve curricular integration, and maintain a psychological atmosphere of competitiveness, tension, fear, and alienation. Others deplore the ideological movement away from the formal organization of education, fearing an abandonment of standards, a dilution of the curriculum, an erosion of intellectual and behavioral discipline, and a decline in adult and institutional authority.

Students of education (whether prospective teachers, practicing professionals, or interested laypeople) must examine closely the assumptions and values underlying alternative positions in order to clarify their own viewpoints. This tri-level task may best be organized around the basic themes of purpose, power, and reform. These themes offer access to the theoretical grounding of actions in the field of education, to the political grounding of such actions, and to the future orientation of action decisions.

A general model for the examination of positions on educational issues includes the following dimensions: identification of the viewpoint, recognition of the stated or implied assumptions underlying the viewpoint, analysis of the validity of the supporting argument, and evaluation of the conclusions and action-suggestions of the originator of the position. The stated or implied assumptions may be derived from a philosophical or religious orientation, from scientific theory, from social or personal values, or from accumulated experience. Acceptance by the reader of an author's assumptions opens the way for a receptive attitude regarding the specific viewpoint expressed and its implications for action. The argument offered in justification of the viewpoint may be based on logic, common experience, controlled experiments, information and data, legal precedents, emotional appeals, and/or a host of other persuasive devices.

Holding the basic model in mind, readers of the positions presented in this volume (or anywhere else, for that matter) can examine the constituent elements of arguments—basic assumptions, viewpoint statements, supporting evidence, conclusions, and suggestions for action. The careful reader will accept or reject the several elements of the total position. One might see reasonableness in a viewpoint and its justification but be unable to accept the assumptions on which it is based. Or one might accept the flow of argument from assumptions to viewpoint to evidence but find illogic or impracticality in the stated conclusions and suggestions for action. In any event, the reader's personal view is tested and honed through the process of analyzing the views of others.

PHILOSOPHICAL CONSIDERATIONS

Historically, organized education has been initiated and instituted to serve many purposes—spiritual salvation, political socialization, moral uplift, societal stability, social mobility, mental discipline, vocational efficiency, social reform. The various purposes have usually reflected the dominant philosophical conception of human nature and the prevailing assumptions about the relationship between the individual and society. At any given time, competing conceptions may vie for dominance—social conceptions, economic conceptions, conceptions that emphasize spirituality, conceptions that stress the uniqueness and dignity of the individual.

These considerations of human nature and individual-society relationships are grounded in philosophical assumptions, and these assumptions find their way to such practical domains as schooling. In Western civilization there has been an identifiable (but far from consistent and clear-cut) historical trend in the basic assumptions about reality, knowledge, values, and the human condition. This trend, made manifest in the philosophical positions of idealism, realism, pragmatism, and existentialism, has involved a shift in emphasis from the spiritual world to nature to human behavior to the social individual to the free individual, from eternal ideas to fixed natural laws to social interaction to the inner person.

The idealist tradition, which dominated much of philosophical and educational thought until the eighteenth and nineteenth centuries, separates the changing, imperfect material world and the permanent, perfect spiritual or mental world. As Plato saw it, for example, human beings and all other physical entities are particular manifestations of an ideal reality which, in material existence, humans can never fully know. The purpose of education is to bring us closer to the absolute ideals, pure forms, and universal standards which exist spiritually by awakening and strengthening our rational powers. For Plato, a curriculum based on mathematics, logic, and music would serve this purpose, especially in the training of leaders whose rationality must exert control over emotionality and baser instincts.

Against this tradition, which shaped the liberal arts curriculum in schools for centuries, the realism of Aristotle, with its finding of the "forms" of things *within* the material world, brought an emphasis on scientific investigation and on environmental factors in the development of human potential. This fundamental view has influenced two philosophical movements in education: "naturalism," based on following or gently assisting nature (as in the approaches of John Amos Comenius, Jean-Jacques Rousseau, and Johann Heinrich Pestalozzi), and "scientific realism," based on uncovering the natural laws of human behavior and shaping the educational environment to maximize their effectiveness (as in the approaches of John Locke, Johann Friedrich Herbart, and Edward Thorndike).

In the twentieth century, two philosophical forces (pragmatism and existentialism) have challenged these traditions. Each has moved primary attention away from fixed spiritual or natural influences and toward the individual as shaper of knowledge and values. The pragmatic position, articulated in America by Charles Sanders Peirce, William James, and John Dewey, turns from metaphysical abstractions toward concrete results of action. In a world of change and relativity, human beings must forge their own truths and values as they interact with their environments and each other. The European-based philosophy of existentialism, emerging from such thinkers as Gabriel Marcel, Martin Buber, Martin Heidegger, and Jean-Paul Sartre, has more recently influenced education here. Existentialism places the burdens of freedom, choice, and responsibility squarely on the individual, viewing the current encroachment of external forces and the tendency of people to "escape from freedom" as a serious diminishment of our human possibilities.

All of these basic philosophical views and many of their countless variations are operative today and provide the grounding of most of the positions on contemporary educational issues, including those presented in this book. The conservative and "liberal arts" tradition, emphasizing the humanities, the cultural heritage, and moral standards, can be easily detected in the words of Robert M. Hutchins (Issue 1), Clifton Fadiman (Issue 2), Edward A. Wynne (Issue 4), and Mortimer J. Adler (Issue 7). The progressive, experimental approach, concentrating on critical intelligence, sociopsychological factors, and social adjustment, is found in the ideas of John Dewey (Issue 1), John Holt (Issue 2), and Lawrence Kohlberg (Issue 4). Modern behaviorism, taking cues from the earlier scientific realism, finds its way into education through the views of B. F. Skinner (Issue 6), while existentialist concerns regarding human subjectivity, self-actualization, and authenticity are aired by Carl R. Rogers (Issue 6) and, perhaps, David Guterson (Issue 10).

And so these many theoretical slants contend for recognition and acceptance as we continue the search for broad purposes in education and as we attempt to create curricula, methodologies, and learning environments which fulfill our stated purposes. This is carried out, of course, in the real world of the public schools in which social, political, and economic forces often predominate.

POWER AND CONTROL

Plato, in the fourth century B.C., found existing education manipulative and confining and, in the *Republic*, described a meritocratic approach designed to nurture intellectual powers so as to form and sustain a rational society. Reform-oriented as Plato's suggestions were, he nevertheless insisted on certain restrictions and controls so that his particular version of the "ideal" could be met.

The ways and means of education have been fertile grounds for power struggles throughout history. Many educational efforts have been initiated by religious bodies, often creating a conflict situation when secular authorities have moved into the field. Schools have usually been seen as repositories of culture and social values and, as such, have been overseen by the more conservative forces in society. To others, bent on social reform, the schools have been treated as a spawning ground for change. Given these basic political forces, conflict is inevitable.

When one speaks of the control of education, the range of influence is indeed wide. Political influences, governmental actions, court decisions, professional militancy, parental power, and student assertion all contribute to the phenomenon of control. And the domain of control is equally broad—school finances, curriculum, instructional means and objectives, teacher certification, accountability, student discipline, censorship of school materials, and determination of access and opportunity, of inclusion and exclusion.

The general topic of power and control leads to a multitude of questions: Who should make policy decisions? Must the schools be puppets of the government? Can the schools function in the vanguard of social change? Can cultural indoctrination be avoided? Can the schools lead the way to full social integration? Can the effects of social class be eradicated? Can and should the schools teach values? Dealing with such questions is complicated by the increasing power of the federal government in educational matters. Congressional legislation has broadened substantially from the early land grants and aid to agricultural and vocational programs to more recent laws covering aid to federally impacted areas, school construction aid, student loans and fellowships, support for several academic areas of the curriculum, work-study programs, compensatory education, employment opportunities for youth, adult education, aid to libraries, teacher preparation, educational research, career education, education of the handicapped, and equal opportunity for females. This proliferation of areas of influence has caused the federal administrative bureaucracy to blossom from its meager beginnings in 1867 into a cabinet-level Department of Education in 1979.

State legislatures and state departments of education have also grown in power, handling greater percentages of school appropriations and controlling basic curricular decisions, attendance laws, accreditation, research, etc. Local school boards, once the sole authorities in policy-making, now share the role with higher governmental echelons as the financial support sources shift away from the local scene. Simultaneously, strengthened teacher organizations and increasingly vocal pressure groups at the local, state, and national levels have forced a widening of the base for policy decisions.

SOME CONCLUDING REMARKS

The schools often seem to be either facing backward or to be completely absorbed in the tribulations of the present, lacking a vision of possible futures which might guide current decisions. The present is inescapable, obviously, and certainly the historical and philosophical underpinnings of the present situation must be understood, but true improvement often requires a break with conventionality, a surge toward a desired future.

The radical reform critique of government-sponsored compulsory schooling has depicted organized education as a form of cultural or political imprisonment which traps young people in an artificial and mainly irrelevant environment which rewards conformity and docility while inhibiting curiosity and creativity. Constructive reform ideas that have come from this critique include the creation of "open" classrooms, the de-emphasis of external motivators, the diversification of educational experience, and the building of a true sense of "community" within the instructional environment.

Starting with Francis Wayland Parker's schools in Quincy, Massachusetts, and John Dewey's laboratory school at the University of Chicago around the turn of the current century, the campaign to make schools into more productive and humane places has been relentless. The duplication of A. S. Neill's Summerhill model in the free school movement in the 1960s, the open classroom/open space trends of recent years, the several curricular variations on applications of "humanistic" ideals, and the emergence of schools without walls, storefront schools, and street academies in a number of urban areas testify to the desire to reform the present system or to build alternatives to it.

The progressive education movement, the development of "life adjustment" goals and curricula, and the "whole person" theories of educational psychology moved the schools toward an expanded concept of schooling which embraced new subject matters and new approaches to discipline during the first half of this century. Since the 1950s, however, pressure for a return to a narrower concept of schooling as intellectual training has sparked new waves of debate. Out of this situation have come attempts by educators and academicians to design new curricular approaches in the basic subject matter areas, efforts by private foundations to stimulate organizational innovations and to improve the training of teachers, and federal government support of the community school model and the career educational curriculum. Yet, criticism of the schools abounds. The schools, according to many who use their services, remain too factorylike, too age-segregated, too custodial. Alternative paths are still sought—paths which allow action-learning, work-study, and a diversity of ways to achieve success.

H. G. Wells has told us that human history becomes more and more a race between education and catastrophe. What is needed in order to win this race is the generation of new ideas regarding cultural change, human relationships, ethical norms, the uses of technology, and the quality of life. These new ideas, of course, may be old ideas newly applied. One could do worse, in thinking through the problem of improving the quality of education, than to turn to the third-century philosopher, Plotinus, who called for an education directed to "the outer, the inner, and the whole." For Plotinus, "the outer" represented the public person, the socioeconomic dimension of the total human being; "the inner" reflected the subjective dimension, the uniquely experiencing individual, the "I"; and "the whole" signified the universe of meaning and relatedness, the realm of human, natural, and spiritual connectedness. It would seem that education must address all of these dimensions if it is to truly help people in the lifelong struggle to shape a meaningful existence. If educational experiences can be improved in these directions, the end result might be people who are not just filling space, filling time, or filling a social role, but who are capable of saying something worthwhile in their lives.

UN Photo

PART 1

Fundamental Issues

The issues discussed in this section are fundamental to any inquiry into education. The answers to the questions raised explore diverse views of human nature, development, religion, economics, morality, equality, and government as they relate to shaping educational policy.

Should Schooling Be Based on Social Experiences?

Should Schools Determine What Is Learned?

Should Curricula Emphasize Commonality Over Multiculturalism?

Should Values Be Developed Rather Than Transmitted?

Is Church-State Separation Being Threatened?

Do External Controls Provide the Best Learning Stimulus?

Does a Common Curriculum Promote Equality?

Should Schools Serve National Economic Needs?

ISSUE 1

Should Schooling Be Based on Social Experiences?

YES: John Dewey, from *Experience and Education* (Macmillan, 1938)

NO: Robert M. Hutchins, from *The Conflict in Education* (Harper & Row, 1953)

ISSUE SUMMARY

YES: Philosopher John Dewey suggests a reconsideration of traditional approaches to schooling, giving fuller attention to the social development of the learner and the quality of his or her total experience.
NO: Noted educator and one time chancellor of the University of Chicago Robert M. Hutchins argues for a liberal arts education geared to the development of intellectual powers.

Throughout history, organized education has served many purposes—the transmission of tradition, knowledge, and skills; the acculturation and socialization of the young; the building and preserving of political-economic systems; the provision of opportunity for social mobility; the enhancement of the quality of life; and the cultivation of individual potential, among others. At any given time, schools pursue a number of such goals, but the elucidation of a primary or overriding goal, which gives focus to all others, has been a source of continuous contention.

Schooling in America has been extended in the last hundred years to vast numbers of young people, and during this time the argument over aims has gained momentum. At the turn of the century, John Dewey was raising serious questions about the efficacy of the prevailing approach to schooling. He believed that schooling was often arid, pedantic, and detached from the real lives of children and youths. In establishing his laboratory school at the University of Chicago, Dewey hoped to demonstrate that experiences provided by schools could be meaningful extensions of the normal social activities of learners, having as their primary aim the full experiential growth of the individual.

In order to accomplish this, Dewey sought to bring the learner into an active and intimate relationship with the subject matter. The problem-solving or inquiry approach that he and his colleagues at Columbia University in New York City devised became the cornerstone of the "new education"—the progressive education movement.

In 1938, Dewey himself (as expressed in his article that follows) sounded a note of caution to progressive educators who may have abandoned too completely the traditional disciplines in their attempt to link schooling with the needs and interests of the learners. Having spawned an educational revolution, Dewey, in his later years, emerges as more of a compromiser.

In that same year, William C. Bagley, in "An Essentialists' Platform for the Advancement of American Education," harshly criticized what he felt were anti-intellectual excesses promulgated by progressivism. In the 1950s and 1960s this theme was elaborated on by other academics, among them Robert M. Hutchins, Hyman Rickover, Arthur Bestor, and Max Rafferty, who demanded a return to intellectual discipline, higher standards, and moral guidance.

Hutchins's critique of Dewey's pragmatic philosophy was perhaps the best reasoned. He felt that the emphasis on immediate needs and desires of students and the focus on change and relativism detracted from the development of the intellectual skills needed for the realization of human potential.

In the following selections, John Dewey charts the necessary shift from the abstractness and isolation of traditional schooling to the concreteness and vitality of the newer concept. Robert M. Hutchins dissects the assumptions underlying Dewey's position and puts forth his own theory based on the premise that human nature is constant and functions the same in every society.

YES   John Dewey

EXPERIENCE AND EDUCATION

Mankind likes to think in terms of extreme opposites. It is given to formulating its beliefs in terms of *Either-Ors*, between which it recognizes no intermediate possibilities. When forced to recognize that the extremes cannot be acted upon, it is still inclined to hold that they are all right in theory but that when it comes to practical matters circumstances compel us to compromise. Educational philosophy is no exception. The history of educational theory is marked by opposition between the idea that education is development from within and that it is formation from without; that it is based upon natural endowments and that education is a process of overcoming natural inclination and substituting in its place habits acquired under external pressure.

At present, the opposition, so far as practical affairs of the school are concerned, tends to take the form of contrast between traditional and progressive education. If the underlying ideas of the former are formulated broadly, without the qualifications required for accurate statement, they are found to be about as follows: The subject-matter of education consists of bodies of information and of skills that have been worked out in the past; therefore, the chief business of the school is to transmit them to the new generation. In the past, there have also been developed standards and rules of conduct; moral training consists of forming habits of action in conformity with these rules and standards. Finally, the general pattern of school organization (by which I mean the relations of pupils to one another and to the teachers) constitutes the school as a kind of institution sharply marked off from other social institutions. Call up in imagination the ordinary schoolroom, its time schedules, schemes of classification, of examination and promotion, of rules of order, and I think you will grasp what is meant by "pattern of organization." If then you contrast this scene with what goes on in the family, for example, you will appreciate what is meant by the school being a kind of institution sharply marked off from any other form of social organization.

The three characteristics just mentioned fix the aims and methods of instruction and discipline. The main purpose or objective is to prepare the

From John Dewey, *Experience and Education* (Macmillan, 1938). Copyright © 1938 by Kappa Delta Pi, An International Honor Society in Education. Reprinted by permission.

young for future responsibilities and for success in life, by means of acquisition of the organized bodies of information and prepared forms of skill which comprehend the material of instruction. Since the subject-matter as well as standards of proper conduct are handed down from the past, the attitude of pupils must, upon the whole, be one of docility, receptivity, and obedience. Books, especially textbooks, are the chief representatives of the lore and wisdom of the past, while teachers are the organs through which pupils are brought into effective connection with the material. Teachers are the agents through which knowledge and skills are communicated and rules of conduct enforced.

I have not made this brief summary for the purpose of criticizing the underlying philosophy. The rise of what is called new education and progressive schools is of itself a product of discontent with traditional education. In effect it is a criticism of the latter. When the implied criticism is made explicit it reads somewhat as follows: The traditional scheme is, in essence, one of imposition from above and from outside. It imposes adult standards, subject-matter, and methods upon those who are only growing slowly toward maturity. The gap is so great that the required subject-matter, the methods of learning and of behaving are foreign to the existing capacities of the young. They are beyond the reach of the experience the young learners already possess. Consequently, they must be imposed; even though good teachers will use devices of art to cover up the imposition so as to relieve it of obviously brutal features.

But the gulf between the mature or adult products and the experience and abilities of the young is so wide that the very situation forbids much active participation by pupils in the development of what is taught. Theirs is to do—and learn, as it was the part of the six hundred to do and die. Learning here means acquisition of what already is incorporated in books and in the heads of the elders. Moreover, that which is taught is thought of as essentially static. It is taught as a finished product, with little regard either to the ways in which it was originally built up or to changes that will surely occur in the future. It is to a large extent the cultural product of societies that assumed the future would be much like the past, and yet it is used as educational food in a society where change is the rule, not the exception.

If one attempts to formulate the philosophy of education implicit in the practices of the new education, we may, I think, discover certain common principles amid the variety of progressive schools now existing. To imposition from above is opposed expression and cultivation of individuality; to external discipline is opposed free activity; to learning from texts and teachers, learning through experience; to acquisition of isolated skills and techniques by drill, is opposed acquisition of them as mean of attaining ends which make direct vital appeal; to preparation for a more or less remote future is opposed making the most of the opportunities of present life; to static aims and materials is opposed acquaintance with a changing world.

Now, all principles by themselves are abstract. They become concrete only in the consequences which result from their application. Just because the principles set forth are so fundamental and far-reaching, everything depends upon the interpretation given them as they are put into practice in the school and the home.

It is at this point that the reference made earlier to *Either-Or* philosophies becomes peculiarly pertinent. The general philosophy of the new education may be sound, and yet the difference in abstract principles will not decide the way in which the moral and intellectual preference involved shall be worked out in practice. There is always the danger in a new movement that in rejecting the aims and methods of that which it would supplant, it may develop its principles negatively rather than positively and constructively. Then it takes its clew in practice from that which is rejected instead of from the constructive development its own philosophy.

I take it that the fundamental unity of the newer philosophy is found in the idea that there is an intimate and necessary relation between the processes of actual experience and education. If this be true, then a positive and constructive development of its own basic idea depends upon having a correct idea of experience. Take, for example, the question of organized subject-matter. . . . The problem for progressive education is: What is the place and meaning of subject-matter and of organization *within* experience? How does subject-matter function? Is there anything inherent in experience which tends towards progressive organization of its contents? What results follow when the materials of experience are not progressively organized? A philosophy which proceeds on the basis of rejection, of sheer opposition, will neglect these questions. It will tend to suppose that because the old education was based on ready-made organization, therefore it suffices to reject the principle of organization *in toto*, instead of striving to discover what it means and how it is to be attained on the basis of experience. We might go through all the points of difference between the new and the old education and reach similar conclusions. When external control is rejected, the problem becomes that of finding the factors of control that are inherent within experience. When external authority is rejected, it does not follow that all authority should be rejected, but rather that there is need to search for a more effective source of authority. Because the older education imposed the knowledge, methods, and the rules of conduct of the mature person upon the young, it does not follow, except upon the basis of the extreme *Either-Or* philosophy, that the knowledge and skill of the mature person has no directive value for the experience of the immature. On the contrary, basing education upon personal experience may mean more multiplied and more intimate contacts between the mature and the immature than ever existed in the traditional school, and consequently more, rather than less, guidance by others. The problem, then, is: how these contacts can be established without violating the principle of learning through personal experience. The solution of this problem requires a well thought-out philosophy of the social factors that operate in the constitution of individual experience.

What is indicated in the foregoing remarks is that the general principles of the new education do not of themselves solve any of the problems of the actual or practical conduct and management of progressive schools. Rather, they set new problems which have to be worked out on the basis of a new philosophy of experience. The problems are not even recognized, to say nothing of being solved, when it is assumed that it suffices to reject the ideas and practices of the old education and then go to the opposite extreme. Yet I am sure that you will appreciate what is meant when I say that many of the newer schools tend to make little or nothing of organized subject-matter of study; to proceed as if any form of direction and guidance by adults were an invasion of individual freedom, and as if the idea that education should be concerned with the present and future meant that acquaintance with the past has little or no role to play in education. Without pressing these defects to the point of exaggeration, they at least illustrate what is meant by a theory and practice of education which proceeds negatively or by reaction against what has been current in education rather than by a positive and constructive development of purposes, methods, and subject-matter on the foundation of a theory of experience and its educational potentialities.

It is not too much to say that an educational philosophy which professes to be based on the idea of freedom may become as dogmatic as ever was the traditional education which is reacted against. For any theory and set of practices is dogmatic which is not based upon critical examination of its own underlying principles. Let us say that the new education emphasizes the freedom of the learner. Very well. A problem is now set. What does freedom mean and what are the conditions under which it is capable of realization? Let us say that the kind of external imposition which was so common in the traditional school limited rather than promoted the intellectual and moral development of the young. Again, very well. Recognition of this serious defect sets a problem. Just what is the role of the teacher and of books in pro-

moting the educational development of the immature? Admit that traditional education employed as the subject-matter for study facts and ideas so bound up with the past as to give little help in dealing with the issues of the present and future. Very well. Now we have the problem of discovering the connection which actually exists *within* experience between the achievements of the past and the issues of the present. We have the problem of ascertaining how acquaintance with the past may be translated into a potent instrumentality for dealing effectively with the future. We may reject knowledge of the past as the *end* of education and thereby only emphasize its importance as a *means*. When we do that we have a problem that is new in the story of education: How shall the young become acquainted with the past in such a way that the acquaintance is a potent agent in appreciation of the living present? . . .

In short, the point I am making is that rejection of the philosophy and practice of traditional education sets a new type of difficult educational problem for those who believe in the new type of education. We shall operate blindly and in confusion until we recognize this fact; until we thoroughly appreciate that departure from the old solves no problems. What is said in the following pages is, accordingly, intended to indicate some of the main problems with which the newer education is confronted and to suggest the main lines along which their solution is to be sought. I assume that amid all uncertainties there is one permanent frame of reference: namely, the organic connection between education and personal experience; or, that the new philosophy of education is committed to some kind of empirical and experimental philosophy. But experience and experiment are not self-explanatory ideas. Rather, their meaning is part of the problem to be explored. To know the meaning of empiricism we need to understand what experience is.

The belief that all genuine education comes about through experience does not mean that all experiences are genuinely or equally educative. Experience and education cannot be directly equated to each other. For some experiences are miseducative. Any experience is miseducative that has the effect of arresting or distorting the growth of further experience. An experience may be such as to engender callousness; it may produce lack of sensitivity and of responsiveness. Then the possibilities of having richer experience in the future are restricted. Again, a given experience may increase a person's automatic skill in a particular direction and yet tend to land him in a groove or rut; the effect again is to narrow the field of further experience. An experience may be immediately enjoyable and yet promote the formation of a slack and careless attitude; this attitude then operates to modify the quality of subsequent experiences so as to prevent a person from getting out of them what they have to give. Again, experiences may be so disconnected from one another that, while each is agreeable or even exciting in itself, they are not linked cumulatively to one another. Energy is then dissipated and a person becomes scatter-brained. Each experience may be lively, vivid, and "interesting," and yet their disconnectedness may artificially generate dispersive, disintegrated, centrifugal habits. The consequence of formation of such habits is inability to control future experiences. They are then taken, either by way of enjoyment or of discontent and revolt, just as they come. Under such circumstances, it is idle to talk of self-control.

Traditional education offers a plethora of examples of experiences of the kinds just mentioned. It is a great mistake to suppose, even tacitly, that the traditional schoolroom was not a place in which pupils had experiences. Yet this is tacitly assumed when progressive education as a plan of learning by experience is placed in sharp opposition to the old. The proper line of attack is that the experiences which were had, by pupils and teachers alike, were largely of a wrong kind. How many students, for example, were rendered callous to ideas, and how many lost the impetus to learn because of the way in which learning was experienced by them? How many acquired special skills by means of automatic drill so that their power of judgment and capacity to act intelligently in new situations was limited? How many came to associate the learning process with ennui and boredom? How many found what they did learn so foreign to the situations of life outside the school as to give them no power of control over the latter? How many came to associate books with dull drudgery, so that they were "conditioned" to all but flashy reading matter?

If I ask these questions, it is not for the sake of wholesale condemnation of the old education. It is for quite another purpose. It is to emphasize the fact, first, that young people in traditional schools do have experiences; and, secondly, that the trouble is not the absence of experiences, but their defective and wrong character—wrong and defective from the standpoint of connection with further experience. The positive side of this point is even more important in connection with progressive education. It is not enough to insist upon the necessity of experience, nor even of activity in experience. Everything depends upon the *quality* of the experience which is had. The quality of an experience has two aspects. There is an immediate aspect of agreeableness or disagreeableness, and there is its influence upon later experiences. The first is obvious and easy to judge. The *effect* of an experience is not borne on its face. It sets a problem to the educator. It is his business to arrange for the kind of experiences which, while they do not repel the student, but rather engage his activities are, nevertheless, more than immediately enjoyable since they promote having desirable future experiences. Just as no man lives or dies to himself, so no experience lives or dies to itself. Wholly independent of desire or intent, every experience lives on in further experiences. Hence the central problem of an education based upon experience is to select the kind of present experiences that live fruitfully and creatively in subsequent experiences.

Later, I shall discuss in more detail the principle of the continuity of experience or what may be called the experiential continuum. Here I wish simply to emphasize the importance of this principle for the philosophy of educative experience. A philosophy of education, like my theory, has to be stated in words, in symbols. But so far as it is more than verbal it is a plan for conducting education. Like any plan, it must be framed with reference to what is to be done and how it is to be done. The more definitely and sincerely it is held that education is a development within, by, and for experience, the more important it is that there shall be clear conceptions of what experience is. Unless experience is so conceived that the result is a plan for deciding upon

subject-matter, upon methods of instruction and discipline, and upon material equipment and social organization of the school, it is wholly in the air. It is reduced to a form of words which may be emotionally stirring but for which any other set of words might equally well be substituted unless they indicate operations to be initiated and executed. Just because traditional education was a matter of routine in which the plans and programs were handed down from the past, it does not follow that progressive education is a matter of planless improvisation.

The traditional school could get along without any consistently developed philosophy of education. About all it required in that line was a set of abstract words like culture, discipline, our great cultural heritage, etc., actual guidance being derived not from them but from custom and established routines. Just because progressive schools cannot rely upon established traditions and institutional habits, they must either proceed more or less haphazardly or be directed by ideas which, when they are made articulate and coherent, form a philosophy of education. Revolt against the kind of organization characteristic of the traditional school constitutes a demand for a kind of organization based upon ideas. I think that only slight acquaintance with the history of education is needed to prove that educational reformers and innovators alone have felt the need for a philosophy of education. Those who adhered to the established system needed merely a few fine-sounding words to justify existing practices. The real work was done by habits which were so fixed as to be institutional. The lesson for progressive education is that it requires in an urgent degree, a degree more pressing than was incumbent upon former innovators, a philosophy of education based upon a philosophy of experience.

I remarked incidentally that the philosophy in question is, to paraphrase the saying of Lincoln about democracy, one of education of, by, and for experience. No one of these words, *of*, *by*, or *for*, names anything which is self-evident. Each of them is a challenge to discover and put into operation a principle of order and organization which follows from understanding what education experience signifies.

It is, accordingly, a much more difficult task to work out the kinds of materials, of methods, and of social relationships that are appropriate to the new education than is the case with traditional education. I think many of the difficulties experienced in the conduct of progressive schools and many of the criticisms leveled against them arise from this source. The difficulties are aggravated and the criticisms are increased when it is supposed that the new education is somehow easier than the old. This belief is, I imagine, more or less current. Perhaps it illustrates again the *Either-Or* philosophy, springing from the idea that about all which is required is *not* to do what is done in traditional schools.

I admit gladly that the new education is *simpler* in principle than the old. It is in harmony with principles of growth, while there is very much which is artificial in the old selection and arrangement of subjects and methods, and artificiality always leads to unnecessary complexity. But the easy and the simple are not identical. To discover what is really simple and to act upon the discovery is an exceedingly difficult task. After the artificial and complex is once institutionally established and ingrained in custom and routine, it is easier to walk in the paths

that have been beaten than it is, after taking a new point of view, to work out what is practically involved in the new point of view. The old Ptolemaic astronomical system was more complicated with its cycles and epicycles than the Copernican system. But until organization of actual astronomical phenomena on the ground of the latter principle had been effected the easiest course was to follow the line of least resistance provided by the old intellectual habit. So we come back to the idea that a coherent *theory* of experience, affording positive direction to selection and organization of appropriate educational methods and materials, is required by the attempt to give new direction to the work of the schools. The process is a slow and arduous one. It is a matter of growth, and there are many obstacles which tend to obstruct growth and to deflect it into wrong lines.

I shall have something to say later about organization. All that is needed, perhaps, at this point is to say that we must escape from the tendency to think of organization in terms of the *kind* of organization, whether of content (or subject-matter), or of methods and social relations, that mark traditional education. I think that a good deal of the current opposition to the idea of organization is due to the fact that it is so hard to get away from the picture of the studies of the old school. The moment "organization" is mentioned imagination goes almost automatically to the kind of organization that is familiar, and in revolting against that we are led to shrink from the very idea of any organization. On the other hand, educational reactionaries, who are now gathering force, use the absence of adequate intellectual and moral organization in the newer type of school as proof not only of the need of organization, but to identify any and every kind of organization with that instituted before the rise of experimental science. Failure to develop a conception of organization upon the empirical and experimental basis gives reactionaries a too easy victory. But the fact that the empirical sciences now offer the best type of intellectual organization which can be found in any field shows that there is no reason why we, who call ourselves empiricists, should be "pushovers" in the matter of order and organization.

NO

Robert M. Hutchins

THE BASIS OF EDUCATION

The obvious failures of the doctrines of adaptation, immediate needs, social reform, and of the doctrine that we need no doctrine at all may suggest to us that we require a better definition of education. Let us concede that every society must have some system that attempts to adapt the young to their social and political environment. If the society is bad, in the sense, for example, in which the Nazi state was bad, the system will aim at the same bad ends. To the extent that it makes men bad in order that they may be tractable subjects of a bad state, the system may help to achieve the social ideals of the society. It may be what the society wants; it may even be what the society needs, if it is to perpetuate its form and accomplish its aims. In pragmatic terms, in terms of success in the society, it may be a "good" system.

But it seems to me clearer to say that, though it may be a system of training, or instruction, or adaptation, or meeting immediate needs, it is not a system of education. It seems clearer to say that the purpose of education is to improve men. Any system that tries to make them bad is not education, but something else. If, for example, democracy is the best form of society, a system that adapts the young to it will be an educational system. If despotism is a bad form of society, a system that adapts the young to it will not be an educational system, and the better it succeeds in adapting them the less educational it will be.

Every man has a function as a man. The function of a citizen or a subject may vary from society to society, and the system of training, or adaptation, or instruction, or meeting immediate needs may vary with it. But the function of a man as man is the same in every age and in every society, since it results from his nature as a man. The aim of an educational system is the same in every age and in every society where such a system can exist: it is to improve man as man.

If we are going to talk about improving men and societies, we have to believe that there is some difference between good and bad. This difference must not be, as the positivists think it is, merely conventional. We cannot tell

From Robert M. Hutchins, *The Conflict in Education* (Harper & Row, 1953). Copyright © 1953 by Harper & Row, Publishers, Inc. Reprinted by permission.

this difference by any examination of the effectiveness of a given program as the pragmatists propose; the time required to estimate these effects is usually too long and the complexity of society is always too great for us to say that the consequences of a given program are altogether clear. We cannot discover the difference between good and bad by going to the laboratory, for men and societies are not laboratory animals. If we believe that there is no truth, there is no knowledge, and there are no values except those which are validated by laboratory experiment, we cannot talk about the improvement of men and societies, for we can have no standard of judging anything that takes place among men or in societies.

Society is to be improved, not by forcing a program of social reform down its throat, through the schools, or otherwise, but by the improvement of the individuals who compose it. As Plato said, "Governments reflect human nature. States are not made out of stone or wood, but out of the characters of their citizens: these turn the scale and draw everything after them." The individual is the heart of society. . . .

Man is by nature free, and he is by nature social. To use his freedom rightly he needs discipline. To live in society he needs the moral virtues. Good moral and intellectual habits are required for the fullest development of the nature of man.

To develop fully as a social, political animal man needs participation in his own government. A benevolent despotism will not do. You cannot expect the slave to show the virtues of the free man unless you first set him free. Only democracy, in which all men rule and are ruled in turn for the good life of the whole community, can be an absolutely good form of government. . . .

Education deals with the development of the intellectual powers of men. Their moral and spiritual powers are the sphere of the family and the church. All three agencies must work in harmony; for, though a man has three aspects, he is still one man. But the schools cannot take over the role of the family and the church without promoting the atrophy of those institutions and failing in the task that is proper to the schools.

We cannot talk about the intellectual powers of men, though we can talk about training them, or amusing them, or adapting them, and meeting their immediate needs, unless our philosophy in general tells us that there is knowledge and that there is a difference between true and false. We must believe, too, that there are other means of obtaining knowledge than scientific experimentation. If knowledge can be sought only in the laboratory, many fields in which we thought we had knowledge will offer us nothing but opinion or superstition, and we shall be forced to conclude that we cannot know anything about the most important aspects of man and society. If we are to set about developing the intellectual powers of man through having them acquire knowledge of the most important subjects, we have to begin with the proposition that experimentation and empirical data will be of only limited use to us, contrary to the convictions of many American social scientists, and that philosophy, history, literature, and art give us knowledge, and significant knowledge, on the most significant issues.

If the object of education is the improvement of men, then any system of education that is without values is a contradiction in terms. A system that seeks bad values is bad. A system that denies the existence of values denies the possibility of education. Relativism, scientism, skepticism, and anti-intellectualism, the four horsemen of the philosophical apocalypse, have produced that chaos in education which will end in the disintegration of the West.

The prime object of education is to know what is good for man. It is to know the goods in their order. There is a hierarchy of values. The task of education is to help us understand it, establish it, and live by it. This Aristotle had in mind when he said: "It is not the possessions but the desires of men that must be equalized, and this is impossible unless they have a sufficient education according to the nature of things."

Such an education is far removed from the triviality of that produced by the doctrines of adaptation, of immediate needs, of social reform, or of the doctrine of no doctrine at all. Such an education will not adapt the young to a bad environment, but it will encourage them to make it good. It will not overlook immediate needs, but it will place these needs in their proper relationship to more distant, less tangible, and more important goods. It will be the only effective means of reforming society.

This is the education appropriate to free men. It is liberal education. If all men are to be free, all men must have this education. It makes no difference how they are to earn their living or what their special interests or aptitudes may be. They can learn to make a living, and they can develop their special interests and aptitudes, after they have laid the foundation of free and responsible manhood through liberal education. It will not do to say that they are incapable of such education. This claim is made by those who are too indolent or unconvinced to make the effort to give such education to the masses.

Nor will it do to say that there is not enough time to give everybody a liberal education before he becomes a specialist. In America, at least, the waste and frivolity of the educational system are so great that it would be possible through getting rid of them to give every citizen a liberal education and make him a qualified specialist, too, in less time than is now consumed in turning out uneducated specialists.

A liberal education aims to develop the powers of understanding and judgment. It is impossible that too many people can be educated in this sense, because there cannot be too many people with understanding and judgment. We hear a great deal today about the dangers that will come upon us through the frustration of educated people who have got educated in the expectation that education will get them a better job, and who then fail to get it. But surely this depends on the representations that are made to the young about what education is. If we allow them to believe that education will get them better jobs and encourage them to get educated with this end in view, they are entitled to a sense of frustration if, when they have got the education, they do not get the jobs. But, if we say that they should be educated in order to be men, and that everybody, whether he is ditch-digger or a bank president, should have this education because he is a man, then the ditch-digger may still feel frustrated, but not because of his education.

Nor is it possible for a person to have too much liberal education, because it is impossible to have too much understanding and judgment. But it is possible to undertake too much in the name of liberal education in youth. The object of liberal education in youth is not to teach the young all they will ever need to know. It is to give them the habits, ideas, and techniques that they need to continue to educate themselves. Thus the object of formal institutional liberal education in youth is to prepare the young to educate themselves throughout their lives.

I would remind you of the impossibility of learning to understand and judge many of the most important things in youth. The judgment and understanding of practical affairs can amount to little in the absence of experience with practical affairs. Subjects that cannot be understood without experience should not be taught to those who are without experience. Or, if these subjects are taught to those who are without experience, it should be clear that these subjects can be taught only by way of introduction and that their value to the student depends on his continuing to study them as he acquires experience. The tragedy in America is that economics, ethics, politics, history, and literature are studied in youth, and seldom studied again. Therefore the graduates of American universities seldom understand them.

This pedagogical principle, that subjects requiring experience can be learned only by the experienced, leads to the conclusion that the most important branch of education is the education of adults. We sometimes seem to think of education as something like the mumps, measles, whooping cough, or chicken pox. If a person has had education in childhood, he need not, in fact he cannot, have it again. But the pedagogical principle that the most important things

can be learned only in mature life is supported by a sound philosophy in general. Men are rational animals. They achieve their terrestrial felicity by the use of reason. And this means that they have to use it for their entire lives. To say that they should learn only in childhood would mean that they were human only in childhood.

And it would mean that they were unfit to be citizens of a republic. A republic, a true *res publica*, can maintain justice, peace, freedom, and order only by the exercise of intelligence. When we speak of the consent of the governed, we mean, since men are not angels who seek the truth intuitively and do not have to learn it, that every act of assent on the part of the governed is a product of learning. A republic is really a common educational life in process. So Montesquieu said that, whereas the principle of a monarchy was honor, and the principle of a tyranny was fear, the principle of a republic was education.

Hence the ideal republic is the republic of learning. It is the utopia by which all actual political republics are measured. The goal toward which we started with the Athenians twenty-five centuries ago is an unlimited republic of learning and a worldwide political republic mutually supporting each other.

All men are capable of learning. Learning does not stop as long as a man lives, unless his learning power atrophies because he does not use it. Political freedom cannot endure unless it is accompanied by provision for the unlimited acquisition of knowledge. Truth is not long retained in human affairs without continual learning and relearning. Peace is unlikely unless there are continuous, unlimited opportunities for learning and unless men continuously avail themselves of them. The world of law and justice for which we yearn, the worldwide political republic, cannot be realized without the worldwide republic of learning. The civilization we seek will be achieved when all men are citizens of the world republic of law and justice and of the republic of learning all their lives long.

POSTSCRIPT

Should Schooling Be Based on Social Experiences?

Intellectual training vs. social-emotional-mental growth—the argument between Dewey and Hutchins reflects a historical debate that flows from the ideas of Plato and Aristotle and which continues today. The positions put forth by Clifton Fadiman and John Holt in Issue 2, "Should Schools Determine What Is Learned?" reflect this continuing debate, as do some of the other selections in this volume. Psychologists, sociologists, curriculum and instruction specialists, and popular critics have joined philosophers in commenting on this central concern.

Followers of Dewey contend that training the mental powers cannot be isolated from other factors of development and, indeed, can be enhanced by attention to the concrete social situations in which learning occurs. Critics of Dewey worry that the expansion of effort into the social and emotional realm only detracts from the intellectual mission which is schooling's unique province.

Was the progressive education movement ruinous, or did it lay the foundation for the education of the future? A reasonably even-handed appraisal can be found in Lawrence Cremin's *The Transformation of the School* (1961). The free school movement of the 1960s, at least partly derived from progressivism, is analyzed in Allen Graubard's *Free the Children* (1973) and Jonathan Kozol's *Free Schools* (1972).

Other sources that represent a wide spectrum of views regarding primary goals for education include Paul Nash's *Models of Man* (1968); Edward J. Power's *Evolution of Educational Doctrine* (1969); Arthur Pearl's *The Atrocity of Education* (1972); Stephen K. Bailey's *The Purposes of Education* (1976); *Doctrines of the Great Educators* (1979), by Robert R. Rusk and James Scotland; Mortimer J. Adler's *The Paideia Proposal* (1982); John I. Goodlad's *A Place Called School* (1984); and Theodore R. Sizer's *Horace's Compromise* (1984).

Questions that must be addressed include: Can the "either/or" polarities of this basic argument be overcome? Is the articulation of overarching general aims essential to the charting of a productive and worthwhile educational experience? And how can the classroom teacher relate to general philosophical aims?

ISSUE 2

Should Schools Determine What Is Learned?

YES: Clifton Fadiman, from "The Case for Basic Education," in James D. Koerner, ed., *The Case for Basic Education* (Council for Basic Education, 1959)

NO: John Holt, from *Escape from Childhood* (E. P. Dutton, 1974)

ISSUE SUMMARY

YES: Writer and editor Clifton Fadiman argues that standardized subject matter rescues the learner from triviality and capriciousness and sets the stage for successful and meaningful interaction in the world.
NO: Educator John Holt feels that an imposed curriculum damages the individual and usurps a basic human right to select one's own path of development.

Controversy over the content of education has been particularly keen since the 1950s. The pendulum has swung from learner-centered progressive education to an emphasis on structured intellectual discipline to calls for radical reform in the direction of "openness" to the recent rally to go "back to basics."

The conservative viewpoint, articulated by such writers as Robert M. Hutchins, Clifton Fadiman, Jacques Barzun, Arthur Bestor, and James Koerner, arises from concerns about the drift toward informalism and the decline in academic achievement in recent decades. Taking philosophical cues from Plato's contention that certain subject matters have universal qualities that prompt mental and characterological development, the "basics" advocates argue against incidental learning, student choice, and diminution of structure and standards. Jacques Barzun summarizes the viewpoint succinctly: "Nonsense is at the heart of those proposals that would replace definable subject matters with vague activities copied from 'life' or with courses organized around 'problems' or 'attitudes.' "

The reform viewpoint, represented by John Holt, Paul Goodman, Ivan Illich, Charles Silberman, Edgar Friedenberg, and others, portrays the typical traditional school as a mindless, indifferent, social institution dedicated to producing fear, docility, and conformity. In such an atmosphere, the viewpoint holds, learners either become alienated from the established curriculum or learn to play the school "game" and thus achieve a hollow success.

Taking cues from the ideas of John Dewey and A. S. Neill, the "radical reformers" have given rise to a flurry of alternatives to regular schooling during recent decades. Among these are free schools, which follow the Summerhill model; urban storefront schools, which attempt to develop a true sense of "community"; "schools without walls," which follow the Philadelphia Parkway Program model; "commonwealth" schools, in which students, parents, and teachers share responsibility; and various "humanistic education" projects within regular school systems, which emphasize students' self-concept development and choice-making ability.

The utilitarian tradition that has descended from Benjamin Franklin, Horace Mann, and Herbert Spencer, Dewey's theory of active experiencing, and Neill's insistence on free and natural development support the reform position. The ideology rejects the factory model of schooling with its rigidly set curriculum, its neglect of individual differences, its social engineering function, and its pervasive formalism. "Basics" advocates, on the other hand, express deep concern over the erosion of authority and the watering down of demands upon students, which result from the reform ideology.

In the following pairing, Clifton Fadiman argues the case for basic education, emphasizing prescribed studies, drawing on his own experience of schooling, and demonstrating the meaningfulness of "old-fashioned" education. In opposition, John Holt goes beyond his earlier concerns about the oppressiveness of the school curriculum to propose complete freedom for the learner to determine all aspects of his or her educational development.

YES

Clifton Fadiman

THE CASE FOR BASIC EDUCATION

The present educational controversy, like all crucial controversies, has its roots in philosophy. One's attitude toward the proposals advanced in this book depends on one's conception of man. It depends on one's view of his nature, his powers, and his reason for existence.

If, consciously or unconsciously, one takes the position that his nature is essentially animal; that his powers lie largely in the area of social and biological adaptation; and that his reason for existence is either unknowable or (should he advance one) a form of self-delusion—then the case for basic education, and consequently for education itself, falls to the ground. By the same token the case for physical, social, and vocational training becomes irrefutable.

On the other hand, if one takes the position that man's nature is both animal *and* rational; that his powers lie not only in the area of adaptation but also in that of creation; and that his reason for existence is somehow bound up with the fullest possible evolution of his mental and spiritual capacities— then the case for basic education, and consequently for education itself, is established; and further discussion becomes a matter, however interesting and important, of detail.

A crisis period is not necessarily marked by disaster or violence or even revolutionary change. It is marked by the absence of any general, tacit adherence to an agreed-upon system of values. It is in such a crisis period that we live. Of the two positions briefly outlined above, a minority adheres to the first. Another minority adheres to the second. But most of us waver between the two or have never reflected on either. Our present educational system quite properly mirrors this uncertainty of the majority. It mirrors our own mental chaos. There is nothing else it *can* do, for ours is a democratic society, and all our institutions are representative.

Now neither of the positions is logically demonstrable, though some have tried to bend them to logic, as well as to propaganda. They are faiths. The scholars whose essays comprise this book deal explicitly with questions of curriculum. Implicitly, however, they are proclaiming the faith by which they live. Furthermore, they are proclaiming that this is the faith by which Western civilization lives.

Because all faiths are attackable, everything they say can be attacked. Indeed everything they say may be wrong. But the attack can only be sustained by the proclamation of an opposing faith. And if they are wrong, they are wrong only in the sense that no faith can be "proved" right.

Thus the *Metaphysics* of Aristotle opens with the well-known statement: "All men by nature desire to know." This is not a statement of fact in the sense that "All men are born with lungs" is a statement of fact. It is not statistically checkable. It is not a self-evident truth. Cursory observation of many men seems to give it the lie. Depending on whether we prefer the language of logic or the language of emotion we may call it either an assumption or a declaration of faith. If the assumption is denied, or the declaration countered by an opposing declaration, this book, as well as education itself, becomes an irrelevancy. But in that case the cultural fruits of civilization also become an irrelevancy, because they would appear to flow, not from some blind process of unending adaptation, but from Aristotle's proposition. Any doubt cast on that proposition also casts doubt on the permanent value of culture.

It may be that the proposition *is* untenable. Perhaps all men do not by nature desire to know. We can then fall back on a second line of defense. We can say that at least men have acted *as if* they did so desire. Aristotle's dictum may be an illusion. But it looks like a creative illusion.

He has another dictum. He tells us that man is a social animal. Put the two statements together. Were man not a social animal but an anarchic animal, his desire

to know would have both its origin and its terminus located in himself. But, as he is a social and not an anarchic animal, he socializes and finally systematizes his desire to know. This socialization and systematization are what we mean by education. The main, though not the only, instrument of education is an odd invention, only three thousand years old, called the school. The primary job of the school is the efficient transmission and continual reappraisal of what we call tradition. Tradition is the mechanism by which all past men teach all future men.

Now arises the question: If all men by nature desire to know, and if that desire is best gratified by education and the transmission of tradition, what should be the character of that education and the content of that tradition? At once a vast, teeming chaos faces us: apparently men desire to know and transmit all kinds of matters, from how to tie a four-in-hand to the attributes of the Godhead.

Obviously this chaos cannot be taught. Hence in the past men have imposed upon it form, order, and hierarchy. They have selected certain areas of knowledge as the ones that, to the exclusion of others, both *can* and *should* be taught.

The structure of this hierarchy is not a matter of accident. Nor is it a matter of preference. The teacher may not teach only what happens to interest him. Nor may the student choose to be taught only what happens to interest him. The criteria of choice are many and far from immutable. But there is an essential one. Basic education concerns itself with those matters which, once learned, enable the student to learn all the other matters whether trivial or complex, that cannot properly be the subjects of elementary and secondary schooling. In other words, both logic and experience suggest that certain subjects have generative power and others do not have generative power. When we have learned to tie a four-in-hand, the subject is exhausted. It is self-terminating. Our knowledge is of no value for the acquisition of further knowledge. But once we have learned to read we can decipher instructions for the tieing of a four-in-hand. Once we have learned to listen and observe, we can learn from someone else how to tie a four-in-hand.

It has, up to our time, been the general experience of men that certain subjects and not others possess this generative power. Among these subjects are those that deal with language, whether or not one's own; forms, figures and numbers; the laws of nature; the past; and the shape and behavior of our common home, the earth. Apparently these master or generative subjects endow one with the ability to learn the minor or self-terminating subjects. They also endow one, of course, with the ability to learn the higher, more complex developments of the master subjects themselves.

To the question, "Just what are these master subjects?" the contributors to this book supply a specific answer. It happens to be a traditional answer. That is, these are, more or less, with modifications in each epoch, the subjects that Western civilization has up to recent times considered basic. That they are traditional is not an argument in their favor. The contributors believe that they are sanctioned not only by use and wont but by their intrinsic value.

The word *intrinsic* is troublesome. Is it possible that, as the environment changes, the number and names of the basic subjects must also change? At a certain time, our own for example, is it possible that driver-education is more basic than his-

tory? Many of us think so, or act as if we thought so. Again I would suggest that if we do think so, or act as if we thought so, it is not because we wish to lower the accident rate (though that is what we say) but because we unconsciously conceive of man primarily as an adaptive animal and not as a rational soul. For if he is primarily the first, then at the present moment in our human career driver-education *is* basic; but if he is primarily the second it is, though desirable, not basic.

I think the authors of this book would concede that with the environmental changes the relative importance of the basic subjects will also change. It is obvious that a post-Newtonian world must accord more attention to the mathematical and physical sciences than did the pre-Newtonian world. But *some* science has at all times been taught. Similarly in a hundred years the American high school student may be universally offered Russian rather than French or German. But this does not affect the principle that *some* systematic instruction in *some* leading foreign language will remain a basic necessity.

In other words, however their forms may be modified, a core of basic or generative subjects exists. This core is not lightly to be abandoned, for once it is abandoned we have lost the primary tools which enable us to make any kind of machine we wish. Other subjects may seem transiently attractive or of obvious utility. It is pleasant to square-dance, for instance and it is useful to know how to cook. Yet we cannot afford to be seduced by such "subjects." Hard though it may be, we must jettison them in favor of the basic subject matters. And there is no time for an eclectic mixture: only a few years are available in which [to] educe, to educate the rational soul. We cannot afford bypaths. We cannot afford pleasure. All education, Aristotle tells us, is accompanied by pain. Basic education is inescapably so accompanied, as well as by that magnificent pleasure that comes of stretching, rather than tickling, the mind.

I have briefly outlined the standard case for basic education insofar as it rests on an unchanging philosophic faith or view of human nature. But there is a more urgent, though less fundamental, argument still to be advanced. In sum it is this: while basic education is *always* a necessity, it is peculiarly so in our own time. . . .

I am a very lucky man, for I believe that my generation was just about the last one to receive an undiluted basic education. As this is written, I am fifty-four years old. Thus I received my secondary school education from 1916 to 1920. Though I was not well educated by European standards, I was very well educated by present-day American ones. . . .

My high school was part of the New York City system. It had no amenities. Its playground was asphalt and about the size of two large drawing rooms. It looked like a barracks. It made no provision for dramatics or square dancing. It didn't even have a psychiatrist—perhaps because we didn't need one. The students were all from what is known as the "underprivileged"—or what we used to call poor—class. Today this class is depended on to provide the largest quota of juvenile delinquents. During my four years in high school there was one scandalous case in which a student stole a pair of rubbers.

Academically my school was neither very good nor very bad. The same was true of me. As the area of elective subjects was strictly limited. I received approximately the same education my fellows did. (Unfortunately Latin was not compulsory: I had to learn it—badly—by myself later on.) Here is what—in addition to the standard minors of drawing, music, art and gym—I was taught some forty years ago:

Four years of English, including rigorous drill in composition, formal grammar and public speaking.
Four years of German.
Three years of French.
Three or four years (I am not sure which) of history, including classical, European and American, plus a no-nonsense factual course in civics. . . .
One year of physics.
One year of biology.
Three years of mathematics, through trigonometry.

That, or its near equivalent, was the standard high school curriculum in New York forty years ago. That was all I learned, all any of us learned, all all of us learned. All these subjects can be, and often are, better taught today—when they are taught at all on this scale. However, I was taught French and German well enough so that in later years I made part of my living as a translator. I was taught rhetoric and composition well enough to make it possible for me to become a practicing journalist. I was taught public speaking well enough to enable me to replace my lower-class accent with at least a passable one; and I learned also the rudiments of enunciation, placing, pitch, and proper breathing so that in after years I found it not too difficult to get odd jobs as a public lecturer and radio-and-television handyman.

I adduce these practical arguments only to explode them. They may seem important to the life-adjuster. They are not important to me. One can make a living without French. One can even make a living without a knowledge of spelling. And it is perfectly possible to rise to high estate without any control whatsoever over the English language.

What *is* important about this old-fashioned basic education (itself merely a continuation and sophistication of the basic education then taught in the primary schools) is not that it prepared me for life or showed me how to get along with my fellow men. Its importance to me and, I believe, to most of my fellow students, irrespective of their later careers, is twofold:

(1) It furnished me with a foundation on which later on, within the limits of my abilities, I could erect any intellectual structure I fancied. It gave me the wherewithal for the self-education that should be every man's concern to the hour of his death.

(2) It precluded my ever becoming Lost.

In drawing the distinction between generative and self-terminating subjects we have already discussed (1).

I want now to explain (2) because the explanation should help to make clear why in our time basic education is needed not only in principle but as a kind of emergency measure. . . .

Considered as a well-rounded American I am an extremely inferior product. I am a poor mechanic. I play no games beyond a little poorish tennis and I haven't played that for five years. I swim, type, dance and drive raggedly, though, with respect to the last, I hope non-dangerously. I have had to learn about sex and marriage without benefit of classroom instruction. I would like to be well-rounded and I admire those who

are. But it is too late. I take no pleasure in my inferiorities but I accept the fact that I must live with them.

I feel inferior. Well and good. It seems to hurt nobody. But, though I feel inferior, I do not feel Lost. I have not felt lost since being graduated from high school. I do not expect ever to feel lost. This is not because I am wise, for I am not. It is not because I am learned, for I am not. It is not because I have mastered the art of getting along with my peers, for I do not know the first thing about it. I am often terrified by the world I live in, often horrified, usually unequal to its challenges. But I am not lost in it.

I know how I came to be an American citizen in 1959; what large general movements of history produced me; what my capacities and limitations are; what truly interests me; and how valuable or valueless these interests are. My tastes are fallible but not so fallible that I am easily seduced by the vulgar and transitory—though often enough I am unequal to a proper appreciation of the noble and the permanent. In a word, like tens of millions of others in this regard, I feel at home in the world. I am at times scared but I can truthfully say that I am not bewildered.

I do not owe this to any superiority of nature. I owe it, I sincerely believe, to the conventional basic education I received beginning about a half century ago. It taught me how to read, write, speak, calculate, and listen. It taught me the elements of reasoning and it put me on to the necessary business of drawing abstract conclusions from particular instances. It taught me how to locate myself in time and space and to survey the present in the light of an imperfect but ever-functioning knowledge of the past. It provided me with great models by which to judge my own lesser perform-ances. And it gave me the ability to investigate for myself anything that in-terested me, provided my mind was equal to it. . . .

The average high school graduate to-day is just as intelligent as my fellow students were. He is just as educable. But he is Lost, in greater or lesser degree.

By that I mean he feels little relation to the whole world in time and space, and only the most formal relation to his own country. He may "succeed," he may be-come a good, law-abiding citizen, he may produce other good, law-abiding citizens, and on the whole he may live a pleasant—that is, not painful—life. Yet during most of that life, and particularly after his fortieth year or so, he will feel vaguely disconnected, rootless, purpose-less. Like the very plague he will shun any searching questions as to his own worth, his own identity. He will die after having lived a fractional life.

Is this what he really wants? Perhaps it is. It all comes round again to what was said at the opening of these remarks. Again it depends on one's particular vi-sion of man. If we see our youngster as an animal whose main function is biolog-ical and social adaptation on virtually a day-to-day basis, then his fractional life is not fractional at all. It is total. But in that case our school curriculum should reflect our viewpoint. It should include the ru-diments of reading so that our high school graduate may decipher highway markers, lavatory signs, and perhaps the headlines of some undemanding news-paper. It should include a large number of electives, changing every year, that may be of use to him in job hunting. And primarily it should include as much play and sport as possible, for these are the proper activities of animals, and our boy is an animal.

Yet the doubt persists. *Is* this really what he wants? And once again the an-swer depends on our faith. For example, the "Rockefeller Report" on Education (published in 1958 and called *The Pursuit of Excellence*) did not issue, except indi-rectly, from surveys, analyses, polls or statistical abstracts. It issued from faith. The following sentences do not comprise a scientific conclusion. They are an ex-pression of faith, like the Lord's Prayer:

"What most people, young or old, want is not merely security or comfort or luxury—although they are glad enough to have these. They want meaning in their lives. If their era and their culture and their leaders do not or cannot offer them great meanings, great objectives, great convictions, then they will settle for shallow and trivial meanings."

There is no compulsion to believe this. If we do not believe it, and unqualifiedly, there is no case for basic education. Which means that, except for the supe-rior intellect, there is no case for tradi-tional education at all. In that event we should at once start to overhaul our school system in the light of a conception of man that sees him as a continually adjusting, pleasure-seeking, pain-avoid-ing animal.

But if we do believe it, and unqual-ifiedly, then the proposals contained [here] might at least be considered as guidelines, subject to discussion and modification.

The root of our trouble does not lie in an unbalanced curriculum, or in an inad-equate emphasis on any one subject, or in poor teaching methods, or in insuffi-cient facilities, or in underpaid instruc-tors. It lies in the circumstance that somehow the average high school graduate does not know who he is, where he is, or how he got there. It lies in the fact that naturally enough he "will settle for shallow and trivial meanings."

NO

John Holt

ESCAPE FROM CHILDHOOD

Young people should have the right to control and direct their own learning, that is, to decide what they want to learn, and when, where, how, how much, how fast, and with what help they want to learn it. To be still more specific, I want them to have the right to decide if, when, how much, and by whom they want to be *taught* and the right to decide whether they want to learn in a school and if so which one and for how much of the time.

No human right, except the right to life itself, is more fundamental than this. A person's freedom of learning is part of his freedom of thought, even more basic than his freedom of speech. If we take from someone his right to decide what he will be curious about, we destroy his freedom of thought. We say, in effect, you must think not about what interests and concerns *you*, but about what interests and concerns *us*.

We might call this the right of curiosity, the right to ask whatever questions are most important to us. As adults, we assume that we have the right to decide what does or does not interest us, what we will look into and what we will leave alone. We take this right for granted, cannot imagine that it might be taken away from us. Indeed, as far as I know, it has never been written into any body of law. Even the writers of our Constitution did not mention it. They thought it was enough to guarantee citizens the freedom of speech and the freedom to spread their ideas as widely as they wished and could. It did not occur to them that even the most tyrannical government would try to control people's minds, what they thought and knew. That idea was to come later, under the benevolent guise of compulsory universal education.

This right to each of us to control our own learning is now in danger. When we put into our laws the highly authoritarian notion that someone should and could decide what all young people were to learn and, beyond that, could do whatever might seem necessary (which now includes dosing them with drugs) to compel them to learn it, we took a long step down a very steep and dangerous path. The requirement that a child go to school, for about six hours a day, 180 days a year, for about ten years, whether or not he learn anything there, whether or not he already knows it or could learn it faster or better somewhere else, is such gross violation of civil liberties that few adults would stand for it. But the child who resists is treated as a criminal. With this requirement we created an industry, an army of people whose whole work was to tell young people what they had to learn and to try to make them learn it. Some of these people, wanting to exercise even more power over others, to be even more "helpful," or simply because the industry is not growing fast enough to hold all the people who want to get into it, are now beginning to say, "If it is good for children for us to decide what they shall learn and to make them learn it, why wouldn't it be good for everyone? If compulsory education is a good thing, how can there be too much of it? Why should we allow anyone, of any age, to decide that he has had enough of it? Why should we allow older people, any more than young, not to know what we know when their ignorance may have bad consequences for all of us? Why should we not *make* them know what they *ought* to know?"

They are beginning to talk, as one man did on a nationwide TV show, about "womb-to-tomb" schooling. If hours of homework every night are good for the young, why wouldn't they be good for us all—they would keep us away from the TV set and other frivolous pursuits. Some group of experts, somewhere, would be glad to decide what we all ought to know and then every so often check up on us to make sure we knew it—with, of course, appropriate penalties if we did not.

I am very serious in saying that I think this is coming unless we prepare against it and take steps to prevent it. The right I ask for the young is a right that I want to preserve for the rest of us, the right *to decide what goes into our minds*. This is much more than the right to decide whether or when or how much to go to school or what school you want to go to. That right is important, but it is only part of a much larger and more fundamental right, which I might call the right to Learn, as opposed to being Educated, *i.e.*, made to learn what someone else thinks would be good for you. It is not just compulsory schooling but compulsory Education that I oppose and want to do away with.

That children might have the control of their own learning, including the right to decide if, when, how much, and where they wanted to go to school, frightens and angers many people. They ask me, "Are you saying that if the parents wanted the child to go to school, and the child didn't want to go, that he wouldn't have to go? Are you saying that if the parents wanted the child to go to one school, and the child wanted to go to another, that the child would have the right to decide?" Yes, that is what I say. Some people ask, "If school wasn't compulsory, wouldn't many parents take their children out of school to exploit their labors in one way or another?" Such questions are often both snobbish and hypocritical. The questioner assumes and implies (though rarely says) that these bad parents are people poorer and less schooled than he. Also, though he appears to be defending the right of children to go to school, what he really is defending is the right of the state to compel them to go whether they want to or not. What he wants, in short, is that children should be in school, not that they should have any choice about going.

But saying that children should have the right to choose to go or not to go to school does not mean that the ideas and wishes of the parents would have no weight. Unless he is estranged from his parents and rebelling against them, a child cares very much about what they think and want. Most of the time, he doesn't want to anger or worry or disappoint them. Right now, in families where the parents feel that they have some choice about their children's schooling, there is much bargaining about schools. Such parents, when their children are little, often ask them whether they want to go to nursery school or kindergarten. Or they may take them to school for a while to try it out. Or, if they have a choice of schools, they may take them to several to see which they think they will like the best. Later, they care whether the child likes his school. If he does not, they try to do something about it, get him out of it, find a school he will like.

I know some parents who for years had a running bargain with their children. "If on a given day you just can't stand the thought of school, you don't feel well, you are afraid of something that may happen, you have something of your own that you very much want to do—well, you can stay home." Needless to say, the schools, with their supporting experts, fight it with all their might— Don't Give into Your Child, Make Him Go to School, He's Got to Learn. Some parents, when their own plans make it possible for them to take an interesting trip, take their children with them. They don't ask the schools' permission, they just go. If the child doesn't want to make the trip and would rather stay in school, they work out a way for him to do that. Some parents, when their child is frightened, unhappy, and suffering in school, as many children are, just take him out.

Hal Bennett, in his excellent book *No More Public School*, talks about ways to do this.

A friend of mine told me that when her boy was in third grade, he had a bad teacher, bullying, contemptuous, sarcastic, cruel. Many of the class switched to another section, but this eight-year-old, being tough, defiant, and stubborn, hung on. One day—his parents did not learn this until about two years later—having had enough of the teacher's meanness, he just got up from his desk and without saying a word, walked out of the room and went home. But for all his toughness and resiliency of spirit, the experience was hard on him. He grew more timid and quarrelsome, less outgoing and confident. He lost his ordinary good humor. Even his handwriting began to go to pieces—it was much worse in the spring of the school year than in the previous fall. One spring day he sat at breakfast, eating his cereal. After a while he stopped eating and sat silently thinking about the day ahead. His eyes filled up with tears, and two big ones slowly rolled down his cheeks. His mother, who ordinarily stays out of the school life of her children, saw this and knew what it was about. "Listen," she said to him, "we don't have to go on with this. If you've had enough of that teacher, if she's making school so bad for you that you don't want to go any more, I'll be perfectly happy just to pull you right out. We can manage it. Just say the word." He was horrified and indignant. "No!" he said, "I couldn't do that." "Okay," she said, "whatever you want is fine. Just let me know." And so they left it. He had decided that he was going to tough it out, and he did. But I am sure knowing that he had the support of his mother and the chance to give it up if it got too much for him gave him the strength he needed to go on.

To say that children should have the right to control and direct their own learning, to go to school or not as they choose, does not mean that the law would forbid the parents to express an opinion or wish or strong desire on the matter. It only means that if their natural authority is not strong enough the parents can't call in the cops to make the child do what they are not able to persuade him to do. And the law may say that there is no limit to the amount of pressure or coercion the parents can apply to the child to deny him a choice that he has a legal right to make.

When I urge that children should control their learning, there is one argument that people bring up so often that I feel I must anticipate and meet it here. It says that schools are a place where children can for a while be protected against the bad influences of the world outside, particularly from its greed, dishonesty, and commercialism. It says that in school children may have a glimpse of a higher way of life, of people acting from other and better motives than greed and fear. People say, "We know that society is bad enough as it is and that children go out into the larger world as soon as they wanted, they would be tempted and corrupted just that much sooner."

They seem to believe that schools are better, more honorable places than the world outside—what a friend of mine at Harvard once called "museums of virtue." Or that people in school, both children and adults, act from higher and better motives than people outside. In this they are mistaken. There are, of course, some good schools. But on the whole, far from being the opposite of, or an antidote to, the world outside, with all its envy, fear, greed, and obsessive competitiveness, the schools are very much like it. If anything, they are worse, a terrible, abstract, simplified caricature of it. In the world outside the school, some work, at least, is done honestly and well, for its own sake, not just to get ahead of others; people are not everywhere and always being set in competition against each other; people are not (or not yet) in every minute of their lives subject to the arbitrary, irrevocable orders and judgement of others. But in most schools, a student is every minute doing what others tell him, subject to their judgement, in situations in which he can only win at the expense of other students.

This is a harsh judgement. Let me say again, as I have before, that schools are worse than most of the people in them and that many of these people do many harmful things they would rather not do, and a great many other harmful things that they do not even see as harmful. The whole of school is much worse than the sum of its parts. There are very few people in the U.S. today (or perhaps anywhere, any time) in *any* occupation, who could be trusted with the kind of power that schools give most teachers over their students. Schools seem to me among the most anti-democratic, most authoritarian, most destructive, and most dangerous institutions of modern society. No other institution does more harm or more lasting harm to more people or destroys so much of their curiosity, independence, trust, dignity, and sense of identity and worth. Even quite kindly schools are inhibited and corrupted by the knowledge of children and teachers alike that they are *performing* for the judgement and approval of others—the children for the teachers; the teachers for the parents, supervisors, school board, or the state. No one is ever free from feeling that he is being judged all the time, or soon may be. Even after the best class experiences teachers must ask themselves, "Were we right to do that? Can we prove we were right? Will it get us in trouble?"

What corrupts the school, and makes it so much worse than most of the people in it, or than they would like it to be, is its power—just as their powerlessness corrupts the students. The school is corrupted by the endless anxious demand of the parents to know how their child is doing—meaning is he ahead of the other kids—and their demand that he be kept ahead. Schools do not protect children from the badness of the world outside. They are at least as bad as the world outside, and the harm they do to the children in their power creates much of the badness of the world outside. The sickness of the modern world is in many ways a school-induced sickness. It is in school that most people learn to expect and accept that some expert can always place them in some sort of rank or hierarchy. It is in school that we meet, become used to, and learn to believe in the totally controlled society. We do not learn much science, but we learn to worship "scientists" and to believe that anything we might conceivably need or want can only come, and someday will come, from them. The school is the closest we have yet been able to come to Huxley's *Brave New World*, with its alphas and betas, deltas and epsilons—and now it even has its soma. Everyone, including children, should have the right to say "No!" to it.

POSTSCRIPT

Should Schools Determine What Is Learned?

The free/open school movement values small, personalized educational settings in which students engage in activities that have personal meaning. One of the movement's ideological assumptions, emanating from the philosophy of Jean-Jacques Rousseau, is that, given a reasonably unrestrictive atmosphere, the learner will pursue avenues of creative and intellectual self-development. This confidence in self-motivation is the cornerstone of Holt's advocacy of freedom for the learner, a position he elaborates upon in his recent books *Instead of Education* and *Teach Your Own*. The argument has gained some potency with recent developments in home-based computer-assisted instruction.

Writers in the field of curriculum theory have been struggling in the past decade to design approaches that can accomplish Holt's goals within the school context. Volumes of articles and essays enunciating this new direction include *Curriculum Theorizing: The Reconceptualists* (1975), edited by William Pinar, and *Curriculum and the Cultural Revolution* (1972), edited by David E. Purpel and Maurice Belanger. These books present a general view that stands for greater emphasis on self-fulfillment, personal liberty, diversity, pluralism, and social justice. A 1975 publication of the Association for Supervision and Curriculum Development, *Schools in Search of Meaning*, edited by James B. Macdonald and Esther Zaret, pursues similar ideological paths toward curricular reform.

A culmination of the Fadiman appraisal of the value of tightly organized schooling and the need for curricular clarity and certainty can be seen in the 1982 publication by the Institute for Philosophical Research of *The Paideia Proposal: An Educational Manifesto*. Written by Mortimer J. Adler, on behalf of

32

a group of distinguished scholars and practitioners, the book charts the essential ingredients of an approach to schooling that aims at instilling in all students the general aspects of culture that will enable them to lead civilized lives. The proposal advocates a uniform course of study built around the acquisition of organized knowledge, the development of learning skills, and the understanding of ideas and values. The Institute for Philosophical Research's 1988 yearbook, *Content of the Curriculum*, edited by Ronald S. Brandt, seems to present a compromise portrait of a revitalized traditional curriculum.

ISSUE 3

Should Curricula Emphasize Commonality Over Multiculturalism?

YES: Richard Rodriguez, from "What Is an American Education?" *Education Week* (September 9, 1987)

NO: Alba A. Rosenman, from "The Value of Multicultural Curricula," *Education Week* (November 11, 1987)

ISSUE SUMMARY

YES: Richard Rodriguez, a well-known contemporary writer and editor, who has written about his own educational experiences as a child from a Spanish-speaking household, presents the case that the United States, as a society of immigrants, must be bound together by knowledge of the dominant cultural heritage, which education can impart.
NO: Alba A. Rosenman, an associate professor of secondary education, counters with an antiassimilationist argument for augmenting a standard curriculum with a point of view that values cultural diversity.

The argument persists over the public school's historical function of increasing social and economic opportunities for all its constituents. The "melting pot" ideology associated with nineteenth-century justifications of public schooling is now seen by many as a convenient myth. The assimilation of diverse cultural groups into a true "melting pot" society would entail a diminution of the dominant group's power and status, a general withering of cultural roots, and the emergence of a less-differentiated societal mass. This has not occurred in America.

Two factors that have worked against the achievement of the ideal (or myth) in the past are the institutional dominance of Anglo-Saxon Protestants who viewed themselves either as the controllers or transformers of minority groups, and the members of those racial and ethnic minorities who were unwilling or unable to reject their cultural heritage in order to accomplish the transformation. These phenomena have been extensively described and analyzed in such works as *Cultural Pluralism and the American Idea* (1956), by Horace M. Kallen; *Beyond the Melting Pot*, 2d ed. (1970), by Nathan Glazer and Daniel P. Moynihan; *The Rise of the Unmeltable Ethnics* (1971), by Michael Novak; *Ethnicity in the United States* (1974), by Andrew M. Greeley; and *Divided Society: The Ethnic Experience in America* (1974), edited by Colin Greer.

Greer, in *The Great School Legend* (1972), examines more specifically the school's role in the assimilation (or transformation) of minority group members. His analysis shows that public school rhetoric promised common experiences that would equip diverse groups for economic prosperity, but that the reality was much to the contrary. The "Americanization" implied in the schooling experience, demanding conformity to avoid "failure," was always narrowly defined by the dominating elite. Greer further contends that, despite the absence of an overt status system, "issues of ethnicity, race, and culture have been superimposed on economic and occupational differences to provide a basis for discrimination, prejudice, and social inequality."

During the past twenty years or so the public schools have been encouraged to embrace multiculturalism as a curricular focus. The "No One Model American" statement (issued by the American Association of Colleges of Teacher Education in 1972) set the tone by rejecting both assimilation and separatism as social goals, calling for an educational effort to support cultural diversity and enhance global understanding.

The conservative swing in the 1980s has given rise to a critique of the aims of multiculturalism. Messages from writers William Bennett, Mortimer J. Adler, E. D. Hirsch, Jr., Allan Bloom, Diane Ravitch, S. I. Hayakawa, and others have rekindled the emphasis on cultural commonality. Richard Rodriguez, author of *Hunger of Memory*, joins this group with a warning that diversity entails fragmentation. In the following selections, Rodriguez makes the case that the classroom is the best setting for the development of a child's public identity based on an understanding of the common culture. Alba A. Rosenman's response is based on the observation that American culture is dynamic and evolving and therefore cannot be anchored by a single set of ideas and values.

YES

Richard Rodriguez

WHAT IS AN AMERICAN EDUCATION?

I am thinking of travel. The difference between a traveler and the nomad is a permanent address. The traveler takes his point of view on tour. The same metaphor has often enough been applied to an education. The student acquires a point of view; he then applies his point of view, his method, to a wider experience.

What is an American education?

The argument is between those who think education should teach that Americans are of one purpose and those who believe that education should teach that Americans are of many purposes but tolerant among ourselves. The debate can be observed as shuttling between right and left, but curiously so. For it is the right urging a communal curriculum, while arguments for individualism—the Protestant arguments—come from the left.

The Study Commission on Global Education, which in May issued its report ("The United States Prepares for Its Future: Global Perspectives in Education"), would probably like to be perceived as brooding over all. However, in emphasizing the need for "global perspective," the commission lists to the left. Members do not wonder (as traditionalists would) whether American students can trace a path back to Thomas Jefferson. The commission is troubled that American students are becoming "global illiterates," unprepared for an international future. The members recommend that the nation's students, from 1st grade to high school, confront the foreign, learn histories, values, tongues.

The commission consists of the sort of people who can be said to inhabit official America, including a state governor, a New York foundation officer, and academic bureaucrats of the first water—deans and college presidents. Several are authors of their own education reports. These are people who attend meetings. These are people who fly the redeye from here to there and who communicate to persons sitting next to them through microphones or by memo. The commission is supported by grants from Exxon and from the Ford Foundation and from Rockefeller.

From Richard Rodriguez, "What Is an American Education?" *Education Week*, vol. 7, no. 1 (September 9, 1987). Copyright © 1987 by Richard Rodriguez. Reprinted by permission of Georges Borchardt, Inc., and the author.

These are people out of touch. Their aim, they say, is to lend support to "pioneers" of global-perspective education—toilers on the earth—with a "continuous flow of suggestions." I doubt if they can have seen a classroom for many a long year, so unfettered is their optimism about what can happen there.

A copy of the report costs $10, and I recommend it to anyone interested in what policymakers and foundations are up to. From its board room, presumably in outer space, the commission beams platitudes: "Teachers should bring to the classroom from their collegiate experiences a broad but integrated education that encourages curiosity about connections among the classroom, the school, and the world at large."

The problem is real. The study commission reminds us how the world beyond our borders is becoming "increasingly interrelated." And within, our country is "increasingly multicultural, multiracial, multiethnic, and mobile." America is more complex than ever; the world is getting smaller. So what is needed, concludes the commission, is not necessarily a new curriculum but the reformation of existing courses "in global perspective." A new curriculum, in other words.

Europe fades from memory. The commission casts its insidiously bland eye toward new continents. At the high-school level, for example, there should be "in-depth study of at least two other cultures, including a non-European culture, in addition to that of the United States. . . ." The objective is to prepare for Tomorrowland.

Few words issue from the commission's 52-page report with more frequency or with less precision than does the word "diversity." The dilemma of our national diversity becomes, with a little choke on

logic, the solution: American educators "must understand diversity." "Appreciate diversity." "Deal constructively with diversity." Pay "greater attention to . . . diversity . . . around the world and within the United States."

The commission is headed by Clark Kerr, former president of the University of California. It has sought a term comparable to the chimerical "multiversity" (Mr. Kerr's famous coinage from the university of the 60's), a term that would at the same time account for the current condition of the American primary classroom and justify the lack of any singular vision of what a classroom ought to be. Diversity is a liquid noun. Diversity admits everything, stands for nothing.

I do not agree that the primary purpose of early education is to teach diversity. I believe something closer to the reverse—that education's primary purpose, its distinguishing obligation, is to foster communality. It is in the classroom that the child comes to learn a public identity. The child learns the skills of numbers and words crucial to public survival, and learns to put on a public self, apart from family or ethnic community.

As education begins, diversity is the enemy of the classroom. Diversity chafes and boogies and blows through the neighborhoods; diversity (the knowledge that I am different from the gringos) is handed down by grandmothers. The classroom is opposite. The classroom is a social fiction; it teaches us that we are communal. As the church is always the last holdout against popular piety, the last to validate the miraculous, so, traditionally, the classroom is skeptical, conservative, admitting only what must be admitted. Only slowly will the academy notice riotous changes outside its door.

Because America is an immigrant society, dynamic, changing, the classroom is always adding to its common text. Martin Luther King Jr. and Susan B. Anthony are inducted into textbooks much as they are canonized by the U.S. Postal Service, not as figures of diversity but as persons who implicate our entire society.

To acknowledge that our national culture changes is not to repudiate the notion of a common culture. I believe that there is a thread, a column, a genious—use what metaphor you will—connecting Greek, Judeo-Christian, Western European thought with wars and kings and dates, an intention, or precise accident, that has shaped America. Such an intention, such an accident, must be what the classroom is prepared to convey.

Americans are no longer aware of much in common. It has been the political right that has most often approved the passing on of "values" in education. But the feminist and the ethnic left have as often sought to cleanse, even to redeem history, by reworking the canon. They seek "role models" from history and exemplary lessons. History becomes a lesson willing to distinguish between the importance of the writer Aphra Behn and the printer Benjamin Franklin.

I submit that America is not a tale for sentimentalists. I read writings of 18th-century white men who powdered their wigs and kept slaves, because they were men who shaped the country that shapes my life. I claim them. I am brown and of Mexican ancestors, one generation into this country. I claim Thomas Jefferson as a cultural forefather.

In 1987, Mr. Kerr's commission reminds: "By around the year 2000, one out of every three Americans will be nonwhite and they will cover a broader socioeconomic range than ever before."

The commission is not what you'd call a radical band. Nevertheless, it has purchased, with foundation money, a remnant of the radical 60's—precisely the notion of diversity. In my opinion, the commission betrays American education. We don't need diversity in the American classroom; we need uniformity.

There are influential educators today, and I have met them, who say that the purpose of American education is to instill in children a pride in their separate ancestral pasts and their home languages. There are university students, and I have met them, who scorn the notion of a shared "Western Civilization" course.

The commission allows that it wants both, uniformity and diversity. Yes, there must be instruction in American history, geography, manners. There should also be a juxtaposition of the national with the international. The question, of course, is how?

It seems to me there is at least a question of sequence, In order to judge, to evaluate, to reject, or to admire, the student first needs a point of view. Not until a student comprehends his own culture and history will he be in a position to confront the foreign with any sophistication.

We read in the newspapers now that American students are unable to pin Japan on a map. I infer that the greatest problem is that American students are unable to make any kind of assessment of Japanese collectivism or Soviet socialism or American individualism. I suspect the triumph of the adolescent shrug.

From the mid-60's, one senses a deflation of American self-esteem. Americans are no longer confident that we are good; we think we are no better than many another place and time. Which perhaps advances us toward a healthier sense of universal failing or of original sin. The pity is that we relinquish a reasonable pride in what America has accomplished.

In the 19th century, as America became an immigrant country, necessity gathered generations of European immigrants in big-city classrooms. Assimilation was an honorable achievement, comparable, in my mind, with opening the plains, building bridges. Should we expect less of our own age because the faces in our classrooms are no longer of Europe? Are we prepared to teach our students that there are values and institutions and customs here that are different, even better, than those in other countries? Are we prepared to help the student arrive at a sense of values?

Perhaps we are not. Very likely we are not. Perhaps we have lost too much faith in our purpose. And our children know it. Our children will become cultural nomads in the 21st century. America's greatest cultural export already is a youthful cynicism, which is the controlling entertainment of the world.

NO

Alba A. Rosenman

THE VALUE OF
MULTICULTURAL CURRICULA

In his reply to the Study Commission on Global Education, Richard Rodriguez sets "communality" of values and "uniformity" of perspective as the proper goals for American schools ("What is an American Education?" Commentary, *Sept. 9, 1987*).

In stressing the importance of communality, Mr. Rodriguez mixes topics and draws erroneous conclusions from the most widespread of assimilationist "common sense" points of view.

It is wrong to assume that one set of values is superior to any other and to try to force all people to share one outlook.

Even if total assimilation were expedient, it could not be effected. Only to a point can people drop their differences and assume new cultural identities. Most of those whose survival and success hang on such a thread will—and do—eventually become dropouts.

Culture evolves; it is dynamic. Such is the definition of ethnogenesis. American culture, like any other, is not what it was nor what it will be. As a reflection of society, schools should be places where a match can be made between the student and his world. A person should feel that society needs his gifts, not that it uses him as an interchangeable part.

An American education should be more than a rehashing of history from the European and "winners' " point of view. In suggesting that "Europe fades from memory," Mr. Rodriguez fails to recognize that the influence of Western civilization is not minimized by looking at the events again, seeing where we have told lies.

The power of Western Civilization is not lost in comparing it with other civilizations, whether or not it compares favorably. The notion that Western civilization is better because it is Western, or because it is ours, is at best ethnocentric.

Mr. Rodriguez says that we "relinquish a reasonable amount of pride in what America has accomplished." He continues that "assimilation was an honorable achievement, comparable, in my mind, with opening the plains. . . ." There is no doubt about the magnitude of what America has achieved against the backdrop of human history. But to say that assimilation was honorable in the way that opening the plains was honorable is a perversion of history.

In fact, the opening of the plains was not honorable but disgraceful. Americans today are not diminished by that event in their history, but they *are* diminished by the loss of memory of what Americans did to those who stood in their way.

Schools should teach our history and at the same time examine the morality of the choices made. We should be a nation with a conscience. Who are we if we don't know who we have been? Will we, in our schools, assimilate minorities in the same "honorable" way we conquered the West?

EDUCATION THAT VALUES CULTURAL DIVERSITY does not say that "diversity admits everything, stands for nothing," as Mr. Rodriguez puts it, but rather that a culture is not wrong because it is different.

Knowledge of other societies and customs gives students choices that may be even more meaningful to them than those offered in our society. It is possible that there are other and better ways to live than those we have grown to know and love. We might yet learn something from that imprecise mass called American "diversity."

While there is nothing wrong with a standard curriculum to promote unity, it is wrong to impose as *correct* a subjective curriculum teaching that the culture in power is better than any other. Even though that culture may make the rules of society and students may have to learn to play by those rules if they are to achieve success within the system, those

majority values are not necessarily superior to other values that children may bring to school.

A multicultural curriculum tries, while valuing differences, to teach a fair curriculum to students with diverse backgrounds. There is no threat to society here, simply a relevant education.

To value different backgrounds is not to applaud individualism; in fact, a sense of community, a basic value of minority groups, is quite the contrary of American individualism, the "Protestant argument," as Mr. Rodriguez calls it. It may well be that the "right" holds out for an assimilationist communality, but to attribute valuing cultural diversity to the "left" and to suggest that this left speaks for the Protestant argument makes no sense. One need not be "left"-thinking to feel that people have a right to have their own point of view.

Differing points of view do not threaten American society; they are the definition of American society.

If schools are to help students arrive at "a sense of values," just who does Mr. Rodriguez suggest will decide what those values are?

Schools should teach communality, says Mr. Rodriguez, so that students will have a point of view from which they can "judge, evaluate, reject, and admire." The development of such a point of view has contributed to the narrow mentality characterizing the judgmental society in which we live. We think that we are best, that it is best to be best, and that anyone who is unlike us must be inferior.

The global-education commission was trying to address the problem of this narrow American view of the world. Mr. Rodriguez says that our children are becoming "cultural nomads" and that their "youthful cynicism" is entertaining the world. I disagree. It is not the youthful cynicism of this country that is entertaining the world, but the intolerance and global ignorance of our population. Our smug isolationism, self-satisfied pride, and ethnocentrism are negating too much of our past greatness.

I agree with Mr. Rodriguez that the primary purpose of an early education should not be "to teach diversity." Its primary purposes are to teach students that in school they will learn how to survive in our society and to solidify their feelings of worth.

Though I am not brown or Mexican, I am a Hispanic who coped with my own set of differences in growing up. While I succeeded probably as well as most within the assimilationist American system, I don't advocate that schools today do to children what was done to me and many others. Schools should offer acceptance and nurturing. They should be places where students feel free to learn and grow, not places where some must every day make an effort not to let anyone know they're different.

I am pleased that Mr. Rodriguez identifies so closely with our founding fathers, but I am not sure that those forward-thinking gentlemen would agree with his argument that we contain and restrict diversity. After all, those men fled the intolerance of Europe. My reading of our history is that they would be more likely to agree that nonjudgmental diversity is our strength as a nation.

POSTSCRIPT

Should Curricula Emphasize Commonality Over Multiculturalism?

In official education circles, the concept and practices of multiculturalism have become quite firmly ingrained. Efforts have been made to improve sensitivity to cultural and social differences, to institute bilingual instruction, and to develop specific ways to assist socially disadvantaged children.

Some feel that the present level of acceptance is due to the absence of an explicit definition of multiculturalism and the lack of a full understanding of the demands on human behavior that pluralism entails. They contend that multiculturalism cannot be simply grafted onto an educational program, for it is based upon a different view of society than that which seems to exist presently. So the question remains: how to foster social unity while preserving cultural diversity?

The education system must increase its efforts to better prepare members of diverse minority groups to function effectively in the cultural mainstream. At the same time, however, the schools must honestly portray the varying values and life-styles that emanate from different quarters of our national life and from all areas of the globe.

A variety of views on this complex issue can be added to those of Rodriguez and Rosenman. Some sources include William Julius Wilson's *The Truly Disadvantaged* (1987); Christine E. Sleeter and Carl A. Grant, "An Analysis of Multicultural Education in the United States," *Harvard Educational Review* (November 1987); James A. Banks, "The Social Studies, Ethnic Diversity, and Social Change," *Elementary School Journal* (May 1987); and Anthony Hartnett and Michael Naish, "Multicultural Education: Paregoric or Panacea?" *Journal of Curriculum Studies* (July–August 1987).

The May 1988 issue of *The Elementary School Journal*, the August 1988 issue of *Education and Urban Society*, and the March 1990 issue of *The Clearing House* feature numerous articles on topics connected with this issue. Finally, recent insightful works are "Empowering Minority Students: A Framework for Intervention," by Jim Cummins, *Harvard Educational Review* (February 1986); Edward T. Hall's "Features of the Cultural Context of Learning," *The Educational Forum* (Fall 1989); and "Narcissus Goes to School," by Chester E. Finn, Jr., *Commentary* (June 1990).

ISSUE 4

Should Values Be Developed Rather Than Transmitted?

YES: Lawrence Kohlberg, from "The Cognitive-Developmental Approach to Moral Education," *Phi Delta Kappan* (June 1975)

NO: Edward A. Wynne, from "The Great Tradition in Education: Transmitting Moral Values," *Educational Leadership* (December 1985/January 1986)

ISSUE SUMMARY

YES: Professor of education Lawrence Kohlberg outlines his theory that, in the tradition of Dewey and Piaget, links value development to cognitive growth.
NO: Professor of education Edward A. Wynne feels that, under the influence of Kohlberg and others, schools have abandoned educational traditions by failing to teach specific moral values.

Do schools have a moral purpose? Can virtue be taught? Should the shaping of character take precedence over the training of the intellect? Is the person possessing a highly developed rationality automatically ethical? Are contemporary schools limited to teaching a secularized morality? Should the schools cease meddling in value-charged matters?

Much of the history of education chronicles how philosophers, theorists, education officials, and the general public have responded to the questions above. In almost all countries, and certainly in early America, the didactic teaching of moral values, often those of a particular religious interpretation, was central to the process of education.

Although the direct connection between religion and schooling has faded, the image of the teacher as a value model persists, and the ethical dimension of everyday activities and human relations insinuates itself into the school atmosphere regardless of any curricular neglect of moral controversy. Normative discourse inundates the educational environment; school is a world of "rights" and "wrongs" and "oughts" and "don'ts."

At present, we must try to define and delineate the moral intentions of public education. Storms of controversy rage over the instructional use of value-laden materials and over methodological approaches that seem to some people to be value-destructive. Localized explosions regarding textbooks, entire curricula, and films bear witness to the volatility of the moral dimension of education.

Additional problems emerge from the attempt to delineate the school's role: can school efforts supplement the efforts of home and church? Can the schools avoid representing a "middle-class morality," which disregards the cultural base of minority group values? Should the schools do battle against the value-manipulation forces of the mass media and the popular culture?

In the 1960s and 1970s a number of approaches to these problems emerged. Lawrence Kohlberg fashioned strategies that link ethical growth to levels of cognitive maturity, tracing a range of moral stages from punishment avoidance to recognition of universal principles. This approach employs discussion of moral dilemmas that demand increasingly sophisticated types of moral reasoning.

Another approach popularized during this period was values clarification, developed and refined by Louis Raths, Merrill Harmin, Sidney Simon, and Howard Kirschenbaum. This moral education program attempts to assist learners in understanding their own attitudes, preferences, and values, as well as those of others, placing emphasis on feelings, emotions, sensitivity, and shared perceptions.

Recent years have seen the marketing of a wide range of materials and games slanted toward moral development objectives. Some of these have been criticized as superficial, others as bordering on the psychoanalytical. With or without prepackaged aids, can teachers navigate the waters of moral education in an organized and effective manner?

Edward A. Wynne, who deplores the tendency in the recent past for schools to avoid the direct transmission of moral values, thinks that teachers can once again fulfill this role. Wynne agrees with former secretary of education William J. Bennett's call for "moral literacy" through clear articulation of cultural ideals and, if necessary, indoctrination.

YES

Lawrence Kohlberg

MORAL GROWTH STAGES

The cognitive-developmental approach was fully stated for the first time by John Dewey. The approach is called *cognitive* because it recognizes that moral education, like intellectual education, has its basis in stimulating the *active thinking* of the child about moral issues and decisions. It is called developmental because it sees the aims of moral education as movement through moral stages. According to Dewey:

> The aim of education is growth or *development*, both intellectual and moral. Ethical and psychological principles can aid the school in the *greatest of all constructions—the building of a free and powerful character*. Only knowledge of the *order and connection of the stages in psychological development can insure this.* Education is the work of *supplying the conditions* which will enable the psychological functions to mature in the freest and fullest manner.

Dewey postulated three levels of moral development: 1) the *pre-moral* or *preconventional* level "of behavior motivated by biological and social impulses with results for morals," 2) the *conventional* level of behavior "in which the individual accepts with little critical reflection the standards of his group," and 3) the *autonomous* level of behavior in which "conduct is guided by the individual thinking and judging for himself whether a purpose is good, and does not accept the standard of his group without reflection."[1]

Dewey's thinking about moral stages was theoretical. Building upon his prior studies of cognitive stages, Jean Piaget made the first effort to define stages of moral reasoning in children through actual interviews and through observations of children (in games with rules). Using this interview material, Piaget defined the pre-moral, the conventional, and the autonomous levels as follows: 1) the *pre-moral stage*, where there is no sense of obligation to rules; 2) the *heteronomous stage*, where the right was literal obedience to rules and an equation of obligation with submission to power and punishment (roughly ages 4–8); and 3) the *autonomous stage*, where the purpose and consequences of following rules are considered and obligation is based on reciprocity and exchange (roughly ages 8–12).[2]

From Lawrence Kohlberg, "The Cognitive-Developmental Approach to Moral Education," *Phi Delta Kappan* (June 1975). Copyright © 1975 by Phi Delta Kappan, Inc. Reprinted by permission.

In 1955 I started to redefine and validate (through longitudinal and cross-cultural study) the Dewey-Piaget levels and stages. The resulting stages are presented in Table 1.

We claim to have validated the stages defined in Table 1. The notion that stages can be *validated* by longitudinal study implies that stages have definite empirical characteristics. The concept of stages (as used by Piaget and myself) implies the following characteristics:

1. Stages are "structured wholes," or organized systems of thought. Individuals are *consistent* in level of moral judgment.

2. Stages form an *invariant sequence.* Under all conditions except extreme trauma, movement is always forward, never backward. Individuals never skip stages; movement is always to the next stage up.

3. Stages are "hierarchical integrations." Thinking at a higher stage includes or comprehends within it lower-stage thinking. There is a tendency to function at or prefer the highest stage available.

Each of these characteristics has been demonstrated for moral stages. Stages are defined by responses to a set of verbal moral dilemmas classified according to an elaborate scoring scheme. Validating studies include:

1. A 20-year study of 50 Chicago-area boys, middle- and working-class. Initially interviewed at ages 10–16, they have been reinterviewed at three-year intervals thereafter.

2. A small, six-year longitudinal study of Turkish villages and city boys of the same age.

3. A variety of other cross-sectional studies in Canada, Britain, Israel, Taiwan, Yucatán, Honduras, and India.

With regard to the structured whole or consistency criterion, we have found that more than 50% of an individual's thinking is always at one stage, with the remainder at the next adjacent stage (which he is leaving or which he is moving into).

With regard to invariant sequence, our longitudinal results have been presented in the *American Journal of Orthopsychiatry*, and indicate that on every retest individuals were either at the same stage as three years earlier or had moved up. This was true in Turkey as well as in the United States.

With regard to the hierarchical integration criterion, it has been demonstrated that adolescents exposed to written statements at each of the six stages comprehend or correctly put in their own words all statements at or below their own stage but fail to comprehend any statements more than one stage above their own. Some individuals comprehend the next stage above their own; some do not. Adolescents prefer (or rank as best) the highest stage they can comprehend.

To understand moral stages, it is important to clarify their relations to stage of logic or intelligence, on the one hand, and to moral behavior on the other. Maturity of moral judgment is not highly correlated with IQ or verbal intelligence (correlations are only in the 30s, accounting for 10% of the variance). Cognitive development, in the stage sense, however, is more important for moral development than such correlations suggest. Piaget has found that after the child learns to speak there are three major stages of reasoning: the intuitive, the concrete operational, and the formal operational. At around age 7, the child enters the stage of concrete logical thought: he can make logical inferences, classify, and handle quantitative relations about

Table 1

Definition of Moral Stages

I. Preconventional level

At this level, the child is responsive to cultural rules and labels of good and bad, right or wrong, but interprets these labels either in terms of the physical or the hedonistic consequences of action (punishment, reward, exchange of favors) or in terms of the physical power of those who enunciate the rules and labels. The level is divided into the following two stages:

Stage 1: *The punishment-and-obedience orientation.* The physical consequences of action determine its goodness or badness, regardless of the human meaning or value of these consequences. Avoidance of punishment and unquestioning deference to power are valued in their own right, not in terms of respect for an underlying moral order supported by punishment and authority (the latter being Stage 4).

Stage 2: *The instrumental-relativist orientation.* Right action consists of that which instrumentally satisfies one's own needs and occasionally the needs of others. Human relations are viewed in terms like those of the marketplace. Elements of fairness, of reciprocity, and of equal sharing are present, but they are always interpreted in a physical, pragmatic way. Reciprocity is a matter of "you scratch my back and I'll scratch yours," not of loyalty, gratitude, or justice.

II. Conventional level

At this level, maintaining the expectations of the individual's family, group, or nation is perceived as valuable in its own right, regardless of immediate and obvious consequences. The attitude is not only one of *conformity* to personal expectations and social order, but of loyalty to it, of actively *maintaining*, supporting, and justifying the order, and of identifying with the person or group involved in it. At this level, there are the following two stages:

Stage 3: *The interpersonal concordance or "good boy-nice girl" orientation.* Good behavior is that which pleases or helps others and is approved by them. There is much conformity to stereotypical images of what is majority or "natural" behavior. Behavior is frequently judged by intention—"he means well" becomes important for the first time. One earns approval by being "nice."

Stage 4: *The "law and order" orientation.* There is orientation toward authority, fixed rules, and the maintenance of the social order. Right behavior consists of doing one's duty, showing respect for authority, and maintaining the given social order for its own sake.

III. Postconventional, autonomous, or principled level

At this level, there is a clear effort to define moral values and principles that have validity and application apart from the authority of the groups or persons holding these principles and apart from the individual's own identification with these groups. This level also has two stages:

Stage 5: *The social-contract, legalistic orientation,* generally with utilitarian overtones. Right action tends to be defined in terms of general individual rights and standards which have been critically examined and agreed upon by the whole society. There is a clear awareness of the relativism of personal values and opinions and a corresponding emphasis upon procedural rules for reaching consensus. Aside from what is constitutionally and democratically agreed upon, the right is a matter of personal "values" and "opinion." The result is an emphasis upon the "legal point of view," but with an emphasis upon the possibility of changing law in terms of rational considerations of social utility (rather than freezing it in terms of Stage 4 "law and order"). Outside the legal realm, free agreement and contract is the binding element of obligation. This is the "official" morality of the American government and constitution.

Stage 6: *The universal-ethical-principle orientation.* Right is defined by the decision of conscience in accord with self-chosen *ethical principles* appealing to logical comprehensiveness, universality, and consistency. These principles are abstract and ethical (the Golden Rule, the categorical imperative); they are not concrete moral rules like the Ten Commandments. At heart, these are universal principles of *justice,* of the *reciprocity* and *equality* of human *rights,* and of respect for the dignity of human beings as *individual persons* ("From Is to Ought," pp. 164, 165).

—Reprinted from *The Journal of Philosophy,* October 25, 1973.

concrete things. In adolescence individuals usually enter the stage of formal operations. At this stage they can reason abstractly, i.e., consider all possibilities, form hypotheses, deduce implications from hypotheses, and test them against reality.[3]

Since moral reasoning clearly is reasoning, advanced moral reasoning depends upon advanced logical reasoning: a person's logical stage puts a certain ceiling on the moral stage he can attain. A person whose logical stage is only concrete operational is limited to the pre-conventional moral stages (Stages 1 and 2). A person whose logical stage is only partially formal operational is limited to the conventional moral stages (Stages 3 and 4). While logical development is necessary for moral development and sets limits to it, most individuals are higher in logical stage than they are in moral stage. As an example, over 50% of late adolescents and adults are capable of full formal reasoning, but only 10% of these adults (all formal operational) display principled (Stages 5 and 6) moral reasoning.

The moral stages are *structures of moral judgment* or *moral reasoning*. Structures of moral judgment must be distinguished from the *content* of moral judgment. As an example, we cite responses to a dilemma used in our various studies to identify moral stage. The dilemma raises the issue of stealing a drug to save a dying woman. The inventor of the drug is selling it for 10 times what it costs him to make it. The woman's husband cannot raise the money, and the seller refuses to lower the price or wait for payment. What should the husband do?

The choice endorsed by a subject (steal, don't steal) is called the *content* of his moral judgment in the situation. His reasoning about the choice defines the

structure of his moral judgment. This reasoning centers on the following 10 universal moral values or issues of concern to persons in these moral dilemmas:

1. Punishment
2. Property
3. Roles and concerns of affection
4. Roles and concerns of authority
5. Law
6. Life
7. Liberty
8. Distributive justice
9. Truth
10. Sex

A moral choice involves choosing between two (or more) of these values as they *conflict* in concrete situations of choice.

The stage or structure of a person's moral judgment defines; 1) *what* he finds valuable in each of these moral issues (life, law), i.e., how he defines the value, and 2) *why* he finds it valuable, i.e., the reasons he gives for valuing it. As an example, at Stage 1 life is valued in terms of the power or possessions of the person involved; at Stage 2, for its usefulness in satisfying the needs of the individual in question or others; at Stage 3, in terms of the individual's relations with others and their valuation of him; at Stage 4, in terms of social or religious law. Only at Stages 5 and 6 is each life seen as inherently worthwhile, aside from other consideration.

MORAL JUDGMENT VS. MORAL ACTION

Having clarified the nature of stages of moral *judgment*, we must consider the relation of moral judgment to moral *action*. If logical reasoning is a necessary but not sufficient condition for mature moral judgment, mature moral judgment is a necessary but not sufficient condition for mature moral action. One cannot follow moral principles if one does not understand (or believe in) moral principles. However, one can reason in terms of principles and not live up to these principles. As an example, Richard Krebs and I found that only 15% of students showing some principled thinking cheated as compared to 55% of conventional subjects and 70% of preconventional subjects. Nevertheless, 15% of the principled subjects did cheat, suggesting that factors additional to moral judgment are necessary for principled moral reasoning to be translated into "moral action." Partly, these factors include the situation and its pressures. Partly, what happens depends upon the individual's motives and emotions. Partly, what the individual does depends upon a general sense of will, purpose, or "ego strength." As an example of the role of will or ego strength in moral behavior, we may cite the study of Krebs: Slightly more than half of his conventional subjects cheated. These subjects were also divided by a measure of attention/will. Only 26% of the "strong-willed" conventional subjects cheated; however, 74% of the "weak-willed" subjects cheated.

If maturity of moral reasoning is only one factor in moral behavior, why does the cognitive-developmental approach to moral education focus so heavily upon moral reasoning? For the following reasons:

1. Moral judgment, while only one factor in moral behavior, is the single most important or influential factor yet discovered in moral behavior.

2. While other factors influence moral behavior, moral judgment is the only distinctively *moral* factor in moral behavior. To illustrate, we noted that the Krebs

study indicated that "strong-willed" conventional stage subjects resisted cheating more than "weak-willed" subjects. For those at a preconventional level of moral reasoning, however, "will" had an opposite effect. "Strong-willed" Stages 1 and 2 subjects cheated more, not less, than "weak-willed" subjects, i.e., they had the "courage of their (amoral) convictions" that it was worthwhile to cheat. "Will," then, is an important factor in moral behavior, but it is not distinctively moral; it becomes moral only when informed by mature moral judgment.

3. Moral judgment change is long-range or irreversible; a higher stage is never lost. Moral behavior as such is largely situational and reversible or "loseable" in new situations.

AIMS OF MORAL AND CIVIC EDUCATION

Moral psychology describes what moral development is, as studied empirically. Moral education must also consider moral philosophy, which strives to tell us what moral development ideally *ought to be*. Psychology finds an invariant sequence of moral stages; moral philosophy must be invoked to answer whether a later stage is a better stage. The "stage" of senescence and death follows the "stage" of adulthood, but that does not mean that senescence and death are better. Our claim that the latest or principled stages of moral reasoning are morally better stages, then, must rest on considerations of moral philosophy.

The tradition of moral philosophy to which we appeal is the liberal and rational tradition, in particular the "formalistic" or "deonotological" tradition running from Immanuel Kant to John Rawls. Central to this tradition is the claim that an adequate morality is *principled*, i.e., that it makes judgments in terms of *universal* principles applicable to all mankind. *Principles* are to be distinguished from *rules*. Conventional morality is grounded on rules, primarily "thou shalt nots" such as are represented by the Ten Commandments, prescriptions of kinds of actions. Principles are, rather, universal guides to making a moral decision. An example is Kant's "categorical imperative," formulated in two ways. The first is the maxim of respect for human personality, "Act always toward the other as an end, not as a means." The second is the maxim of universalization, "Choose only as you would be willing to have everyone choose in your situation." Principles like that of Kant's state the formal conditions of a moral choice or action. In the dilemma in which a woman is dying because a druggist refuses to release his drug for less than the stated price, the druggist is not acting morally, though he is not violating the ordinary moral rules (he is not actually stealing or murdering). But he is violating principles: He is treating the woman simply as a means to his ends of profit, and he is not choosing as he would wish anyone to choose (if the druggist were in the dying woman's place, he would not want a druggist to choose as he is choosing). Under most circumstances, choice in terms of conventional moral rules and choice in terms of principles coincide. Ordinarily, principles dictate not stealing (avoiding stealing is implied by acting in terms of a regard for others as ends and in terms of what one would want everyone to do). In a situation where stealing is the only means to save a life, however, principles contradict the ordinary rules and would dictate stealing. Unlike rules which are supported by social authority,

principles are freely chosen by the individual because of their intrinsic moral validity.[4]

The conception that a moral choice is a choice made in terms of moral principles is related to the claim of liberal moral philosophy that moral principles are ultimately principles of justice. In essence, moral conflicts are conflicts between the claims of persons, and principles for resolving these claims are principles of justice, "for giving each his due." Central to justice are the demands of *liberty, equality*, and *reciprocity*. At every moral stage, there is a concern for justice. The most damning statement a school child can make about a teacher is that "he's not fair." At each higher stage, however, the conception of justice is reorganized. At Stage 1, justice is punishing the bad in terms of "an eye for an eye and a tooth for a tooth." At Stage 2, it is exchanging favors and goods in an equal manner. At Stages 3 and 4, it is treating people as they desire in terms of the conventional rules. At Stage 5, it is recognized that all rules and laws flow from justice, from a social contract between the governors and the governed designed to protect the equal rights of all. At Stage 6, personally chosen moral principles are also principles of justice, the principles any member of a society would choose for that society if he did not know what his position was to be in the society and in which he might be the least advantaged. Principles chosen from this point of view are, first, the maximum liberty compatible with the like liberty of others and, second, no inequalities of goods and respect which are not to the benefit of all, including the least advantaged.

As an example of stage progression in the orientation of justice, we may take judgments about capital punishment.

Capital punishment is only firmly rejected at the two principled stages, when the notion of justice as vengeance or retribution is abandoned. At the sixth stage, capital punishment is not condoned even if it may have some useful deterrent effect in promoting law and order. This is because it is not a punishment we would choose for a society if we assumed we had as much chance of being born into the position of a criminal or murderer as being born into the position of a law abider.

Why are decisions based on universal principles of justice better decisions? Because they are decisions on which all moral men could agree. When decisions are based on conventional moral rules, men will disagree, since they adhere to conflicting systems of rules dependent on culture and social position. Throughout history men have killed one another in the name of conflicting moral rules and values, most recently in Vietnam and the Middle East. Truly moral or just resolutions of conflicts require principles which are, or can be, universalizable.

ALTERNATIVE APPROACHES

We have given a philosophic rationale for stage advance as the aim of moral education. Given this rationale, the developmental approach to moral education can avoid the problems inherent in the other two major approaches to moral education. The first alternative approach is that of indoctrinative moral education, the preaching and imposition of the rules and values of the teacher and his culture on the child. In America, when this indoctrinative approach has been developed in a systematic manner, it has usually been termed "character education."

Moral values, in the character education approach, are preached or taught in terms of what may be called the "bag of virtues." In the classic studies of character by Hugh Hartshorne and Mark May, the virtues chosen were honesty, service, and self-control. It is easy to get superficial consensus on such a bag of virtues— until one examines in detail the list of virtues involved and the details of their definition. Is the Hartshorne and May bag more adequate than the Boy Scout bag (a Scout should be honest, loyal, reverent, clean, brave, etc.)? When one turns to the details of defining each virtue, one finds equal uncertainty or difficulty in reaching consensus. Does honesty mean one should not steal to save a life? Does it mean that a student should not help another student with his homework?

Character education and other forms of indoctrinative moral education have aimed at teaching universal values (it is assumed that honesty or service are desirable traits for all men in all societies), but the detailed definitions used are relative; they are defined by the opinions of the teacher and the conventional culture and rest on the authority of the teacher for their justification. In this sense character education is close to the unreflective valuings by teachers which constitute the hidden curriculum of the school.[5] Because of the current unpopularity of indoctrinative approaches to moral education, a family of approaches called "values clarification" has become appealing to teachers. Values clarification takes the first step implied by a rational approach to moral education: the eliciting of the child's own judgment or opinion about issues or situations in which values conflict, rather than imposing the teacher's opinion on him. Values clarification, however, does not attempt to go further than eliciting awareness of values; it is assumed that becoming more self-aware about one's values is an end in itself. Fundamentally, the definition of the end of values education as self-awareness derives form a belief in ethical relativity held by many value-clarifiers. As stated by Peter Engel, "One must contrast value clarification and value inculcation. Value clarification implies the principle that in the consideration of values there is no single correct answer." Within these premises of "no correct answer," children are to discuss moral dilemmas in such a way as to reveal different values and discuss their value differences with each other. The teacher is to stress that "our values are different," not that one value is more adequate than others. If this program is systematically followed, students will themselves become relativists, believing there is no "right" moral answer. For instance, a student caught cheating might argue that he did nothing wrong, since his own hierarchy of values, which may be different from that of the teacher, made it right for him to cheat.

Like values clarification, the cognitive-developmental approach to moral education stresses open or Socratic peer discussion of value dilemmas. Such discussion, however, has an aim: stimulation of movement to the next stage of moral reasoning. Like values clarification, the developmental approach opposes indoctrination. Stimulation of movement to the next stage of reasoning is not indoctrinative, for the following reasons:

1. Change is in the way of reasoning rather than in the particular beliefs involved.

2. Students in a class are at different stages; the aim is to aid movement at each to the next stage, not convergence on a common pattern.

3. The teacher's own opinion is neither stressed nor invoked as authoritative. It enters in only as one of many opinions, hopefully one of those at a next higher stage.

4. The notion that some judgments are more adequate than others is communicated. Fundamentally, however, this means that the student is encouraged to articulate a position which seems most adequate to him and to judge the adequacy of the reasoning of others.

In addition to having more definite aims than values clarification, the moral development approach restricts value education to that which is moral or, more specifically, to justice. This is for two reasons. First, it is not clear that the whole realm of personal, political, and religious values is a realm which is non-relative, i.e., in which there are universals and a direction of development. Second, it is not clear that the public school has a right or mandate to develop values in general.[6] In our view, value education in the public schools should be restricted to that which the school has the right and mandate to develop: an awareness of justice, or of the rights of others in our constitutional system. While the Bill of Rights prohibits the teaching of religious beliefs, or of specific value systems, it does not prohibit the teaching of the awareness of rights and principles of justice fundamental to the Constitution itself.

When moral education is recognized as centered in justice and differentiated from value education or affective education, it becomes apparent that moral and civic education are much the same thing. This equation, taken for granted by the classic philosophers of education from

Plato and Aristotle to Dewey, is basic to our claim that a concern for moral education is central to the educational objectives of social studies.

NOTES

1. These levels correspond roughly to our three major levels: the preconventional, the conventional, and the principled. Similar levels were propounded by William McDougall, Leonard Hobhouse, and James Mark Baldwin.

2. Piaget's stages correspond to our first three stages; Stage 0 (pre-moral), Stage 1 (heteronomous), and Stage 2 (instrumental reciprocity).

3. Many adolescents and adults only partially attain the stage of formal operations. They do consider all the actual relations of one thing to another at the same time, but they do not consider all possibilities and form abstract hypotheses. A few do not advance this far, remaining "concrete operational."

4. Not all freely chosen values or rules are principles, however. Hitler chose the "rule," "exterminate the enemies of the Aryan race," but such a rule is not a universalizable principle.

5. As an example of the "hidden curriculum," we may cite a second-grade classroom. My son came home from this classroom one day saying he did not want to be "one of the bad boys." Asked "Who are the bad boys?" he replied, "The ones who don't put their books back and get yelled at."

6. Restriction of deliberate value education to the moral may be clarified by our example of the second-grade teacher who made tidying up of books a matter of moral indoctrination. Tidiness is a value, but it is not a moral value. Cheating is a moral issue, intrinsically one of fairness. It involves issues of violation of trust and taking advantage. Failing to tidy the room may under certain conditions be an issue of fairness, when it puts an undue burden on others. If it is handled by the teacher as a matter of cooperation among the group in this sense, it is a legitimate focus of deliberate moral education. If it is not, it simply represents the arbitrary imposition of the teacher's values on the child.

NO

Edward A. Wynne

THE GREAT TRADITION IN EDUCATION: TRANSMITTING MORAL VALUES

Within the recent past, American education substantially disassociated itself from what may be called the great tradition in education: the deliberate transmission of moral values to students. Despite this separation, many education reforms are being considered or are under way to increase the academic demands made on students. These reforms can be generally helpful; however, unless they are sensitive to the implications of our break with the great tradition, their effect on student conduct and morality may be transitory or even harmful. To understand the significance of the great tradition, we must engage in a form of consciousness-raising by enriching our understanding of the past and by understanding the misperceptions that pervade contemporary education.

The transmission of moral values has been the dominant educational concern of most cultures throughout history. Most educational systems have been simultaneously concerned with the transmission of cognitive knowledge—skills, information, and techniques of intellectual analysis—but these admittedly important educational aims, have rarely been given priority over moral education. The current policies in American education that give secondary priority to transmitting morality represent a sharp fracture with the great tradition.

Our break with the past is especially significant in view of the increase since the early 1950s of youth disorder: suicide, homicide, and out-of-wedlock births. Patterns revealed by statistics coincide with popular conceptions about these behaviors. For instance, in 16 of the past 17 Gallup Polls on education, pupil discipline has been the most frequent criticism leveled against public schools. One may wonder if better discipline codes and more homework are adequate remedies for our current school problems, or whether these dysfunctions are more profound and should be treated with more sensitive and complex remedies. Although literacy and student diligence are unquestionably worthy of pursuit, they are only a part of the process of communicating serious morality. If we want to improve the ways

From Edward A. Wynne, "The Great Tradition in Education: Transmitting Moral Values," *Educational Leadership*, vol. 43, no. 4 (December 1985/January 1986), pp. 4–9. Copyright © 1985 by the Association for Supervision and Curriculum Development. Reprinted by permission. All rights reserved.

we are now transmitting morality, it makes sense to recall the way morality was transmitted before youth disorder became such a distressing issue.

SOME DEFINITIONS

The term "moral values" is ambiguous and requires some definition. It signifies the specific values that particular cultures generally hold in regard. Such values vary among cultures; during World War II, a Japanese who loved his homeland was likely to be hostile to Americans, and vice versa. Value conflicts along national or ethnic lines are common, although most cultures treat the characteristic we call "patriotism" as a moral value, and treat "treason" with opprobrium. Comparable patterns of value govern interpersonal relations in cultures: beliefs about proper family conduct or the nature of reciprocal relationships. Such beliefs are laden with strong moral components.

In sum, common "moral values" are the vital common beliefs that shape human relations in each culture. Often these values—as in the Ten Commandments—have what is popularly called a religious base. Whether their base is religious, traditional, or secular, however, such values are expected to be widely affirmed under most circumstances.

The term "educational systems" also is somewhat obscure. Contemporary Americans naturally think in terms of formal public or private schools and colleges. But for most history, and all prehistory, formal agencies were a minute part of children's and adolescents' education. In traditional cultures, education was largely transmitted by various formal and informal nonschool agencies: nuclear and extended families; religious institutions; "societies" for the young organized and monitored by adults. In addition, the complex incidental life of preindustrial rural and urban societies, and the demands of work in and out of the family socialized young persons into adult life. Many of these agencies still play important educational roles in contemporary America; nonetheless, in the modern period, the gradual replacement of such agencies by schools has been a strong trend.

TRANSMITTING MORAL VALUES

Whether the dominant educational system has been formal or informal, the transmission of moral values has persistently played a central role. This role has been necessary and universal for two reasons.

1. Human beings are uniquely adaptable animals and live in nearly all climates and in diverse cultural systems. But, as the anthropologist Yehudi Cohen (1964) put it, "No society allows for the random and promiscuous expression of emotions to just anyone. Rather, one may communicate those feelings, either verbally, physically, or materially, to certain people." Because our means of communicating emotions are socially specific, slow maturing young persons must be socialized gradually to the right—or moral—practices appropriate to their special environment.

2. Without effective moral formation, the human propensity for selfishness—or simply the advancement of self-interest—can destructively affect adult institutions. Thus, moral formation is necessary to cultivate our inherent, but moderate, propensity for disinterested sacrifice. The institutions of any persisting society must be organized to ensure

that people's "unselfish genes" are adequately reinforced.

The general modes of moral formation have remained relatively stable throughout all cultures. To be sure, social class and sex-related differences have influenced the quantity and nature of moral formation delivered to the young; for instance, in many environments, limited resources have restricted the extent and intensity of the education provided to lower-class youths. Furthermore, the substance of the moral training transmitted to older youths has varied among cultures: according to Plato, Socrates was put to death because the Athenians disapproved of the moral training he was offering to Athenian young men. But such variations do not lessen the strength of the general model. Despite his affection for Socrates, Plato, in *The Republic* (circa 390 B.C.) emphasized the importance of constraining the learning influences on children and youths, to ensure appropriate moral outcomes.

Although secular and church-related educators have disputed the *means* of moral formation since the nineteenth century both, until comparatively recently, have agreed on their programs' behavioral *ends*. Children should be moral: honest, diligent, obedient, and patriotic. Thus, after the American Revolution, deists and secularists such as Thomas Jefferson and John Adams felt democracy would fail unless citizens acquired an unusually high degree of self-discipline and public spiritedness. They termed this medley of values "republican virtue." After the revolution, many of the original 13 states framed constitutions with provisions such as " . . . no government can be preserved to any people, but by a firm adherence to justice, moderation, temperance, frugality,

and virtue."[1] The founders believed that popular education would be a means of developing such precious traits. As the social historians David J. And Sheila Rothman have written, "The business of schools [in our early history] was not reading and writing but citizenship, not education but social control." The term "social control" may have a pejorative sound to our modern ears, but it simply and correctly means that schools were concerned with affecting conduct, rather than transmitting information or affecting states of mind.

CHARACTERISTICS OF THE GREAT TRADITION

Although issues in moral formation posed some conflicts in traditional societies, there were great areas of congruence around the great tradition of transmitting moral values. Documents generated in historical societies as well as ethnographic studies of many ancient and primitive cultures reveal through anecdote and insight the principles that characterize the tradition. Since the principles are too often ignored in contemporary education, we should consider them in some detail.

• *The tradition was concerned with good habits of conduct as contrasted with moral concepts or moral rationales.* Thus, the tradition emphasized visible courtesy and deference. In the moral mandate, "Honor thy father and mother," the act of *honoring* can be seen. It is easier to observe people *honoring* their parents than *loving* them. Loving, a state of mind, usually must be inferred.

• *The tradition focused on day-to-day moral issues: telling the truth in the face of evident temptation, being polite, or obeying legitimate authority.* It assumed that most moral challenges arose in mundane situations, and that people were often prone to act improperly.

• *The great tradition assumed that no single agency in society had the sole responsibility for moral education.* The varieties of moral problems confronting adults and youths were innumerable. Thus, youths had to be taught to practice morality in many environments. One agency, for example, the nuclear family or the neighborhood, might be deficient, so considerable redundancy was needed. In other words, there could be no neutrality about educating the young in morality: youth-serving agencies were either actively promoral or indifferent.

• *The tradition assumed that moral conduct, especially of the young, needed persistent and pervasive reinforcement.* To advance this end, literature, proverbs, legends, drama, ritual, and folk tales were used for cautionary purposes. Systems of symbolic and real rewards were developed and sustained: schools used ribbons, awards, and other signs of moral merit; noneducational agencies used praise and criticism as well as many symbolic forms of recognition.

• *The tradition saw an important relationship between the advancement of moral learning and the suppression of wrong conduct.* Wrong acts, especially in the presence of the young, were to be aggressively punished, as punishment not only suppressed bad examples, but also corrected particular wrongdoers. The tradition also developed concepts such as "scandal," a public, immoral act that also lowered the prestige of a person or institution. Conversely, since secret immoral acts were less likely to confuse or misdirect innocent persons, they received less disapproval.

• *The tradition was not hostile to the intellectual analysis of moral problems.*

Adults recognized that life occasionally generates moral dilemmas. In the Jewish religious tradition, learned men were expected to analyze and debate Talmudic moral issues. Other cultures have displayed similar patterns. But such analyses typically relied on a strong foundation of habit-oriented, mundane moral instruction and practice. Instruction in exegetical analysis commenced only after the selected neophyte had undergone long periods of testing, memorized large portions of semididactic classics, and displayed appropriate deference to exegetical experts.

• *The great tradition assumed that the most important and complex moral values were transmitted through persistent and intimate person-to-person interaction.* In many cases, adult mentors were assigned to develop close and significant relationship with particular youths. The youths might serve as apprentices to such persons, or the mentors might accept significant responsibilities for a young relative. In either case, constructive moral shaping required a comparatively high level of engagement.

• *The tradition usually treated "learners,"* who were sometimes students, as members of vital groups, such as teams, classes, or clubs. These groups were important reference points for communicating values, among them, group loyalty, and the diverse incidents of group life provided occasions for object lessons. The emphasis on collective life contrasts sharply with the individualism that pervades contemporary American education, and which is often mistaken for "humanism."

• *The tradition had a pessimistic opinion about the perfectibility of human beings, and about the feasibility or value of breaking with previous socialization patterns.* The tradition did not contend that whatever "is" is necessarily right, but it did assume that the persistence of certain conduct over hundreds of years suggested that careful deliberation should precede any modification or rejection.

As schooling spread, the tendency was to present the formal curriculum in a manner consistent with the tradition, and thus to focus on the transmission of correct habits and values. We should not assume that the interjection of moral concern was necessarily cumbersome. The famous *McGuffey's Reader* series featured stories and essays by substantial writers, such as Walter Scott and Charles Dickens. The literary quality of such writings was appropriate to the age of the student. Significantly, both the materials and their authors supported the development of certain desired traits.

CHARACTER EDUCATION

The most recent efflorescence of the great tradition in America can be found in the "character education" movement in our public schools between 1880 and about 1930. That movement attempted to make public schools more efficient transmitters of appropriate moral values.

The efforts to foster character education assumed schools had to operate from a purely secular basis, which posed special challenges for moral formation. Whereas some earlier education reformers had semisecular sympathies, in previous eras their impact had been tempered by the proreligious forces concurrently affecting schools. Before 1900, for example, probably 15-25 percent of American elementary and secondary school pupils attended either private or public schools that were explicitly religious; another 25-50 percent attended public schools that were tacitly religious. For example,

they used readings from the *King James Bible*.

The character education movement articulated numerous traditional moral aims: promptness, truthfulness, courtesy, and obedience. The movement strove to develop elementary and secondary school programs to foster such conduct. It emphasized techniques such as appropriately structured materials in history and literature; school clubs and other extracurricular activities; rigorous pupil discipline codes; and daily flag salutes and frequent assemblies. Many relatively elaborate character education plans were designed and disseminated to schools and school districts. Often the plans were adopted through the mandate of state legislatures or state boards of education. Some modern authorities, such as James Q. Wilson (1973), have perceived a strong relationship between the character education movement and the relatively high levels of youth order in America during the nineteenth century.

AN UNFAVORABLE EVALUATION

From the first, the supporters of character education emphasized rational organization and research. Despite such attempts, much of the research was superficial. Nonetheless, the research persisted because of the importance attributed to character, and gradually its quality improved. During the mid-1920s, researchers led by Hugh Hartschorne and Mark A. May concluded that the relationship between pupil good conduct and the application of formal character education approach was slight. Good conduct appeared to be relatively situation-specific: a person might routinely act correctly in one situation and incorrectly in another slightly different one. A person could cheat on exams, for example, but not steal money from the class fund. This situational specificity meant that good character was not a unified trait that could be cultivated by any single approach.

Despite this research, character education was never formally abandoned. Few educators or researchers have ever said publicly that schools should *not* be concerned with the morality or character of their pupils. Indeed, recent research and statistical reanalysis of earlier data has contended that Hartschorne and May's findings were excessively negative. Still, their research was a turning point in the relationship between American public education and the great tradition of moral values. Before the research many schools were fully concerned with carrying forward that tradition, and the intellectual forces affecting schools were in sympathy with such efforts. Even after the 1930s, many schools still reflexively maintained their former commitment to moral formation; the prevailing intellectual climate among researchers and academics, however, was indifferent or hostile to such efforts. Gradually, a disjunction arose between what some educators and many parents thought was appropriate (and what some of them applied), and what was favored by a smaller, more formally trained group of experts.

Ironically, the research findings of Hartschorne and May did not refute conflict with the major intellectual themes of the great tradition. The tradition emphasized that moral formation was complex. To be effective, it had to be incremental, diverse, pervasive, persistent, and rigorous. Essentially, it relied on probabilistic principles: the more frequent and more diverse techniques applied, the more

likely that more youths would be properly formed; but even if all techniques were applied, some youths would be "missed." Given such principles, it logically follows that the measured long-term effect of any limited program of "moral instruction" would be minute.

The Hartschorne and May findings demonstrated that American expectations for character education were unrealistic, a proposition not inconsistent with expectations we seem to have for *any* education technique. This does not mean that education's effects are inconsequential, but that Americans often approach education from a semi-utopian perspective. We have trouble realizing that many things happen slowly, and that not all problems are solvable.

NEW APPROACHES TO MORAL INSTRUCTION

During the 1930s, 1940s, and 1950s, there was little intellectual or research concern with moral formation in America. Schools continued to be engaged in moral instruction, both deliberately or incidentally, but the in-school process relied on momentum stimulated by earlier perspectives. In other words, moral instruction went on, but without substantial intellectual underpinning.

Since the 1960s, a number of different—perhaps more scientific—approaches to moral instruction have evolved. Many of these approaches have been described by the term "moral education." Among these have been values clarification, identified with Louis L. Raths and Sidney B. Simon, and the moral development approach identified with Lawrence Kohlberg and his colleagues. Despite the variations among contemporary approaches, almost all the more recent techniques have had certain common elements. Their developers were not school teachers, ministers, or education administrators, but college professors who sought to emphasize the scientific base for their efforts. But, most important, the approaches disavowed the great tradition's persistent concern with affecting *conduct*. The moral dilemmas used in some exercises were highly abstract and probably would never arise in real life. Their aim was to cause students to feel or reason in particular ways rather than to practice right conduct immediately.

The developers of the new systems were conscious of Hartschorne and May's research. They recognized the difficulty of shaping conduct and presumably felt that shaping patterns of reasoning was more feasible. Furthermore, many of the moral education approaches were designed as curriculum materials that could be taught through lectures and class discussion. Such designs facilitated their adoption by teachers and schools. Had the approaches aimed to pervasively affect pupil day-to-day conduct, they would have been more difficult to disseminate. Finally, both the researchers and the proponents of the new approaches felt it was morally unjustifiable to apply the vital pressures needed to actually shape pupil's conduct, feeling such pressures would constitute "indoctrination." On the other hand, methods of moral reasoning apparently might be taught as routine school subjects with the tacit consent of the pupils involved.

The anti-indoctrination stance central to the new approaches invites amplification. Obviously, the great tradition regarded the issue of indoctrination as a specious question. Proponents of the great tradition say, "Of course indoctrination happens. It is ridiculous to be-

lieve children are capable of objectively assessing most of the beliefs and values they must absorb to be effective adults. They must learn a certain body of 'doctrine' to function on a day-to-day basis in society. There is good and bad doctrine, and thus things must be weighed and assessed. But such assessment is largely the responsibility of parents and other appropriate adults."

It is hard to articulate fairly the position of the anti-indoctrinators. Although they are against indoctrination, they provide no clear answer as to how children are given many real choices in a relatively immutable world necessarily maintained by adults. The anti-indoctrinators also do not say what adults are to do when children's value choices and resulting potential conduct are clearly harmful to them or others. After all, punishments for bad value choices are, in effect, forms of indoctrination. And the idea of presenting pupils with any particular approach to moral education in a school is inherently indoctrinative: the pupils are not allowed to refuse to come to school, or to hear seriously the pros and cons articulated by sympathetic spokespersons (or critics) for moral education or to freely choose among various approaches to them. Providing such choices is antithetical to the operation of any school.

To consider another perspective, the secular nature of the typical public school obviously indoctrinates pupils against practicing religion in that environment, although most religions contend that some religious practices of a public nature are inextricably related to day-to-day life. This "reality" of separating religion and public education is understandable. However, it is disingenuous to call this policy nonindoctrinative. Thus, it is specious to talk about student choices. The point is that, *on the whole, school is and should and must be inherently indoctrinative*. The only significant questions are: Will the indoctrination be overt or covert, and what will be indoctrinated?

The great tradition has never died. Many administrators and teachers in public and private schools have continued practices consistent with its principles. Given the increased support from academics and intellectuals, . . . these principles deserve widespread professional support.

NOTE

1. The Virginia Constitution.

REFERENCES

Cohen, Y. *The Transition from Childhood to Adolescence*. Chicago: Aldine, 1964.

Hartschorne, H., and May, M. A. *Studies in Deceit, Studies in Service and Self-Control*, and *Studies in the Organization of Character*. New York: Macmillan, 1928, 1929, 1930.

Klapp. O. *The Collective Search for Identity*. New York: Holt, Rinehart, and Winston, 1969.

Meyers, E. *Education in the Perspective of History*. New York: Harper & Row, 1960.

Rothman, D. J., and Rothman, S. M. *Sources of American Social Tradition*. New York: Basic, 1975.

Wilkinson, R. *Governing Elites*. New York: Oxford University Press, 1969.

Wilson, J. Q. "Crime and American Culture." *The Public Interest* 70 (Winter 1973): 22–48.

Wynne, E. A. *Looking at Schools*. Lexington, MA.: Heath/Lexington, 1980.

Yulish, S. M. *The Search for a Civic Religion*, Lanham, Md.: University Press of America, 1980.

POSTSCRIPT

Should Values Be Developed Rather Than Transmitted?

One of the questions concerning school-developed morality is whether or not the system effectively transmits the desired values. According to Philip W. Jackson, in "The School as Moral Instructor: Deliberate Efforts and Unintentional Consequences," *The World and I* (March 1988), schools generally respond to societal problems by creating extra courses to specifically address them. He cites such examples as driver education for traffic safety problems and sexuality education in response to the rising rate of teenage pregnancies. Jackson supports this reaction as a logical curricular solution, but feels that gauging the effectiveness of such courses is impossible.

In addition to not knowing if students are learning the desired material, Jackson wonders what moral signals students may pick up that are not intentionally taught. Do day-to-day school routines arbitrarily transmit undesired morals? Again, there is little evidence to base an answer on.

For a full view of the educational problems and alternatives bearing on the values domain, one must sample widely. Some sources that may help clarify this difficult area are Abraham Maslow's *New Knowledge in Human Values* (1959); Milton Rokeach's *The Nature of Human Values* (1973); and a collection of essays presented by Robert Coles in *The Moral Life of Children* (1986).

Other sources that may be illuminating are Philip Phenix's "The Moral Imperative in Contemporary American Education," *Perspectives on Education* (Winter 1969), and John Dewey's *Moral Principles in Education* (1911).

Of more recent vintage are Thomas Lickona's practical guidebook *Raising Good Children* (1983); John A. Howard's article, "Re-opening the Books on Ethics: The Role of Education in a Free Society," *American Education* (October 1984); and Jerome Kagan's chapter on "Establishing a Morality" in his book *The Nature of the Child* (1984). The December 1985/January 1986 issue of *Educational Leadership* is devoted to the schools' role in the development of character. Harold Howe II offers some challenging ideas in his article "Can Schools Teach Values?" *Teachers College Record* (Fall 1987). The latest books on the topic are *Theories of Moral Development* (1985), by John Martin Rich and Joseph DeVitts; *Schools and Meaning: Essays on the Moral Nature of Schooling* (1985), edited by David E. Purpel and H. Svi Shapiro; and *No Ladder to the Sky: Education and Morality* (1987), by Gabriel Moran.

Perhaps columnist Jonathan Yardley added a necessary dimension to the continuing controversy: "The prevailing sense that the country is morally rudderless is well-founded and disturbing. But throwing the problem onto the schools is hardly the answer."

ISSUE 5

Is Church-State Separation Being Threatened?

YES: R. Freeman Butts, from "A History and Civics Lesson for All of Us," *Educational Leadership* (May 1987)

NO: Robert L. Cord, from "Church-State Separation and the Public Schools: A Re-evaluation," *Educational Leadership* (May 1987)

ISSUE SUMMARY

YES: Professor emeritus of education R. Freeman Butts warns that current efforts to redefine the relationship between religion and schooling are eroding the Constitution's intent.
NO: Professor of political science Robert L. Cord offers a more accommodating interpretation of this intent, one which allows for the school practices that Butts condemns as unconstitutional.

The religious grounding of early schooling in America certainly cannot be denied. Nor can the history of religious influences on the conduct of our governmental functions and our school practices. In the nineteenth century, however, protests against the prevailing Protestant influence in the public schools were lodged by Catholics, Jews, nonbelievers, and other groups, giving rise to a number of issues that revolve around interpretations of the "establishment of religion" and the "free exercise of religion" clauses of the Constitution.

Twentieth-century U.S. Supreme Court cases, such as *Cochran* (1930), *Everson* (1947), *McCollum* (1948), *Zorach* (1952), *Engel* (1962), and *Murray* (1963), attempted to clarify the relationship between religion and schooling. Most of these decisions bolstered the separation of church and state position. Only recently has a countermovement, led in some quarters by the Moral Majority organization of Reverend Jerry Falwell, sought to sway public and legal opinion toward an emphasis on the "free exercise" clause and toward viewing the influence of secular humanism in the schools as "an establishment of religion."

At both the legislative and judicial levels, attempts have been made in the 1980s to secure an official place in public education for voluntary prayer, moments of silent meditation, and creationism in the science curriculum. Censorship of textbooks and other school materials, access to facilities by religious groups, and the right of parents to withdraw their children from instruction deemed to be morally offensive and damaging have also been promoted. Humanists (who may be either religious or nonreligious) find a good deal of distortion in these recent attacks on the "secularization" of schooling, and they argue that the materials used in the schools are consistent with the historical goals of character development while also being in tune with the realities of the present times.

John Buchanan of People for the American Way argues that public schools are places where young people of differing backgrounds and beliefs can come together and learn tolerance. He and others worry that parental veto power will undermine decision-making and impair school effectiveness. Bill Keith of the Creation Science Legal Defense Fund contends that a parent's liberty with regard to a child's education is a fundamental right, an enduring American tradition.

Resolution of the philosophical questions regarding the content and conduct of public education has become increasingly politicized. Who should control the school curriculum and its materials—school boards, professional educators, community groups, the federal or state governments, parents, or students? Should censorship boards operate at the local, state, or national level—or none of the above? Where does the line get drawn between benevolent intervention and thought control? Can schools be value-neutral?

In the articles presented here, R. Freeman Butts makes the case that legal and historical scholarship points to the broader, separatist, and secular meaning of the First Amendment, which controls the answers to many of these questions. Robert L. Cord bases his argument for a more accommodating interpretation on his findings in primary historical sources and on the actions of the framers of the Constitution.

YES

R. Freeman Butts

A HISTORY AND CIVICS LESSON
FOR ALL OF US

As chairman of the Commission on the Bicentennial of the U.S. Constitution, former Chief Justice Warren E. Burger urges that the occasion provide "a history and civics lesson for all of us." I heartily agree, but the lesson will depend on which version of history you read—and believe.

From May 1982, when President Reagan advocated adoption of a constitutional amendment to permit organized prayer in public schools, Congress has been bitterly divided during the repeated efforts to pass legislation aimed either at amending the Constitution or stripping the Supreme Court and other federal courts of jurisdiction to decide cases about prayers in the public schools. Similar controversies have arisen over efforts of the Reagan administration to promote vouchers and tuition tax credits to give financial aid to parents choosing to send their children to private religious schools.

SCHOOL/RELIGION CONTROVERSIES

I would like to remind educators that the present controversies have a long history, and the way we understand that history makes a difference in our policy judgments. A watershed debate occurred, for example, in 1947 when the Supreme Court spelled out the meaning of the part of the First Amendment which reads, "Congress shall make no law respecting an establishment of religion." The occasion was a challenge to a New Jersey law giving tax money to Catholic parents to send their children by bus to parochial schools. The Court split 5-4 in that case, *Everson* v. *Board of Education*, on whether this practice was, in effect, "an establishment of religion" and thus unconstitutional, but there was no disagreement on the principle. Justice Hugo Black wrote for the majority.

> The "establishment of religion" clause of the First Amendment means at least this: Neither a state nor the Federal Government can pass laws which aid one religion, aid all religions, or prefer one religion over another. . . . No tax in

From R. Freeman Butts, "A History and Civics Lesson for All of Us," *Educational Leadership*, vol. 44, no. 8 (May 1987), pp. 21-25. Copyright © 1987 by the Association for Supervision and Curriculum Development. Reprinted by permission. All rights reserved.

any amount, large or small, can be levied to support any religious activities or institutions, whatever they may be called, or whatever form they may adopt to teach or practice religion. . . . In the words of Jefferson, the clause against establishment of religion by law was intended to erect "a wall of separation between Church and State."[1]

The *Everson* majority accepted this broad principle, but decided, nevertheless, that bus fares were merely welfare aid to parents and children and not aid to the religious schools themselves. The 1948 *McCollum* case prohibited released time for religious instruction in the public schools of Champaign, Illinois, because it violated the *Everson* principle.

These two cases set off a thunderous denunciation of the Supreme Court and calls for impeachment of the justices. They also sent historians of education scurrying to original sources to see how valid this broad and liberal interpretation was.

ESTABLISHMENT PRINCIPLE

The two books at that time that gave most attention to the establishment principle as it related to education were James M. O'Neill's *Religion and Education Under the Constitution*[2] and my own, *The American Tradition in Religion and Education*.[3] O'Neill found the Court's interpretation appalling; I found it basically true to Madison and the majority of the framers of the First Amendment. My book was cited in 1971 in the concurring opinions of Justices Brennan, Douglas, and Black in *Lemon* v. *Kurtzman*.[4] Chief Justice Burger summarized for a unanimous court the accumulated precedents since *Everson* and listed three tests of constitutional state action in education: a secular purpose; neither advancement

nor inhibition of religion; and no excessive government entanglement with religion.

With that decision, I concluded that my views of the framers' intentions had been pretty well accepted: namely, that "an establishment of religion" in the 1780s was "a multiple establishment" whereby public aid could go to several churches, and that this is what the majority of framers, particularly Madison, intended to prohibit in the First Amendment.

Indeed, single religious establishments had existed in nine of the early colonies, but by 1789 when the First Congress drafted the First Amendment, religious diversity had become such a powerful political force that seven states, which included the vast majority of Americans, had either disestablished their churches or had never established any. Only six state constitutions still permitted "an establishment of religion," and all six provided tax funds for several churches, not just one.[5] Naturally, some representatives and senators from those states did not want their multiple establishment threatened by a Bill of Rights in the new federal government. But Madison did.

Madison had prevented just such a multiple establishment in Virginia in 1785 and 1786 and managed instead the passage of Jefferson's powerful Statute for Religious Freedom. In his speech of 8 June 1789, when he introduced his Bill of Rights proposals in the House, he made a double-barreled approach to religious freedom. He proposed (1) to prohibit Congress from establishing religion on a national basis, and (2) to prohibit the states from infringing "equal rights of conscience."

After considerable discussion and some changes of language, the House of Representatives approved both of Madison's proposals and sent them to the Senate. The Senate, however, did not approve the prohibition on the states. Furthermore, a minority in the Senate made three attempts to narrow the wording of the First Amendment to prohibit Congress from establishing a single church or giving preference to one religious sect or denomination. The majority, however, rejected all such attempts to narrow Madison's proposal, and the Senate finally accepted the wording of Madison's conference committee. This was then finally adopted by both houses. Madison's broad and liberal interpretation of the establishment clause as applied to Congress had won.[6]

Neither Madison nor the majority of framers intended for government to disdain religion. They intended that republican government guarantee equal rights of conscience to all persons, but it took some 150 years before Madison's views were applied specifically to the states through the Fourteenth Amendment. That is what the Supreme Court did in *Everson*.

FRAMERS' INTENTIONS REDEFINED

But today, "a jurisprudence of original intention" has revived the debates of the 1940s and 1950s, expounding much the same views as those of O'Neill namely that "the framers" intended only to prohibit Congress from establishing a single national church, but would permit aid to all religions on a nonpreferential basis and would even permit the states to establish a single church if they wished. These arguments are now being resurrected or reincarnated (to use the secular meaning of those terms) with even more sophisticated scholarship by such au-thors as Walter Berns of Georgetown University, Michael Malbin of the American Enterprise Institute, and Robert L. Cord of Northeastern University.[7]

Their works have been cited in legal briefs in several state actions and in at least one federal district court decision, while an increasingly vigorous campaign has been launched by conservative members of Congress and the Reagan administration to appeal to the history of "original intention."

These efforts reached a crescendo of confrontation in summer and fall of 1985, following two Supreme Court decisions. In *Wallace* v. *Jaffree* on 4 June 1985, the Court reversed Federal Judge W. Brevard Hand's decision that Alabama's laws providing for prayer in the public schools were, indeed, permissible and did not violate the First Amendment's prohibition against "an establishment of religion." Relying in part on Cord's version of history, Judge Hand argued that the Supreme Court had long erred in its reading of the original intention of the framers of the First Amendment. He said that they intended solely to prevent the federal government from establishing a single national church such as the Church of England; therefore, the Congress could aid all churches if it did not give preference to any one; that a state was free to establish a state religion if it chose to do so and, thus, could require or permit prayers in its public schools.

The Supreme Court reversed this decision (6-3), and Justice John Paul Stevens, writing for the Court, rebuked Judge Hand by referring to his "newly discovered historical evidence" as a "remarkable conclusion" wholly at odds with the firmly established constitutional provision that "the several States have no greater power to restrain the individual freedoms protected by the First Amendment than does the Congress of the United States." Justice Stevens emphasized that the Court had confirmed and endorsed time and time again the principle of incorporation, by which the Fourteenth Amendment imposes the same limitations on the states that it imposes on Congress regarding protection of civil liberties guaranteed by the First Amendment and the original Bill of Rights.[8]

However, the confrontations between these views of history were not over. In his long dissenting opinion in *Jaffree*, Associate Justice William H. Rehnquist, now Chief Justice, reasserted an "accommodationist" view of church and state relations. Relying on O'Neill's and Cord's version of history, he argued that the "wall of separation between church and state" is a metaphor based on bad history and that the *Everson* principle "should be frankly and explicitly abandoned." Justice Byron R. White's dissent also supported such "a basic reconsideration of our precedents."

Soon after, on 1 July 1985, the Supreme Court ruled in *Aguilar v. Fenton* (5-4) that the practices of New York City and Grand Rapids, Michigan, in sending public school teachers to private religious schools to teach remedial and enhancement programs for disadvantaged children, were also unconstitutional. Justice William J. Brennan, delivering the Court's opinion, cited the *Everson* principle that the state should remain neutral and not become entangled with churches in administering schools. Dissents were written by the Chief Justice and Justices Sandra Day O'Connor, White, and Rehnquist.[9]

These Supreme Court decisions were greeted with some surprise and considerable elation by liberals and with dis-

may by conservatives. Attorney General Edwin Meese III quickly and forcefully responded on 10 July 1985 in a speech before the American Bar Association. He explicitly criticized the Court's decisions on religion and education as a misreading of history and commended Justice Rehnquist's call for overruling *Everson*. Secretary of Education William Bennett echoed the complaint that the Supreme Court was misreading history. And, then, in October 1985 Justices Brennan and Stevens both gave speeches sharply criticizing the Attorney General's campaign for a "jurisprudence of original intention."

In addition, the White House, the Attorney General, the Justice Department, the Secretary of Education, the former Republican majority of the Senate Judiciary Committee, the new Chief Justice, and the conservative justices of the Supreme Court, by public statements are now ranged against the liberal and centrist members of the Supreme Court and such notable constitutional scholars as Laurence Tribe of Harvard, Herman Schwartz of American University, A. E. Dick Howard of the University of Virginia, and Leonard W. Levy of the Claremont Graduate School. They all appeal to history, but whose version of history do you read—and believe?

All in all, I think it fair to say that the predominant stream of constitutional, legal, and historical scholarship points to the broader, separatist, and secular meaning of the First Amendment against the narrower, cooperationist, or accommodationist meaning. A nonspecialist cannot encompass the vast literature on this subject, but a valuable and readily available source of evidence is the recently published book by Leonard Levy, professor of humanities and chairman of the Claremont University Graduate Faculty of History. He is editor of the *Encyclopedia of the American Constitution* and the author of a dozen books devoted mostly to the Bill of Rights.

In his book on the First Amendment's establishment clause Levy concludes, and I fully agree, that the meaning of "an establishment of religion" is as follows:

> After the American Revolution seven of the fourteen states that comprised the Union in 1791 authorized establishments of religion by law. Not one state maintained a single or preferential establishment of religion. An establishment of religion meant to those who framed and ratified the First Amendment what it meant in those seven states, and in all seven it meant public support of religion on a nonpreferential basis. It was specifically this support on a nonpreferential basis that the establishment clause of the First Amendment sought to forbid.[10]

Acceptance of a narrow, accommodationist view of the history of the establishment clause must not be allowed to be turned into public policies that serve to increase public support for religious schools in any form: vouchers, tax credits, or aid for extremes of "parental choice." They must not be allowed to increase the role of religion in public schools by organized prayer, teaching of Creationism, censorship of textbooks on the basis of their "secular humanism" or "opting out" of required studies in citizenship on the grounds that they offend any sincerely held religious belief, as ruled by Federal District Judge Thomas Hull in Greeneville, Tennessee, in October 1986.[11]

These practices not only violate good public policy, but they also vitiate the thrust toward separation of church and state which, with minor exceptions, marked the entire careers of Madison and Jefferson. William Lee Miller, professor of religious studies at the University of Virginia, wrote the following succinct summary of their views:

> Did "religious freedom" for Jefferson and Madison extend to atheists? Yes. To agnostics, unbelievers, and pagans? Yes. To heretics and blasphemers and the sacrilegious? Yes. To the Jew and the Gentile, the Christian and Mohametan, the Hindoo, and infidel of every denomination? Yes. To people who want freedom *from* religion? Yes. To people who want freedom *against* religion? Yes. . . .
>
> Did this liberty of belief for Jefferson and Madison entail separation of church and state? Yes. A ban on tax aid to religion? Yes. On state help to religion? Yes. Even religion-in-general? Yes. Even if it were extended without any favoritism among religious groups? Yes. The completely voluntary way in religion? Yes.
>
> Did all the founders agree with Jefferson and Madison? Certainly not. Otherwise there wouldn't have been a fight.[12]

The fight not only continues, but seems to be intensifying on many fronts. So, it behooves educators to study these issues in depth, to consider the best historical scholarship available, and to judge present issues of religion and education accordingly.

NOTES

1. *Everson v. Board of Education*, 330 U.S. 1 (1947). Black was joined by Chief Justice Vinson and Justices Douglas, Murphy, and Reed.

2. James M. O'Neill, *Religion and Education Under the Constitution* (New York: Harper, 1949). O'Neill was chairman of the department of speech at Queens College, New York. See also Wilfrid Parsons, S.J., *The First Freedom: Considerations on Church and State in the United States* (New York: Declan X. McMullen, 1948).

3. R. Freeman Butts, *The American Tradition in Religion and Education* (Boston: Beacon Press, 1950). I was professor of education at Teachers College, Columbia University, teaching courses in the history of education. See O'Neill's review of my book in *America*, 9 September 1950, pp. 579–583. See also Leo Pfeffer, *Church, State, and Freedom* (Boston: Beacon Press, 1953) for views similar to mine.

4. *Lemon v. Kurtzman*, 403 U.S. 602 (1971). The law struck down in Pennsylvania would have paid part of the salaries of private school teachers of nonreligious subjects.

5. Those six states were Massachusetts, Connecticut, New Hampshire, Maryland, South Carolina, and Georgia.

6. R. Freeman Butts, *Religion, Education, and the First Amendment: The Appeal to History* (Washington, D.C.: People for the American Way, 1985),35. R. Freeman Butts, "James Madison, the Bill of Rights, and Education," *Teachers College Record* 60, 3 (December 1958): 123–128.

7. Walter Berns, *The First Amendment and the Future of American Democracy* (New York: Basic Books, 1976). Michael J. Malbin, *Religion and Politics: The Intentions of the Authors of the First Amendment* (Washington, D.C.: American Enterprise Institute, 1978). Robert L. Cord, *Separation of Church and State: Historical Fact and Current Fiction* (New York: Lambeth Press, 1982) with a Foreword by William F. Buckley, Jr.

8. *Wallace v. Jaffree*, 105 S.Ct. 2479 (1985).

9. *Aguilar v. Felton*, 105 S.Ct. 3232 (1985).

10. Leonard W. Levy, *The Establishment Clause: Religion and the First Amendment* (New York: Macmillan, 1986), p. xvi.

11. *Mozert v. Hawkins*, U.S. District Court for Eastern District of Tennessee, 24 October 1986.

12. *The Washington Post National Weekly Edition*, 13 October 1986, pp. 23–24.

NO

Robert L. Cord

CHURCH-STATE SEPARATION AND THE PUBLIC SCHOOLS: A RE-EVALUATION

For four decades—since the *Everson* v. *Board of Education*[1] decision in 1947—a volatile national debate has raged about the meaning and scope of the First Amendment's establishment clause that mandates separation of church and state. Many of the U.S. Supreme Court's decisions about this matter involve education; therefore, their importance is great to school administrators and teachers who establish and execute policy.

Because of the vagueness of Supreme Court decision making in this important area of constitutional law, public school educators have been accused of violating the First Amendment by allowing or disallowing, for example, the posting of the Ten Commandments, a meeting on school property of a student religious club, or a moment of silent meditation and/or prayer. Today even the very textbooks that students read have become a subject of litigation by parents against a school system, a controversy most likely to end before the Supreme Court.

As this national debate rages, most scholars generally agree that the Founding Fathers' intentions regarding church-state separation are still extremely relevant and important. While the framers of the Constitution and the First Amendment could not foresee many twentieth century problems—especially those growing from advanced technology—many church-state concerns that they addressed in 1787 and 1789 are similar to those we face today.

CONSTITUTION'S WORDS NOT TRIVIAL

Further, if a nation, such as the United States, proclaims that its written Constitution protects individual liberties and truly provides legal restrictions on the actions of government, the words of that organic law—and the principles derived from them—cannot be treated as irrelevant trivia by those who temporarily govern. That is the surest single way to undo constitutional government, for constitutional government requires that the general power of government be defined and limited by law *in fact* as well as in theory.[2]

From Robert L. Cord, "Church-State Separation and the Public Schools: A Re-evaluation," *Educational Leadership*, vol. 44, no. 8 (May 1987), pp 26–32. Copyright © 1987 by the Association for Supervision and Curriculum Development. Reprinted by permission. All rights reserved.

Published in 1979 to the praise of many respected constitutional scholars, the encyclopedic *Congressional Quarterly's Guide to the U.S. Supreme Court* provided the following meaning of the establishment clause.

> The two men most responsible for its inclusion in the Bill of Rights construed the clause *absolutely*. Thomas Jefferson and James Madison thought that the prohibition of establishment meant that a presidential proclamation of Thanksgiving Day was just as improper as a tax exemption for churches.[3]

Despite this authoritative statement, the historical facts are that, as President, James Madison issued at least four Thanksgiving Day proclamations—9 July 1812, 23 July 1813, 16 November 1814, and 4 March 1815.[4] If Madison interpreted the establishment clause absolutely, he violated both his oath of office and the very instruments of government that he helped write and labored to have ratified.[5]

Similarly, if President Thomas Jefferson construed the establishment clause absolutely, he also violated his oath of office, his principles, and the Constitution when, in 1802, he signed into federal law tax exemption for the churches in Alexandria County, Virginia.[6]

Since Jefferson and Madison held the concept of separation of church and state most dear, in my judgment, neither man—as president or in any other public office under the federal Constitution—was an absolutist and neither violated his understanding of the First Amendment's establishment clause. For me, it therefore logically follows that President Madison did not think issuing Thanksgiving Day Proclamations violated the constitutional doctrine of church-state separation, and that President Jefferson held the same view about tax exemption for churches.

Whoever wrote the paragraph quoted from the prestigious *Guide to the U.S. Supreme Court*, I assume, did not intend to deceive, but evidently did not check primary historical sources, was ignorant of Madison's and Jefferson's actions when each was president, and mistakenly relied on inadequate secondary historical writings considered authoritative, as no doubt the paragraph from the *Guide* is, too. This indicates that much misunderstanding and/or misinformation exists about the meaning of the constitutional concept of separation of church and state.

In that context, I examine ideas critical of my writing published in a monograph—*Religion, Education, and the First Amendment: The Appeal to History*—by the eminent scholar, R. Freeman Butts. There he characterized my book, *Separation of Church and State: Historical Fact and Current Fiction*, as a manifestation of some "conservative counterreformation," the purpose of which is "to attack once again the [U.S. Supreme] Court's adherence to the principle of separation between church and state" by characterizing that principle as a "myth" or a "fiction" or merely "rhetoric."[7] The very first paragraph of my book refutes this erroneous characterization.

> Separation of Church and State is probably the most distinctive concept that the American constitutional system has contributed to the body of political ideas. In 1791, when the First Amendment's prohibition that "Congress shall make no law respecting an establishment of religion" was added to the United States Constitution, no other country had provided so carefully to prevent the combination of the power of religion with the power of the national government.[8]

While primary historical sources exist that substantiate the Founding Fathers' commitment to church-state separation, other primary sources convince me that much of what the United States Supreme Court and noted scholars have written about it is historically untenable and, in many instances, sheer fiction at odds with the words and actions of the statesmen who placed that very principle in our Constitution.

ABSOLUTE SEPARATION V. "NO PREFERENCE" DOCTRINE

In the 40-year-old *Everson* case the Supreme Court justices, while splitting 5-4 over the immediate issue, were unanimous in proclaiming that the purpose of the establishment clause—and the intention of its framers in the First Congress—was to create a "high and impregnable" wall of separation between church and state.[9]

Unlike the *Everson* Court, Professor Butts, and all "absolute separationist" scholars, I think the full weight of historical evidence—especially the documented public words and deeds of the First Amendment's framers, including James Madison and our early presidents and Congresses—indicates that they embraced a far narrower concept of church-state separation. In my judgment, they interpreted the First Amendment as prohibiting Congress from (1) creating a national religion or establishment, and (2) placing any one religion, religious sect, or religious tradition in a legally preferred position.[10]

Simply put, the framers of the establishment clause sought to preclude discriminatory government religious partisanship, not nondiscriminatory government accommodation or, in some instances, government collaboration with religion. When this "no religious preference" interpretation of the establishment clause is substituted for the Supreme Court's "high and impregnable wall" interpretation, it is easier to understand many historical documents at odds with the absolutists' position. They substantiate that all our early Congresses, including the one that proposed to the states what subsequently became the First Amendment, and all our early presidents, including Jefferson and Madison, in one way or another used sectarian means to achieve constitutional secular ends.

EVERSON CASE

In the *Everson* case, writing the Court's opinion, Justice Black sought to bolster his "high and impregnable wall" dictum with appeals to some carefully chosen actions of Madison, Jefferson, the Virginia Legislature of 1786, and the framers of the First Amendment. Omitted from all of the *Everson* opinions are any historical facts that run counter to that theory. In his writings, I think Professor Butts employs a similar technique of "history by omission." By this I mean that he fails to address indisputable historical facts that are irreconcilable with his absolute separationist views. A few examples will substantiate this extremely important point.

Mentioning Madison's successful Virginia battle against the "Bill Establishing a Provision for Teachers of the Christian Religion" and "Jefferson's historic statute for religious freedom in 1786,"[11] Professor Butts does not explain away Jefferson's Virginia "Bill for Punishing Disturbers of Religious Worship and Sabbath Breakers," which was introduced by

Madison in the Virginia Assembly in 1785 and became law in 1786.[12] Further, while he emphasizes Madison's role in introducing and guiding the Bill of Rights through the First Congress,[13] Professor Butts does not explain why the "absolutist" Madison served as one of six members of a Congressional Committee which, without recorded dissent, recommended the establishment of a Congressional Chaplain System. Adopting the Committee's recommendation, the First Congress voted a $500 annual salary from public funds for a Senate chaplain and a like amount for a House chaplain, both of whom were to offer public prayers in Congress.[14]

Nor does Professor Butts explain why, as an absolute separationist, James Madison would, as president, issue discretionary proclamations of Thanksgiving, calling for a day "to be set apart for the devout purposes of rendering the Sovereign of the Universe and the Benefactor of Man [identified earlier in the proclamation by Madison as "Almighty God"] the public homage due to His holy attributes. . . ."[15]

Unexplained also is why Professor Butts' absolute separationist version of Thomas Jefferson would, as president, conclude a treaty with Kaskaskia Indians which, in part, called for the United States to build them a Roman Catholic Church and pay their priest, and subsequently would urge Congress to appropriate public funds to carry out the terms of the treaty.[16] An understanding of what the framers of our Constitution thought about church-state separation would also be furthered if we had explanations of why Presidents Washington, John Adams, and Jefferson apparently did not think they were breaching the "high and impregnable" wall when they signed into law Congressional bills that, in effect, purchased with enormous grants of federal land, in controlling trusts, the services of the "Society of the United Brethren for propagating the Gospel among the Heathen" to minister to the needs of Christian and other Indians in the Ohio Territory.[17] Like the majority of the Supreme Court, Professor Butts does not comment on these historical documents and events.

When all the historical evidence is considered, I think it relatively clear that the establishment clause was designed to prevent Congress from either establishing a national religion or from putting any one religion, religious sect, or religious tradition into a legally preferred position. In *Everson*, the Supreme Court interpreted the Fourteenth Amendment as prohibiting state legislatures, or their instrumentalities such as school boards, from doing likewise. As a result, the interpretation of the establishment clause by Supreme Court decisions governs the permissible range of both state and federal legislative authority.

Professor Butts thinks my definition of an "establishment of religion" too narrow, and the prohibition which I think the framers intended "plausible but false."[18] Plausible because in the sixteenth and seventeenth centuries, establishments in Europe and in the early American colonies usually meant the establishment of a single church. False because Professor Butts contends that, by the end of the eighteenth century, in America the term "establishment of religion" had taken on a different meaning.

His argument is that "the idea of a single church as constituting 'an establishment of religion' was no longer embedded in the legal framework of any American state when the First Amendment was being debated in Congress in the summer of 1789." Adding that in all of the states that still retained establishments, "multiple establishments were the rule," Professor Butts concludes that "the founders and the framers could not have been ignorant of this fact; they knew very well that this is what the majority in the First Congress intended to prohibit at the federal level."[19]

BUTTS' ARGUMENT UNTENABLE

This argument is simply untenable when considered with the primary historical record. Professor Butts virtually ignored the documents most crucial to an understanding of what the religion clauses were designed to prohibit at the federal level—the suggested constitutional amendments from the various State Ratifying Conventions. Those documents show that they feared, among other things, that important individual rights might be infringed by the powerful new national legislature authorized by the adoption of the federal Constitution.

Their amendments indicate that the states feared interference with the individual's right of conscience and an exclusive religious establishment, *not a multiple national establishment*, as Professor Butts wants us to believe. Typical was the Maryland Ratifying Convention's proposed amendment stating "that there will be no national religion established by law; but that all persons be equally entitled to protection in their religious liberty."[20]

The Virginia Ratifying Convention proposed a "Declaration of Bill of Rights" as amendments to the Constitution that was echoed by North Carolina, Rhode Island, and New York Conventions. Virginia's Article Twenty, adopted 27 June 1788, stated:

> That religion, or the duty which we owe to our Creator, and the manner of discharging it, can be directed only by reason and conviction, not by force or violence; and therefore all men have an equal, natural, and unalienable right to the free exercise of religion, according to the dictates of conscience, and that no particular religious sect or society ought to be favored or established, by law, in preference to others.[21]

STATES WANTED NONPREFERENCE

In short, when it came to religious establishments, the State Ratifying Conventions proposed "nonpreference" amendments.

With these proposals in mind, it is easier to understand the wording of Madison's original religion amendment: "The Civil rights of none shall be abridged on account of religious belief or worship, nor shall any national religion be established, nor shall the full and equal rights of Conscience be in any manner, or on any pretext, infringed."[22] Madison wanted the Constitution to forbid the federal government from interfering with the rights of conscience or establish an exclusive national religion—not religions—and the record said so.

The "nonpreference" interpretation is further bolstered by Madison's original wording of his own establishment clause and his later interpretation on the floor of the House of Representatives of the intended prohibitions of the amendment. On 15 August 1789, using virtually the same words employed by the petitioning State Ratifying Conventions,

> Mr. Madison said, he apprehended the meaning of the words to be, that

Congress should not establish a religion, and enforce the legal observation of it by law, nor compel men to worship God in any manner contrary to their conscience. Whether the words are necessary or not, he did not mean to say, but . . . he thought it as well expressed as the nature of the language would admit.[23]

Further, the House record indicates that Madison said that "he believed that the people feared one sect might obtain a preeminence, or two combine together, and establish a religion to which they would compel others to conform."[24] Certainly Madison's statements from the record of the First Congress and the other primary documents mentioned here run contrary to the "multiple establishment" thesis.

IMPLICATIONS FOR THE PUBLIC SCHOOLS

Professionals in education may wonder appropriately what the impact would be on public education should the U.S. Supreme Court now choose to reverse some of its major rulings and adopt the narrower interpretation of church-state separation which I believe was intended and embraced by the First Amendment's framers.

First, the establishment clause would continue to prohibit Congress and individual states from creating, in Madison's words, "a national religion."

Second, in keeping with the framers' intent, the establishment clause's "no preference" doctrine, applied directly to the federal government and to the states by the Fourteenth Amendment, would constitutionally preclude all governmental entities from placing any one religion, religious sect, or religious tradition into a preferred legal status. As a consequence,

in public schools, the recitation of the Lord's Prayer or readings taken solely from the New Testament would continue to be unconstitutional because they place the Christian religion in a preferred position.

Similarly, the posting of the Ten Commandments only or reading only from the Old Testament would place the Judeo-Christian tradition in an unconstitutionally favored religious status. However, unendorsed readings or postings from many writings considered sacred by various religions, such as the Book of Mormon, the interpretative writings of Mary Baker Eddy, the Bible, the Koran, the Analects of Confucius, would be constitutional. A decision to teach only "creationism" or Genesis would be unconstitutional, while a course in cosmology, exploring a full range of beliefs about the origin of life or the nature of the universe—religious, areligious, or nonreligious—would not violate the First Amendment any more than would a course on comparative religions without teacher endorsement.

In all circumstances where the state is pursuing a valid educational goal, and is religiously nonpartisan in doing so, the professional leadership of the educational unit would decide, as in any other policy, whether such an activity was educationally appropriate or desirable. This would be the case whether the educational unit was a school, a school district, or an entire state educational system. Consequently, adherence to the "no preference" doctrine would return many policy decisions to the appropriate educational authorities, elected or appointed, and reduce the all too frequent present pattern of government by judiciary.

Third, although the First Amendment's free exercise of religion clause would not be contracted by the "no preference" principle, that interpretation would, in some instances, expand the individual's free exercise of religion and other First Amendment rights. This would happen where "equal access" is currently denied public school students.

EQUAL ACCESS ACT

The Equal Access Act of 1984 (Public Law 98-377) prohibits public high schools receiving federal aid from preventing voluntary student groups, including religious ones, from meeting in school facilities before and after class hours or during a club period, if other extracurricular groups have access.[25] The constitutionality of refusing "equal access" to voluntary student religious organizations was litigated in the lower courts[26] before reaching the U.S. Supreme Court in *Bender* v. *Williamsport* in March 1986.[27]

In deciding equal access cases, the lower federal courts applied the Supreme Court's "three part *Lemon*" test to determine whether the establishment clause had been violated. Under this test, first described in *Lemon* v. *Kurtzman*, the Supreme Court held that in order to pass constitutional muster under the establishment clause, the challenged governmental policy or activity must (1) have a secular purpose, (2) be one that has a principal or primary effect which neither advances nor inhibits religion, and (3) not foster an excessive government entanglement with religion.[28]

The "no preference" doctrine, on the other hand, would provide a relatively clearer and easier-to-apply test. Alleged violations would be measured by two simple questions: (1) Is the governmental action within the constitutional power of the acting public body? and (2) Does the

governmental action elevate any one religion, religious sect, or religious tradition into a preferred legal status? Either a "no" to the first question or a "yes" to the second would make the policy unconstitutional.

Unlike the *Lemon* interpretation, the "no preference" interpretation poses less danger to a student's individual First and Fourteenth Amendment liberty. The Third U.S. Circuit Court's decision in *Bender* v. *Williamsport* illustrates this point. There the court held that it was constitutional for a school board to refuse to permit a student-initiated nondenominational prayer club to meet during the regularly scheduled activity period in a public school room.[29] As I see it, that decision subordinated three First Amendment freedoms—free exercise of religion, freedom of speech, and voluntary assembly—to one misinterpreted First Amendment guarantee. Under the "no preference" doctrine, equal access would be guaranteed to *all* religious or, for that matter, irreligious student groups under the same conditions that apply to any other voluntary student group.

Application of the "no preference" interpretation also avoids enormous dangers to an "open society" possible under the *Lemon* test. Can we not see that a court which can hold today that a classroom could not be used by a voluntary religious student group because that use may have as its primary effect the advancement of religion, can tomorrow, by the same logic, bar meeting rooms to students who want to discuss atheism or a book negative about religion, such as Bertrand Russell's *Why I Am Not a Christian*, because the primary effect there might be said to inhibit religion. By the use of *Lemon's* "primary effect" test, books about religion or those said to be irreligious can be removed from public school libraries. Is C. S. Lewis' *The Screwtape Letters* safe? And what about *Inherit the Wind*, or Darwin's *Origin of the Species*? Are we so frightened of ourselves that we are willing to disallow, in our institutions of learning, scrutinization of ultimate issues and values because of fear about where an open marketplace of ideas may eventually take the nation?

Finally, while some actions such as an uncoerced moment of silence for mediation and/or prayer in a public schoolroom[30] or the teaching of educationally deprived students from low-income families for several hours each week in a parochial school by public school teachers, recently held unconstitutional,[31] would be constitutional under the "no preference" interpretation, that does not mean they would automatically become educational policy. In all public educational entities, large or small, what would become policy would be up to the legally empowered decision makers in each of those entities.

NOTES

1. 330 U.S. 1 (1947).
2. Charles H. McIlwain, *Constitutionalism: Ancient and Modern*, rev. ed. (Ithaca, N.Y.: Great Seal Books, 1958), 19-22.
3. *Congressional Quarterly's Guide to the United States Supreme Court* (Washington, D.C.: Congressional Quarterly, Inc., 1979), 461. Emphasis added. The First Amendment has two religion clauses, the "establishment" clause and the "free exercise" clause. U.S. Constitution Amendment I: "Congress shall make no law respecting an establishment of religion, or prohibiting the free exercise thereof. . . ."
4. These proclamations, in their entirety, are published in James D. Richardson, *A Contemplation of the Messages and Papers of the Presidents, 1789-1897*, vol. I (Washington, D.C.: Bureau of National Literature and Art, 1901), 34-35; and Robert L. Cord, *Separation of Church and State: Historical Fact and Current Fiction* (Grand Rapids, Michigan: Baker Book House, 1988), 257-260.

5. After he had left the presidency, and toward the end of his life, Madison wrote a document commonly known as the "Detached Memoranda," which was first published as recently as 1946 in *William and Mary Quarterly* 3 (1946): 534. In it Madison *does* say that Thanksgiving Day proclamations are unconstitutional, as are chaplains in Congress. In light of his actions in public office, these were obviously not his views as a congressman and president. For a fuller discussion of Madison's "Detached Memoranda," see Cord, *Separation*, 29-36.
6. 2 *Statutes at Large* 194, Seventh Congress, Sess. 1, Chap. 52. Jefferson *did* believe Thanksgiving Proclamation violated the First Amendment and, unlike Washington, John Adams, and James Madison, declined to issue them.
7. R. Freeman Butts, *Religion, Education, and the First Amendment: The Appeal to History* (Washington, D.C.: People for the American Way, 1986), 9. Butts, an educational historian, is William F. Russell Professor Emeritus, Teachers College, Columbia University; Senior Fellow of the Kettering Foundation; and Visiting Scholar at the Hoover Institution, Stanford University.
8. Cord, *Separation*, XIII.
9. For an extensive critique of the *Everson* case and its interpretation of the establishment clause, see Cord, *Separation*, 103-133.
10. For in-depth study of the "no preference" principle, see Robert L. Cord, "Church-State Separation: Restoring the 'No Preference' Doctrine of the First Amendment," *Harvard Journal of Law & Public Policy* 9 (1986): 129.
11. Butts, *Religion*, 18.
12. Cord, *Separation*, 215-218.
13. Butts, *Religion*, 18-21.
14. Cord, *Separation*, 22-26.
15. Quoted from President Madison's "Proclamation" of "the 9th day of July A.D. 1812." This proclamation is republished in its entirety in Cord, *Separation*, 257.
16. For the entire text of the treaty, see Ibid., 261-263.
17. The full texts of these laws are republished in Cord, 263-270.
18. Butts, *Religion*, 16.
19. Ibid., 18.
20. Jonathan Elliott, *Debates on the Federal Constitution*, vol. II (Philadelphia: J.B. Lippincott Co., 1901), 553.
21. Ibid., vol. III, 659.
22. *Annals of the Congress of the United States, The Debates and Proceedings in the Congress of the United States*, vol. I, Compiled from Authentic Materials, by Joseph Gales, Senior (Washington, D.C.: Gales and Seaton, 1834), 434.
23. Ibid., 730.
24. Ibid., 731.

25. *Congressional Quarterly Weekly Report*, vols. 42, p. 1545, 1854; 43, p. 1807.

26. *Brandon* v. *Board of Education*, 635 F. 2nd 971 (2d Cir. 1980); *cert. denied*, 454 U.S. 1123 (1981); *Lubbock Civil Liberties Union* v. *Lubbock Independent School District*, 669 F. 2d 1038 (5th Cir. 1982), *cert. denied*, 459 U.S. 1155 (1983).

27. *Bender* v. *Williamsport*, 475 U.S. 534, 89 L.Ed. 2d 501 (1986). While the Third Circuit Court dealt with the "equal access" question, the Supreme Court did not reach that constitutional issue because one of the parties to the suit in the Circuit Court lacked standing and, therefore, that Court should have dismissed the case for want of jurisdiction. Ibid., 516.

28. *Lemon* v. *Kurtzman*, 403 U.S. 602, 612, 613 (1971).

29. *Bender* v. *Williamsport*, 741 F. 2d 538, 541 (3rd Cir. 1984).

30. In *Wallace* v. *Jaffree*, 105 S. Ct. 2479 (1985), the U.S. Supreme Court held such a law unconstitutional.

31. In *Grand Rapids* v. *Ball*, 473 U.S. 373, 87 L.Ed. 2d 267 (1985) and *Aguilar* v. *Felton*, 473 U.S. 402, 87 L.Ed. 2d 290 (1985), the Supreme Court held similar programs unconstitutional.

POSTSCRIPT

Is Church-State Separation Being Threatened?

If the Constitution is indeed a document that attempts to guarantee the protection of minority opinions from a possibly oppressive majority, can it be applied equally to all parties in any value-laden dispute such as those involving the relationship of church and state? An exhaustive review of historical cases dealing with manifestations of this basic problem may be found in Martha McCarthy's article "Religion and Public Schools," in the August 1985 issue of the *Harvard Educational Review*.

An extremely wide variety of articles is available on this volatile area of concern, including "Stepchildren of the Moral Majority," by Daniel Yankelovich, *Psychology Today* (November 1981); "The Crusade to Ban Books," by Stephen Arons, *Saturday Review* (June 1981); "Textbook Censorship and Secular Humanism in Perspective," by Franklin Parker, *Religion & Public Education* (Summer 1988); Rod Farmer's "Toward a Definition of Secular Humanism," *Contemporary Education* (Spring 1987); Mel and Norma Gabler's "Moral Relativism on the Ropes," *Communication Education* (October 1987); and Donald Vandenberg's "Education and the Religious," *Teachers College Record* (Fall 1987).

Three other provocative sources of insights are these: Thomas W. Goodhue's "What Should Public Schools Say About Religion?" *Education Week* (April 23, 1986); "How Prayer and Public Schooling Can Coexist," by Eugene W. Kelly, Jr., *Education Week* (November 12, 1986); and Edward A. Wynne's "The Case for Censorship to Protect the Young," *Issues in Education* (Winter 1985). Goodhue, while admitting book banning is bad, states that "when teachers, curriculum writers, and publishers minimize or omit the role of religion in history, art, music, literature, science, and other fields, they give students the false impression that religious influence has been slight." Kelly counsels that parents can teach their children how to have silent moments of prayer during the school day, tying prayer to "caring and respect for others, diligence in learning, helpfulness in common tasks, strength in rejecting destructive behavior, and patience in failing and starting over."

Other excellent sources are these: Warren A. Nord, "The Place of Religion in the World of Public School Textbooks," and Mark G. Yudof, "Religion, Textbooks, and the Public Schools," both in *The Educational Forum* (Spring 1990), and James Davison Hunter's "Modern Pluralism and the First Amendment," *The Brookings Review* (Spring 1990).

In the end, the main problem is one of finding an appropriate balance between the two First Amendment clauses within the context of public schooling and making that balance palatable and realizable at the local school level.

ISSUE 6

Do External Controls Provide the Best Learning Stimulus?

YES: B. F. Skinner, from *Beyond Freedom and Dignity* (Bantam, 1972)

NO: Carl R. Rogers, from *Freedom to Learn* (Merrill, 1983)

ISSUE SUMMARY

YES: B. F. Skinner, influential proponent of behaviorism and professor of psychology, critiques the concept of "inner freedom" and links learning and motivation to the influence of external forces.
NO: Professor of psychology and psychiatry Carl R. Rogers offers the "humanistic" alternative to behaviorism, insisting on the reality of subjective forces in human motivation.

Intimately enmeshed with considerations of aims and purposes and determination of curricular elements are the psychological base that affects the total setting in which learning takes place and the basic means of motivating learners. Historically, the atmosphere of schooling has often been characterized by harsh discipline, regimentation, and restriction. The prison metaphor often used by critics in describing school conditions rings true all too often.

Although calls to make schools pleasant have been sounded frequently, they have seldomly been heeded. Roman rhetorician Marcus Fabius Quintilian (ca. A.D. 35–ca. 100) advocated a constructive and enjoyable learning atmosphere. John Amos Comenius in the seventeenth century suggested a gardening metaphor in which learners were given kindly nurturance. Johann Heinrich Pestalozzi established a model school in the nineteenth century that replaced authoritarianism with love and respect.

Yet school as an institution retains the stigma of authoritarian control—attendance is compelled, social and psychological punishment is meted out, and the decision-making freedom of students is limited and often curtailed. These practices lead to rather obvious conclusions: either the prevailing belief is that young people are naturally evil and wild and therefore must be tamed in a restricting environment, or that schooling as such is so unpalatable that people must be forced and cajoled to reap its benefits—or both.

Certainly philosopher John Dewey (1895–1952) was concerned about this circumstance, citing at one time the superintendent of his native Burlington,

Vermont, school district as admitting that the schools were a source of "grief and mortification" and were "unworthy of patronage." Dewey rejected both the need for "taming" and the defeatist attitude that the school environment must remain unappealing. He hoped to create a motivational atmosphere that would engage learners in real problem-solving activities, thereby sustaining curiosity, creativity, and attachment. The rewards were to flow from the sense of accomplishment and freedom, which was to be achieved through the disciplined actions necessary to solve the problem at hand.

More recent treatment of the allied issues of freedom, control, and motivation has come from the two major camps in the field of educational psychology: the behaviorists (rooted in the early twentieth-century theories of Pavlov, Thorndike, and Watson) and the humanists (emanating from the Gestalt and field theory psychologies developed in Europe and America earlier in this century).

B. F. Skinner has been the dominant force in translating behaviorism into recommendations for school practices. The humanistic viewpoint has been championed by Carl R. Rogers, Abraham Maslow, Fritz Perls, Rollo May, and Erich Fromm, most of whom ground their psychological theories in the philosophical assumptions of existentialism and phenomenology.

Skinner believes that "inner" states are merely convenient myths, that motives and behaviors are shaped by environmental factors. These shaping forces, however, need not be negative, nor must they operate in an uncontrolled manner. Our present understanding of human behavior allows us the freedom to shape the environmental forces, which in turn shape us. With this power, Skinner contends, we can replace aversive controls in schooling with positive reinforcements that heighten the students' motivation level and make learning more efficient. Skinner deals with the problem of freedom and control in the selection that follows.

Carl R. Rogers, representing humanistic psychology, critiques Skinner's behaviorist approach and sets forth his argument supporting the reality of freedom as an inner human state that is the wellspring of responsibility, will, and commitment.

YES

B. F. Skinner

FREEDOM THROUGH CONTROL

Almost all living things act to free themselves from harmful contacts. A kind of freedom is achieved by the relatively simple forms of behavior called reflexes. A person sneezes and frees his respiratory passages from irritating substances. He vomits and frees his stomach from indigestible or poisonous food. He pulls back his hand and frees it from a sharp or hot object. More elaborate forms of behavior have similar effects. When confined, people struggle ("in rage") and break free. When in danger they flee from or attack its source. Behavior of this kind presumably evolved because of its survival value; it is as much a part of what we call the human genetic endowment as breathing, sweating, or digesting food. And through conditioning similar behavior may be acquired with respect to novel objects which could have played no role in evolution. These are no doubt minor instances of the struggle to be free, but they are significant. We do not attribute them to any love of freedom; they are simply forms of behavior which have proved useful in reducing various threats to the individual and hence to the species in the course of evolution.

A much more important role is played by behavior which weakens harmful stimuli in another way. It is not acquired in the form of conditioned reflexes, but as the product of a different process called operant conditioning. When a bit of behavior is followed by a certain kind of consequence, it is more likely to occur again, and a consequence having this effect is called a reinforcer. Food, for example, is a reinforcer to a hungry organism; anything the organism does that is followed by the receipt of food is more likely to be done again whenever the organism is hungry. Some stimuli are called negative reinforcers; any response which reduces the intensity of such a stimulus—or ends it—is more likely to be emitted when the stimulus recurs. Thus, if a person escapes from a hot sun when he moves under cover, he is more likely to move under cover when the sun is again hot. The reduction in temperature reinforces the behavior it is "contingent upon"—that is, the behavior it follows. Operant conditioning also occurs when a person simply avoids a hot sun—when, roughly speaking, he escapes from the *threat* of a hot sun.

Negative reinforcers are called aversive in the sense that they are the things organisms "turn away from." The term suggests a spatial separation—moving or running away from something—but the essential relation is temporal. In a standard apparatus used to study the process in the laboratory, an arbitrary response simply weakens an aversive stimulus or brings it to an end. A great deal of physical technology is the result of this kind of struggle for freedom. Over the centuries, in erratic ways, men have constructed a world in which they are relatively free of many kinds of threatening or harmful stimuli—extremes of temperature, sources of infection, hard labor, danger, and even those minor aversive stimuli called discomfort.

Escape and avoidance play a much more important role in the struggle for freedom when the aversive conditions are generated by other people. Other people can be aversive without, so to speak, trying; they can be rude, dangerous, contagious, or annoying, and one escapes from them or avoids them accordingly. They may also be "intentionally" aversive—that is, they may treat other people aversively because of what follows. Thus, a slave driver induces a slave to work by whipping him when he stops; by resuming work the slave escapes from the whipping (and incidentally reinforces the slave driver's behavior in using the whip). A parent nags a child until the child performs a task; by performing the task the child escapes nagging (and reinforces the parent's behavior). The blackmailer threatens exposure unless the victim pays; by paying, the victim escapes from the threat (and reinforces the practice). A teacher threatens corporal punishment or failure until his students pay attention; by pay-ing attention the students escape from the threat of punishment (and reinforce the teacher for threatening it). In one form or another intentional aversive control is the pattern of most social coordination—in ethics, religion, government, economics, education, psychotherapy, and family life.

A person escapes from or avoids aversive treatment by behaving in ways which reinforce those who treated him aversively until he did so, but he may escape in other ways. For example, he may simply move out of range. A person may escape from slavery, emigrate or defect from a government, desert from an army, become an apostate from a religion, play truant, leave home, or drop out of a culture as a hobo, hermit, or hippie. Such behavior is as much a product of the aversive conditions as the behavior the conditions were designed to evoke. The latter can be guaranteed only by sharpening the contingencies or by using stronger aversive stimuli.

Another anomalous mode of escape is to attack those who arrange aversive conditions and weaken or destroy their power. We may attack those who crowd us or annoy us, as we attack the weeds in our garden, but again the struggle for freedom is mainly directed toward intentional controllers—toward those who treat others aversively in order to induce them to behave in particular ways. Thus, a child may stand up to his parents, a citizen may overthrow a government, a communicant may reform a religion, a student may attack a teacher or vandalize a school, and a dropout may work to destroy a culture.

It is possible that man's genetic endowment supports this kind of struggle for freedom: when treated aversively people tend to act aggressively or to be reinforced by signs of having worked aggressive damage. Both tendencies should have had evolutional advantages, and they can easily be demonstrated. If two organisms which have been coexisting peacefully receive painful shocks, they immediately exhibit characteristic patterns of aggression toward each other. The aggressive behavior is not necessarily directed toward the actual source of stimulation; it may be "displaced" toward any convenient person or object. Vandalism and riots are often forms of undirected or misdirected aggression. An organism which has received a painful shock will also, if possible, act to gain access to another organism toward which it can act aggressively. The extent to which human aggression exemplifies innate tendencies is not clear, and many of the ways in which people attack and thus weaken or destroy the power of intentional controllers are quite obviously learned.

What we may call the "literature of freedom" has been designed to induce people to escape from or attack those who act to control them aversively. The content of the literature is the philosophy of freedom, but philosophies are among those inner causes which need to be scrutinized. We say that a person behaves in a given way because he possesses a philosophy, but we infer the philosophy from the behavior and therefore cannot use it in any satisfactory way as an explanation, at least until it is in turn explained. The literature of freedom, on the other hand, has a simple objective status. It consists of books, pamphlets, manifestoes, speeches, and other verbal products, designed to induce people to act to free themselves from various kinds of intentional control. It does not impart a philosophy of freedom; it induces people to act.

The literature often emphasizes the aversive conditions under which people live, perhaps by contrasting them with conditions in a freer world. It thus makes the conditions more aversive, "increasing the misery" of those it is trying to rescue. It also identifies those from whom one is to escape or those whose power is to be weakened through attack. Characteristic villains of the literature are tyrants, priests, generals, capitalists, martinet teachers, and domineering parents.

The literature also prescribes modes of action. It has not been much concerned with escape, possibly because advice has not been needed; instead, it has emphasized how controlling power may be weakened or destroyed. Tyrants are to be overthrown, ostracized, or assassinated. The legitimacy of a government is to be questioned. The ability of a religious agency to mediate supernatural sanctions is to be challenged. Strikes and boycotts are to be organized to weaken the economic power which supports aversive practices. The argument is strengthened by exhorting people to act, describing likely results, reviewing successful instances on the model of the advertising testimonial, and so on.

The would-be controllers do not, of course, remain inactive. Governments make escape impossible by banning travel or severely punishing or incarcerating defectors. They keep weapons and other sources of power out of the hands of revolutionaries. They destroy the written literature of freedom and imprison or kill those who carry it orally. If the struggle for freedom is to succeed, it must then be intensified.

The importance of the literature of freedom can scarcely be questioned. Without help or guidance people submit to aversive conditions in the most surprising way. This is true even when the aversive conditions are part of the natural environment. Darwin observed, for example, that the Fuegians seemed to make no effort to protect themselves from the cold; they wore only scant clothing and made little use of it against the weather. And one of the most striking things about the struggle for freedom from intentional control is how often it has been lacking. Many people have submitted to the most obvious religious, governmental, and economic controls for centuries, striking for freedom only sporadically, if at all. The literature of freedom has made an essential contribution to the elimination of many aversive practices in government, religion, education, family life, and the production of goods.

The contributions of the literature of freedom, however, are not usually described in these terms. Some traditional theories could conceivably be said to define freedom as the absence of aversive control, but the emphasis has been on how the condition *feels*. Other traditional theories could conceivably be said to define freedom as a person's condition when he is behaving under nonaversive control, but the emphasis has been upon a state of mind associated with doing what one wants. According to John Stuart Mill, "Liberty consists in doing what one desires." The literature of freedom has been important in changing practice (it has changed practices whenever it has had any effect whatsoever), but it has nevertheless defined its task as the changing of states of mind and feelings. Freedom is a "possession." A person escapes from or destroys the power of a controller in order to feel free, and once he feels free and can do what he desires, no further action is recommended and none is prescribed by the literature of freedom, except perhaps eternal vigilance lest control be resumed.

The feeling of freedom becomes an unreliable guide to action as soon as would-be controllers turn to nonaversive measures, as they are likely to do to avoid the problems raised when the controllee escapes or attacks. Nonaversive measures are not as conspicuous as aversive and are likely to be acquired more slowly, but they have obvious advantages which promote their use. Productive labor, for example, was once the result of punishment: the slave worked to avoid the consequences of not working. Wages exemplify a different principle; a person is paid when he behaves in a given way so that he will continue to behave in that way. Although it has long been recognized that rewards have useful effects, wage systems have evolved slowly. In the nineteenth century it was believed that an industrial society required a hungry labor force; wages would be effective only if the hungry worker could exchange them for food. By making labor less aversive—for instance, by shortening hours and improving conditions—it has been possible to get men to work for lesser rewards. Until recently teaching was almost entirely aversive: the student studies to escape the consequences of not studying, but nonaversive techniques are gradually being discovered and used. The skillful parent learns to reward a child for good behavior rather than punish him for bad. Religious agencies move from the threat of hellfire to an emphasis on God's love, and governments turn from aversive sanctions to various kinds of inducements, as we shall note again shortly. What the layman calls a reward is a "positive reinforcer," the effects of which have been exhaustively studied in the experimental analysis of operant behavior. The effects are not as easily recognized as those of aversive contingencies because they tend to be deferred, and applications have therefore been delayed, but techniques as powerful as the older aversive techniques are now available. . . .

The literature of freedom has never come to grips with techniques of control which do not generate escape or counterattack because it has dealt with the problem in terms of states of mind and feelings. In his book *Sovereignty*, Bertrand de Jouvenel quotes two important figures in that literature. According to Leibnitz, "Liberty consists in the power to do what one wants to do," and according to Voltaire, "When I can do what I want to do, there is my liberty for me." But both writers add a concluding phrase: Leibnitz, " . . . or in the power to want what can be got," and Voltaire, more candidly, " . . . but I can't help wanting what I do want." Jouvenel relegates these comments to a footnote, saying that the power to want is a matter of "interior liberty" (the freedom of the inner man!) which falls outside the "gambit of freedom."

A person wants something if he acts to get it when the occasion arises. A person who says "I want something to eat" will presumably eat when something becomes available. If he says "I want to get warm," he will presumably move into a warm place when he can. These acts have been reinforced in the past by whatever was wanted. What a person *feels* when he feels himself wanting something depends upon the circumstances. Food is reinforcing only in a state of deprivation, and a person who wants something to eat may feel parts of that state—for example, hunger pangs. A person who wants to get warm presumably feels cold. Conditions associated with a

high probability of responding may also be felt, together with aspects of the present occasion which are similar to those of past occasions upon which behavior has been reinforced. Wanting is not, however, a feeling, nor is a feeling the reason a person acts to get what he wants. Certain contingencies have raised the probability of behavior and at the same time have created conditions which may be felt. Freedom is a matter of contingencies of reinforcement, not of the feelings the contingencies generate. The distinction is particularly important when the contingencies do not generate escape or counterattack. . . .

The literature of freedom has encouraged escape from or attack upon all controllers. It has done so by making any indication of control aversive. Those who manipulate human behavior are said to be evil men, necessarily bent on exploitation. Control is clearly the opposite of freedom, and if freedom is good, control must be bad. What is overlooked is control which does not have aversive consequences at any time. Many social practices essential to the welfare of the species involve the control of one person by another, and no one can suppress them who has any concern for human achievements. We shall see later that in order to maintain the position that all control is wrong, it has been necessary to disguise or conceal the nature of useful practices, to prefer weak practices just because they can be disguised or concealed, and—a most extraordinary result indeed!—to perpetuate punitive measures.

The problem is to be free men, not from control, but from certain kinds of control, and it can be solved only if our analysis takes all consequences into account. How people feel about control, before or after the literature of freedom has worked on their feelings, does not lead to useful distinctions.

Were it not for the unwarranted generalization that all control is wrong, we should deal with the social environment as simply as we deal with the nonsocial. Although technology has freed men from certain aversive features of the environment, it has not freed them from the environment. We accept the fact that we depend upon the world around us, and we simply change the nature of the dependency. In the same way, to make the social environment as free as possible of aversive stimuli, we do not need to destroy that environment or escape from it; we need to redesign it.

Man's struggle for freedom is not due to a will to be free, but to certain behavioral processes characteristic of the human organism, the chief effect of which is the avoidance of or escape from so-called "aversive" features of the environment. Physical and biological technologies have been mainly concerned with natural aversive stimuli; the struggle for freedom is concerned with stimuli intentionally arranged by other people. The literature of freedom has identified the other people and has proposed ways of escaping from them or weakening or destroying their power. It has been successful in reducing the aversive stimuli used in intentional control, but it has made the mistake of defining freedom in terms of states of mind or feelings, and it has therefore not been able to deal effectively with techniques of control which do not breed escape or revolt but nevertheless have aversive consequences. It has been forced to brand all control as wrong and to misrepresent many of the advantages to be gained from a social environment. It is unprepared for the next step, which is not to free men from control but to analyze and change the kinds of control to which they are exposed.

NO
Carl R. Rogers

FREEDOM AND COMMITMENT

One of the deepest issues in modern life, in modern man, is the question as to whether the concept of personal freedom has any meaning whatsoever in our present-day scientific world. The growing ability of the behavioral scientist to predict and to control behavior has brought the issue sharply to the fore. If we accept the logical positivism and strictly behavioristic emphases which are predominant in the American psychological scene, there is not even room for discussion. . . .

But if we step outside the narrowness of the behavioral sciences, this question is not only *an* issue, it is one of the primary issues which define modern man. Friedman in his book (1963, p. 251) makes his topic "the problematic of modern man—the alienation, the divided nature, the unresolved tension between personal freedom and psychological compulsion which follows on 'the death of God'." The issues of personal freedom and personal commitment have become very sharp indeed in a world in which man feels unsupported by a supernatural religion, and experiences keenly the division between his awareness and those elements of his dynamic functioning of which he is unaware. If he is to wrest any meaning from a universe which for all he knows may be indifferent, he must arrive at some stance which he can hold in regard to these timeless uncertanties.

So, writing as both a behavioral scientist and as one profoundly concerned with the human, the personal, the phenomenological and the intangible, I should like to contribute what I can to this continuing dialogue regarding the meaning of and the possibility of freedom.

MAN IS UNFREE

. . . In the minds of most behavioral scientists, man is not free, nor can he as a free man commit himself to some purpose, since he is controlled by factors outside of himself. Therefore, neither freedom nor commitment is even a possible concept to modern behavioral science as it is usually understood.

To show that I am not exaggerating, let me quote a statement from Dr. B. F. Skinner of Harvard, who is one of the most consistent advocates of a strictly behavioristic psychology. He says,

> The hypothesis that man is not free is essential to the application of scientific method to the study of human behavior. The free inner man who is held responsible for his behavior is only a prescientific substitute for the kinds of causes which are discovered in the course of scientific analysis. All these alternative causes lie *outside* the individual (1953, p.477).

This view is shared by many psychologists and others who feel, as does Dr. Skinner, that all the effective causes of behavior lie outside of the individual and that it is only through the external stimulus that behavior takes place. The scientific description of behavior avoids anything that partakes in any way of freedom. For example, Dr. Skinner (1964, pp. 90–91) describes an experiment in which a pigeon was conditioned to turn in a clockwise direction. The behavior of the pigeon was "shaped up" by rewarding any movement that approximated a clockwise turn until, increasingly, the bird was turning round and round in a steady movement. This is what is known as operant conditioning. Students who had watched the demonstration were asked to write an account of what they had seen. Their responses included the following ideas: that the pigeon was conditioned to *expect* reinforcement for the right kind of behavior; that the pigeon *hoped* that something would bring the

food back again; that the pigeon *observed* that a certain behavior seemed to produce a particular result; that the pigeon *felt* that food would be given it because of its action; that the bird came to *associate* his action with the click of the food dispenser. Skinner ridicules these statements because they all go beyond the observed behavior in using such words as *expect, hope, observe, felt,* and *associate.* The whole explanation from his point of view is that the bird was reinforced when it emitted a given kind of behavior; the pigeon walked around until the food container again appeared; a certain behavior produced a given result; food was given to the pigeon when it acted in a given way; the click of the food dispenser was related in time to the bird's action. These statements describe the pigeon's behavior from a scientific point of view.

Skinner goes on to point out that the students were undoubtedly reporting what they would have expected, felt and hoped under similar circumstances. But he then makes the case that there is no more reality to such ideas in the human being than there is in the pigeon, that it is only because such words have been reinforced by the verbal community in which the individual has developed, that such terms are used. He discusses the fact that the verbal community which conditioned them to use such terms saw no more of their behavior than they had seen of the pigeon's. In other words the internal events, if they indeed exist, have no scientific significance.

As to the methods used for changing the behavior of the pigeon, many people besides Dr. Skinner feel that through such positive reinforcement human behavior as well as animal behavior can be "shaped up" and controlled. In his book *Walden Two,* Skinner says,

Now that we know how positive reinforcement works and how negative doesn't, we can be more deliberate and hence more successful in our cultural design. We can achieve a sort of control under which the controlled, though they are following a code much more scrupulously than was ever the case under the old system, nevertheless *feel free*. They are doing what they want to do, not what they are forced to do. That's the source of the tremendous power of positive reinforcement—there is no restraint and no revolt. By a careful cultural design we control not the final behavior but the *inclination* to behave—the motives, the desires, the wishes. The curious thing is that in that case *the question of freedom never arises* (1948, p. 218).

. . . I think it is clear from all of this that man is a machine—a complex machine, to be sure, but one which is increasingly subject to scientific control. Whether behavior will be managed through operant conditioning as in *Walden Two* or whether we will be "shaped up" by the unplanned forms of conditioning implied in social pressure, or whether we will be controlled by electrodes in the brain, it seems quite clear that science is making out of man an object and that the purpose of such science is not only understanding and prediction but control. Thus it would seem to be quite clear that there could be no concept so foreign to the facts as that man is free. Man is a machine, man is unfree, man cannot commit himself in any meaningful sense; he is simply controlled by planned or unplanned forces outside of himself.

MAN IS FREE

I am impressed by the scientific advances illustrated in the examples I have given. I regard them as a great tribute to the ingenuity, insight, and persistence of the individuals making the investigations. They have added enormously to our knowledge. Yet for me they leave something very important unsaid. Let me try to illustrate this, first from my experience in therapy.

I think of a young man classed as schizophrenic with whom I had been working for a long time in a state hospital. He was a very inarticulate man, and during one hour he made a few remarks about individuals who had recently left the hospital; then he remained silent for almost forty minutes. When he got up to go, he mumbled almost under his breath, "If some of *them* can do it, maybe I can too." That was all—not a dramatic statement, not uttered with force and vigor, yet a statement of choice by this young man to work toward his own improvement and eventual release from the hospital. It is not too surprising that about eight months after that statement he was out of the hospital. I believe this experience of responsible choice is one of the deepest aspects of psychotherapy and one of the elements which most solidly underlies personality change.

I think of another young person, this time a young woman graduate student, who was deeply disturbed and on the borderline of a psychotic break. Yet after a number of interviews in which she talked very critically about all of the people who had failed to give her what she needed, she finally concluded: "Well, with that sort of a foundation, it's really up to *me*. I mean it seems to be really apparent to me that I can't depend on someone else to *give* me an education." And then she added very softly: "I'll really have to get it myself." She goes on to explore this experience of important and responsible choice. She finds it a frightening experience, and yet one which gives her a feeling of strength. A force seems to surge up within her which is big and strong, and yet she also feels very much alone and sort of cut off from support. She adds: "I am going to begin to do more things that I know I should do." And she did.

I could add many other examples. One young fellow talking about the way in which his whole life had been distorted and spoiled by his parents finally comes to the conclusion that, "Maybe now that I *see* that, it's up to *me*." . . .

For those of you [who] have seen the film *David and Lisa*—and I hope that you have had that rich experience—I can illustrate exactly what I have been discussing. David, the adolescent schizophrenic, goes into a panic if he is touched by anyone. He feels that "touching kills," and he is deathly afraid of it, and afraid of the closeness in human relationships which touching implies. Yet toward the close of the film he makes a bold and positive choice of the kind I have been describing. He has been trying to be of help to Lisa, the girl who is out of touch with reality. He tries to help at first in an intellectually contemptuous way, then increasingly in a warmer and more personal way. Finally, in a highly dramatic movement, he says to her, "Lisa, take my hand." He *chooses*, with obvious conflict and fear, to leave behind the safety of his untouchableness, and to venture into the world of real human relationships where he is literally and figuratively in *touch* with another. You are an unusual person if the film does not grow a bit misty at this point.

Perhaps a behaviorist could try to account for the reaching out of his hand by saying that it was the result of intermit-tent reinforcement of partial movements. I find such an explanation both inaccurate and inadequate. It is the *meaning* of the *decision* which is essential to understanding the act.

What I am trying to suggest in all of this is that I would be at a loss to explain the positive change which can occur in psychotherapy if I had to omit the importance of the sense of free and responsible choice on the part of my clients. I believe that this experience of freedom to choose is one of the deepest elements underlying change.

THE MEANING OF FREEDOM

Considering the scientific advances which I have mentioned, how can we even speak of freedom? In what sense is a client free? In what sense are any of us free? What possible definition of freedom can there be in the modern world? Let me attempt such a definition.

In the first place, the freedom that I am talking about is essentially an inner thing, something which exists in the living person quite aside from any of the outward choices of alternatives which we so often think of as constituting freedom. I am speaking of the kind of freedom which Viktor Frankl vividly describes in his experience of the concentration camp, when everything—possessions, status, identity—was taken from the prisoners. But even months and years in such an environment showed only "that everything can be taken from a man but one thing: the last of the human freedoms—to choose one's own attitude in any given set of circumstances, to choose one's own way" (1959, p. 65). It is this inner, subjective, existential freedom which I have observed. It is the realization that "I can live myself, here and now, by my own choice." It is the quality of courage which enables a person to step into the uncertainty of the unknown as he chooses himself. It is the discovery of meaning from within oneself, meaning which comes from listening, sensitively and openly to the complexities of what one is experiencing. It is the burden of being responsible for the self one chooses to be. It is the recognition of a person that he is an emerging process, not a static end product. The individual who is thus deeply and courageously thinking his own thoughts, becoming his own uniqueness, responsibly choosing himself, may be fortunate in having hundreds of objective outer alternatives from which to choose, or he may be unfortunate in having none. But his freedom exists regardless. So we are first of all speaking of something which exists within the individual, something phenomenological rather than external, but nonetheless to be prized.

The second point in defining this experience of freedom is that it exists not as a contradiction of the picture of the psychological universe as a sequence of cause and effect, but as a complement to such a universe. Freedom rightly understood is a fulfillment by the person of the ordered sequence of his life. The free man moves out voluntarily, freely, responsibly, to play his significant part in a world whose determined events move through him and through his spontaneous choice and will.

I see this freedom of which I am speaking, then, as existing in a different *dimension* than the determined sequence of cause and effect. I regard it as a freedom which exists in the subjective person, a freedom which he courageously uses to live his potentialities. The fact that this type of freedom seems completely irrec-

oncilable with the behaviorist's picture of man is something which I will discuss a bit later. . . .

THE EMERGENCE OF COMMITMENT

I have spoken thus far primarily about freedom. What about commitment? Certainly the disease of our age is lack of purpose, lack of meaning, lack of commitment on the part of individuals. Is there anything which I can say in regard to this?

It is clear to me that in therapy, as indicated in the examples that I have given, commitment to purpose and to meaning in life is one of the significant elements of change. It is only when the person decides, "I am someone; I am someone worth being: I am committed to being myself," that change becomes possible.

At a very interesting symposium at Rice University recently, Dr. Sigmund Koch sketched the revolution which is taking place in science, literature and the arts, in which a sense of commitment is again becoming evident after a long period in which that emphasis has been absent.

Part of what he meant by that may be illustrated by talking about Dr. Michael Polanyi, the philosopher of science, formerly a physicist, who has been presenting his notions about what science basically is. In his book, *Personal Knowledge*, Polanyi makes it clear that even scientific knowledge is personal knowledge, committed knowledge. We cannot rest comfortably on the belief that scientific knowledge is impersonal and "out there," that it has nothing to do with the individual who has discovered it. Instead, every aspect of science is pervaded by disciplined personal commitment, and Polanyi makes the case very persuasively that the whole attempt to divorce science from the person is a completely unrealistic one. I think I am stating his belief correctly when I say that in his judgment logical positivism and all the current structure of science cannot save us from the fact that all knowing is uncertain, involves risk, and is grasped and comprehended only through the deep, personal commitment of a disciplined search.

Perhaps a brief quotation will give something of the flavor of his thinking. Speaking of great scientists, he says:

So we see that both Kepler and Einstein approached nature with intellectual passions and with beliefs inherent in these passions, which led them to their triumphs and misguided them to their errors. These passions and beliefs were theirs, personally, even universally. I believe that they were competent to follow these impulses, even though they risked being misled by them. And again, what I accept of their work today, I accept personally, guided by passions and beliefs similar to theirs, holding in my turn that my impulses are valid, universally, even though I must admit the possibility that they may be mistaken (1959, p.145).

Thus we see that a modern philosopher of science believes that deep personal commitment is the only possible basis on which science can firmly stand. This is a far cry indeed from the logical positivism of twenty or thirty years ago, which placed knowledge far out in impersonal space.

Let me say a bit more about what I mean by commitment in the psychological sense. I think it is easy to give this word a much too shallow meaning, indicating that the individual has, simply by conscious choice, committed himself to one course of action or another. I think the meaning goes far deeper than that. Commitment is a total organismic direction involving not only the conscious mind but the whole direction of the organism as well.

In my judgment, commitment is something that one *discovers* within oneself. It is a trust of one's total reaction rather than of one's mind only. It has much to do with creativity. Einstein's explanation of how he moved toward his formulation of relativity without any clear knowledge of his goal is an excellent example of what I mean by the sense of commitment based on a total organismic reaction. He says:

"During all those years there was a feeling of direction, of going straight toward something concrete. It is, of course, very hard to express that feeling in words but it was decidedly the case and clearly to be distinguished from later considerations about the rational form of the solution" (quoted in Wertheimer, 1945, p. 183-184).

Thus commitment is more than a decision. It is the functioning of an individual who is searching for the directions which are emerging within himself. Kierkegaard has said, "The truth exists only in the process of becoming, in the process of appropriation" (1941, p.72). It is this individual creation of a tentative personal truth through action which is the essence of commitment.

Man is most successful in such a commitment when he is functioning as an integrated, whole, unified individual. The more that he is functioning in this total manner the more confidence he has in the directions which he unconsciously chooses. He feels a trust in his experiencing, of which, even if he is fortunate, he has only partial glimpses in his awareness.

Thought of in the sense in which I am describing it, it is clear that commitment is an achievement. It is the kind of purposeful and meaningful direction which is only gradually achieved by the individual who has come increasingly to live closely in relationship with his own experiencing—a relationship in which his unconscious tendencies are as much respected as are his conscious choices. This is the kind of commitment toward which I believe individuals can move. It is an important aspect of living in a fully functioning way.

THE IRRECONCILABLE CONTRADICTION

I trust it will be very clear that I have given two sharply divergent and irreconcilably contradictory points of view. On the one hand, modern psychological science and many other forces in modern life as well, hold the view that man is unfree, that he is controlled, that words such as purpose, choice, commitment have no significant meaning, that man is nothing but an object which we can more fully understand and more fully control. Enormous strides have been and are being made in implementing this perspective. It would seem heretical indeed to question this view.

Yet, as Polanyi has pointed out in another of his writings (1957), the dogmas of science can be in error. He says:

In the days when an idea could be silenced by showing that it was contrary to religion, theology was the greatest single source of fallacies. Today, when any human thought can be discredited by branding it as unscientific, the power previously exercised by theology has passed over to science; hence science has become in its turn the greatest single source of error.

So I am emboldened to say that over against this view of man as unfree, as an object, is the evidence from therapy, from subjective living, and from objective research as well, that personal freedom and responsibility have a crucial significance, that one cannot live a complete life without such personal freedom and responsibility, and that self-understanding and responsible choice make a sharp and measurable difference in the behavior of the individual. In this context, commitment does have meaning. Commitment is the emerging and changing total direction of the individual, based on a close and acceptant relationship between the person and all of the trends in his life, conscious and unconscious. Unless, as individuals and as a society, we can make constructive use of this capacity for freedom and commitment, mankind, it seems to me, is set on a collision course with fate. . . .

A part of modern living is to face the paradox that, viewed from one perspective, man is a complex machine. We are every day moving toward a more precise understanding and a more precise control of this objective mechanism which we call man. On the other hand, in another significant dimension of his existence, man is subjectively free; his personal choice and responsibility account for the shape of his life; he is in fact the architect of himself. A truly crucial part of his existence is the discovery of his own meaningful commitment to life with all of his being.

POSTSCRIPT

Do External Controls Provide the Best Learning Stimulus?

The freedom-determinism or freedom-control argument has raged in philosophical, political, and psychological circles down through the ages. Is freedom of choice and action a central, perhaps *the* central, characteristic of being human? Or is freedom only an illusion, a refusal to acknowledge the external shaping of all human actions?

Moving the debate into the field of education, John Dewey depicts a developmental freedom that is acquired through improving one's ability to cope with problems. A. S. Neill sees a more natural, inborn freedom in human beings, which must be protected and allowed to flourish. B. F. Skinner refuses to recognize this "inner autonomous man," but sees freedom resulting from the scientific reshaping of the environment that influences us. Skinner ends *Beyond Freedom and Dignity* with the challenging statement, "We have not yet seen what man can make of man."

Just as Skinner has struggled to remove the stigma from the word "control," arguing that it is the true gateway to freedom, John Holt, in *Freedom and Beyond* (1972), points out that freedom and free activities are not "unstructured"—indeed, that the structure of an open classroom is vastly more complicated than the structure of a traditional classroom.

If both of these views have validity, then we are in a position, as Dewey counselled, to go beyond either-or polemics on these matters and build a more constructive educational atmosphere. Jerome S. Bruner has consistently suggested ways in which free inquiry and subject matter structure can be effectively blended. Arthur W. Combs, in journal articles and in a report titled *Humanistic Education: Objectives and Assessment* (1978), has helped to bridge the ideological gap between humanists and behaviorists by demonstrating that subjective outcomes can be assessed by direct or modified behavioral techniques.

Other sources that offer different perspectives on the basic psychological environment in education include John D. Nolan's defense of a moderate behaviorism in "The True Humanist: The Behavior Modifier," *Teachers College Record* (December 1974); Gerald Weinstein and Mario Fantini's *Toward Humanistic Education—A Curriculum of Affect* (1970); William Glasser's "reality therapy" approach as described in his *Schools Without Failure* (1969); and Philip W. Jackson's *Life in Classrooms* (1968). Two popular treatments of the issue are *The Brain Changers*, by Maya Pines (1973), and *The People Shapers*, by Vance Packard (1977).

ISSUE 7

Does a Common Curriculum Promote Equality?

YES: Mortimer J. Adler, from "The Paideia Proposal: Rediscovering the Essence of Education," *The American School Board Journal* (July 1982)

NO: Floretta Dukes McKenzie, from "The Yellow Brick Road of Education," *Harvard Educational Review* (November 1983)

ISSUE SUMMARY

YES: Mortimer J. Adler, director of the Institute of Philosophical Research, contends that equality of educational opportunity can be attained in qualitative terms by establishing uniform curricular objectives for all.
NO: Former superintendent of public schools Floretta Dukes McKenzie, in a critique of *The Paideia Proposal*, points out Adler's faulty assumptions about the learning process and his lack of attention to the realities of contemporary society.

Quality and equality have been dominant themes in discourse about education in recent decades. Equality of educational opportunity has been dealt with through judicial and legislative means, which have served to break down existing barriers and to provide new means of access and support for groups previously excluded or discriminated against.

Only in recent years has there been concern expressed about making qualitative factors in the educational services available to increasing numbers of students. This has gone hand in hand with an accelerated concern for quality and excellence in general. The question for the 1990s is: Can quality and equity be gained simultaneously and, if so, how?

The search for academic excellence pervades most of the thinking contained in recent reports on schooling in this country: the Carnegie Foundation report on high schools; John I. Goodlad's eight-year study of schooling; the Twentieth Century Fund's report on education policy; the College Board's Project Equality; Theodore Sizer's study of high schools; the Action for Excellence plan of the Education Commission of the States; and, of course, Nation at Risk recommendations of the National Commission for Excellence in Education.

It was philosopher Mortimer J. Adler, however, who brought the questions of quality and equality together in a most provocative manner in his educational manifesto *The Paideia Proposal* and subsequent elaborations. Drawing on principles developed some decades back with his University of Chicago colleague Robert M. Hutchins, Adler, as spokesman for the members of the Paideia Group, outlines a plan for providing the same essential schooling for all students regardless of background. This common schooling is to be based on the development of thinking skills, the acquisition of necessary organized information, and the sustenance of intellectual inquiry.

It is Adler's position that we may as well abandon our hope of developing a truly democratic society if we cannot, through our educational institutions, bring all of our citizens to levels of understanding and performance that will ensure thoughtful participation in the processes of government. What we need desperately, the Paideia Group contends, is a renewal of the ancient Greek concept of *paideia*, a community of contributing individuals held together by a sense of common culture and productive intellectual discourse.

The Adler proposal has been widely discussed since its release. While some critics have attacked the philosophical assumptions that undergird the document, more have raised serious questions regarding the practicality and feasibility of the changes that would be necessitated by widespread adoption of the proposal. Could teachers qualified to carry out the various aspects of the program be found or developed? Would "nonacademic" students be more inclined to drop away from the rigorous intellectual training implied by the proposal? Would students and parents be willing to alter their prevailing view of the schools as an occupational preparation agency?

In the articles that follow, Mortimer J. Adler summarizes the thinking that went into the Paideia Group's proposals for educational reform. Floretta Dukes McKenzie examines and refutes both the theoretical and practical aspects of the Adler position.

YES

Mortimer J. Adler

THE PAIDEIA PROPOSAL

In the first 80 years of this century, we have met the obligation imposed on us by the principle of equal educational opportunity, but only in a quantitative sense. Now, as we approach the end of the century, we must achieve equality in qualitative terms.

This means a completely one-track system of schooling. It means, at the basic level, giving all the young the same kind of schooling, whether or not they are college bound.

We are aware that children, although equal in their common humanity and fundamental human rights, are unequal as individuals, differing in their capacity to learn. In addition, the homes and environments from which they come to school are unequal—either predisposing the child for schooling or doing the opposite.

Consequently, the Paideia Proposal, faithful to the principle of equal educational opportunity, includes the suggestion that inequalities due to environmental factors must be overcome by some form of preschool preparation—at least one year for all and two or even three for some. We know that to make such preschool tutelage compulsory at the public expense would be tantamount to increasing the duration of compulsory schooling from 12 years to 13, 14, or 15 years. Nevertheless, we think that this preschool adjunct to the 12 years of compulsory basic schooling is so important that some way must be found to make it available for all and to see that all use it to advantage.

THE ESSENTIALS OF BASIC SCHOOLING

The objectives of basic schooling should be the same for the whole school population. In our current two-track or multitrack system, the learning objectives are not the same for all. And even when the objectives aimed at those on the upper track are correct, the course of study now provided does not adequately realize these correct objectives. On all tracks in our current system, we fail to cultivate proficiency in the common tasks of learning, and we especially fail to develop sufficiently the indispensable skills of learning.

From Mortimer J. Adler, "The Paideia Proposal: Rediscovering the Essence of Education," *The American School Board Journal* (July 1982). Copyright © 1982 by the National School Boards Association. Reprinted by permission. All rights reserved.

The uniform objectives of basic schooling should be threefold. They should correspond to three aspects of the common future to which all the children are destined: (1) Our society provides all children ample opportunity for personal development. Given such opportunity, each individual is under a moral obligation to make the most of himself and his life. Basic schooling must facilitate this accomplishment. (2) All the children will become, when of age, full-fledged citizens with suffrage and other political responsibilities. Basic schooling must do everything it can to make them good citizens, able to perform the duties of citizenship with all the trained intelligence that each is able to achieve. (3) When they are grown, all (or certainly most) of the children will engage in some form of work to earn a living. Basic schooling must prepare them for earning a living, but not by training them for this or that specific job while they are still in school.

To achieve these three objectives, the character of basic schooling must be general and liberal. It should have a single, required, 12-year course of study for all, with no electives except one—an elective choice with regard to a second language, to be selected from such modern languages as French, German, Italian, Spanish, Russian, and Chinese. The elimination of all electives, with this one exception, excludes what *should* be excluded—all forms of specialization, including particularized job training.

In its final form, the Paideia Proposal will detail this required course of study, but I will summarize the curriculum here in its bare outline. It consists of three main columns of teaching and learning, running through the 12 years and progressing, of course, from the simple to the more complex, from the less difficult to the more difficult, as the students grow older. Understand: The three columns (see chart on next page) represent three distinct modes of teaching and learning. They do not represent a series of courses. A specific course or class may employ more than one mode of teaching and learning, but all three modes are essential to the overall course of study.

The first column is devoted to acquiring knowledge in three subject areas: (A) language, literature, and the fine arts; (B) mathematics and natural science; © history, geography, and social studies.

The second column is devoted to developing the intellectual skills of learning. These include all the language skills necessary for thought and communication—the skills of reading, writing, speaking, listening. They also include mathematical and scientific skills; the skills of observing, measuring, estimating, and calculating; and skills in the use of the computer and of other scientific instruments. Together, these skills make it possible to think clearly and critically. They once were called the liberal arts—the intellectual skills indispensable to being competent as a learner.

The third column is devoted to enlarging the understanding of ideas and values. The materials of the third column are books (*not* textbooks), and other products of human artistry. These materials include books of every variety—historical, scientific, and philosophical as well as poems, stories, and essays—and also individual pieces of music, visual art, dramatic productions, dance productions, film or television productions. Music and works of visual art can be used in seminars in which ideas are discussed; but as with poetry and fiction, they also are to be experienced aesthetically, to be

The Paideia Curriculum

	Column One	Column Two	Column Three
Goals	Acquisition of Organized Knowledge	Development of Intellectual Skills and Skills of Learning	Improved Understanding of Ideas and Values
	by means of	*by means of*	*by means of*
Means	Didactic Instruction, Lecturing, and Textbooks	Coaching, Exercises, Supervised Practice	Maieutic or Socratic Questioning and Active Participation
	in these three subject areas	*in these operations*	*in these activities*
Subject Areas, Operations, and Activities	Language, Literature, and Fine Arts; Mathematics and Natural Science; History, Geography, and Social Studies	Reading, Writing, Speaking, Listening, Calculating, Problem Solving, Observing, Measuring, Estimating, Exercising Critical Judgment	Discussion of Books (Not Textbooks) and Other Works of Art; Involvement in Music, Drama, and Visual Arts

The three columns do not correspond to separate courses, nor is one kind of teaching and learning necessarily confined to any one class.

enjoyed and admired for their excellence. In this connection, exercises in the composition of poetry, music, and visual works and in the production of dramatic works should be used to develop the appreciation of excellence.

The three columns represent three different kinds of learning on the part of the student and three different kinds of instruction on the part of teachers.

In the first column, the students are engaged in acquiring information and organized knowledge about nature, man, and human society. The method of instruction here, using textbooks and manuals, is didactic. The teacher lectures, invites responses from the students, monitors the acquisition of knowledge, and tests that acquisition in various ways.

In the second column, the students are engaged in developing habits of performance, which is all that is involved inthe development of an art or skill. Art,

skill, or technique is nothing more than a cultivated, habitual ability to do a certain kind of thing well, whether that is swimming and dancing, or reading and writing. Here, students are acquiring linguistic, mathematical, scientific, and historical *know-how* in contrast to what they acquire in the first column, which is *know-that* with respect to language, literature, and the fine arts, mathematics and science, history, geography, and social studies. Here, the method of instruction cannot be didactic or monitorial; it cannot be dependent on textbooks. It must be coaching, the same kind used in the gym to develop bodily skills; only here it is used by a different kind of coach in the classroom to develop intellectual skills.

In the third column, students are engaged in a process of enlightenment, the process whereby they develop their understanding of the basic and controlling ideas in all fields of subject matter and come to appreciate better all the human values embodied in works of art. Here, students move progressively from understanding less to understanding more—understanding better what they already know and appreciating more what they already have experienced. Here, the method of instruction cannot be either didactic or coaching. It must be the Socratic, or maieutic, method of questioning and discussing. It should not occur in any ordinary classroom with the students sitting in rows and the teacher in front of the class, but in a seminar room, with the students sitting around a table and the teacher sitting with them as an equal, even though a little older and wiser.

Of these three main elements in the required curriculum, the third column is completely innovative. Nothing like this is done in our schools, and because it is completely absent from the ordinary curriculum of basic schooling, the students never have the experience of having their minds addressed in a challenging way or of being asked to think about the important ideas, to express their thoughts to defend their opinions in a reasonable fashion.

The only thing that is innovative about the second column is the insistence that the method of instruction here must be coaching carried on either with one student at a time or with very small groups of students. Nothing else can be effective in the development of a skill, be it bodily or intellectual. The absence of such individualized coaching in our schools explains why most of the students cannot read well, write well, speak well, listen well, or perform well any of the other basic intellectual operations.

The three columns are closely interconnected and integrated, but the middle column—the one concerned with linguistic, mathematical, and scientific skills—is central. It both supports and is supported by the other two columns. All the intellectual skills with which it is concerned must be exercised in the study of the three basic subject-matters and in acquiring knowledge about them, and these intellectual skills must be exercised in the seminars devoted to the discussion of books and other things.

In addition to the three main columns in the curriculum, ascending through the 12 years of basic schooling, there are three adjuncts: One is 12 years of physical training, accompanied by instruction in bodily care and hygiene. The second, running through something less than 12 years, is the development of basic manual skills, such as cooking, sewing, carpentry, and the operation of all kinds of machines. The third, reserved for the last year or two, is an introduction to the whole world of work—the range of occupations in which human beings earn their livings. This is not particularized job training. It is the very opposite. It aims at a broad understanding of what is involved in working for a living and of the various ways in which that can be done. If, at the end of 12 years, students wish training for specific jobs, they should get that in two-year community or junior colleges, or on the job itself, or in technical institutes of one sort or another.

Everything that has not been specifically mentioned as occupying the time of the school day should be reserved for after-hours and have the status of extra-curricular activities.

Please, note: The required course of study just described is as important for what it *displaces* as for what it introduces. It displaces a multitude of elective courses, especially those offered in our secondary schools, most of which make little or no contribution to general, liberal education. It eliminates all narrowly specialized job training, which now abounds in our schools. It throws out of the curriculum and into the category of optional extracurricular activities a variety of things that have little or no educational value.

If it did not call for all these displacements, there would not be enough time in the school day or year to accomplish everything that is essential to the general, liberal learning that must be the content of basic schooling.

THE QUINTESSENTIAL ELEMENT

So far, I have set forth the bare essentials of the Paideia Proposal with regard to basic schooling. I have not yet mentioned the quintessential element—the *sine qua non*—without which nothing else can possibly come to fruition, no matter how sound it might be in principle. The heart of the matter is the quality of learning and the quality of teaching that occupies the school day, not to mention the quality of the homework after school.

First, the learning must be active. It must use the whole mind, not just the memory. It must be learning by discovery, in which the student, never the teacher, is the primary agent. Learning by discovery, which is the only genuine learning, may be either unaided or aided. It is unaided only for geniuses. For most students, discovery must be aided.

Here is where teachers come in—as aids in the process of learning by discovery not as knowers who attempt to put the knowledge they have into the minds of their students. The quality of the teaching, in short, depends crucially upon how the teacher conceives his role in the process of learning, and that must be as an aid to the student's process of discovery.

I am prepared for the questions that must be agitating you by now: How and where will we get the teachers who can perform as teachers should? How will we be able to staff the program with teachers so trained that they will be competent to provide the quality of instruction required for the quality of learning desired?

The first part of our answer to these questions is negative: We *cannot* get the teachers we need for the Paideia program from schools of education *as they are now constituted*. As teachers are now trained for teaching, they simply will not do. The ideal—an impracticable ideal—would be to ask for teachers who are, themselves, truly educated human beings. But truly educated human beings are too rare. Even if we could draft all who are now alive, there still would be far too few to staff our schools.

Well, then, what can we look for? Look for teachers who are actively engaged in the process of *becoming* educated human beings, who are themselves deeply motivated to develop their own minds. Assuming this is not too much to ask for the present, how should teachers be schooled and trained in the future? First, they should have the same kind of basic schooling that is recommended in the Paideia Proposal. Second, they should have additional schooling, at the college and even the university level, in which the same kind of general, liberal learning is carried on at advanced levels—more deeply, broadly, and intensively than it can be done in the first 12 years of schooling. Third, they must be given something analogous to the clinical experience in the training of physicians. They must engage in practice-teaching under supervision, which is another way of saying that they must be *coached* in the arts of teaching, not just given didactic instruction in educational psychology and in pedagogy. Finally, and most important of all, they must learn how to teach well by being exposed to the performances of those who are masters of the arts involved in teaching.

It is by watching a good teacher at work that they will be able to perceive what is involved in the process of assisting others to learn by discovery. Perceiving it, they must then try to emulate what they observe, and through this process, they slowly will become good teachers themselves.

The Paideia Proposal recognizes the need for three different kinds of institutions at the collegiate level: The two-year community or junior college should offer a wide choice of electives that give students some training in one or another specialized field, mainly those fields of study that have something to do with earning a living. The four-year college also should offer a wide variety of electives, to be chosen by students who aim at the various professional or technical occupations that require advanced study. Those elective majors chosen by students should be accompanied, for all students, by one required minor, in which the kind of general and liberal learning that was begun at the level of basic schooling is continued at a higher level in the four years of college. And we should have still a third type of collegiate institution—a four-year college in which general, liberal learning at a higher level constitutes a required course of study that is to be taken by all students. *It is this third type of college, by the way, that should be attended*

by all who plan to become teachers in our basic schools.

At the university level, there should be a continuation of general, liberal learning at a still higher level to accompany intensive specialization in this or that field of science or scholarship, this or that learned profession. Our insistence on the continuation of general, liberal learning at all the higher levels of schooling stems from our concern with the worst cultural disease that is rampant in our society—*the barbarism of specialization.*

There is no question that our technologically advanced industrial society needs specialists of all sorts. There is no question that the advancement of knowledge in all fields of science and scholarship, and in all the learned professions, needs intense specialization. But for the sake of preserving and enhancing our cultural traditions, as well as for the health of science and scholarship, we need specialists who also are generalists—generally cultivated human beings, not just good plumbers. We need truly educated human beings who can perform their special tasks better precisely because they have general cultivation as well as intensely specialized training.

Changes indeed are needed in higher education, but those improvements cannot reasonably be expected unless improvement in basic schooling makes that possible.

THE FUTURE OF OUR FREE INSTITUTIONS

I already have declared as emphatically as I know how that the quality of human life in our society depends on the quality of the schooling we give our young people, both basic and advanced. But a marked elevation in the quality of human life is not the only reason improving the quality of schooling is so necessary—not the only reason we must move heaven and earth to stop the deterioration of our schools and turn them in the opposite direction. The other reason is to safeguard the future of our free institutions.

They cannot prosper, they may not even survive, unless we do something to rescue our schools from their current deplorable deterioration. Democracy, in the full sense of that term, came into existence only in this century and only in a few countries on earth, among which the United States is an outstanding example. But democracy came into existence in this century only in its initial conditions, all of which hold out promises for the future that remain to be fulfilled. Unless we do something about improving the quality of basic schooling for all and the quality of advanced schooling for some, there is little chance that those promises ever will be fulfilled. And if they are not, our free institutions are doomed to decay and wither away.

We face many insistently urgent problems. Our prosperity and even our survival depend on the solution of those problems—the threat of nuclear war, the exhaustion of essential resources and of supplies of energy, the pollution or spoilage of the environment, the spiraling of inflation accompanied by the spread of unemployment.

To solve these problems, we need resourceful and innovative leadership. For that to arise and be effective, an educated populace is needed. Trained intelligence—not only on the part of leaders, but also on the part of followers—holds the key to the solution of the problems our society faces. Achieving peace, prosperity, and plenty could put us on the threshold of an early paradise. But a much better educational system than now exists also is needed, for that alone can carry us across the threshold. Without it, a poorly schooled population will not be able to put to good use the opportunities afforded by the achievement of the general welfare. Those who are not schooled to enjoy society can only despoil its institutions and corrupt themselves.

NO

Floretta Dukes McKenzie

THE YELLOW BRICK ROAD
OF EDUCATION

Like Dorothy in *The Wizard of Oz*, educators hold a vision that somewhere—perhaps over the rainbow—a place exists that is free from all the knotty and nagging problems of everyday life. For teachers and school administrators, this "Oz" includes classrooms of endlessly inquisitive and motivated youngsters; instructors with a bottomless reservoir of energy, dedication, and talent; and schools free from yearly political haggles over funds needed to buy the texts, hire staff, and heat buildings. Frontline educators—classroom teachers, principals, and the like—as well as researchers and theorists, work toward the attainment of such an educational paradise. However, as evidenced in *The Paideia Proposal*, a fundamental difference in perspective distinguishes the practitioners' and the academicians' approaches to educational improvement.

To extend *The Wizard of Oz* analogy a bit further, Mortimer Adler regards the educational Oz as Dorothy viewed the Emerald City. Disgruntled with the problems at Aunt Em's farm, Dorothy believed in a better place; she could envision and describe it but lacked a way to get there. Speaking for the Paideia Group—primarily comprising noted college presidents, "think tankers," and foundation officials—Adler also complains about the "present deplorable condition" of schooling and depicts an idyllic state of education, yet offers little direction for reaching it.

On the other hand, far too many educators in the daily business of schooling have lost the excitement and hope Oz offered to Dorothy. After many trials and tribulations, Dorothy discovers that the Wizard is really an illusion; she longs to return to Kansas and is content to face farm life without the wonders of technicolor. Practicing educators, perhaps hardened over the years by too many trips down a yellow brick road of so-called "educational reform," likewise no longer believe in miracles. They frequently rely on teaching children in perhaps outmoded but familiar ways, viewing educational excellence as something that only a few schools can attain.

As the *Proposal* accurately points out, this disparaging attitude toward educational prospects is a tragic problem which contributes to the debilitating notion that public schooling can make only limited improvements in children's lives. Ironically, however, the *Proposal* itself, with its wholesale condemnation of present educational practices, further erodes the public confidence vital to any attempts at educational reform, particularly one that would prove as costly as the *Proposal*.

The Paideia Proposal claims that U.S. education has only won "half the battle—the quantitative half" of the goal to provide equal educational opportunity to all. Currently, 75 percent of all students graduate from high school compared to only 55 percent as recently as 1950. Although the number of years a child spends in school is not a reliable measure of the quality of education that child has received, this increase indicates more than a mere tally of the classroom hours students are logging in. A number of economists have estimated that between 25 to 50 percent of the increase in the Gross National Product in the last twenty years is due to the increased educational level of the work force.[1] This cannot be attributed simply to the amount of time students spend sitting in schools; it is an indication that schools have succeeded to a commendable degree in teaching meaningful, life-enhancing skills to the young.

Minimizing this country's tremendous gains in providing access to education, as the *Proposal* does, is a serious flaw in any analysis of U.S. education. It is specifically this commitment to educational access which led to the rich diversity in

teaching strategies that is essential to meeting the schooling needs of an equally diverse student population.

Educators should not be lured into the popular but mistaken belief that the national emphasis on educational access has not been accompanied by significant improvements in quality. The *Proposal* contends, without offering any supporting evidence, that "basic schooling in America does not now achieve the fundamental objective of opening the doors to the world of learning and providing the guidelines for exploring it." The *Proposal* goes further to suggest—again without examples or data—that U.S. education "used to do so for those who completed high school at the beginning of this century."

One of the few long-range studies of reading achievement indicates that, in 1944, Indiana's sixth- and tenth-grade students did not read as well as their counterparts did in 1976. Clearly, reading is a vital key to opening those doors to the world of learning, and if this ability among students has increased over time, the *Proposal's* claim that education was better in the "good old days" is highly suspect. As the Indiana study indicates, even though access to education has increased greatly, our schools are educating our youth to a much higher standard than they were able to do with only 30 to 40 percent of the student population four decades ago.[2]

Although *The Paideia Proposal's* failure to acknowledge education's accomplishments undermines the basis of the manifesto's suggested reforms, it is not the work's most serious flaw. The *Proposal* reflects assumptions about the learning process that disregard what educators have come to know through years of practice and research. Granted, all children are educable, innately possessing curiosity and an interest in learning. Although educators know this, they must work vigorously to ensure that this idea is incorporated into practice at all times for all children. The *Proposal*, however, makes a quantum conceptual leap by presuming that this belief in children's educability dictates a uniformity in instruction.

"The best education for the best is the best education for all" should not be the guiding principle for instruction, as the *Proposal* contends. As almost any teacher can testify, the methods which work well with the brightest and most eager students do not necessarily spark the interest of children who, for whatever reason, are not achieving as well. This belief, that what is best for the best is best for all, is a dangerously elitist tenet which may destroy the potential of countless young minds. Granted, as the *Proposal* suggests, students need clear direction as to what is expected of them, and the schools must do a better job in this arena. However, contrary to the *Proposal*, higher expectations of students do not necessarily translate into higher student achievement.

All children do not learn in the same fashion, for there is great variety in ways of acquiring and integrating information. Therefore, in almost all cases, rigid prescriptions for instruction invariably fail. Many teachers already have, and many more teachers need, competence in that comprehensive range of instructional strategies—such as didactic, coaching, and Socratic methods—that the *Proposal* details. However, such skills are needed to better meet students' varying levels of instructional needs rather than to reach the suggested single-track core curriculum. Although the *Proposal* decries

teachers' narrow repertoire of instructional skills, it is silent on a definitive means of better equipping teachers with such abilities.

Like its questionable assumptions about children's learning processes, the *Proposal's* suppositions concerning the composition of an ideal curriculum are out of touch with both education's proven knowledge base and the realities of contemporary society. As the *Proposal* indicates, "to live well in the fullest human sense involves learning as well as earning." But the key words in this phrase, which the *Proposal* subsequently disregards, are "as well as." By vehemently urging the elimination of almost all vocational training in basic schooling, the Paideia Group has chosen to overlook the very real need and growing demand for students in a technological society to be trained in specific skill areas. Ideally, such well-trained students would also possess the ability and desire for continued learning throughout their lives, which the *Proposal* accurately identifies as the major goal of education. But this goal will not be within students' grasp simply by disposing of specific career training.

Furthermore, the age-old complaint from U.S. business and industry has been that schools—including colleges—let students graduate who lack not only necessary general skills but also specific skills for employment. Historically, U.S. employers have only reluctantly taken on the role of providing the technical training for generally-educated new employees. The *Proposal* apparently overlooks the facts that vocational education arose out of a societal demand for career-trained graduates, that this demand is increasing with the expanding new technologies, and that the business sector will resist taking the responsibility for specific skill training.

Necessary vocational education, the *Proposal* contends, can be obtained after the first twelve years of schooling at either four-year or community colleges. Such postponement of entry into the work force is economically unfeasible for countless young people. The *Proposal* ignores today's reality that post-secondary education is increasingly an expense that fewer and fewer families can bear.

The *Proposal's* failure to recognize career training in schools as a development born, in part, of a strong societal demand highlights one of its other shortcomings: a naive treatment of education's political and economic circumstances. Undoubtedly, superintendents and administrators would eagerly endorse the *Proposal's* call for a debureaucratization of schools. The business of schooling is learning and teaching; however, given the requirements of democracy and the structure for financing public education, schools are also political institutions. Over the last few decades, demands for schools to assume the roles and functions once the sole province of home, church, and government has heavily contributed to the politicization of education. The *Proposal's* simplistic solution to this problem is to hand over greater control to local school principals. Giving principals more authority over the selection and dismissal of school staff and the discipline of students might be a wise and productive change for some school districts, but such actions would do little to remove education from the political sphere.

In today's world, the partner to politics is economics. The *Proposal* admits that, to be successful, its implementation will require higher teacher salaries, better teacher training, smaller class sizes, indi-

vidual student coaching, more remedial education, and publicly funded preschool for one- to three-year-olds. Yet, despite a national and local climate that favors sharp reductions in educational support, the *Proposal* makes no suggestions for financing the costs of its remedies.

A local example hints at the magnitude of the Paideia price tag. In the District of Columbia public school system, the cost of reducing class size by just one student per class is $4 million a year. To provide preschool classes for only one-third of the 18,000 three- and four-year-olds in the city, the school district's budget would have to be increased by $16 million each year.

Speculation and discussion on needed improvements in U.S. education are healthy and beneficial. Such exercises, however, must not only name the desired destinations but must also consider if the routes to those goals are compatible with existing knowledge based on practice and research. The *Proposal* is very strong on detailing what should be but ignores the reality of what already is. The *Proposal* cites increased parental involvement in education and decreased disruptive student behavior as vital to securing quality education for all. These are not issues which schools heretofore have overlooked; they are the time-worn problems with which educators grapple daily. The *Proposal* does not venture a single idea—tried or untried—on how to resolve these and many other longstanding problems.

The *Proposal* forthrightly communicates to the public some often neglected messages which probably cannot be broadcast too loudly or too frequently: quality education is the key to quality living; the survival of our democratic society depends on the existence of an educated electorate; and education is the gateway to equality for all people. *The Paideia Proposal* is as strong as Dorothy's determination to return to Kansas; as a constructive plan of action for educational improvement, it is as specious as the Wizard's magic powers.

NOTES

1. Harold Hodgkinson, "What's Still Right With Education," *Phi Delta Kappan*, 64 (1982), 233.

2. These statistics came from Harold Hodgkinson, a former director of the National Institute for Education, delivered in a presentation to the Executive Council of the District of Columbia Public Schools, April 1983.

POSTSCRIPT

Does a Common Curriculum Promote Equality?

Throughout most of the history of formal, institutionalized education, the tendency has been to expand the curriculum to meet the needs of a growing constituency. In twentieth-century America the public schools have added great numbers of courses and functions to its original set of obligations to serve the needs of young people and the needs of society in general. Educational reform has often been thought of as an addition process.

Some critics see this general tendency as the primary contributing factor in what is seen as a fragmented, shallow, and purposeless system of schooling. Adler's call for a unified curricular and methodological approach that is clearly focused on the development of the mind has its roots in earlier works: Albert Lynd's *Quackery in the Public Schools*; Arthur Bestor's *Educational Wastelands*; Mortimer Smith's *The Diminished Mind*; Admiral Hyman Rickover's *Swiss Schools and Ours*; James Koerner's *The Miseducation of American Teachers*; and Paul Copperman's *The Literacy Hoax*.

The basic question is: Is this line of criticism of public education valid and are the ideas suggested for reform right and workable? McKenzie doesn't think so, and a number of other writers in the November 1983 issue of the *Harvard Educational Review* join her. Of special interest are "The Peter Pan Proposal," by Ronald Gwiazda, and "Education, Democracy, and Social Conflict," by Martin Carnoy.

The debate about the appropriateness of curricular commonality has been fueled in recent years by former secretary of education William Bennett's recommendations for a prototypical elementary school and high school, put forth during the final year of his tenure in his book *James Madison Elementary School: A Curriculum for American Students,* and *What Do Our 17-Year-Olds Know?* (1987), by Diane Ravitch and Chester Finn, Jr. Two widely discussed works that directly reflect *paideia* concerns are *The Closing of the American Mind* (1987), by Allan Bloom, and *Cultural Literacy: What Every American Needs to Know* (1987), by E. D. Hirsch, Jr.

ISSUE 8

Should Schools Serve National Economic Needs?

YES: James B. Hunt, Jr., from "Education for Economic Growth: A Critical Investment," *Phi Delta Kappan* (April 1984)

NO: Joel Spring, from "Education and the Sony War," *Phi Delta Kappan* (April 1984)

ISSUE SUMMARY

YES: James B. Hunt, Jr., former governor of North Carolina, argues that students must learn the skills that are necessary for the improvement of the American economy.
NO: Professor of education Joel Spring contends that schools are becoming increasingly captive to the profit motives of business and industry.

Social, political, and economic aims for education would certainly seem to be natural and acceptable both historically and on the contemporary scene. Government-supported schools are expected to serve the predominant goals of society, including those of economic development.

In recent years, a large number of national reports appear to have placed economic reconstruction and growth firmly in the driver's seat when it comes to reconsidering educational objectives and making curricular decisions. These reports include the National Commission on Excellence in Education's *A Nation at Risk*, the Education Commission of States' *Action for Excellence*, the Twentieth Century Fund's *Making the Grade*, and the National Science Foundation's *Educating Americans for the 21st Century*.

These reports focus on the means for ensuring quality products through curricular standardization, teacher improvement, and the strengthening of graduation requirements. They contend that the present crisis situation demands crash programs to increase scientific literacy, upgrade mathematical skills, reduce drop-out rates, and eliminate "unnecessary" subject matter.

James B. Hunt, Jr., served as chairman of the Task Force on Education for Economic Growth for the Education Commission of the States. He therefore is an appropriate spokesman for this type of prioritization of aims. Specifically, the *Action for Excellence* report recommends the establishment of state task forces to improve the schools' ability to train young people for worthwhile occupations and the building of productive partnerships with the business community. International competition, the increasing obsolescence of American industry, and the challenge of new technologies are given as justification for this emphasis.

The "nation at risk" portrayal has set off a wave of "reforms" in school systems across the land. Some commentators view this with alarm; among them is Joel Spring, who fears the "single-mindedness" of the movement and the growing pervasiveness of "corporate control" in the process of schooling. Spring views the current effort primarily as a means to expand the pool of potential employees holding technological qualifications. The schools, seeing in the movement a possibility for better levels of financial support, are eagerly jumping on the bandwagon. Students and their parents, seeing possibilities for more lucrative employment, fail to cast a critical eye upon the decisions that are being made.

Echoing the sentiments expressed by Samuel Bowles and Herbert Gintis in their 1976 book, *Schooling in Capitalist America: Educational Reform and the Contradictions of Economic Life,* Spring argues that school "reforms" have never been successful in dealing with social and economic ills and, in fact, cover up the systemic origins of the maladies and steer us away from the identification of true reform needs at the wider societal level.

In the articles that follow, Hunt and Spring offer a detailing of their positions on the efficacy of economic aims for American schooling.

YES

James B. Hunt, Jr.

EDUCATION FOR ECONOMIC GROWTH

Americans believe in education. It is the public enterprise that is closest to the hearts and most important to the lives of Americans. Ultimately, education is crucial to success in everything we attempt as a nation.

Time and again in its history, the U.S. educational system has been challenged to meet the changing needs of a growing, complex society. Yet not since the Russian launching of Sputnik in 1957 has education in America faced a greater challenge than the one it faces today, for today America is in danger of losing the worldwide economic and technological leadership that it has built up over generations.

During the 1970s Japan, France, and West Germany began to outstrip the U.S. in the rate of growth of productivity.[1] Today we are told that we have become less competitive and that our factories are crumbling into obsolescence. Our economic future is in danger because our students, unlike those in other leading industrial nations, are not learning the fundamental skills they need in a modern economy.

Last May *Newsweek* reported that "on most levels, U.S. students suffer in comparison with those in other industrialized nations at a time when American standing in world markets, in terms of both products and ideas, is threatened."[2] Indeed, our curriculum, particularly at the primary and secondary levels, is much less demanding than that of other leading nations. For example, all high school students in the Soviet Union take four years of chemistry (including one year of organic chemistry)[3] and two years of calculus.[4] In contrast, half of all high school graduates in the U.S. take no science or math beyond the 10th grade.[5] Japan, now with the highest literacy rate in the world, graduates 95% of its teenagers from high school; only 74% of U.S. teenagers graduate from high school. Such statistics clearly indicate that, without a shift in our educational direction, America will soon have difficulty competing in a world that demands new knowledge and higher levels of skills from its workforce.

The U.S. economic system is undergoing fundamental change today. Technology greatly affects how we do our work, and other countries have

From James B. Hunt, Jr., "Education for Economic Growth: A Critical Investment," *Phi Delta Kappan* (April 1984). Copyright © 1984 by Phi Delta Kappan, Inc. Reprinted by permission.

become major competitors with the U.S. for the world market. The majority of workers in the United States are now engaged not in industrial production, but in service occupations such as trade, transportation, banking, public utilities, and so on. In 1950, 55% of the U.S. workforce was employed by industry; today that figure has fallen to 20%. In contrast, in 1950, 30% of our workforce held service and information jobs; today that figure has climbed to 70%.

This shift is sure to continue. In fact, it's fairly common to see estimates predicting that 15 million American manufacturing jobs will disappear in the coming decade. We must respond to this shift with a renaissance in education. We must educate our young people for the jobs of tomorrow, the jobs that will be available when they leave high school or college. And we must begin now to develop the skills that will be required tomorrow.

Certainly those jobs promising upward mobility will require the mastery of skills that go beyond today's definition of "the basics." To adequately prepare our young people for these jobs, we must expand our idea of the basics to include not only the abilities to read, write, and compute at a rudimentary level, but also the ability to put to creative use more complex skills.

Basic competence in reading, for example, must be expanded to include the ability to analyze, summarize, and interpret written passages. Competence in writing must encompass the ability to select, organize, and develop ideas. Competence in mathematics must include the ability to compute—with whole numbers, fractions, decimals, and percentages—and to use basic concepts of probability and statistics. Most important, students must acquire such "learning to learn" skills as analysis and problem solving, which will enable them to acquire new skills.

All jobs in the future will by no means require higher-order skills. Yet the growth of technology will change both job opportunities and job requirements, and jobs promising advancement will increasingly be those that require not just mastery of the more advanced skills, but also the ability to use them creatively in the workplace.[6]

Our American educational ethic demands that we provide all students, not just a selected elite, with the opportunity and encouragement to develop more sophisticated skills. We must give everyone both a choice and a genuine chance in life. We must begin immediately to invest more in our human resources by strengthening the education and training of *all* our students. To achieve sound economic growth, we must make these investments now.

We Americans want to insure that we can continue to compete in the world economy. We want our economic productivity increased, our technological capability enhanced, and our standing in the world restored.[7] Our quality of life and the future of our children depend on our ability to pursue this new ethic of educational excellence. We are, of course, concerned about the enormous task of training and retraining that lies before us. Clearly our educational system is being called upon to meet a new challenge. We must equip our citizens to be scientifically and technologically literate if our nation is to participate in a technology-based world economy. In short, we must "maximize human potential through education."[8]

Lately we have heard bleak reports on the quality of education in America. Doomsayers have chronicled its weaknesses and claimed that we have squandered previous gains and produced a generation of Americans inadequately prepared to meet the demands of the future.[9]

A national emergency is clearly upon us. Yet we must not forget that there have been notable positive achievements in American education in recent years. Performance of the historically lower-achieving students improved dramatically during the 1970s as a result of efforts to provide equal educational opportunities to the economically disadvantaged. Data gathered by the National Assessment of Educational Progress indicate that—though there are students who still must be better served if they are to master the basics of literal comprehension, writing mechanics, and whole-number computation—we made great progress during the 1970s in increasing the average performance in reading and math of lower-achieving students.

There is much that is excellent in our public schools. What has become increasingly evident, however, is the fact that we must act now to better educate our young people for future job markets. We must act now to improve our educational system and prove that Americans can still outwork, outproduce, outinvent, and outcompete any nation in the world.

Recent studies of our educational system have awakened Americans to this challenge, and the call for educational reform reflects a national confidence in our capacity to respond yet again. We must take advantage of the current momentum to accomplish something of substance. We must translate our concern into commitment and action, and we must give educational reform top priority on our national, state, and local agendas.

This past year I had the privilege of chairing the Task Force on Education for Economic Growth, sponsored by the Education Commission of the States. Our task force included leaders from the fields of government, business, education, labor, and science.

The fundamental belief of the members of our task force was that education is the key to economic growth in this nation. Our charge was to make the public aware of the link between good schools and good jobs. And our ultimate goal was the renewal of a commitment to excellence in education.

We did not focus primarily on what is wrong within our educational system, but rather on what can be done to make it better—that is, more responsive to the demands of a changing workplace. We assessed the critical role that education must play in the economic growth of the nation. We explored how excellence in education is vital to the strength and prosperity of America, and we dramatized how the challenge of technology must be met in the classroom.

Our report, *Action for Excellence*, presents a blueprint for reform: an eight-point plan for mobilizing all of our resources in the pursuit of education for economic growth. We are convinced that this plan can shape lasting and positive changes within the structure of education.

Our chief recommendation is that each governor join with legislators, state and local boards of education, business and labor leaders, and others in the creation of a state task force. Each state task force should assess statewide and local needs and develop an action plan for improving that state's schools. Each plan should focus on education for jobs and economic growth and should set forth specific objectives, timetables, and methods for measuring progress.[10] Each plan should be comprehensive, straightforward, and understandable: a cohesive master plan for improving education in that state. Piecemeal efforts are doomed to failure.

We also recommend the creation of partnerships between education, business, and government to improve education for economic growth.[11] A central element of our plan is the involvement of business as a genuine partner with the schools, to help determine what is taught, to assist in marshaling the resources needed to provide top-quality education, and to convey to educators the skills that are needed in the workplace. Because we are preparing young people for the jobs of tomorrow, we must make business a full partner in educating those young people. We must tell the business community that, if it wants better employees and higher profits, it must be involved in what the schools teach and how they teach it.

We recommend the more efficient use of existing resources available to our school systems. Furthermore, we must increase our investment in the financial, human, and institutional resources that will promote excellence in education.[12] We must tell taxpayers that excellence will cost money, but we must also guarantee that we will invest that money in efforts that boost quality.

We call for a renewed respect for teachers and for the profession of teaching. This effort is long overdue. The crucial importance of the teaching profession to our national welfare must be emphasized, and both the individual and the collective dignity of our teachers must be recognized. Every state and every local school district must drastically improve its methods of recruiting, train-

ing, and paying teachers.[13] Teacher pay must be made competitive with compensation in other jobs and professions. Teachers need opportunities to assume varying levels and types of responsibilities, and they should be paid accordingly.

We must examine ways to improve the classroom environment—the working conditions for teachers and the learning conditions for students. Classrooms must be orderly places in which teachers are free to teach, unburdened by administrative trivia, and in which students are expected and encouraged to learn.

Teachers must also be given the opportunity to improve and grow professionally. The only limit should be that the best teachers spend most of their time teaching and working with young people. We must not lose our best teachers to nonteaching assignments.

We recommend an intensive effort to make the academic experience more rigorous and more effective. Specifically, we recommend the establishment of explicit requirements regarding discipline, attendance, homework, and grades, for the purpose of improving student performance.[14] We must strengthen the curriculum in such critical areas as mathematics and science, and we must encourage the mastery of both basic and more complex skills.

We must also institute some quality-control measures if we are to insure excellence and effectiveness in our schools. We must establish methods of measuring the effectiveness of teachers and improving the process by which they are certified. Student progress must be monitored through periodic achievement testing.[15] We must tell teachers and students alike that we want better performance.

We must improve the leadership and management of our schools. Principals must be placed in charge of the quality of education in their schools, and, like teachers, they must be rewarded for superior performance. Programs must be established to train principals in the latest techniques of educational management.[16]

Finally, we recommend that each state and local system try to address the needs of student populations that are now unserved or underserved.[17] We must investigate the needs of women, minorities, and the exceptionally gifted, to name a few, and we must invest more in developing their knowledge and skills. If we are to grow economically, we must make a substantial investment in the education and training of *all* our people.

Now the talking is over. The blueprint for reform is before us. Now is the time to act on these recommendations, to seize the opportunity to make deep and lasting changes in American education.

Happily, many states have already begun to answer the call for reform. This effort is particularly notable in the Southeast, where, under the able leadership of Govs. Richard Riley of South Carolina, Lamar Alexander of Tennessee, Robert Graham of Florida, and Charles Robb of Virginia, extraordinary initiatives aimed at improving education are already under way.

North Carolina, too, has responded to the challenge. Already we have moved ahead on the chief recommendation of the ECS task force by putting in place the North Carolina Commission on Education for Economic Growth, a counterpart to the national effort. I am chairing this 50-member commission, which is made up of legislators, top business and corporate leaders, teachers, principals, superintendents, media representatives, local school board members, parents, and students.

Our commission is working at the state and local levels to create a broad public awareness of the link between good schools and good jobs. We are determined to promote new partnerships between education and business and government. We will translate to the state level the recommendations of the national task force, and we will build on efforts already under way to improve education in North Carolina.

North Carolina boasts a legacy of commitment to education. Years ago we recognized the fundamental truths that education is essential for economic growth and that the best route to good jobs and success in life is through education. Since then our strategy has been to invest in education—to take the initiative in developing first-rate innovative educational opportunities for our students.

We point with pride to the initiatives we have undertaken in recent years. In 1975 we instituted a program to provide intensive reading instruction in the primary grades. Class size in the program is limited to 26, and each class is staffed by two adults—a teacher and an aide—providing a student/adult ratio of 13 to 1. Reading is emphasized, and rigorous diagnostic and achievement tests are administered. Test results indicate that North Carolina students are scoring well above national norms.

We have made free public kindergarten available to every child in the state. At the same time, we have maintained the student/adult ratio of 13 to 1.

In 1977 we began a statewide program of annual achievement testing for students in the "transition grades" (first, second, third, sixth, and ninth). Our students' scores have exceeded the national average in all subject areas for three years in a row (1981 through 1983).

We have begun to require potential high school graduates to pass a minimum competency test in reading and mathematics to insure that they have mastered basic skills. This year, for the first time, the competency test will include a writing section to assess whether students have mastered the principles of effective communication. We have also increased the requirements for graduation from 18 to 20 units, beginning with the class of 1987.

We have established a tuition-free residential public high school for those students gifted in mathematics and science. This three-year-old institution, the North Carolina School of Science and Mathematics, brings exceptional students to its campus in Durham for rigorous instruction not only in science and mathematics, but in the arts and humanities as well. Last year, out of a senior class of only 208, the school produced 62 semifinalists in the National Merit Scholarship Program.

We honor our outstanding students through the "North Carolina Scholars" program. Students who become North Carolina Scholars must earn at least 22 credits and maintain high grades in academic subjects. This statewide program is one of only three of its kind in the nation.

We are putting more emphasis on the teaching of mathematics and science. We have recently established summer institutes to offer additional training to junior high school science and mathematics teachers. We have also acquired the funds to hire 100 new math, science, and computer science teachers, and we employ "lead" high school math and science teachers for an additional six weeks in the summer.

We are instituting a Quality Assurance Program within our colleges and universities that train teachers. This program, now in the pilot stage, establishes specific testing requirements for entrance into and exit from teacher education programs. It also mandates stiffer standards for the approval of teacher training programs. The process of entering the profession that is now being tested extends teacher training beyond the undergraduate program to include a two-year period of full-time provisional teaching in the schools, after which an evaluation of a teacher's performance is conducted to determine eligibility for continuing certification. Following successful completion of the program, a beginning teacher is awarded full certification. The Quality Assurance Program is a cooperative effort between the North Carolina State Board of Education and the Board of Governors of the University of North Carolina.

We have involved North Carolina businesses and industries in the schools to an unprecedented degree. We formed the North Carolina Business Committee on Math/Science Education to enlist the participation of the business community in improving state and local education programs. This committee of business leaders from throughout the state is charged specifically with expanding the involvement of business in math and science education in the public schools.

We are confident in North Carolina that the challenges facing education today can be met. They *must* be met. However, meeting them will require an ongoing cooperative effort on the part of all sectors of our society.

We must not be discouraged by the magnitude of the task at hand. It is not necessary for each state to reinvent the wheel. The plan set forth by the National Task Force on Education for Economic Growth is exciting and comprehensive, and it can firmly point the educational systems of all the states in the right direction for a sound economic future. It is up to us now to share strategies, draw on one another's strengths, and build on one another's successes.

State and local governments must accept the ultimate responsibility for improving education. Yet a commitment to this goal at the federal level is imperative if state efforts are to succeed. Unfortunately, this commitment has been conspicuously absent from the federal agenda during the present Administration. Despite praiseworthy efforts on the state level to strengthen education, the Reagan administration has failed to put the federal government at the center of the action.

The cause of improving education will fail without national leadership. The federal government need not assume full responsibility for all that needs to be accomplished, but appropriate federal support to complement state efforts is essential.

First, the President must provide the national leadership required to draw attention to what needs to be done and to mobilize state and local governments, the education system, and business. But providing symbolic leadership at the federal level will not be enough. Several categories of *primary* federal responsibility do exist, including the responsibilities for supporting research and development, insuring an appropriate education for special populations, identifying trends and areas deserving special attention, and providing resource materials to assist state and local educational organizations. In these areas especially,

the federal government must take the lead.

The U.S. economy today has no greater need than trained hands and educated minds. Training and education are investments that will yield higher productivity, higher profits, and a better quality of life.

The challenge before us is to revitalize the schools of the nation. It is a challenge we must greet with the same enthusiasm that Charles B. Aycock, former governor of North Carolina, brought to the noble cause of education. In 1912 Aycock insisted on the "equal right of every child born on earth to have the opportunity to burgeon out all that is within him." Today, we must continue to champion Gov. Aycock's commitment to excellence in education for every student, for every life.

NOTES

1. Task Force on Education for Economic Growth, *Action for Excellence* (Denver: Education Commission of the States, 1983), p. 13.
2. *Newsweek*, 9 May 1983, p. 50.
3. *Action for Excellence*, p. 24.
4. James B. Hunt, Jr., "Academia, Industry, and Government: The Organizational Frontier of Science Today," in James Botkin, Dan Dimancescu, and Ray Stata, eds., *Global Stakes: The Future of High Technology in America* (New York: Harper & Row, 1982), p. 165.
5. *Action for Excellence*, p. 23.
6. Ibid., pp. 15–17.
7. See reference to pollster Louis Harris in Hunt, p. 165.
8. Botkin, Dimancescu, and Stata, p. 48.
9. From the *Newsweek* analysis of *A Nation at Risk* (the report of the National Commission on Excellence in Education), 9 May 1983, p. 50.
10. *Action for Excellence*, p. 34.
11. Ibid., p. 35.
12. Ibid., p. 36.
13. Ibid., p. 37.
14. Ibid., p. 38.
15. Ibid., p. 39.
16. Ibid., p. 40.
17. Ibid.

NO

Joel Spring

EDUCATION AND THE SONY WAR

In the early 1960s one would have been quickly branded a radical for arguing that the U.S. educational system was geared to meet the needs of international corporate competition. Times have certainly changed. The recent reports from federal, state, and private groups demanding an increase in academic standards in the public schools, particularly in science and mathematics, are unanimous in the contention that higher standards in the schools will help keep America competitive in foreign markets.[1]

It is important to ask why a groundswell of opinion supporting the idea that the public schools should be geared to meet the needs of high technology is cresting now. What has happened to the U.S. economy to cause educational concerns to shift from the problem of widespread unemployment that dominated the 1970s to a demand for increased academic requirements? The answer lies in the demographic changes of the last two decades and the response of U.S. business to those changes. The connection between changes in educational policy and industrial needs is direct.

The Seventies were years of declining growth in productivity, dwindling capital investment by U.S. industry, and relatively high unemployment, particularly among young workers. But there was no decrease in the demand for workers during this period. Instead, the high unemployment figures during the Seventies were caused by the large numbers of youth—members of the postwar baby boom—entering the labor market.[2] This flooding of the labor market caused wages to decline, particularly for entry-level occupations. In the 1970s and into the early 1980s young people in the U.S. have had a difficult time finding employment at wages comparable to those of the previous decade.[3]

Because of these circumstances, government educational policy in the 1970s concentrated on the problem of youth unemployment. Career education and vocational education became major educational concerns of all levels of government. Federal policy was typified by the Youth Employment Act of 1977, which provided training and employment opportunities.[4] The response of the U.S. business community to a labor surplus and declining wages was to become more labor intensive and to decrease capital outlays.[5] For instance, a company might choose to increase production by adding a second or third shift, rather than by investing in new equipment.

These changes in labor use and capital investment led to the decline in the growth of productivity of U.S. industry. Productivity may be simply defined as the level of output divided by the amount of labor needed to produce it within a certain time. Under this definition, the increased use of labor naturally led to reduced growth in productivity. By 1977 the level of labor productivity in the U.S. was the same as it had been in 1960. On the other hand, Japan increased its labor productivity during the same period by approximately 255%.[6]

The trends in the early 1980s have been almost the exact opposite of those of the 1970s. With the passing of the baby boom, fewer youths are now entering the labor market. One set of figures shows that the average number of new workers entering the labor force in the 1970s was approximately 2.5 million per year and that, by the late 1980s, this number will decline to approximately 1.5 million workers per year.[7] Another forecast estimates a 14% decline in the 1980s in the number of persons between 14 and 24 years old and a 20% decline in high school enrollments and graduates.[8] Col. George Bailey, former director of continuing education for the U.S. Army, argues that "during the next decade, the military, the colleges, and business and industry will all be competing for the same limited supply of people."[9]

The response of business and industry to the end of the baby boom has been twofold. On the one hand, employers are concerned about the decrease in the number of qualified employees for entry-level jobs. This dwindling pool of workers threatens to drive up wages. Thus business has been working with the schools to maximize the size of the labor pool by improving the education of those students who would have been marginally employable in the 1970s. This newfound interest in education is reflected in adopt-a-school programs, Jobs for America's Graduates, and local alliances between businesses and schools. It has also led to increased emphasis on career preparation in the schools themselves. In his study for the Carnegie Corporation, Michael Timpane details the extent of these new cooperative programs and argues that they have sprung up primarily in response to the growing shortage of entry-level workers. "For the first time in a generation," Timpane writes, "there will probably be, in several urban locations, an absolute shortage of labor supply for entry-level positions. Urban employers already report great difficulty in locating qualified employees for entry-level positions."[10]

On the other hand, the U.S. business community finds itself in difficulty because of delayed capital investments and declining productivity. Both business and political leaders have called for greater technological development to meet the growth of international competition. With regard to educational policy, this has meant a call for increased graduation requirements in mathematics, science, and other academic fields. Policy makers hope that these new graduates will lead U.S. industry to victory in the worldwide technological competition.

Both of these trends in educational policy are designed to provide U.S. business with an expanded pool of potential employees—and consequently a decline in wages. This will be particularly true if high unemployment continues to characterize the 1980s. If these two trends are successful, the market will be flooded with high school graduates with good work attitudes and minimum basic skills for entry-level positions and with highly qualified scientists and engineers.

Meeting the short-term needs of U.S. business and industry does not necessarily result in economic benefits either to the economy or to the individual. After all, the decision of business not to invest in new plants and equipment in the 1970s and instead to reap short-term profits is partly responsible for the present technological crisis. *The failure of the public schools did not cause the problem.* Indeed, it is hard to predict the social, political, and economic needs of the world that the first high school graduates to have completed 12 years of schooling under the present educational proposals will face in 1995.

In fact, if the schools continue to be geared to meet the changing needs of U.S. business, we can expect still another change in educational policy in the next decade to meet those changing desires. Thus the public school system becomes a captive of the profit motive of U.S. industry. And, let me emphasize again, this relationship guarantees neither an improved economy nor a higher standard of living for individuals. Indeed, such a close connection between education and industry might lead to *lower* wages, as different segments of the labor market are flooded by workers channeled there by the public school system. In effect, American business would be using the public school system to exploit the American worker.

Educators have been quick to accept the demands that business makes on the schools because of the constant promise of more money for education. Over the last three decades U.S. educators have been willing to accept the extravagant claims that public schooling can win the cold war, end poverty, and eliminate unemployment. Although all of these claims have been built on shaky premises, educators have seen them as ways of convincing the public of the worth of the schools and of the need for more money. In other words, extravagant claims about the power of public education provide an important means of public relations for public school educators.

The report of the National Commission on Excellence in Education is a case in point. It stresses both the importance of future investment in education and of an educational plan to meet the current needs of industry. The report argues that investment in public education is the key to solving the economic problems of the U.S. "If only to keep and improve on the slim competitive edge we still retain in world markets," the report urges, "we must rededicate ourselves to the reform of our educational system for the benefit of all. . . ." In language designed to frighten readers into shelling out more money for public education, the report states, "If an unfriendly foreign power had attempted to impose on America the mediocre educational performance that exists today, we might well have viewed it as an act of war."[11] The picture painted in *A Nation at Risk* is that of a tired giant losing a global trade war because of the failure of its public schools. The solution to the problems of international trade, according to the report, is the reform of public schooling.

In making these claims, the National Commission offered no evidence that public schooling can solve the problems of international trade and economic development. Indeed, the commissioners seem to have assumed that the economic problems of the U.S. are not being caused by problems in the economic system itself but by problems in the development of human capital. Again, they offered no proof. Ample proof is offered of the decline of public schools but not of the relationship of this decline to economic problems.

All the historical evidence from the last three decades of federal involvement in public schools suggests that public schooling is *not* the answer to social and economic problems. In the 1950s the public schools were called on to win the cold war against the Soviet Union by providing more mathematicians and scientists. (The parallels between today's rhetoric and that of the 1950s should be noted.) In the 1950s the key to our technological race with the Soviet Union was believed to be the public schools. The National Defense Education Act was passed in 1958 to provide more funding for science, mathematics, and foreign language instruction. This legislation was very similar to several bills now pending in Congress. In addition, there was a five-fold increase in funding to the National Science Foundation to develop new curricula for the schools.[12]

What was the result of this federal involvement? There is no evidence that it won the military/technological war with the Soviet Union. In fact, all the evidence marshaled by the National Commission indicates that the public schools actually declined shortly after the National Defense Education Act was passed. Though it cannot be proved, there may even be a causal relationship between federal involvement and the academic decline of the schools.

In the 1960s Presidents Kennedy and Johnson called on the public schools to end poverty and improve the economic conditions of minority groups. The major piece of federal legislation in this "war on poverty" was the Elementary and Secondary Education Act of 1965. In the 1970s Presidents Nixon and Ford tried to solve the problems of unemployment by expanding career and vocational education programs. Despite all of these efforts to solve social and economic problems through public schooling, the U.S. still faces high unemployment and chronic poverty.

Now we face another demand: change the educational system to fit the national goal of increased technological development for improved international trade. The National Commission recommends that state and local requirements for high schools be changed to include, as a minimum, what the report calls the "five new basics." These new basics include four years of English, three years of mathematics, three years of science, three years of social studies, and one-half year of computer science.

The proposals of the National Commission parallel exactly what is happening as states try to improve their economic conditions by requiring more math and science courses as a means of attracting high-technology industries. As of May 1983 the Oregon state legislature was considering the establishment of a state high school for science and mathematics; Wyoming was considering scholarships for math and science teachers; New York was considering training programs and special scholarships for math and science teachers; and Connecticut was considering some form of loan program for math and science teachers. In all, 30 states were considering some form of special aid for math and science teaching. In addition, Congress was considering a $425 million math and science education bill.[13]

There is a certain irony in the fact that these proposals are designed to correct problems resulting from earlier proposals linking public goals with academic requirements. Most existing state-mandated academic standards are the products of some previous effort to achieve political, economic, or social goals. After its survey of trends in the high school curriculum, the National Commission concluded that "secondary school curricula, have been homogenized, diluted, and diffused to the point that they no longer have a central purpose. But because the Commission does not analyze the causes for this diffuse curriculum, it travels down the same path that brought the schools to their present predicament.

Through the years the states and the federal government have continually added to and subtracted from the curriculum according to social, political, and economic needs. The public schools have been asked to solve problems ranging from driver safety to fighting communism. As Gene Maeroff writes, "Schools have been viewed by Congress primarily as instruments of social change. It is perhaps flattering to public education that it was awarded so pivotal a role in the perfecting of society, but the responsibility is a burden nonetheless."[14]

What this rush to save U.S. international trade means is that the public school curriculum is being biased toward yet another goal: namely, technological development. But is this the only problem faced by the United States? One could argue that the economic problems of the U.S. have been primarily political in origin. For instance, U.S. economic problems could be related to the high deficits and runaway inflation caused by the Vietnam war and the federal government's handling of the energy crisis of the 1970s. If this were true, then one might argue for more political education in the schools. But the point is that it is wrong to bias public school curricula in *any* one direction when there is no proof as to what are the most important social, economic, and political problems—much less their solutions.

This issue becomes clearer when one considers possible alternatives to raising academic requirements for secondary schools. Suppose America's problems stemmed from an inability of the population to think through important issues clearly. If this were true, why not have all secondary schools require three years of philosophy? Suppose the problem is the inability of the population to understand and act on political, social, and economic issues. One might then replace the meaningless hodgepodge of social studies courses with a requirement that all secondary students take three years of sociology, three years of economics, and three years of political science. Or suppose society has been ruined by too much technology and not enough appreciation of the arts and humanities. If this were true, why not require three years of music, three years of art, and three years of literature? All of these curricula could be defended in terms of some national need or purpose.

Until the federal government and the state legislatures stop making curriculum changes on the basis of social, political, and economic needs, the curriculum of the public schools will continue to be in a state of flux and chaos. The real question regarding the curriculum is, What knowledge is of most worth? In a democratic society, the answer to that central question should be given by individuals, not by governments. State legislatures must stop establishing academic requirements, and the federal government must stop trying to influence the curriculum to serve national policy objectives.

The recommendations of the National Commission offer no real hope for a reform that will cure the ills of U.S. education. All the problems addressed by the report have their origin in the present structure of public schooling. Merely changing academic requirements to suit the latest whim of the government—to serve some particular policy goal—will do nothing to alter that basic structure.

How long will the American public continue to believe extravagant claims about the value of public schooling? How many more generations will accept the public relations strategy of public school educators, as they offer their product as a panacea for practically every social, political, or economic ill? How many more years will Congress and the state legislatures go along with the grandiose claims of the lobbyists for public education? Perhaps society will see through the current fog of rhetoric that envelops the recommendations of these new commissions; perhaps this time the public will realize that the public schools cannot solve such problems as the weakened position of the U.S. in international trade or the failure of the domestic economy. Indeed, we might even harbor the hope that someday the public schools will no

longer be captives of the profit motive of U.S. industry and that the education of Americans will not be determined by the economic goals of business.

NOTES

1. Three of the major reports are Education Commission of the States, *Action for Excellence: A Comprehensive Plan to Improve Our Nation's Schools* (Denver: ECS, 1983); Twentieth Century Fund Task Force on Federal Elementary and Secondary Education Policy, *Making the Grade* (New York: Twentieth Century Fund, 1983); and National Commission on Excellence in Education, *A Nation at Risk: The Imperative for Educational Reform* (Washington, D.C.: U.S. Government Printing Office, 1983).

2. See Daniel Quinn Mills, "Decisions About Employment in the 1980s: Overview and Underpinning," and Michael Wachter, "Economic Challenges Posed by Demographic Changes," in Eli Ginzberg et al., eds., *Work Decisions in the 1980s* (Boston: Auburn House, 1982).

3. "For example, while males 20 to 24 years old earned $73 for every $100 by prime-age males in 1955, they earned only $58 for every $100 in 1977," according to Wachter, p. 43.

4. For a discussion of the Youth Employment Act of 1977, see Joel Spring, *American Education,* 2nd ed. (New York: Longman, 1982), pp. 117–21.

5. "In fact, in the mid-1970s American manufacturing firms were cautious about capital investment, but relatively expansive about employment. . . . In the most telling comparison, American manufacturers and manufacturers in France, Japan, and Germany increased output between 1972 and 1978 by somewhat similar amounts. During the same period employment fell in France by 2.2%, in Japan by 4.7%, and in Germany by 12%; but in the United States, manufacturers increased employment by 615%," according to Mills, pp. 8–9.

6. Ibid., p. 5.

7. Wachter, pp. 35–42.

8. Michael Timpane, *Corporations and Public Education,* report distributed by Teachers College, Columbia University (New York: Carnegie Corporation, May 1982), pp. 8–9.

9. Quoted in Anne C. Lewis, "Washington Report: The Military Enters the Competition for Technically Trainable Graduates," *Phi Delta Kappan,* May 1983, p. 603.

10. Timpane, p. 8.

11. *A Nation at Risk*, p. 5.

12. A history of federal involvement in public schools after World War II can be found in Joel Spring, *The Sorting Machine* (New York: Longman, 1976).

13. "State Proposals to Bolster Math and Science Teaching," *Education Week*, 18 May 1983, pp. 14–16.

14. Gene Maeroff, *Don't Blame the Kids: The Trouble with America's Public Schools* (New York: McGraw-Hill, 1982), p. 8.

POSTSCRIPT

Should Schools Serve National Economic Needs?

The very founding of organized public schooling in this country was abetted by Horace Mann's promise that the schools would help produce efficient and compliant workers and would become the "balance wheel" of the social machinery. Although many people still see the schools as performers of this function, there is concern that Herbert Spencer's 1860 question, "What knowledge is of most worth?" cannot be answered by either the national government or by business interests.

In support of schools producing workers, Ralph C. Weinrich, in "Meeting Our Commitment to Employment-Bound Youth," *NASSP Bulletin* (February 1990), proposes a system of schooling that would eliminate nonemployable graduates. He feels that, by the time they reach high school, students may sufficiently be placed into either a college-bound or a vocational category. By dividing the schools into two distinct branches, each concentrating on one category or the other, and assigning each student to the curriculum that best suits him or her, those who had no plans for either higher education or for entering the job market after high school would be forced to make a choice. General education curricula would no longer exist. Under this model, schools would serve no other purpose but to prepare young people for work. If effected, would this economics-controlled education be desirable?

Joel Spring's critique of political and economic purposes in education has been a central theme of his research. Elaborations upon this theme may be found in his books *The Sorting Machine, American Education* (particularly Chapter One), and *Educating the Worker-Citizen*, which includes chapters on political theories of education, the economic state, the production of knowledge, and the control of schooling. A more technical treatment of these and related issues may be found in *Power and Ideology in Education* (1977), edited by Jerome Karabel and A. H. Halsey.

Further analyses of political and economic influences on educational decision-making can be found in the books and articles of Michael W. Kirst and in the following works: Frank Musgrove's *School and the Social Order* (1980); *Education and American Culture* (1980), edited by Elisabeth Steiner, Robert Arnove, and B. Edward McClellan; Michael Fullan's *The Meaning of Educational Change* (1982); and Seymour B. Sarason's *Schooling in America* (1983).

Spring's recent work, *Conflict of Interests: The Politics of American Education* (1988), examines special interest groups in "the knowledge industry" and political control factors at the federal, state, and local levels.

Among other recent books that analyze various facets of the economic dimension of education are these: *A Pedagogy for Liberation* (1986), by Ira Shor and Paulo Freire; Freire's *Politics of Education: Culture, Power, and Liberation* (1985), a collection of essays that attempts to chart a theoretical grounding; James S. Coleman's *The Asymmetrical Society* (1981); and *Education and Work* (1983), published by the Organization for Economic Cooperation and Development.

In 1990 the National Governors' Association released reports on state actions and on goals for the year 2000, and the Association for Supervision and Curriculum Development issued its "Guidelines for Business Involvement in the Schools."

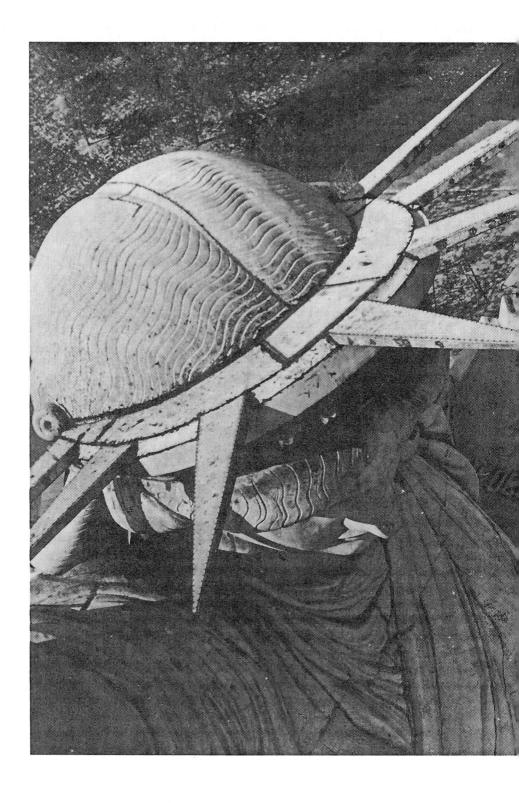

PART 2
Specific Issues

In this section, the issues debated probe concerns that currently face educators and policy makers. How these debates are resolved will affect the future direction of education in our society.

ISSUE 9

Should "Choice" Plans Include Private Schools?

YES: John E. Coons, from " 'Choice' Plans Should Include Private Option," *Education Week* (January 17, 1990)

NO: Dennis L. Evans, from "The Risks of Inclusive 'Choice' Plans," *Education Week* (February 14, 1990)

ISSUE SUMMARY

YES: Professor of law John E. Coons argues that the next step in giving parents the right to choose their children's schools is to extend the option to private schools.
NO: Public school principal Dennis L. Evans criticizes this renewed attempt to provide government aid to private and parochial education.

One of the more heated educational debates in recent years has been the one concerned with finding ways to provide parents and learners with a greater range of choices in schooling. Some people see the public school system as a monolithic structure that runs roughshod over individual inclinations and imposes a rigid social philosophy on its constituents. Others feel that the reduced quality of public education, particularly in large urban areas, demands that parents be given support in their quest for better learning environments. Still others agree with sociologist James S. Coleman's contention that "the greater the constraints imposed on school attendance—short of dictating place of residence and prohibiting attendance at private schools— the greater the educational gap between those who have the money to escape the constraints and those who do not."

Measures that emphasize freedom of choice abound and are often connected with desegregation and school reform goals. Some jurisdictions have developed a system of magnet schools to serve the dual purposes of equality and quality; some districts now allow parents to send their children to any public school under their control; and a few urban districts (notably Milwaukee and Kansas City) are experimenting with funding plans to allow private school alternatives.

Two of the most-discussed ideas of dealing with this last possibility are tuition tax credits and voucher plans. The first, provided by the federal, state, or local government, would expand the number of families able to send their children to the school of their choice and would, according to advocates, improve the quality of public schooling by encouraging competition. Voucher plans, first suggested in 1955 by conservative economist Milton Friedman, are designed to return tax monies to parents of school-aged children for use in a variety of authorized public and private educational settings. Opponents of either approach take the position that such moves will turn the public schools into an enclave of the poor and will lead to further racial, socio-economic class, and religious isolation. The question of church-state separation looms large in the minds of those who oppose these measures. (See Issue 5 for further discussion of this aspect.)

A recent Gallup poll shows that 71 percent of the respondents feel that parents should have the right to choose among public schools and that 44 percent believe that private and parochial schools should be included among the alternatives. The U.S. Department of Education favors the expansion of choice, and some 40 states have initiated "choice" plans, most of which limit the choice to public alternatives. A recently released study funded by the Brookings Institution, *Politics, Markets, and America's Schools*, by John E. Chubb and Terry M. Moe, puts forth a new plan for chartering any group or organization as a public school if certain minimum criteria are met.

The problem of "choice" provides an exhilarating example of the interlocking forces of history, social change, public policy, and educational theory. Some of these forces are alluded to in the following articles. John E. Coons, long an advocate of voucher plans, tuition tax credits, and other measures designed to facilitate parental selection of private alternatives for schooling, argues the case further in light of the pressing need for offering maximum alternatives for disadvantaged families in urban areas. Dennis L. Evans provides a poignant rebuttal of the private school inclusion position, finding that both public schools and private institutions would be gravely damaged by such a change in policy.

YES

John E. Coons

'CHOICE' PLANS SHOULD INCLUDE PRIVATE OPTION

When government adopts educational choice as sound policy, should it help parents choose private as well as public schools? Or should it instead continue its effective monopoly over the schooling of those who cannot afford to pay for an education?

So far in the debate over choice, the President, the governors, spokesmen for the public schools, and the teachers' union have assumed that only state-operated schools would participate. Curiously, no one has tried to justify the exclusion of private schools. Some protagonists self-consciously evade the question; one well-known figure even resorts to code, signaling that private is taboo merely by italicizing the word *public*. Even those who have long praised private schools as educators of the poor duck the issue of their inclusion. This mute boycott of the obvious has been criticized as political cowardice. Is there a benign interpretation?

The explanation cannot be that any comprehensive system of choice would discriminate against government schools. No politically sane proposal could allow unregulated private academies to "cream off" the brightest prospects and charge extra tuition, leaving public schools with red tape, regulation, and rejects. If there were to be a private option, both politics and good sense require that the playing field be level or even tipped toward the state schools. Specifically, the subvention for state schools would have to equal or exceed that for the private sector. And, except for the teaching of religion, public schools would have to be deregulated to enjoy the same freedom as private schools in management, style, and content. Conversely, every private and public school would accept the new responsibility of admitting a substantial share of low-income children; poor families could not be excluded by unregulated charges beyond the state subsidy.

Adjust the details to your satisfaction. Once the system is neutral between sectors, the case for government monopoly is thin. Private education obviously works well enough for those who now use it—and especially for the poor. No one doubts that low-budget religious schools are effective with disadvantaged children. Of course, the populations of these successful schools are "self-selected," but that is precisely the point. Poverty does not destroy the parental capacity to choose well, and the waiting lists at such institutions demonstrate that those who have already chosen are not the only parents who know what they are doing.

Nor is the private sector a special instrument for segregation by race and class. To the contrary, it offers a neglected opportunity for dismantling the de facto segregation that is typically imposed by government schools. Imagine what scholarships could achieve in the hands of parents in the depressed neighborhoods of, say, Los Angeles or the District of Columbia.

In Kansas City—a similar urban setting—black families have petitioned the federal court to order the deliberately segregated school district to provide scholarships so that their children can vindicate their 14th Amendment rights in integrated private schools. Why do they need private schools? First, there are too few whites—25 percent—left in the public schools of the defendant district; second, the contiguous districts will not accept transfers. By contrast, 50 neighboring private schools—Catholic, Lutheran, Episcopal, and secular—have offered over 4,000 spaces in their own integrated student bodies. The sole condition they would impose is that applicants not have a record of repeated violent behavior. The average per-pupil cost of such schools is about $2,000; the Kansas City public schools spend three times as much.

Are private schools, then, a problem or a solution? If they stand ready to reduce segregation, will they nevertheless be red-lined because of some occult objection to what they do?

FOR MANY POLICYMAKERS AND EDUCATORS, the answer is yes. It simply does not matter to them how effective the private schools are in educating the poor and in producing integration by class and race. Indeed, if private schools are efficient at way they do, this only makes them worse. For the real objection is that they teach the wrong ideas. Children of the underclass can get the "right" ideas only in institutions that combine a common curriculum with state monopoly.

This one right way for the poor was contrived in another epoch. It was designed to provide a specific therapy for the uncommon curricula of 19th-century immigrants, with their loyalties to strange gods and old cultures. Its patrician founders feared that toleration of exotic doctrines would have two consequences: Error would proliferate and endure, and ideological factions would war with one another as they had in the Old World. The imposition of a common curriculum would thus serve both a "truth" function and a social function.

The truth function has evaporated. The curriculum can no longer be "common" in the sense of a set of accepted propositions, for there are too many versions of reality and of the good life. The message can be only a vector of these many visions of truth. And so we witness creationists and evolutionists battling to exhaustion, assuring thereby that the ideas of neither can be preached; creationism is out, but evolution can be taught only as a theory.

This temperate outcome is typical of the state's resolution of controversial questions. Public schools are left to teach the compromises that emerge from the clashes of labor, minorities, feminists, churches, homosexuals, nationalists, and business. On many of life's interesting issues of fact and morality, the public schools offer not truth but rather whatever propositions are allowed by the bland treaties forged by politics. By its nature, the common curriculum must be narrow, riskless, and—very often—silent.

The politics of pluralism thus imposes a kind of peaceable agnosticism on the public schools as their civic duty. This intellectual repose becomes so familiar that it is sometimes mistaken as a good in itself. By extension, those who teach truth as they see it can appear almost uncivil. By trafficking in specific answers to controversial questions, they threaten the American covenant. And such answers are precisely what many private schools offer their students on crucial issues of fact and morality. They teach particular descriptions of God, intellect, will, human immortality, and the limits of science; they address directly such concerns as abortion, chastity, social responsibility, individualism, nationalism, and the pursuit of money.

The vanilla curriculum of public education must endure, and it is an appropriate diet for those who prefer it. But a policy of irenic censorship in the public sector must not be misunderstood as a national philosophy of knowledge. The menu provided by the state is no criterion of truth but a makeshift necessary for this peculiarly political institution. No argument appears here for discriminating against private schools that teach distinct ideas on which Americans disagree.

The other historical justification for public monopoly was the social function of schools. And there is still a consensus—which I share—that schools should nourish civic virtue in two senses: Graduates should be prepared to participate in government and society, and they should be tolerant of diversity. Now, no one imagines that private schools violate the first mandate. Their alumni participate as voters and public servants and are no more likely to go to jail or commit suicide than the rest of us. The objection rather boils down to the 19th-century fear that, because they promote ideas that must be censored in the sanitized public curriculum, private schools will breed intolerance.

What do we know of the relative effects of public and private schooling on tolerance? There is no evidence that graduates of private schools typically aim to throttle the civil rights of others. What we do know of them cuts exactly the other way. Meanwhile, the really successful merchant of intolerance may be the public system of assignment, in which the poor have choice of neither school nor curriculum. The inner-city clients of that system see plainly that *their* views of the good and the true are despised; they, in turn, have little reason to tolerate the views of others. What Horace Mann actually achieved in the lobbied curriculum was a plausible design for social division.

A choice of private schools well might make things better. Parents who found themselves liberated and trusted by society would at last have a reason to support the system and to transmit their sense of belonging to the child. The effect of systematic indoctrination on the individual child is, of course, not predictable. And, in a system of choice, a very few schools would hope to teach intolerance—they do now in both sectors.

We know, nonetheless, that children profit in a general way from a school that is committed to the ideals of a community chosen by the family. If tolerance has not been a conspicuous product of the public curriculum, could it be that this virtue, like others, is best learned from humans who embody some freely chosen version of the good? Perhaps children must learn respect for the ideals of others by first grasping those of their own parents. There is certainly no evidence to the contrary.

I find nothing in our national experience or in our understanding of childhood that justifies the exclusion of private schools from any system of subsidized parental choice.

NO

Dennis L. Evans

THE RISKS OF INCLUSIVE 'CHOICE' PLANS

In spite of consistent opposition from the general public, legislative and judicial bodies, and the vast majority of educators—all of whom are strongly committed to our heritage of church-and-state separation—John E. Coons continues to play lobbyist for a private school voucher system (" 'Choice' Plans Should Include Private Option," Commentary, *Jan. 17, 1990*).

In his Commentary, Mr. Coons attempts to revive his tired rhetoric regarding vouchers by linking that concept with the public-school "choice" movement. But even if the fundamental constitutional issues could be resolved, Mr. Coons's proposals would deserve to remain moribund.

Choice within the public-school system is a quantum leap from Mr. Coons's notion of governmental support for private and parochial schools. The movement for choice is founded on the presumption that competition for students will improve public education. While that position may be arguable, it at least speaks to the crucial importance of public education.

Mr. Coons, on the other hand, believes that public education has, at best, outlived its original purposes: "The imposition of a common [public] curriculum would thus serve both a 'truth' function and a social function. The truth function has evaporated."

And at worst, Mr. Coons suggests that public education contributes to anti-intellectualism and social stratification: "The vanilla curriculum of public education must endure, and it is an appropriate diet for those who prefer it. . . . What Horace Mann actually achieved in the lobbied [public] curriculum was a plausible design for social division."

Mr. Coons's cure for what he sees as the malaise created by the "sanitized public curriculum" is to underwrite, with tax dollars, the individual philosophies and educational panaceas of private-school proprietors who, in his words, will "teach truth as they see it." Most reasonable choice plans do not propose, as does Mr. Coons, to give new money to parents so that they might shop at the educational mall. Rather, the plans would provide for the redistribution of existing monies to those public schools that are affected by enrollment changes due to parental choice.

The logical extension of Mr. Coons's argument would be that parents could keep the cash from the state and tutor their children at home. While home schooling may well be appropriate for some, should it be subsidized by the state? What about issues such as governance and accreditation?

It seems somewhat ironic, albeit understandable, that Mr. Coons appears willing to sell out the traditional freedoms of private education to receive government subsidies. He states that "every private and public school would accept the new responsibility of admitting a substantial share of low-income children."

Whom would Mr. Coons suggest—other than the government—as an appropriate regulatory body to see that such responsibilities are carried out? Would private schools adhere to the guidelines of accrediting associations or to state regulations regarding teacher licensing? If not, how would unsuspecting parents and children be protected from unscrupulous entrepreneurs out for a quick voucher? Perhaps we would need a "Better School Bureau."

MR. COONS'S IDEAS WOULD TREMENdously increase the total cost of education to benefit those who have already opted for private schooling. Or does he imagine that only new enrollees would receive the vouchers? Hardly. His program would either destroy private education as it currently exists, by requiring accreditation, licensing, and other government regulations, or it would ask the public to indiscriminately support all manners and forms of unsupervised schooling.

Mr. Coons's elitist remarks notwithstanding, public schools need to be improved, not dismantled. More than ever, our public schools must perform functions that no other institution can. Contrary to his assertion that a form of "irenic censorship" dictates public-education curricula, the schools actually provide the only forum where all viewpoints regarding a particular issue receive consideration and scrutiny without the a priori biases found in private education. Public schooling is the only educational enterprise dedicated, by design, to offering a program that respects the myriad outlooks and values held by all of the children of all of the people.

In Mr. Coons's view, it is lamentable that public schools "teach the compromises that emerge from the clashes of labor, minorities, feminists, churches, homosexuals, nationalists, and business." Some of us would suggest that such an approach is far preferable to the type of sectarian, special-interest, private education that he extols as teaching "particular descriptions of God, intellect, will, human immortality, and the limits of science."

But the beauty of our current approach to education is that both systems exist. Mr. Coons's proposals would irreparably damage one of them by diverting much needed funding from it, while unalterably changing the other by subsidizing it with public monies and thus subjecting it to government regulation and control.

POSTSCRIPT

Should "Choice" Plans Include Private Schools?

Which side truly speaks for American ideals? Which position will bring a better quality of education to the greatest number of young people in this society? Which approach is most in tune with the evolving conception of cultural pluralism?

Questions such as these cannot be answered by considering the issue of choice alone. The companion topics of compulsory attendance laws, home schooling (see Issue 10), private school funding, voucher plans, church-state separation (see Issue 5), desegregation, magnet schools, and urban education (see Issue 11) all come into play in questions of this depth.

The availability of controversial viewpoints on these many topics is almost limitless. A detailed overview may be gained from *School Finance and Education Policy: Enhancing Educational Efficiency, Equality, and Choice*, 2d ed. (1988), by James W. Guthrie, Walter I. Garms, and Lawrence C. Pierce. An excellent treatment of wider issues related to choice may be found in Peter S. Hlebowitch's "Schools of Choice and the Sociopolitical Context," *Equity and Excellence* (Summer 1990).

Further considerations of choice as a reform mechanism are contained in these articles: "The Bottom Line for School Reform," by Hugh B. Price, vice president of the Rockefeller Foundation, *Phi Delta Kappan* (November 1990); Joe Nathan's "More Public School Choice Can Mean More Learning" and Ann Bastian's "Choice Is a Double-Edged Tool," *Educational Leadership* (October 1989); and "Educational Vouchers: A Viable Option for Urban Settings," by Sandler and Kapel, *Urban Review* (Winter 1988).

A variety of books and pamphlets are available, among them *Public Schools of Choice* (1990), by ASCD; *Magnet Schools: An Approach to Desegregation* (1980), by Phi Delta Kappa; and *The Carrot or the Stick for School Desegregation Policy* (1988), by AERA. Numerous articles can be found in the July 1989 issue of *The American School Board Journal,* the Spring 1989 issue of *Public Interest,* and the December 1990/January 1991 issue of *Educational Leadership.*

Will the 1990s see further expansion of the concept and policy of parental choice, further eroding the traditional barriers to public funding of private schools, or will such expansion bring with it increased public control of private schooling, resulting in a blending of the two realms?

ISSUE 10

Is Home Schooling a Viable Alternative?

YES: David Guterson, from "When Schools Fail Children: An English Teacher Educates His Kids at Home," *Harper's* (November 1990)

NO: William Konnert and Josef Wendel, from "Here's What Your Board Should Know When Parents Ask About Home Schooling," *The American School Board Journal* (May 1988)

ISSUE SUMMARY

YES: David Guterson, a public school teacher, explains why he and his wife educate their own children at home.

NO: Professor of educational administration William Konnert and public school principal Josef Wendel raise legal and logistical issues concerning this option.

Historically, compulsory school attendance laws have been justified in a variety of ways—parental inability or unwillingness to educate their offspring, a social need to elevate the level of moral behavior, the need to maintain the social and economic machinery, the desire to widen opportunities for social mobility, the need to acculturate an immigrant population, and the need to pass on the cultural heritage and "civilize" the young. Compulsory attendance laws in this country date back to 1852, and only in recent decades have they come under serious attack.

The first barrage came primarily from the radical reformers of the 1960s and 1970s. Paul Goodman's *Compulsory Mis-education and the Community of Scholars* (1964), Ivan Illich's *Deschooling Society* (1970), and many books written by John Holt demanded that government monopolization of the paths of learning be demolished. According to Illich, compulsory, government-controlled schooling treats knowledge as a commodity, deadens the individual's will to learn, and establishes an artificial structure for "success" that socially damages those who are unable to take advantage of the system. He further contends that "the whole enterprise of formal education is based on the false assumption that learning will be assured, maximized, and made more efficient if it is administered by specially prepared professionals in a special place at a prescribed time according to a preconceived plan to a group of children of a certain age."

The second assault came primarily from the Christian fundamentalists in the 1980s who saw the secularism of the public schools as a threat to the values being taught at home. Using the U.S. Supreme Court decision in *Wisconsin v. Yoder* (1972), which exempted the Amish sect from compliance with compulsory attendance laws, increasing numbers of parents engaged in home schooling on religious grounds. Support groups, such as the Christian Liberty Academy, provided parents with materials for conducting school at home. By the mid-1980s almost every state had given permission for some form of home schooling. Some jurisdictions mandated strict controls, some liberalized existing attendance laws, some clarified "home schooling" as a fulfillment of the law while upholding the right of the state to enforce regulations, while still others virtually abandoned their compulsory attendance laws.

What this leaves us with in the 1990s, according to Patricia M. Lines in "An Overview of Home Instruction," *Phi Delta Kappan* (March 1987), is a "small but vigorous and diverse" movement. Although estimates vary widely, the home-schooling movement serves about one percent of the total school-age population. Lines reports that the current reasons parents give for educating their children at home include concern about the methods and materials used in the schools, the child's inability to adapt to formal schooling, concerns about a lack of moral climate in the schools, and the inability of the schools to provide individualized attention to their children's needs.

This specific issue is related to the somewhat broader issue of parental choice (see Issue 9) and the fundamental problems involved in the relationship between church and state (see Issue 5). In the selections that follow, public school teacher David Guterson provides an in-depth analysis of his reasons for keeping his own children away from formal schooling. While not arguing directly against the rights of parents to select such an option, educators William Konnert and Josef Wendel examine some of the difficulties involved in choosing that course of action.

YES

David Guterson

WHEN SCHOOLS FAIL CHILDREN

Although it remains unarticulated among us, we Americans share an allegiance to schools, an assumption that schools are the foundation of our meritocracy and the prime prerequisite to a satisfying existence. In fact, to the oft-cited triumvirate of what is ineluctable in life—birth, death, and taxes—we are prone to add an unspoken fourth: education in classrooms.

In my classroom at a public high school in an upper-middle-class milieu where education is taken relatively seriously, we read with great purpose precisely those stories that tacitly reaffirm this loyalty to schools: In *Lord of the Flies* a pack of schoolboys degenerate into killers because no teachers are around to preserve the constraints of civilization. In *To Kill a Mockingbird* the venerable Atticus Finch insists that, for all of its shortcomings—and despite the fact that his daughter, Scout, is best educated by his own good example and by life in the larger web of Maycomb County—Maycomb Elementary is *mandatory*. *The Catcher in the Rye* is in large part the story of its protagonist's maladjustment to schools, and J. D. Salinger is highly critical of the hypocrisy behind a good education; still he ultimately offers up Mr. Antolini—an English teacher—as Holden Caulfield's last best hope.

The doctrine that school is necessary, which we early imbibe while within the very belly of the beast, is inevitably reinforced after we are disgorged. The daily implacability with which the media report the decline of schools, the constant knell of ominous statistics on the sorry state of American education, the curious popularity of such books as E. D. Hirsch's *Cultural Literacy* and Allan Bloom's *Closing of the American Mind*, are signs and portents, yes—but they also serve to bolster our shared assumption that school is required not merely because we attended it but also because our common life is in such a precarious state. Our national discussion about education is a desperate one, taking place, as it does, in an atmosphere of crisis, but it does not include in any serious way a challenge to the notion that *every child should attend school*. Why? Because, quite simply, there is no context for such a challenge: We live in a country where a challenge to the universal necessity of schools is not merely eccentric, not merely radical, but fundamentally un-American.

Yet there *are* those who have challenged not exactly the schools' raison d'être but the reason for their children's being *in* them. The children of such people have come to be called by a powerful misnomer, by a Newspeak conjoining: "homeschoolers." These children are not really *home*schoolers at all but rather young persons who do not go to school and are educated outside of institutions, persons best defined by what they don't do as opposed to what they do. There are currently about 300,000 homeschoolers in the United States—truants from one perspective, but, from another, following in the footsteps of Thomas Jefferson, Thomas Edison, Woodrow Wilson, Margaret Mead, and Andrew Wyeth.

A substantial majority of homeschooling parents in America are fervently religious and view schools as at odds with Christian doctrine. Overall, however, they are a diverse lot—the orthodox and the progressive, the Fundamentalist Christian and the libertarian, the urban, the rural, the social skeptic, the idealist, the self-sufficient, and the paranoid. And studies show little or no correlation between the degree of religious content in a homeschooling program or the level of its formal structure—ranging from orthodox "structuralists," with homes set up as miniature schools, to informal programs guided only by a child's ability to learn—or the education or affluence of homeschooling parents (or lack of affluence; the median annual income of homeschooling families is somewhere between $20,000 and $30,000) and the surprising academic success of homeschooled children, who tend to score well above average on standardized achievement tests.

But despite this—and despite the fact that teaching one's own was the norm in the United States until the 1850s—home-schooling today is little more than a fringe movement, an uprising perceived by many as a sort of insult and by others as a severe admonishment: *Take more interest in your children, like us!* (A Gallup revealed that 70 percent of the American population disapproved of homeschooling.) The movement inspires guilt in the hearts of too many parents—a lot of them baby boomers energetically seeking money and success yet worried that their children are growing up estranged from them—guilt and the sort of rage normally reserved for heretics and cultists.

Few people realize that the home-schooling movement is populated by a large number of educators or ex-educators—parents who teach or who have taught in the schools but keep their children out of them. Their paradoxical behavior makes them at first a curiosity and finally an affront to the schools that hired them; their students are confounded by their apparent hypocrisy; their colleagues are apt to tread delicately around the subject. So saying, I'll add my own confession: I am one of these walking contradictions. I teach my neighbors' children in my high school classroom, but my wife and I teach ours at home.

WE CAME TO THIS DECISION, I SHOULD admit from the outset, viscerally, with our understanding incomplete, pondering no more than a year's trial run. We were like most parents in the turmoil we felt far in advance of our oldest son's first step onto the school bus but unlike most in our response to it: We became existentially worried.

At first it seemed this anxiety signified that something was fundamentally wrong with us. Were we overzealous, overprotective, paranoid? It was our duty, we tried to tell ourselves, to override our parental instincts; school, after all, was ineluctable. And so my wife attempted to visit the local kindergarten (to no avail—its principal's policy forbade such visits) in order to assure herself that nothing dreadful might occur within its walls. Meanwhile I sought to convince myself that my own experience of student life as nightmarishly dreary and an incomparable waste of time was my own experience, only that, and that nothing legitimate could be deduced from it. And this was true: I could deduce nothing.

I wish I could write that my wife and I had excellent reasons for deciding to homeschool. We didn't: It was in the gut, and the gut, we knew, could be wrong either way. In May of 1986 we read books, in June we talked, July we wrung hands, August felt deep and hot and still, September came, and then one morning the big yellow bus arrived, waited a minute with its doors open, and our child did not get on it.

That fall we took to answering our inquisitors—friends, acquaintances, siblings, grandparents—with the all-purpose and ultimately evasive assertion that to hold a child out of kindergarten was not really so unusual, that many people do it.

Not schoolteachers, they replied.

But since then, each of our three sons has missed the bus, so to speak, and we find ourselves flung headlong into a life neither of us would have predicted.

AS IT TURNS OUT, IT IS A LIFE OUR FAMILY likes, and this is our chief reason for continuing to homeschool. Our days and our children's days are various. They pass with no sense that learning is separate from life, an activity that begins at a specific point in the morning and arbi-trarily ends at another in the afternoon. Instead, learning proceeds *from* our children, spurred by their interests and questions. A winter day on which snow falls is the natural starting point for discussion and reading about meteorology, weather fronts, road salts, sloped roofs, Alaska, polar bears, the invention of touring skis. A spring evening spent on a blanket in the yard as the stars begin to show themselves is a proper time for talk of constellations, for bringing out a star chart, for setting up a telescope, for questions about satellites, eclipses, comets, meteors, navigation, Columbus, the Apollo space program. When the weather is poor for roaming out of doors, our boys—five, seven, and nine—might spend hours playing Scrabble or chess, or read to one another, or draw pictures, or comb through atlases and encyclopedias because the maps and pictures interest them. At dinner, if it is impending war in the Middle East that is in the news, the atlases and encyclopedias might end up on the table, and we might be there for two hours or more, eating, asking questions, looking up precise answers, discovering how oil is formed in the ground, why people fight over it, how Islam differs from other religions, why a person has to drink more water when it's hot, and why camels have humps.

There are hours in the morning—two at most—when my wife sits down with our nine-year-old and is systematic about writing and mathematics; later, they will practice violin together. Evenings are my time for nurturing our children's interest in geography, for discussing the day's news, and for reading poems to them before they go to bed. We try to be consistent about these matters, and yet no two days are ever much alike, and the curriculum is devised by us according to our children's needs and implemented by us according to our strengths and weaknesses as parents and teachers. Thus:

AUGUST 30: Reading: *The Wooden Horse;* violin: *Witches' Dance;* writing: letter to Adam, final draft; science: gas cannon, carbon dioxide.
SEPTEMBER 26: Visit to the chicken-butchering plant and Point Defiance Zoo; violin practice; journal and writing.
OCTOBER 16: Neighborhood recycling; banking; violin practice; Chess Club; finished letter to Aunt Mary.
NOVEMBER 7: *Mouse and the Motorcycle,* Chapters 3 and 4; math drill, multiplying by 4 and 5; violin practice; cursive writing; swimming with Nathan.

What else? An ant farm, a bug jar, a pair of field glasses, a rabbit cage, old appliances to take apart. An aquarium, a terrarium, a metronome, a collection of petrified wood, another of shells, a globe, a magnifying glass, a calculator, a microscope. Felt pens, watercolors, dry cell batteries, paper-airplane kits. Swimming teachers, lithographers, bakers, canoe builders, attorneys, inventors, flutists, fishermen. And time to ponder all of them. To read the information on the backs of baseball cards, dig butter clams, dye rice paper, weave on a homemade frame loom. To plant potatoes, tell tall tales, watch birds feed. To fashion a self in silence.

And people too, many of them, a large and shifting variety. Friends from Little League and music lessons, acquaintances made on the basketball court and in art classes. The group of homeschoolers with whom our boys put on plays, beachcomb at low tide, play chess.

And salmon. Perhaps it began, one night, with merely eating one. Or with reading *Red Tag Comes Back.* Or with the man at the side of the road with the purse seine laid out in his yard. At any rate, the salmon life-cycle exhibit at the Seattle Aquarium and walking among the gill-netters at Fisherman's Terminal. And cleaning debris from a salmon stream, standing in it, one Saturday. Visiting the hatchery on the Elwha River, the fish ladders at the Rocky Reach Dam, the Pacific Science Center display on the Nootka people. Then seeing their grandfather's catch from the Hakai Peninsula, the bones and organs, the digestive tracts of fish—the blood and murder—and mulling over eating what was once living and the relative ethics of sportfishing. And then one day, abruptly—perhaps a plane has flown overhead or they have seen from the yard a crow fly—it is *flight* that interests them, the Wright Brothers, Charles Lindbergh, Amelia Earhart, draft and lift and thrust and wingspan, the Museum of Flight, the Boeing plant, pitch, yaw, and roll. . . .

Their education is various, alive, participatory, whole—and, most of all, *theirs.* Quite frankly, no school can hope to match it. It is an education tuned to their harmonies, local and intimate as opposed to generic and imposed. They have not learned to be fearful of learning, to associate it with pain and dreariness, with competition, anxiety, dread. My wife and I hope that they will continue in this, that adolescence will find them earnestly seeking, that they will see enough of schools—by visiting them—to know what they are missing. We hope that colleges, if college is what they want, will recognize their strengths without school transcripts. (Admissions boards, incidentally, increasingly recognize homeschooled children as legitimate candidates.) And that their social lives will continue to be vigorous and sane, will continue to include people of all sorts and all ages. And finally that the life we have developed as a family will sustain itself on through *their* children, that our intimacy will not end when *they* are parents.

It is not always, of course, so idyllic, so wonderful, so easy to wax romantic over. Much of the time, though, it is satisfying and full, a fruitful existence for us all. We recognize that in the long run it may have drawbacks, but in the long run no life is perfect. We can't know, finally, if this is what is best for our children and, like all parents, we are playing it by ear to some extent, hoping to guess correctly what it is we should *do*. We do know that homeschooling has given us a life we wouldn't otherwise have, and we are thankful for that.

AT THE SAME TIME, I GO ON TEACHING English in a public high school. There my students might bemoan the dreary meaninglessness of classroom life and rail against its absurdities but also profess skepticism at the very mention of homeschooling. How are your kids going to make friends? they ask. Who's going to teach them algebra? How do you expect them to get into college? When do you find time to teach them anyway? What if you weren't a teacher—could you do it? Why are you *here*, Mr. Guterson?

Excellent questions, I say, sooner or later, in the approving voice of a high school English teacher. But answering them I feel the orbit of my reasoning widen—what high school students call "digression"—because in the end you can't discuss homeschooling as if it were divorced from other raging social issues. In fact, bring it up with your students' parents and you're soon fending off a touchy debate about such sacred matters as work, children, money, leisure time, and, above all, the self. Before long you are listening to hysterical pronouncements about democracy, capitalism, enculturation, the Japanese, and nearly everything else.

Let's take, for example, the assertion that children who don't go to school won't be "socialized." Most people believe school is the primary training ground for the social life we experience when we emerge from school: In its halls and classrooms, these skeptics recollect with mixed emotions, one sorts out the broad panoply of human types and then adjusts oneself to them, finds ways to modulate one's persona in the face of the great shifting tide of humanity. In this vision of things, the homeschooled child figures as an eternal outsider who, because he or she never attended school, will remain forever uninitiated in the tricky nuances of adult society. He will miss his cues at cocktail parties, he will not understand the subtleties of behaviors that come his way at the office or on the bus.

Furthermore, say homeschooling's detractors, homeschooling is *undemocratic*. They take at face value the portrait of schools as the irreplaceable agents of enculturation and, as E. D. Hirsch would have it, of cultural literacy. Jefferson's vision, after all, was that school would be democracy's proving ground, a place where all comers would take their best shot at the American Dream and where that dream would ultimately find its most basic and most enduring sustenance. Not to show up at all—at all!—is thus to give in to the forces of cultural decline, to withdraw at the moment of national crisis, and to suggest openly that if Rome is really burning, the best response is not to douse the flames or even to fiddle away beside the baths but to go home and lock the door.

Critics of homeschooling are likely to add that for America to work we must act in concert to repair our schools; that few parents are, in fact, well qualified to teach children the broad range of things they need to know; that homeschooling allows the bigoted and narrow-minded to perpetuate their types; that despite all the drawbacks to a peer-dominated world, such a world is required if children are to grapple with relationships more egalitarian than family ones. And more: Send your child to the school of hard knocks, they say, where some bigger boy will shove him from his place in line or steal his blocks or vandalize his fingerpaintings, where he will learn forbearance and self-reliance and meet in the form of his teacher an adult who is less than perfect and less than fully attentive to his every need—where, in short, life in all of its troubling glory will present itself daily to him. A dark inversion, perversely true, of Robert Fulghum's *All I Really Need to Know I Learned in Kindergarten.*

LET ME ADDRESS THESE CRITICISMS IN ORDER. Evidence in support of homeschooling's academic virtues is both overwhelming and precisely what we would expect if we gave the matter some reflection. Public educators have complained, into a steady, implacable wind, that with much smaller classes and more one-to-one contact they might make better academic headway. Small wonder, then, that homeschoolers score consistently well above the norm on standardized achievement tests: They're learning under the ideal conditions—alone or in groups small enough to make real learning possible—that schoolteachers persistently cry out for.

Recently, a strong case has been made that achievement tests don't tell us anything that matters, because they are culturally biased and because they are *tests*—and tests are attended by various levels of anxiety and a wide range of test-taking habits. Here some facts about homeschoolers are in order: They come predominantly from the very middle-class backgrounds that standardized achievement tests reportedly favor, and their parents are, for the most part, deeply interested in their education as well as themselves better educated than the average American adult. Thus, homeschoolers' test scores might best be compared with those of schoolchildren who come from similar test-favoring backgrounds and whose parents also are well educated and involved. Furthermore, it's true that some homeschooling parents teach "to" standardized tests—some classroom teachers do also—because states require that their children take them or because college entry is largely contingent on test scores in the absence of a school grade-point average. (Harvard, for example, admits homeschooled children and takes their SAT scores very seriously.)

Researchers have probed as well the more slippery question of whether homeschooled children are properly socialized. John Wesley Taylor V, using the Piers-Harris Self-Concept Scale—a measure of the "central core of personality"—concluded that "few homeschooling children are socially deprived." Mona Maarse Delahooke placed them in the "well-adjusted" range on a personality measure known as the Roberts Apperception Test for Children; Jon Wartes, in surveys of 219 Washington State homeschoolers, found that at least half spent more than twenty hours a month in organized community activities and that more than two thirds spent twenty to thirty plus hours a month with other children of varying ages. Linda Montgomery, after studying the leadership skills of homeschooled children, concluded that "homeschooling is not generally repressive of a student's potential leadership, and may in fact nurture leadership at least as well as does the conventional system." In my experience, homeschoolers are less peer-dependent than schoolchildren and less susceptible to peer pressure. In this regard, the research merely corroborates what seems to most observers obvious.

But although homeschooling may work, it is by no means easy. Most American adults are fully competent, of course, to learn whatever they have to learn—facts, skills, methods, strategies—in order to teach their children. But should they want to do it, they should strive to be good at it, and they should face the endeavor seriously. It should bring them satisfaction; it should feel like important work. *No one* should undertake to homeschool without coming to terms with this fundamental truth: It is the fabric of your own life you are deciding about, not just your child's education.

THIS MATTER — THE FABRIC OF A HOMEschooling life—is the concern of some critics who assert that in practice homeschooling is patently sexist, that its most obvious result is the isolation of women in the home, away from the fulfillments of the workplace. (That there may be fulfillments in the home, for both sexes, as educators of children, is another issue entirely.) Yet the question of who does what in a relationship is no more or less important with regard to homeschooling than with regard to anything else: who works outside the home, who works inside, who does the dishes, changes oil in the car, shops for food, flies to Miami on a business trip. The question of *who does what* remains: who takes responsibility for the child's introduction to long division, drives her to swimming lessons, teaches him to throw a baseball, shows her how to use a calculator. Homeschooling is, in fact, no more inherently sexist than anything else in a marriage (and is less so than schools), and if in many homeschooling families the mother is the prime mover and first cause of education and the father an addendum and auxiliary, this is a reflection on the culture at large and not on the phenomenon of homeschooling.

There are others who assert that although homeschooling might serve well for the American middle class, other groups—the poor, the disenfranchised, the immigrant—need schools to flourish. After all, the public schools have historically been a crucial conduit of upward mobility, they say, and point out the Vietnamese immigrants of the last twenty years, whose kids get full scholarships from places like the University of Texas and Columbia. Yet the mobility they describe is next to nonexistent; a permanent underclass is the reality in this country, and schools do as much as any other institution to reinforce this state of affairs. By systematizing unfairness, inequality, and privilege, schools prepare the children of the underclass to accept as inevitable the coming drudgery of their adult lives. At my school, for example, "basic" students are more likely to serve meals in Foods I while "honors" students join an organization called Future Business Leaders of America and enroll in courses like Leadership and Humanities. In both its social and academic structure, my school best instructs the disenfranchised in the cruel truth that disenfranchisement is permanent.

To say that homeschoolers, for the sake of American democracy, *must* be institutionalized is an undemocratic proposition. Both the courts and state governments recognize this, for homeschooling is legal in one form or another everywhere in the United States. The Supreme Court thus far has not ruled in any explicit way on homeschooling. The closest it came, in 1972, was to declare that Wisconsin's compulsory-education law could not, in fact, compel three Amish families to send their children to high school. Yet legal tension about homeschooling persists—mostly as First, Ninth, and Fourteenth Amendment issues: freedom of religion and the right to privacy—for the states have an interest in seeing children educated and are, rightly, concerned that in at least some cases "homeschool" ends up meaning no school. (When homeschooling parents in question are deemed incompetent, the courts have consistently—and properly—ruled against them.) Moreover, and more importantly, does anyone really believe that schools make students better democrats? Do they serve the individual and democratic society? I give them an A only for prompting peer-group relations of a sort conducive to the workings of our *economy:* Schools are in their social fabric nasty, competitive, mean-spirited, and status-conscious in the manner of the adult institutions they mimic.

Could there be something in the very nature of the school as an institution that prevents it from fully realizing its mandate to inform, educate, and develop both the individual and his or her society? Or, to put it another way, could there be something in its *manner* of being that prevents it from realizing its *reason* for being? At the high school where I teach, as at most, students come and go

in sets of thirty or so at approximately one-hour intervals, an arrangement convenient to the daunting task of administering a crowd of more than 800 young people but not necessarily conducive to their education or in the best interests of society. The arrangement is instead both relatively expedient and indicative of the schools' custodial function—in essence, their primary one, since we have structured schools in such a manner as to allow this function to precede all others. Schools *keep* students first, and any education that happens along the way is incidental and achieved against the odds. It may be, finally, that schools temporarily *prevent* us from getting the education we persist in getting outside and beyond schools, where the conditions of life provide more natural motivations and learning is less abstract. *Never let your schooling get in the way of your education,* advised Mark Twain, who never attended school.

THE SCHOOL I TEACH IN IS FORTUNATE TO employ some excellent teachers, honorable and earnest men and women who are quietly heroic for the sake of their students and whose presence does much to salvage some good from an otherwise untenable institution. They bring humanity to an inhumane setting and pit it against the *design* of schools, which were envisioned as factories dedicated to the efficient production of predictable, formulaic human beings.

But I find myself, like many teachers, beating my head against the classroom wall on a daily, even hourly, basis. My students are compelled to herd themselves from room to room, to sit in daily confinement with other people of precisely their age and approximately their social class, to hear me out on "Sailing to

Byzantium" whether or not they are ready. They are scrutinized, sorted, graded, disciplined, and their waking hours are consumed by this prison life: thirty hours a week, thirty-six weeks a year, seven to ten hours a week of "homework" twelve years running—the heart of their young lives consumed by it. What can we expect of them as adults, other than that they become, as New York City Teacher of the Year John Taylor Gatto says, "dependent human beings, unable to initiate lines of meaning to give substance and pleasure to their existence"? Penned up and locked away, shaped by television and school instead of by their community, they must struggle as adults for a satisfying life they can neither grasp nor envision.

CONFINING CHILDREN TO SCHOOL IS EMblematic of the industrialized twentieth century, but it is also convenient for our current generation of young parents, which might best be characterized in general terms as terrifyingly selfish, persistently immature, and unable to efface its collective ego for the sake of the generation that will follow it and is *already* following it. While these people go about the business of saving the world—or of extracting everything they can from it— their children (they can hardly believe they have children, can hardly grasp the privilege of nurturing them when they are so thoroughly occupied by their attentions to themselves) need *someplace* to go. The truth is that for too many contemporary parents the school system is little more than convenient day care— day care they can feel good about as long as they don't reflect on it too deeply.

Many parents I know put more hours into their golf games or their wardrobes or into accumulating enough capital for the purchase of unnecessary luxuries than into their child's education. Because they are still children themselves, it simply doesn't occur to them to take an active role in their child's learning—in part because they expect the schools to do it all, in part because there isn't room in their souls for anybody to loom as large as themselves. For many the solution is simply to buy an education as one buys a BMW—your child's school as yet another commodity to show off. So when I talk about homeschooling I am talking about choosing less affluence in the name of more education. I am talking about giving matters intense and vital thought before one ships one's child off to school.

And while it's easy—and understandable—for parents to protest that one hasn't the time or energy for homeschooling, there is much, short of pulling children out of school, that parents can undertake today. Homeschooling is only the extreme form of a life in which all of us can and should take part. The notion of parents as educators of their children is, in the broad sense, neither extreme nor outlandish, and we should consider how instinctively parents engage in the instruction of their children—at the dinner table, for example—and how vital a role an expanded homeschooling movement might play in repairing families. We should think clearly about the problems of schools, ask ourselves why every attempt to correct them seems doomed to fail, replace in our hearts the bankrupt notion of "quality time" with a reassessment of our role as parents. We should recognize that schools will never solve the bedrock problems of education because the problems are problems of *families*, of cultural pressures that the schools reflect and thus cannot really remedy.

Today it is considered natural for parents to leave their children's education entirely in the hands of institutions. In a better world we would see *ourselves* as responsible and our schools primarily as resources. Schools would cease to be *places* in the sense that prisons and hospitals are places; instead, education would be embedded in the life of the community, part of the mechanics of our democracy, and all would feel a devotion to its processes. Parents would measure their inclinations and abilities and immerse themselves, to varying degrees and in varying ways, in a larger educational system designed to *assist* them. Schools—educational resource centers—would provide materials, technology, and expertise instead of classrooms, babysitters, and bureaucrats.

Admittedly, I am a professional educator, part of this vast bureaucracy. Yet I see no contradiction in what I am doing: coming each day to where young people are, attempting within the constraints of the institution to see to their education. Each year I come to admire many of my students, to like them so well that I am sad to see them go; each year there are moments in which I am gratified, even moved, by a sentence a student has written in an essay, by a question somebody asks. Yet for all this, for all the quiet joys of the classroom, I am forever aware of some amorphous dissatisfaction, some inkling that things might be better. It seems to me that many of my students should simply be elsewhere, that they would be better served by a different sort of education, that their society would be better served by it, too. I believe this education is one their parents can best provide and that they should expect schools to assist them. These parents love their children with a depth that,

finally, I can't match—and finally, teaching is an act of love before it is anything else.

NO

William Konnert and
Josef Wendel

LEGAL AND POLICY BARRIERS ABOUND

Dissatisfied with public and private schools alike, an increasing number of parents in the U.S. are opting to educate their children at home. It's difficult to get a firm fix on just how many children are involved in this phenomenon: The U.S. Department of Education estimates that between 120,000 and 260,000 children are educated at home, but other estimates run as high as a million.

Whatever the number, your school system sooner or later runs a good chance of being faced with a request for home schooling. A variety of reasons might prompt parents to take this step: Objecting to the standard curriculum on religious grounds probably is the most common reason, but some families opt for home schooling because they refuse to subject their children to forced busing for purposes of achieving racial integration within the school system, because they believe the schools' academic standards are too low, or because they're worried about drugs, alcohol, vandalism, and student safety. Home schoolers don't necessarily agree on appropriate education objectives for their children, but they all want greater control over their children's education than they would have in public schools.

What they—and many members of the public—often fail to realize is that education is a state responsibility. Even in the landmark 1972 decision in *Wisconsin v. Yoder*, which established a precedent for religious exemptions from compulsory education laws, the U.S. Supreme Court took care to emphasize the state's right to "impose reasonable regulations for the control and duration of basic education." Indeed, courts consistently have supported the state's authority to legislate and enforce education standards.

State statutes on compulsory education generally form the framework, provide guidelines, and contain some reference to the type of schooling or education program that will satisfy the intent of the law. Compulsory education laws differ from state to state, however, and in some states, they have been the target of lawsuits brought by advocates of home schooling. . . . This rise in litigation has focused renewed attention on home schooling.

A FEW KEY ISSUES

Don't wait for dissatisfied parents to take their children out of your schools to find out about home schooling. Arm yourself in advance with an understanding of the key issues involved:

1. *Do your state statutes permit home schooling as an educational alternative?* If so, what requirements and conditions do laws place on home schooling? Courts have ruled that parental rights must be measured against the state's vested interest in the child's education. To date, no higher court has limited the state's power to insist that any form of alternative education—including home schooling—be approved by an official state agency, such as a local school board.

2. *Is home schooling adequate?* Home schoolers argue that a school is simply a place where instruction is imparted and that neither the number of children being taught nor the location of the facility has a bearing on whether it is in fact a school. Advocates of public or other formal schooling, on the other hand, claim that no home or parent can hope to match the kinds of educational resources or experiences available in a formal school. They argue that the process of education is too complex to be carried on at home by parents who lack specialized preparation and equipment.

3. *How does the state regulate instruction?* In states where home schooling is permitted, the state's authority to regulate that instruction sometimes is a point of contention. There is no question that the state legitimately may exercise reasonable control over education; the question is what is reasonable. For example,

some home schoolers have challenged state requirements for home visits by school administrators or for standardized tests for children taught at home.

4. *Is the state in violation of First Amendment religious freedom guarantees if it authorizes only formal schooling, be it public or private?* Many home schoolers have argued that any insistence on state standards for schooling is an invasion of religious freedom. The courts have ruled, however, that the parents' freedom to act on their beliefs is not immune from state-imposed regulations. Freedom of religion is not threatened by the state's insistence on appropriate academic standards.

LEGAL GUIDELINES

States and local school boards vary greatly in their reactions to the home schooling movement. But despite these variations, any approach to home schooling must come within some well-established constitutional and judicial guidelines.

First, where and to what degree a child is educated is based on a delicate balance between parental and state interests. Second, the state retains the power to impose minimum uniform curriculum requirements regardless of whether a child attends a public or private school or is educated at home. Third, the state has the power to require that all children attend school of some kind and that all children have access to a good education. In 1923, the Supreme Court ruled in *Meyer v. State of Nebraska* that "the education of youth is a matter of such vital importance to the democratic state and to the public weal that the state may do much, may go very far indeed, by way of limiting the control of the parent over the education of the child."

Just how far the state may go has been the subject of much litigation, and the courts consistently have upheld specific, educationally sound state statutes regulating various aspects of alternative schooling. The courts have upheld state regulations in the following areas: hours of actual instruction (this does not mean working on the family farm or traveling around the world), regularity of instruction, comparability of instruction at home with what is offered in public schools, use of curriculum materials, maintenance of educational and health records, teacher competence, and measures of academic achievement.

In states whose statutes specifically permit home schooling, parents who want to teach their children at home are entitled to procedural due process. That means parents who request home schooling have the right to prior notice of the form and substance of their hearing before school officials. They also have the right to examine witnesses, the right to be represented by counsel, the right to be heard by an impartial body, and the right to obtain a transcript of the hearing. School officials are obliged to comply with applicable open-meeting laws; moreover, if the request is denied, school officials must give the parents, in writing, specific reasons for the decision.

WHAT YOU CAN DO

Most home schooling advocates are sincere and emotional in their beliefs, and it is prudent to address home schooling issues before the heat of battle. As you and your board attorney develop or revise home schooling policies that reflect the board's philosophy, address the key issues, and comply with constitutional and judicial guidelines as well as the laws of your state, you might find the following advice and information helpful:

• It's a good idea to require parents to submit requests for home schooling in writing. It's also a good idea to ask parents to include their reasons for the request as well as the course of home study they propose. Religious dogma is not the only acceptable reason for home schooling, but whatever the reason, the proposed course of study should be reviewed by someone in your school system. Keep the reviewer's name and the results of the review on file. And, if it's permitted in your state, grant home schooling approval for only one year at a time.

• According to the laws of some states, the superintendent or school board must ensure that home instruction is provided by a person who is "qualified" to teach. But that doesn't mean you have to look for home teachers who meet the same certification requirements public school teachers must meet. The courts have held that a baccalaureate degree from an accredited institution is sufficient for home instructors other than parents. For parents, a high school diploma usually is considered sufficient.

• In many states that permit home schooling, the home curriculum must conform to minimum standards prescribed by the state board of education. Your school system might pride itself on academic requirements that are considerably above state-mandated minimums, but you cannot use your higher expectations as a standard by which to deny a home schooling request. Home schoolers often contract with an outside firm (often one with a religious orientation) to provide curriculum materials and tests. If the curriculum materials meet minimum state standards, they usually are acceptable for home schooling. When home instruction is carried out via a correspondence course, the educational objectives of the course should be clearly defined, simply stated, and appropriate to study by mail. The courses offered at home should be sufficiently comprehensive, accurate, and up to date.

• The home where the instruction takes place should meet fire, safety, health, and sanitation codes, and equipment and facilities should be suitable and appropriate for implementing the curriculum.

• Local school officials should identify precisely what educational and health records must be maintained for children educated at home. These records should be subject to inspection by a representative of your school board at any time during the home schools' scheduled hours of operation.

• Finally, testing can be a thorny issue in home schooling—especially in states that have adopted academic competency tests for students. There is no question that your board can require testing to monitor the progress of the child who is taught at home. The tests you require should be comparable to those required in your schools. Frequently, school boards accept the tests supplied by the firms that supply instructional materials for home schooling.

As a school board member, you have some obligations to all of the children who live in your district—not only to those who attend the public schools. As this brief overview suggests, thoughtful and informed deliberations on the issues involved in home schooling will serve you—and all the children in your school district—well.

POSTSCRIPT

Is Home Schooling a Viable Alternative?

A recent Gallup poll shows that the majority of respondents is opposed to home schooling. Yet many of the reasons that home-schooling parents give are shared by many others who are unable to join the movement. A new wave of court actions related to home schooling is anticipated in the 1990s, which will call into question the legality of strict state or district regulations imposed on home schoolers (the state of Missouri, for example, stipulates 1,000 hours of instruction per year, 600 of which must be devoted to reading, language arts, mathematics, social studies, and science, and 400 of which must be accommodated at the home-school site).

Some questions that must be considered as the controversy over home schooling gets ironed out in the coming years are these: Do home-schooling parents exert too much mind control over their children? Is the "peer independence" of home-schooled children a gain or a loss for them? What effects do the lack of facilities and extracurricular activities have? Should home-schooling parents receive financial aid or tax benefits?

These and other questions are addressed in a wide variety of books and articles on the subject. Two classic works are *School Can Wait* (1979), by Raymond and Dorothy Moore, and *Teach Your Own* (1981), by John Holt. Holt's newsletter *Growing Without Schooling* is also an interesting source.

Among recent articles, these are recommended: "The New Pioneers of the Home-Schooling Movement," by Diane Divoky, *Phi Delta Kappan* (February 1983); "Compulsory Education and Home Schooling: Truancy or Prophecy?" by Mary Anne Pitman, *Education and Urban Society* (May 1987); "Home Schooling and Compulsory School Attendance," by Josef Wendel et al.,

School Law Bulletin (Summer 1986); and "Home Schooling Litigation Tests State Compulsory Education Laws," by Sally Banks Zakariya, *The American School Board Journal* (May 1988).

Collections of articles addressing the topic are presented in the Winter 1988 issue of *Religion and Public Education,* the November 1988 issue of *Education and Urban Society,* and the February 1989 issue of *Educational Review.* The January 1988 issue of *Education and Urban Society* also offers two excellent overviews: "The Context of Home Schooling in the United States," by J. Gary Knowles, and "Home Schools: A Synthesis of Research on Characteristics and Learner Outcomes," by B. D. Ray.

ISSUE 11

Can Schools Prevent Urban Dropouts?

YES: Larry Cuban, from "At-Risk Students: What Teachers and Principals Can Do," *Educational Leadership* (February 1989)

NO: Paul Woodring, from "A New Approach to the Dropout Problem," *Phi Delta Kappan* (February 1989)

ISSUE SUMMARY

YES: Professor of education and former school superintendent Larry Cuban offers some basic assumptions and specific guidelines for dealing with the urban dropout problem.
NO: Paul Woodring, an emeritus professor of educational psychology, attacks the conventional wisdom and turns his attention outside the schools.

The present nationwide dropout rate in American schools is somewhere in the vicinity of 25 percent by most calculations. In large urban districts and among certain minority groups the figures are closer to 50 percent. President Bush has declared a goal of a 90 percent high school completion rate by the year 2000. There are those who agree with the president that a dramatic turnaround is possible; but even among those who support the president's goal, there is a great deal of disagreement regarding the best way to accomplish such a goal. There are also those who believe that not only is the goal unrealistic but that the completion of the type of schooling that now prevails is not a desirable aim for many young people. Rutgers University professor Jackson Toby, for one, contends that "stay-ins" damage the quest for excellence in public education and often pose a threat to students who really want to learn. "Isn't it better for everybody," he states, "if some students drop out?"

The reasons why students drop out are many: personal or family problems, excessive absence or truancy, lack of interest or motivation, desire for or need of a job, failing grades, difficulty communicating with school professionals, and low levels of identification with school goals and activities. To deal with the situation, school systems have developed early detection programs and prevention and recovery programs. The former place an emphasis on working with the family to provide support and encouragement, building self-esteem through positive social interaction with peers and teachers, and providing alternative courses that may trigger a more enthusiastic response. The latter focus on better health and counseling centers, better teacher training, a more personalized school atmosphere, and full-time evening schools.

Approximately 80 percent of the nation's larger school districts provide opportunities to attend alternative schools for those students who are not responding well to the standard offerings. Harlem Prep in New York City, which originated in 1967; Philadelphia's Parkway Program, begun in 1968; and numerous "school-without-walls" programs have established long records of success. More recently, magnet schools, challenge programs, and special schools for those who have already dropped out have been initiated.

More research has been done on the dropout phenomenon in the last couple of years than in the previous 20, according to Robert DeBlois in "Keep At-Risk Students in School: Toward a Curriculum for Potential Dropouts," *NASSP Bulletin* (April 1989). Drawing on the ideas of philosopher John Dewey and the practices of dropout prevention approaches that are currently successful, DeBlois lists these essential components of good alternative schools: a meaningful vocational orientation, a focus on interdisciplinary team projects, and an emphasis on mastery learning in a continuous process curriculum that is individualized and flexible. While these components are directed at potential dropouts, a case could be made for their applicability to programs for all students.

In the articles that follow, Larry Cuban contends that, even though much of the educational reform movement of the 1980s missed urban schools, there is still hope for improvement of their programs and a reduction in dropout rates. The key to this is the creation of a true sense of attachment between students and the schools. Paul Woodring does not share this optimism and, in fact, contends that prolonging the schooling of some children has already contributed greatly to disorder in the schools and has made the high school diploma almost meaningless.

YES

Larry Cuban

AT-RISK STUDENTS: WHAT TEACHERS
AND PRINCIPALS CAN DO

You want to know what is happening in big city classrooms? Ask a teacher, talk to an assistant principal, visit a school and listen to students. Whatever you do, don't be fooled by the buzzwords from today's policymakers: *school-site management, high academic standards, core curriculum, restructured schools, teacher-run schools,* and the like. The buzzwords give a skewed picture of what occurs daily in classrooms; real school improvement has yet to penetrate most urban schools.

The truth is that recent state reforms have largely bypassed millions of students in urban schools across the nation (Carnegie Foundation for the Advancement of Teaching 1988, Committee for Economic Development 1987, and Ford Foundation, 1987). I said "largely." There are, of course, numerous efforts under way. The above reports note instances of gifted teachers' and principals' producing results that are outstanding in any situation but mind-boggling in the face of daily conditions in at-risk schools (Corcoran, Walker, and White, 1988). Turnaround schools, where staffs have converted educational disasters into schools where parents clamor for entry, do exist. Teachers like Garfield High's Jaime Escalante and Rabun Gap's Eliot Wigginton inspire and educate their students year after year. Administrators like Harlem's Deborah Meier and Los Angeles' George McKenna help teachers put forth their best again and again. Such successes are reported, then amplified like an echo in a cavern. But in numbers, they are a faint sound in the Grand Canyon of hundreds of thousands of classrooms and millions of students' lives.

I say this not to disparage these successes or the intentions of the reformers; I say this only to point out that recent reforms aimed at school and classroom improvement sailed over urban schools. Furthermore, I distinguish between slogans and the gritty realities facing teachers daily. Policymakers and headline writers frequently assume that changes in school governance, district boundaries, curriculum, or decision-making authority

From Larry Cuban, "At-Risk Students: What Teachers and Principals Can Do," *Educational Leadership*, vol. 46, no. 5 (February 1989), pp. 29–32. Copyright © 1989 by the Association for Supervision and Curriculum Development. Reprinted by permission. All rights reserved.

automatically lead to classroom changes in urban schools. Not so. The historical record unforgivingly documents such flawed assumptions in the stale buzz-words of earlier decades: *decentralization, teacher-proof curriculum, merit pay, individualized instruction*, and so on. We must tell policymakers that we know they cannot mandate or direct what matters in schools and classrooms.

After spending a quarter-century in classrooms and schools, I have reached a few conclusions, my operating assumptions.

- The future of urban schools is the primary issue facing the nation's educational system. If the system is left as it is, the social and individual costs of inadequate schooling will severely corrode the social fabric of the nation.
- The students in these schools, like students everywhere, bring strengths to their classrooms and dream dreams of academic success.
- There are teachers and principals who not only want to improve what occurs in their schools but have done so in the face of massive obstacles.
- As grim as some of the working conditions are, as complicated and tough as the children's lives are, there is a slim but significant margin of constructive change available to teachers and principals who are determined to stretch the minds and fashion the character of low-income, ethnic, and language-minority children.

To practitioners who share these assumptions, I ask two questions: (1) Is there sufficient knowledge available to make fundamental changes in a classroom and school? (2) What can principals and teachers do that will improve what children experience in urban schools?

IS SUFFICIENT KNOWLEDGE AVAILABLE?

Yes, it is. Drawing on practitioner wisdom accumulated through experience and on research findings, we have sufficient knowledge to make changes in schools and classrooms. Some of our practitioner wisdom is captured in the work of gifted principals and teachers who simply know what has to be done and do it. Some of our knowledge appears in syntheses of research such as the U.S. Department of Education's booklet *Schools That Work: Educating Disadvantaged Children.*

We know about the necessary conditions that have to be in place for improvement to occur. We know about the importance of a school culture where both children and adults share common values about respect, intellectual achievement, and caring for one another. We know that key decisions in curriculum, instruction, and school organization need to occur at the school site with the substantial participation of the entire staff.

But no pat formulas to grow effective schools yet exist. Knowing how to put together the right combination of people, things, and ideas to create a productive setting that supports at-risk students and the adults that work with them remains just out of our reach so far. It is the difference between having all the parts of a car lying around and knowing exactly how to put them together to make the car run. We know the necessary parts of an effective school, but we lack the know-how to put them together in just the right order. Still, knowing what the right pieces are is a solid advance (Purkey and Smith 1983).

HOW, THEN, CAN PRINCIPALS AND TEACHERS IMPROVE URBAN SCHOOLS?

By *improve*, I mean *create* schools and classrooms that build attachment in students toward completing school, increase the students' desire to learn, build self-esteem, and enhance academic performance. Let me take up the features of programs that have appeared in the literature and that coincide with practitioner wisdom about what works with at-risk students in urban schools (Comer 1980, Leinhardt and Bickel 1987).

1. *Size.* Successful schools and programs enroll as few as 50 students but seldom more than a few hundred. This smallness helps to foster enduring relationships among adults and students; in these programs, everyone knows everyone else, at least to some extent. Also, the potential for students to participate in activities is greater in small programs. Further, a class size of 15–20 students per teacher permits a level of personalizing instruction unavailable in more crowded settings. In secondary schools these programs can be housed as schools-within-a-school or separated from the main building. For example, Bret Harte Intermediate School in Los Angeles, Orr High School in Chicago, and Theodore Roosevelt High School in the Bronx adopted "houses" and similar arrangements to combat largeness and anonymity (Carnegie 1988).

2. *Staff.* Teachers often *choose* to work in these programs and classes, thus making a commitment to at-risk students in their decisions to volunteer. When this kind of commitment is wedded to personal and cultural knowledge about these pupils and a willingness to experiment with methods and techniques, these like-minded teachers develop into a spirited professional cadre who enjoy working together. Principals of these programs endorse classroom changes and provide tangible and emotional support. Further, district officials, the superintendent, and the school board actively nourish such endeavors and provide resources to help the program accomplish its purposes. Chambers Academy, a small public school in New York City, has 11 teachers who spend at least three hours a week with small groups of students in advisory sessions in addition to teaching two or more courses to the very same students (Carnegie 1988).

3. *Flexibility.* Because the program is small and the purpose is to rescue kids from what appears to be a grim future, teachers and principals usually employ varied nontraditional approaches. There is seldom any ability grouping. Few, if any, distinctions are made between students other than, perhaps, age. Tests are used to figure out what kind of match is needed between the student and the difficulty level of materials and between the student and teacher methods. In effect, these successful programs reflect the concept of continuous progress or nongradedness. Passing and failing are not public displays where some students move ahead and others stay behind; mastery and achievement become personal benchmarks along a trail toward larger goals.

Time is restructured into schedules quite different from regular school: secondary teachers frequently spend unusual amounts of time each day with students; team teaching is common for larger chunks of the school day. One teacher may work with a group of students not for a semester or even a year, but for two or even three years; the same high school teacher may teach three subjects. In-school learning is frequently mixed with out-of-school work or other tasks. Finally, these programs often coordinate an array of social services that the students need. The teacher, adviser, or special staff make linkages with social services, and the pressing needs of each student are dealt with by people who know the child (Lotto 1982, Wehlage 1983).

4. *School As Community*. These programs avoid the conventional model of school, where the teachers' primary concern is academic achievement, where students remain anonymous or emotionally distant from the teacher, and where rewards and penalties dominate the relationship between teacher and students. Rather, these small, flexible programs have in common a model of a community, an extended family where achievement is important and so is caring for one another. Building a sense of belonging to a group—in effect, a supportive environment—is consciously sought as a means of increasing self-esteem and achievement. Of course, the community model exists in regular schools, especially in small elementary schools or on high school athletic teams, clubs, bands, and drill teams; programs for at-risk students work hard to cultivate this community spirit and group cohesion so crucial to their success (Comer 1980).

OPTIONS FOR INSTRUCTION

When we move from matters of organization and climate to instruction, there are at least three directions teachers can consider. First, the literature on teacher effectiveness links certain teaching practices to test score gains. The pedagogy called *direct instruction* or *active teaching*, for example, claims that if teachers of at-risk students use these practices in teaching reading and math at certain elementary grades, achievement test scores will increase. This model of teaching has frequently been folded into efforts aimed at building effective schools (Brophy and Good 1986).

Direct instruction has a fairly large body of research evidence to support its use of very specific teaching tactics for certain skills in elementary classrooms; it seems to fit at-risk students, and it particularly fits the inclinations of teachers familiar with the characteristics of such children.

However, critics of direct instruction have pointed out its deficits in content, its emphasis on routine work that proves tedious, its emphasis on test scores as the only measure of learning, its low expectations for teaching reasoning and critical thinking at the elementary level, and its inapplicability to secondary school subjects. Yet this approach, harnessed to the folk wisdom of veteran teachers, suggests that familiar techniques of managing a class, introducing and explaining material, will have some payoff in higher test scores—if that is the goal.

Second, there are instructional approaches that build on the strengths that children bring to school, instructional strategies that make linkages with life experiences of students and exploit a growing knowledge about active learning and the importance of student involvement in developing higher-order thinking skills. Such ways of teaching at-risk children (for example, whole language programs) further develop children's store of language, connect abstract ideas with children's background, and move back and forth between student experiences and school concepts (Au 1980, Heath 1983, Banks 1987).

Third, there is a growing body of evidence that mixed ability and multi-age groupings within and across classrooms have positive effects on student motivation and learning. Cooperative learning approaches that target culturally different children have demonstrated an array of positive outcomes including test score gains. By contrast, pullout programs or within-class grouping by ethnicity or aptitude often have unintended negative effects on students' learning (Leinhardt and Bickel 1987, Slavin 1983, Cohen 1986, Kennedy et al. 1986).

What these three alternatives mean for classroom teachers is that they can choose among them or blend them into their own individual repertoires. Teachers making these choices also need to know the cultural backgrounds of their students, show skill in connecting subject matter to student experiences, and construct classroom activities in which students participate actively in acquiring what is to be learned.

KEEN SATISFACTIONS

Are the resulting schools or programs very different from the familiar ones where silence, mixed with reprimands, worksheets and order, dominates the school day? Indeed, they are. Does this mean more work for principals and teachers? Indeed, it does. Will this produce keen satisfactions from seeing growth in students? Indeed, it will. The rewards are intensely personal and sharply felt; they last a lifetime.

There is, then, a window of opportunity open to teachers and principals who can still gather their courage, wits, and energy to improve the lives of at-risk children. But the work must be accomplished by teachers and administrators.

We cannot look to policies, regulations, and slogans to do the job.

REFERENCES

Au, K. (1980). "Participation Structures in a Reading Lesson with Hawaiian Children: Analysis of a Culturally Appropriate Instructional Event." *Anthropology and Education Quarterly* 11: 91–115.

Banks, J. (1987). "Ethnicity, Class, and Cognitive Styles: Research and Teaching Implications." Paper presented at American Educational Research Association, Washington, D.C.

Brophy, J., and T. Good. (1986). "Teacher Behavior and Student Achievement." In *Handbook of Research on Teaching,* edited by Merlin Wittrock. New York: Macmillan.

Carnegie Foundation for the Advancement of Teaching. (1988). *The Imperiled Generation.* New York: Carnegie Foundation for the Advancement of Teaching.

Cohen, E. (1986). *Designing Groupwork.* New York: Teachers College Press.

Comer, J. (1980). *School Power.* New York: Free Press.

Committee For Economic Development. (1987). *Children in Need: Investment Strategies for the Educationally Disadvantaged.* New York: Committee for Economic Development.

Corcoran, T., L. Walker, and L. White. (1988). *Working in Urban Schools.* Washington, D.C.: Institute for Educational Leadership.

Ford Foundation. (1987). *The Forgotten Half: Non-College Youth in America.* New York: Ford Foundation.

Heath, S. B. (1983). *Ways With Words.* New York: Cambridge University Press.

Kennedy, M., R. Jung, and M. Orland. (1986). *Poverty, Achievement and the Distribution of Compensatory Education Services.* Washington, D.C.: U.S. Department of Education.

Leinhardt, G., and W. Bickel. (1987). "Instruction's the Thing Wherein to Catch the Mind That Falls Behind." *Educational Psychologist* 22: 177–207.

Lotto, L. S. (1982). "The Holding Power of Vocational Curricula: Characteristics of Effective Dropout Prevention Programs." *Journal of Vocational Education Research* 7, 4: 39–49.

Purkey, S., and M. S. Smith. (1983). "Effective Schools: A Review." *Elementary School Journal* 40: 427–452.

Slavin, R. (1983). *Cooperative Learning.* New York: Longman.

Wehlage, G. (1983). *Effective Programs for the Marginal High School Student.* Bloomington, Ind.: Phi Delta Kappa Educational Foundation.

NO

Paul Woodring

A NEW APPROACH TO THE DROPOUT PROBLEM

The nationwide drive to keep all adolescents in high school until they graduate—to "cut the dropout rate to zero by the year 2000"—undoubtedly has the support of millions of Americans who have not thought deeply about the consequences. Unfortunately, the results of such an effort are certain to be disappointing, even in the unlikely event that the goal is achieved.

In 1951 Robert Ulich of the Harvard Graduate School of Education warned us that "prolongation of school age is not in itself a blessing, but may even be a curse to civilization, unless there goes together with the prolongation a revolutionary rethinking and restructuring of the total program from the secondary school upward" [Robert Ulich, *Crisis and Hope in American Education* (Boston: Beacon Press, 1951), p. 28]. This warning has not been heeded. No such rethinking or restructuring has occurred. Instead, we have persisted in thinking that just keeping all boys and girls in school longer will solve the problems of illiteracy, crime, and unemployment. In reality, while it has solved none of these problems, the prolongation of schooling has already contributed greatly to disorder in the schools and has made the high school diploma almost meaningless.

More years in school will not cure illiteracy. Anyone who has survived 10 years of schooling without learning to read is not likely to become literate as a result of sitting in classes for two more years. If high school teachers are required to spend their time trying to teach adolescents to read, they will have no time for the more advanced education that the rest of their students need, want, and are ready for. The achievement of literacy is the task of the elementary school or of a remedial program for adults.

Keeping juvenile delinquents in school does not prevent crime. It brings crime into the schools. The cliché "school keeps them off the streets" is nonsense. At best, school keeps adolescents off the streets for only five or six hours a day for half the days of the year. This leaves ample time for those who are so disposed to engage in gang warfare and other illegal and antisocial activities. It seems safe to say that potential dropouts do not spend much time on homework.

While it is true that dropouts have trouble finding jobs, there is no persuasive evidence that the same individuals would be any more employable after more years in school. In the past, vocational education programs kept many students in school while preparing them for employment. But such programs do not solve the problems of today's urban dropouts. Courses that prepare students for the skilled trades, for secretarial work, or for scientific agriculture require intelligence and high levels of motivation; they are not designed for slow or reluctant learners.

Moreover, the conviction that high school diplomas are essential for everyone is of recent origin. Edison, Carnegie, Rockefeller, and Ford became high achievers in an industrial society without high school diplomas. Throughout the 19th century, many senators, governors, merchants, and even Presidents of the United States had only a few years of schooling. The fact that Abraham Lincoln was able to compose the Gettysburg Address without the aid of speechwriters is evidence that it is possible to become highly literate without much formal education.

In most parts of the U.S., free public high schools did not come into existence until the last quarter of the 19th century. In 1900 only 6% of the appropriate age group graduated from high school. Somewhere along the way, the other 94% dropped out. In the 1920s only half of our young people even entered high school, and half of those who did enter did not stay for four years. In other words, 75% were dropouts. In 1950, 41% dropped out.

Estimates of the percentage of young people who drop out today range from 14% to 27%, depending on whose figures you choose to accept. (William James once observed that the chief use of statistics is to refute the figures of other statisticians.) The 14% figure comes from the U.S. Census Bureau, which counts as a dropout anyone past the age of 18 who has not graduated from high school and who is no longer enrolled. This is probably the best national figure we can obtain because different school districts count dropouts in different ways, while some do not count them at all.

In any case, it seems clear that the present percentage of dropouts is the lowest in history. The much higher figures often bruited about in the media are for selected cities, not for the entire nation. It is notable that the highest rates are now in the major metropolitan areas, whereas, a generation or two ago, they were in the rural areas. This may explain why dropouts are getting more attention today: most editors and writers live in cities.

THE EFFORT TO KEEP ALL ADOLESCENTS IN high school until they graduate is now on a collision course with the equally insistent demand for higher standards for promotion and graduation. Some of today's school reformers see no conflict. They persist in believing that all adolescents could master the traditional academic disciplines if only they were sufficiently "challenged." They demand a single high school curriculum for all that would include foreign languages, mathematics through calculus, three years of science, three years of social studies, and four years of literature that would include translations of the greatest literature of the western world.

Such a curriculum would be splendid for the academically talented, but it shows no evidence of the kind of rethinking and restructuring advocated by Ulich. The only teachers who think this curriculum could be made effective for all students are those who teach in highly selective private schools that avoid the problem of educating slow learners by not admitting them in the first place. Public school teachers, who face the full range of intellectual capacity in their classrooms, laugh at the idea of teaching Dostoevski and differential calculus to *all* their students. They doubt the wisdom of teaching foreign languages to students who are still having trouble with English. They know that requiring such a program of everyone would cause the number of dropouts to rise.

While some students drop out because they are unable to comprehend what is being taught, many leave for other reasons. Those who are emotionally disturbed might be helped by the services of a good school psychologist, but the prospects are less bright for those who have become addicted to drugs at an early age. Some students drop out in the hope of finding jobs to support their families, only to discover that no jobs are available. Nearly a million teenage girls become pregnant each year, and half of them never finish high school.

But this still leaves a substantial number who, when asked their reasons for leaving, are prone to say that they are bored and that they "can't stand being cooped up in a classroom all day." Such adolescent restlessness is not at all unusual, even among those of good intelligence. In an earlier era, these young people could have gone West, though many were content to return to the farm where they could take pride in doing the work of adults. Because such opportunities are no longer available, today's dropouts pose a growing social problem.

If all reluctant learners were *required* to remain in school—and if we could recruit enough truant officers to enforce the requirement—the schools would become custodial rather than educational institutions. Indeed, some high schools in our major cities have already moved a long way in that direction, as is indicated by falling standards, growing disorder, and despair among teachers. Because the schools cannot solve this problem without endangering the education of those students who are ready and eager to learn, we must look beyond the schools for a solution.

WHAT URBAN DROPOUTS MOST NEED IS A complete change of environment. They need an environment that takes them out of the city slums with their pervasive crime and readily available drugs. One possible way of doing this might be the establishment of a revised version of the Civilian Conservation Corps (CCC) of the 1930s. In the CCC young men were organized into companies of about 200, under the direction of reserve army officers, and sent to national parks and national forests to build roads, trails, and bridges; to construct campgrounds for tourists; and to fight forest fires. They were provided good food and medical services.

Each CCC company had an education officer who offered evening courses, and many boys who had been restless in school found it much more interesting to study geology, biology, surveying, and astronomy while living in a tent in a mountain valley. Men who are now of retirement age recall the CCC experience as a turning point in their lives. Many later returned to school and prospered there. I have known several as colleagues on university faculties. (The new CCC might have two or three education officers in each company, instead of one.)

Today, there should also be a similar program for women. Many girls who find high schools too confining would love the experience of building mountain trails or engaging in other activities that were once considered "men's work." The success of the Women's Army Corps (WACs) in World War II gave clear evidence that women could thrive under wilderness conditions. Those WACs whom I knew in New Guinea and other South Sea islands had higher morale than the men, and many of them were only a little older than today's dropouts.

The CCC program of the 1930s provided work and valuable learning experience for about three million men. At its peak it enrolled about half a million a year—approximately equal to the yearly number of dropouts today. If we could afford such a program during the years of the Great Depression, surely we can afford it in today's more affluent society. It would relieve high schools of the responsibility for the boys and girls who are profiting least from what high schools now provide and who are most likely to cause problems for teachers and for other students. At the same time, it would provide the dropouts with experience that would make them more employable when they return to their homes.

I am not proposing a new version of the CCC as a panacea for all the ills of schooling; there are no panaceas for problems so complex. I offer it as an example of the kind of rethinking that becomes possible once we reject the conventional wisdom that simply keeping everyone in school longer will solve our problems.

POSTSCRIPT

Can Schools Prevent Urban Dropouts?

"Withered Hopes, Stillborn Dreams: The Dismal Panorama of Urban Schools" is the title of a 1988 article by Gene Maeroff. It represents the feelings of many—experts and laypeople alike—that we are nearing the time when many of our big city public school systems will become inoperable.

Nevertheless, a recent stream of opinion and research and experimentation keeps hopes glimmering. A 1988 study by the Grant Foundation, *The Forgotten Half*, charts a path which includes greater flexibility in allowing people to return to school, expansion of work-study programs, development of community service projects, better career information and counseling, and the provision of tutors and mentors. Other proposals for action flow from books, such as *Illiterate America* (1985), by Jonathan Kozol; *Before It's Too Late* (1988), by Anne Wheelock and Gayle Dorman; and *School Dropouts: Patterns and Policies* (1986), by Gary Natriello. The most recent attempt to shed light on the problem is a book featuring interviews of teenagers by teenagers, *When I Was Young I Loved School: Dropping Out and Hanging In* (1989), edited by Anne Sheffield and Bruce Frankel.

Recent journal articles such as the following take a variety of stances on the issue: "The Dropout Controversy: Dropouts and Grownups—Coercion or Choice?" by Chester Finn and Jackson Toby, *Public Interest* (Summer 1989); "Dropout Prevention: Trinkets and Gimmicks or Deweyan Reconstruction," by Joseph Gerics and Miriam Westheimer, *Teachers College Record* (Fall 1988); "Rich Schools, Poor Schools: The Persistence of Unequal Education," by Arthur Wise, *College Board Review* (Spring 1989); "The Student Incentive Plan: Mitigating the Legacy of Poverty," by George Richmond, *Phi Delta Kappan* (November 1990); and "Educating Poor Minority Children," by James P. Comer, *Scientific American* (November 1988).

A number of journals have devoted issues to the dropout theme: the May 1987 issue of *Education and Urban Society*, which contains specific studies of black and Hispanic students and a fine article by Margaret D. LeCompte on the cultural context; the May/June 1988 issue of *Black Scholar*; the February 1989 issue of *Educational Leadership*; and the June 1990 issue of *Phi Delta Kappan*. Finally, the October 1989 issue of *Phi Delta Kappan* includes a summary of the Phi Delta Kappa study of students at risk by Jack Frymier and Bruce Gansneder.

ISSUE 12

Should Preschoolers Receive Academic Instruction?

YES: Siegfried and Therese Engelmann, from *Give Your Child a Superior Mind* (Simon & Schuster, 1981)

NO: David Elkind, from "Formal Education and Early Childhood Education: An Essential Difference," *Phi Delta Kappan* (May 1986)

ISSUE SUMMARY

YES: Professor of education Siegfried Engelmann and attorney Therese Engelmann, as advocates of teaching academic skills to preschool children, offer a program through which parents can positively shape the learning environment of their children.

NO: Professor of child study David Elkind, a leading critic of "superkid" programs, insists that formal instruction does not fit the preschooler's unique modes of learning, and that early instruction may actually harm very young children.

Social and economic changes in recent decades have brought about an increased need for care of preschool children and a need for "getting a leg up" in an increasingly competitive world. This has led to the "designer children" phenomenon and the "superkids" syndrome among members of the upper middle class. Among lower-class children, it has meant a "head start." These changes have created a major conflict in the field of early childhood education, a conflict between those who feel that very young children can and should respond intellectually to a prepared environment and those who hold that there is no legitimate need to rush into academic accomplishment and that, in fact, it may be dangerous.

Glenn Doman's "gentle revolution," kicked off by the success of his 1963 book *How to Teach Your Baby to Read*, was based on the belief that a one-year-old can be taught to read, do math, and understand a foreign language; that a 28-month-old can write stories and plays; that a newborn can learn how to swim; and that an 18-month-old can play the violin and do gymnastics and dance ballet—and all joyfully.

Also in the 1960s, Siegfried Engelmann and his colleague Carl Bereiter developed programs to increase the life chances of poor children by employing early intervention techniques. Their book, *Teaching Disadvantaged Children in the Preschool* (1968), contributed to the "head start" movement.

The backlash to this early academics ideology came in the form of Raymond and Dorothy Moore's 1979 book *School Can Wait;* Louise Bates Ames and Joan Ames Chase's *Don't Push Your Preschooler;* and David Elkind's *The Hurried Child* (1981). The emphasis here was often on the natural development of the individual child and the enjoyment of childhood. Whereas the Doman and Engelmann approaches sometimes seem "pushy," the Ames and Chase approach seems to hold extremely low expectations. Such modest expectations may also be found in Paul Copperman's *Taking Books to Heart* (1986), in which first graders are held to one-syllable words and sentences without commas.

As social pressures mount for all-day kindergartens and programs for four-year-olds, research shows that many later reading problems are the result of children being taught to read too early. The national focus on day care and early intervention presents an opportunity to examine the issue of appropriate methodology and to make some serious recommendations.

The belief that we humans use too little of our brain power leads us toward the Doman-Engelmann approach. The Rousseauian belief that natural development must be protected from artificial imposition leads us in the direction of Elkind's approach. One might look to the ideas of Dr. Maria Montessori for a middle ground. In any event, Siegfried and Therese Engelmann and David Elkind strike the basic argument in the selections that follow.

YES

**Siegfried and
Therese Engelmann**

SUPERIOR MINDS

This book presents a detailed program for teaching academic skills—reading, language, arithmetic—to your preschool child, an endeavor that may seem intimidating to you. There are three reasons for teaching academic skills to your preschool child. These are:

1. If your child learns these skills as a preschooler, your child will be smarter than the average child and will be in a position to learn new skills at a faster rate.

2. The schools are not well designed to teach every child academic skills. If you leave the teaching to the schools, your child may be a school failure and may learn to hate school and academic work.

3. Perhaps most important, teaching your child is a very nice and natural thing to do. The most basic relationship among humans is the transmission of knowledge from parent to child. Parents teach other important skills, such as dressing and eating. They direct the child's activities. Academic skills are important, and the child will be engaged in them for a lifetime. When the skills are taught in a home-teaching situation, the child is shown that the parent is interested in these skills and that they are part of the parent-child relationship.

Teaching your child is not easy, but it is probably not as difficult as you imagine. Initially, your child may balk, just as the child may have balked about getting dressed in some situations or following some of the other rules that you had established. Even though teaching academic skills requires some preparation, a schedule, and a commitment, it can be a very rewarding part of the day, a basis for the most intimate kind of sharing.

Regarding your ability to teach: If you can teach your child how to dress, you should be able to teach academic skills. Follow the same format of helping the child and not expecting the child to do everything at once.

Regarding your child's ability to learn: Even if your child gives no sign of being exceptionally bright, your child can learn to read and learn to perform arithmetic operations before entering the first grade. Furthermore, if you work with your child, your child will become very smart.

THE PHYSICAL ENVIRONMENT—
THE FIRST TEACHER

The child's rate of early learning is limited by practical considerations. Before learning more sophisticated skills, the child must learn the basic ones. The environment for infants is usually quite similar, because children must learn the same skills. A child raised in Nebraska makes the same babbling sounds as a baby in Peru. These children learn to walk at about the same age and they learn basic hand-eye operations at about the same age. The most potent environment conceivable could not seriously accelerate their performance through infancy because the physical environment is teaching them at a very high rate. The physical environment gives them feedback as to whether they are moving their hands appropriately. The physical environment teaches the behaviors associated with walking. Failure to follow these rules leads to punishment. If the child does not maintain an appropriate center of balance when trying to walk, the physical environment will be very consistent. If the child tries to walk inappropriately seventy-eight times, the physical environment will punish the child seventy-eight times. Plop. The environment is not moved by sympathy or tears. It does not care how charming the infant is or how good the child has been at doing some other things. The seventy-eighth trial is met with the same response the others received—plop.

For the physical environment to be an effective teacher of infants, very little conscious manipulation by adults is needed. If the child has freedom to attempt to do things, the child's wired-in tendencies to explore, imitate, and create changes in the environment will interact with the environment and produce good learning. During this learning, the environment plays the role of an overbearing authoritative agent that constantly monitors the child, lavishly correcting any errors the child makes and reinforcing the child for appropriate behaviors. The reinforcement takes the form of permission. If the child appropriately observes the rules of maintaining balance, the environment permits the child to walk.

When the overbearing physical environment is stripped of authority and transformed into a more gentle thing, learning becomes severely retarded. Imagine a place that is designed to handcuff the physical environment, a monotonous place, with no great range of things to see or hear, with nothing very hard or very soft, very loud or very subtle. Put infants on their backs in shallow cribs, make a rule that we never turn them over, rarely pick them up (even when we feed or change them) and give them the barest human contact. Attendants will not talk to them. In such a place, the physical environment would be handcuffed.

This description refers to a real place, a foundling home in Teheran, described by Wayne Dennis in *Journal of Genetic Psychology* (1960). Only 14 percent of the children were able to crawl *at the age of one to two years.* Only 42 percent of them could sit alone at this age. And only 15 percent of them could walk alone *at the age of three to four years!*

THE SOCIAL ENVIRONMENT

The physical environment effectively teaches the first skills the child must master. But it stops dramatically at this point. It does not teach the mental skills the child is expected to learn—language concepts, reading and arithmetic skills, and social skills. These skills are far beyond the domain of the physical environment. Consider the physical environment's responses to a child's attempt at reading the word *mat*. Let's assume that the child wants to read the word accurately and that the child calls the word "egg." Would the physical environment throw the child to the ground or perhaps prevent the child from saying the word? No. Would the environment provide the child with any information that the response is inappropriate? No. The environment that had been so typical when the child was engaged in learning to walk, ride a bike, open doors, and put on clothing is now mute. It does not respond because these incredible mental operations are not part of the physical environment. They don't exist in the same way that walking or opening a door exists.

By observing the physical environment, we discover what an effective teaching environment must do. If the physical environment is successful at teaching physical skills, it seems reasonable to believe that an environment modelled after it would be effective for teaching mental skills. The difference would be that human agents would have to perform feedback and correction functions that the physical environment performs for physical skills. When the child attempts to open a door, the physical environment "corrects" the child. Only a certain set of behaviors will lead to an open door. The physical environment rejects all others. (If the child tries to push on the door without first turning the knob, the door does not open.)

An effective environment for mental skills would provide similar feedback. Just as the physical environment rejects inappropriate attempts to open the door, the effective social environment would have to reject inappropriate attempts to read a word. The social environment should not be nasty, but it should recognize that there is no natural environment for learning cognitive skills. This environment is a creation. If it does not make demands that are beyond the child's capacity and if it monitors and corrects the child's initial attempts to perform on new learning activities, it will work, which means that it will be capable of teaching a wider variety of skills, and it will teach more during a given period of time.

Once we view the environment for cognitive skills as an unnatural contrivance, we can appreciate the notion that we should design it carefully. We should design communications that are effective and unambiguous, design practice so that it is productive, and design interactions so that they reinforce or "turn on" the child. . . .

FACTS ABOUT TEACHING PRESCHOOLERS

We began working on academic skills with young children in 1958. We have seen a generation of them grow up. And observing them has confirmed the adage that as the twig is bent, so grows the tree. Although these young adults are individuals and are quite different from each other in many ways, they share a few common features. They are unusually skilled in specific academic pursuits. The children who completed the arithmetic program outlined in this book are extremely talented in arithmetic, although they received very little special teaching after they entered public school. Two former students received a fairly extensive program in absolute pitch. We taught them to identify notes played on a musical instrument. As adults, they retain this talent, although one of them has very little involvement with music.

A preschool academic program is not a panacea. It merely directs the twig in a particular direction by reinforcing some skills and by prompting particular mental organizations—awareness of specific discriminations or details. It does not automatically make children superior in social situations that involve their peers. To become facile with peers, children should associate with peers and learn the rules of that particular game. Without such exposure, the children will have no opportunity to learn the subtle cues that indicate when to kid around and when to shut up and the vast set of taboos that characterize social situations (how close you stand to another person, how long you look at his face, how loudly you talk, which gestures you use, and so forth). If children receive no training in these areas, the children will grow up with incredible social deficiencies. The deficiencies will be no larger than they would be if the children had received no intensive academic work as preschoolers; however, you must recognize that the academic program is not a substitute for social learning. The academic program must be something that is *added* to the child's activities, not a substitute for other activities.

Since 1964, we have been involved with programs that teach young children (first through the University of Illinois; later through the University of Oregon). In one of the larger projects, the University of Oregon provided a most successful demonstration with disadvantaged children in kindergarten through third grade. This program involved over ten thousand children in communities across the United States. Other studies have dealt with disadvantaged preschoolers, young children with low IQ's (under 85), deaf children, and gifted preschoolers. In Oregon, we have operated a learning center since 1970. We have specialized in problems and in so doing have probably had as much experience with young children as anybody. We have never seen a young child who could not be taught to read within a reasonable period of time (such as a school year). We have never seen a "dyslexic" child. We have never seen a child who had normal skills who could not be taught arithmetic or other academic skills. A somewhat hackneyed-sounding motto tells it the way it is: The children are capable of learning if we are capable of teaching.

Do Preschoolers Learn Faster Than School-Age Children?

No, and it's a myth that they do. They learn more slowly. Expect them to be slow. Remember that if the capacity of humans were judged on the rate of their initial learning, humans would be the dumbest of all animals. Chimpanzees, squirrels, dogs, and goats all learn initial skills at a faster rate than humans. Typically, girls learn faster than boys. Naturally, there is a range of variation among girls and boys; however, the average girl baby will talk better and sooner, will learn faster, and will adapt better to changes in situations. We had three boys followed by our only daughter. We kept careful logs of their performance, and we were extremely proud of our boys' progress. If our children had come in the opposite order (with the girl first), we might have wondered what was wrong with the boys. At the age of three years, our boys were very, very average. They were beginning to produce three-word utterances, such as "Go with Mommie?" At the same age, the girl was producing sentences such as, "Can I wear my blue coat when I go to the store with you, Mommie?"

Quicker learning makes for more rapid progress because complex skills are composed of simpler skills. Although faster learning is an obvious advantage, a slow start does not mean that the child is slow or that the child is incapable of learning as much as the child who is initially faster. The child's learning rate will increase with each new related skill. When we are required to learn generically new skills, our initial performance is very slow. This fact was dramatized in a new learning experiment conducted by Oregon Research Institute. The subjects in this experiment were required to identify spoken words that were transformed into patterns of tactual vibration and that were presented to the forearms, not the ears. The purpose of this experiment was to demonstrate how people learn generically new skills—those skills that are highly different from virtually anything they have previously learned. The subjects in this experiment were bright young adults. The task was to learn to identify twelve tactually-presented words. The number of trials required by the average subject was about 2,000—dramatically confirming the difficulty of the task.

Two subjects in this experiment had received an intensive preschool education. As preschoolers, these boys had been slow. (In fact, they were developmentally slow—not walking until after fourteen months; not talking until after eighteen months.) As young adults, however, these boys learned the tactually-presented words in far fewer trials

than the other subjects, even though the other subjects were very bright.

The effects of the early instruction these young men had received were apparent in the tactual learning experiment. These young men outperformed their peers by a large margin. One mastered the twelve words in seven hundred trials, about one-third the number of trials required by the average subject. This rate of new learning would not have been predicted by the boy's behavior when he was two years old. His preschool instruction, however, taught him more than facts. It taught him how to learn. By the time he was five, he was extremely smart. As a young adult, he retained not only information, but that important ability to learn new skills.

In summary, children are ready to learn academic skills when they are quite young; their initial learning may be slow, but we should not become upset over initially slow learning. The pattern will change dramatically with practice.

Will Early Reading and Academic Work Injure the Child?

Somehow, the age of six-and-a-half became the American age at which formal education is begun. Somehow, this age became the so-called "age of readiness." Unfortunately, the notion of readiness is circular. A six-and-a-half-year-old child is quite easy to teach, far easier to teach than a three-year-old. The six-and-a-half-year-old learns faster, generalizes more readily, and knows more, which means that it is easier to communicate with this child. If our criterion for teaching children is the ease with which we can teach, we should wait until the child has a mental age of six-and-a-half. Better yet, why not wait until the child's mental age is ten or fourteen?

If we view the problem differently, however, we see that the gains a child achieves during the preschool years gives the child a real head start. If the child who receives early instruction has mastered more skills by the age of six than the average six-year-old, the child with the preschool instruction is ahead in two ways: the child knows more and the child is capable of learning additional skills more rapidly. If both receive "average" opportunities beyond this age, the child who received early stimulation should continue to maintain a lead over the average child.

There is no evidence that early reading will injure the eyes, that early learning will put a lid on the child's capacity to learn, or that the early focus on academic activities will distort the child's personality in any way. Certainly you can overdo a good thing, turning it into a charade that could injure the child. But spending twenty minutes a day on academic skills will certainly not warp the child's psyche.

It could be argued that if the child reads extremely small print and spends hours each day in this activity, the eyes will become egg-shaped. However, most of what the child will read is presented in very large print. The print is not excessively close to the child. And it is hard to imagine how looking at the printed page for short periods of time would be any more damaging to the eyes than looking at a picture book, a jigsaw puzzle, or the display of an electronic game.

The biggest possible harm that could come from early reading is early failure. But if you use a program that keeps pace with the child's capabilities and that develops skills in steps that are manageable for the child, early academic experience will instill confidence and the knowledge that "I can do it."

Will the Early Learning Create a Strain on the Parent-Child Relationship?

The program that we suggest will work, but it is not magic. If you have trouble managing children (getting them to do what you want them to do) you will have a strained relationship whether or not you teach academic skills. The reason is that the child, not you, controls most situations. The child trains *you* to be solicitous, to bribe, and to avoid situations that are not palatable to the child. Here is the formula for managing children in academic situations:

1. Make the rules of the situation very clear. Tell them what you want them to do and possibly what sort of reward they will receive for doing it the right way.

2. Set the stage for praising the children. When children perform, you will praise them. The praise is much more potent or reinforcing, however, if you set the stage so that the children will probably perform *beyond your expectations*. Therefore, state your expectations so they are less than you believe can be achieved. For instance, if you think that the child may make one mistake in reading a group of letters, you tell the child: "These letters are very hard. If you can read them without making more than three mistakes, you will do a very good job." If you think that the child should remember something that you had worked on, such as the name of a dinosaur, tell the child: "This is a hard name. I remember it because I'm super-smart. But it's so hard, you probably don't remember it."

3. Act surprised and pleased if the child exceeds your expressed expectations. "Wow, I didn't know you knew your letters that well . . ."; "I thought I was the only one who could remember the name of stegosaurus." Remember, it's far more reinforcing to exceed somebody's expectations—to really show them—than it is to meet expectations.

These rules are simple in principle, but require practice before you become fluent at applying them. So practice. You will find that you can nicely apply variations of the techniques to non-academic situations. For example, if you're going to go on a trip and you suspect that the child will become restless after about 30 minutes in the car, state your expectation that the child will understandably become restless after about 30 minutes. "This is a long trip, and I know how hard it will be to sit quietly. I'll bet if you try hard, you can do it almost all the way from here to the highway." If the child exceeds this expectation, you respond with surprise: "Look at that, you're still sitting still and we're already on the highway!"

Don't over-use the technique or it will become a hollow ploy. Remember, however, that the most important reinforcer you can use is praise. If you are pleased with what the child has done and if the accomplishment is not something that the child perceives as something that is obviously simple, your child will work very hard for your praise. Do not give it so freely that it means nothing. If you praise for every trivial thing the child does, your praise for real accomplishments has very little credibility.

In some situations, you may use tangible rewards. You may give a monetary reward for every lesson the child completes (with the understanding that the child works well during the lesson). Or you may reward the child with something like smiling-face stamps, washable "tattoos," or other symbols that children like. These rewards are reasonable, and issuing them is not bribery. Bribery occurs when you "negotiate" after a problem has occurred. If you set up the rules for earning smiling faces or pictures of animals before the lesson, you're not bribing. You're giving the child a salary for working hard. Whether the child earns the salary is basically the child's decision. And the rules for the behaviors that lead to the salary are clear.

Working on academic skills with a preschooler is counter to much of what you have read and heard about children. Unfortunately, these fatalistic philosophies are not consonant with what we know about children and how they learn. Children respond to the environment. Their capacity to learn and the content of what they learn depends on what the environment teaches. IQ correlates with just about every available measure of the environment's activity level, from the age of the parents (with older parents producing smarter kids) to the per-capita number of telephones in the state where the child is raised. It correlates with the value of the property, the size of the community, and with what the parents do. These facts about the environment suggest that the environment is flexible and that we can mold it to be more effective in maximizing the capacity of our children. Instead of relying on the traditional environment that is rich in learning opportunities for the child, we can take the environment a step further and mold it into a purposeful instrument that teaches and that guarantees your child will have a superior mind.

NO

David Elkind

AN ESSENTIAL DIFFERENCE

Young children do not learn in the same ways as older children and adults. Because the world of things, people, and language is so new to infants and young children, they learn best through direct encounters with their world rather than through formal education involving the inculcation of symbolic rules. The fact of this difference is rooted in the observations of such giants of child study as Froebel, Montessori, and Piaget, and it is consistently supported by the findings of research in child development.[1] This fact was also recognized by the ancients, who described the child of 6 or 7 as having attained the "age of reason."

Given the well-established fact that young children learn differently, the conclusion that educators must draw is a straightforward one: the education of young children must be in keeping with their unique modes of learning. If we accept this conclusion, what is happening in the U.S. today is truly astonishing. In a society that prides itself on its openness to research and on its respect for "expert" opinion, parents, educators, administrators, and legislators are blatantly ignoring the facts, the research, and the consensus of experts about how young children learn and how best to teach them.

All across the country, educational programs devised for school-age children are being applied to the education of young children, as well. In such states as New York, Connecticut, and Illinois, administrators are advocating that children enter formal schooling at age 4. The length of many kindergarten programs has been extended to a full day, and nursery school programs have become prekindergartens. Moreover, many of these kindergartens have introduced curricula (including workbooks and papers) once reserved for first-graders. And a number of writers, in books addressed to parents, advocate the teaching of reading and math to infants and very young children.[2]

This transformation of thinking regarding early childhood education raises at least three questions that I will attempt to answer here. First, why is this

From David Elkind, "Formal Education and Early Childhood Education: An Essential Difference," *Phi Delta Kappan* (May 1936). Copyright © 1936 by Phi Delta Kappan, Inc. Reprinted by permission.

happening? As we have seen, both theory and research consistently agree that young children learn differently from older children and adults. And no one really questions the principle that education should be adapted to the learning abilities of the students to be instructed. Why is the special character of learning in early childhood being ignored by so many people who should know better?

The second question depends on the first. Even if young children are being taught in the manner of older children, what harm is there in that? After all, it could be that we have merely been coddling young children by not introducing them to a rigorous academic program at an early age. Doesn't the new research on infants and young children substantiate their eagerness to learn and the importance of the early years for intensive instruction? We will see below that this is not quite the case.

The third question follows from the first two. If it can be demonstrated that early, formal instruction does more harm than good, what can we do about it? After all, that is the direction, however mistaken, in which U.S. society as a whole is heading. Formal instructional programs for infants and young children are expanding not only in academic areas but also in sports, the arts, and computer science. To oppose these trends is to ignore the social consensus and to run counter to the culture at large. We live in a democratic society in which the majority rules, so what can a minority do even if it wants to?

WHY BEGIN SO SOON?

In America, educational practice is determined by economic, political, and social considerations much more than it is by what we know about what constitutes good pedagogy for children. Until the 1960s, however, early childhood education was an exception to this general rule. Early childhood education programs were, for the most part, privately run and well adapted to the developmental needs of the children they served. Even kindergartens in public schools had a special status and were generally free of the social pressures that influenced the rest of elementary and secondary education.

All of that changed in the 1960s, however, when early childhood education was abruptly shoved into the economic, political, and social spotlight. At that moment, early childhood education lost its innocence and its special status. Like elementary and secondary education, early childhood education became a ground on which to fight social battles that had little or nothing to do with what was good pedagogy for children. The formal symbol of this mainstreaming of early childhood education came with the passage by Congress of the Head Start legislation in 1964. For the first time, early childhood programs were being funded by the federal government.

What brought about this change during the Sixties? In many ways early childhood education was the scapegoat of the social movements of that turbulent decade. Elementary and secondary education were already under attack on two different fronts. First, such events as the launching of Sputnik I in 1957, the demise of progressive education, and the publication of such books as *Why Johnny Can't Read* focused the spotlight of criticism on American education. One explanation (actually, a rationalization) for the problems that such close scrutiny revealed was that children were poorly prepared for school and that early childhood education should be more academically rigorous so that children could move more rapidly once they entered school.

The second front on which education was trying to fight a rear-guard action was in the arena of the civil rights movement. One of the main issues taken up by this movement was the unequal schooling of minorities. Schools for black children, for example, were obviously inferior in quality to those for white children. Again, one explanation (rationalization) was that black children were poorly prepared for school. It wasn't the schools, the argument ran, but the preparation that led to the lower achievement levels of black children. The Head Start legislation was one response to this claim.

One major consequence of this institutionalization of early childhood education was the introduction of a new conception of infants and young children. Educational practice is not alone in being determined by the social, economic, and political tenor of the times. The conception of the child changes with the times as well. For example, a dominant conception of the child in the 19th century—dictated by the religious orthodoxy of the time—was the notion of the "sinful child." Educating the sinful child necessarily involved "breaking the will" by whatever harsh means were needed to do so.

The advent of Freudian psychology in the early 20th century, along with the continuing secularization and urbanization of American society, gradually replaced the concept of the sinful child with the concept of the "sensual child." Freud's depiction of infantile sexuality and his theories regarding the central role of sexuality in the formation of neuroses focused attention on the development of a "healthy personality."[3] Progressive education had as one of its aims the open, spontaneous expression of feelings and emotions (judged to be healthy) rather than their suppression or repression (judged to be unhealthy). During the reign of the sensual child, there was less concern with the child's intellectual development, which, in an emotionally healthy child, was presumed to take care of itself.

The intellectual importance given early childhood education by the civil rights movement and the education reform movement of the 1970s was inconsistent with the concept of the sensual child. A new concept of infants and young children was, therefore, required. This new concept had to be in keeping with the new significance attached to academic education during the early years. What emerged was the concept of the "competent infant." Unwittingly, perhaps, social scientists of the time, caught up in the emotion of the social movements, fostered this conception through unwarranted reinterpretations of established facts about the cognitive development of young children.

Jerome Bruner, for example, though he was not trained in child development or in education, became a guru of the education reform movement of the day.[4] His totally unsubstantiated claim that "you can teach any child any subject matter at any age in an intellectually honest way" became a touchstone of the new conception of the "competent infant." In the same way, Benjamin Bloom's ambiguous statement that a young child attains half of his or her intellectual ability by the age of 4 (based on well-known correlations between I.Q. scores attained by the same subjects at different ages) was another foundation for the conception of the "competent infant."[5] Finally, James McV. Hunt's idea of the malleability of I.Q. (an idea that had always been accepted by reputable psychometricians) was presented as a new idea that was in opposition to the mental testing establishment's supposed advocacy of a fixed I.Q.[6]

Thus the conception of the competent infant and young child was dictated by social and political forces rather than by any new data or findings about the modes of learning of young children. Whatever psychological theory or educational research that was brought to bear to reinforce this conception had been carefully selected and interpreted to support the notion of early childhood competence. Contrary evidence was ignored. The facts were made to fit the hypothesis rather than the hypothesis being changed to accommodate the facts. In short, our conception of the child at any point in history has been much more dependent on social, political, and economic considerations than on the established facts and theories of child development.

The concept of the competent infant was also congruent with the changing lifestyles of American middle-class families. During the reign of the sensual child, middle-class values dictated that mothers stay at home and rear their children, lend support to their husbands, and run the home. Home economics became a major department for women in most colleges and universities of the time and reflected these values. Within that set of middle-class values, the concept of a sensual infant who was in need of a mother's ministrations fit quite comfortably.

In the past two decades, however, thanks partly to the women's movement and partly to the shift in U.S. society from an industrial to a postindustrial economy, the middle-class value system has changed dramatically. The women's movement accentuated women's need for choice in the matter of whether to stay home or to pursue a career. At the same time, a postindustrial economy can make use of more women in the workforce than an industrial economy. In the past, factory work required the large muscles of men, but, with the miniaturization of modern technology, the small motor skills and dexterity of women are in greater demand. Likewise, now that our economy is becoming primarily a service economy, the social skills of women are also much in demand.

Another change in the circumstances of the middle class has contributed to the growing number of middle-class women in the workforce. As divorce has become socially acceptable, divorce rates have soared, and it is now expected that more than half of all marriages will end in divorce. In more than 90% of these cases, it is the mother who retains custody of the children. And because alimony and child support are rarely enough to live on, divorced mothers swell the ranks of working women.

One result of these changes in lifestyle and values has been that middle-class women are entering the workforce in ever-increasing numbers. More than 50% of U.S. women are now employed outside the home, and it is estimated that by the year 2000 between 80% and 90% of women will be in the workforce. One consequence of this social movement is that increasing numbers of infants and young children are being cared for outside the home. Current estimates place the number of children under the age of 6 who are receiving one or another form of out-of-home care at six million.

The conception of the competent infant is clearly more in keeping with these contemporary family styles than is the conception of the sensual infant. A competent infant can cope with the separation from parents at an early age. He or she is able to adjust with minimal difficulty to baby sitters, day-care centers, full-day nursery schools, and so on. If some parents feel residual pangs of guilt about leaving their young offspring in out-of-home care, they can place their youngster in a high-pressure academic program. If the child were not in such a program, the parents tell themselves, he or she would fall behind peers and would not be able to compete academically when it is time to enter kindergarten. From this perspective, high-pressure academic preschool programs are for the young child's "own good."

The social dynamics behind the pressure to place young children in educational programs appropriate for school-age children now become painfully clear. The truth is that the many changes in our society have not been accompanied by adequate provisions for the out-of-home care of all the young children who require it. Consequently, parents are putting pressure on elected officials to provide more early childhood care. This has been the primary motivation for full-day kindergartens, starting school at age 4, and so on. Although the avowed reasons for these proposals are to be found in "new" research showing the need for early childhood education, the "new" data consist of nothing more than the "old" (and always dubious) data from the 1960s. The real reason for these programs is that elected officials are feeling pressure from voters to offer out-of-home care for young children.

There is another motive for introducing formal instruction in early childhood programs. This comes from our intuitive psychology regarding technology and human behavior. Much intuitive psychology derives from emotions and feelings rather than from reason and balanced judgment. Nonetheless, such intuitions seem so obviously correct that one thinks it foolish even to question them. (The so-called "gambler's fallacy" is a case in point: the gambler believes that the number of previous losses increases his or her probability of winning, while, in fact, there is no relationship between the two.)

The intuition regarding human behavior and technology is equally fallacious. The intuition is that human potentials are altered by technology. With respect to children, this intuition is often expressed by saying that, thanks to such innovations as television and computers, children today are brighter and more sophisticated than children in the past. This intuition has reinforced and supported the conception of the competent infant and has been used to rationalize the formal instruction of preschool children.

Technology, however, neither changes human potential nor accelerates human development. Technology extends and amplifies our human potentials, but it does not alter them. The telephone extends our hearing; television extends our vision; computers extend our memories. But neither our capacity for hearing, nor our capacity for seeing, nor our capacity for remembering have been changed by the technology. Modern weaponry may have amplified our ability to express our aggression, but it has neither heightened nor lessened our tendency to be aggressive. There is simply no truth in the intuitive belief that technology alters human potential.

Exactly the same holds true with respect to children. Computers have not improved children's intellectual capacities; they have only amplified the limitations of young children's thinking. Consider "turtle geometry," an application of the computer language Logo, created by Seymour Papert for use with preschool and school-age children.[7] Children learn to write programs that move the cursor in different directions to draw figures on a video screen. The sequence of directions then becomes an elementary program for drawing the figure. One instruction, however, gives young children a great deal of trouble. This is the instruction to rotate the cursor in different directions without moving it. Young children do not easily understand that you can change direction while standing still, and they have difficulty grasping this command. Thus the use of the technology only amplifies the limitations of young children's thinking.

Television provides another example. Programs such as "Sesame Street" and "The Electric Company" were supposed to make learning to read easier for young children. However, the rapid presentation of material on these programs is much too fast for the information-processing abilities of young children. It could be that these programs, geared to the information-processing speeds of adults and older children, have amplified the attentional limitations of young children, with negative consequences for their reading abilities. These programs have been on the air for almost 20 years, and during that time "attentional deficits" have become the leading form of learning disability. Yet most people continue to believe that these programs have improved children's reading abilities. Such intuitive belief that children today are brighter and more sophisticated than previous generations tops off the list of commonly accepted reasons for the formal instruction of young children.

THE HARM OF EARLY INSTRUCTION

What harm is there in exposing young children to formal instruction involving the inculcation of symbolic rules? The harm comes from what I have called "miseducation."[8] We miseducate children whenever we put them at risk for no purpose. The risks of miseducating young children are both short- and long-term. The short-term risks derive from the stress, with all its attendant symptoms, that formal instruction places on children; the long-term risks are of at least three kinds: motivational, intellectual, and social. In each case, the potential psychological risks of early intervention far outweigh any potential educational gain.

Short-term risks. Stress is a demand for adaptation. In this broad sense, of course, stress is coincident with life itself. In a narrower, clinical sense, however, stress refers to any excessive demand for adaptation. What is excessive, in turn, depends on both the individual and the demands made.

Elsewhere I have suggested that each individual has two sources of energy with which to cope with stress.[9] One of these is what I call "clock energy." This is the energy that we use up in pursuing the tasks of daily living, and it is replenished by food and rest. By contrast, what I call "calendar energy" is the energy involved in growth and development that is given us in a more or less fixed quantity and that determines our total life span.

The early symptoms of stress are those associated with clock energy: fatigue, loss of appetite, and decreased efficiency. When the excessive demands continue without adequate time for replenishment, an individual must draw on his or her calendar energy. When this happens, such psychosomatic stress symptoms as headaches and stomachaches that can injure the organism and shorten the life span begin to appear. In young children exposed to formal instruction, both types of stress symptoms are frequently seen.

The reason for this is not difficult to understand. Formal instruction puts excessive demands on young children. A concrete example may help make this point. The learning of young children is "permeable" in the sense that they do not learn in the narrow categories defined by adults, such as reading, math, science, and so on. At the level at which young children learn, there are no sharp boundaries. When young children make soup, for example, they learn the names of vegetables (language), how to measure ingredients (math), the effects of heat on the hardness and softness of the vegetables (science), and the cross-sectional shapes of the vegetables (geometry). It would be nonsense, however, to single out any one of these learnings as a separate lesson in any of the subjects listed in parentheses.

The focus on a specific learning task, as demanded by formal instruction, is thus at variance with the natural mode of learning of the young child. From the viewpoint of formal instruction, the multiple learning potential of the young child is seen as evidence of distractability or the currently more fashionable phrase, attentional deficit. The pressure to focus on one avenue of learning, such as letter or word identification, is very stressful for young children. Pediatricians around the country report an increase in stress-related symptoms in young children.[10] A pediatrician I met at a meeting of the National Academy of Pediatrics told me that he is treating a 4-year-old who has peptic ulcers.

To be sure, formal instruction is but one of the many demands made on a young child in a formal program of education. The child is also separated from his or her parents, a second stress; is in a new and unfamiliar place with strange children and adults, a third stress; and is required to learn new rules of conduct, still another stress. Although the demands of formal instruction may not be sufficient in themselves to overstrain the young child's reservoir of clock energy, the combination of stresses associated with formal schooling can be sufficient to produce symptoms.

By contrast, young children in a sound program of early childhood education have the support of activities nicely suited to their learning styles. This eliminates the stresses occasioned by the curriculum and the stilted teacher/student interactions inherent in formal instruction.

Long-term effects. One long-term danger of early instruction is the potential harm it can do to the child's motivation to learn. In addition to being permeable, the spontaneous learning of young children is self-directed. Children learn their native language not because anyone "teaches" them that language in a formal way but because they have both the need and the capacity to learn language. They use the language models and verbal interactions provided by their environment to acquire this most complicated skill. Young children have their own set of learning priorities.

Certainly some things need to be taught to very young children. For example, they need to learn what might be called the "healthy" fears: for example, not to touch fire, not to insert fingers in electrical sockets, and not to cross streets without looking both ways. Such learning is not self-directed, but it is necessary for survival. On the intellectual plane, however, children's natural curiosity about the world around them is a strong directive for learning the basic categories and concepts of the physical world. Sound early childhood education encourages children's self-directed learning by providing an environment that is rich in materials to explore, manipulate, and talk about.

When adults intrude in this self-directed learning and insist on their own learning priorities, such as reading or math, they interfere with the self-directed impulse. Children can learn something from this instruction, but it may be something other than what the adults intended. A child may learn to become dependent on adult direction and not to trust his or her own initiative. Erik Erikson has described early childhood as the period when the balance is struck between the sense of initiative and the sense of guilt.[11] *And this balance has consequences for a lifetime.*

A child whose self-directed learning is encouraged will develop a sense of initiative that will far outweigh a sense of guilt about getting things started. On the other hand, a child whose self-directed learning is interfered with, who is forced to follow adult learning priorities, may acquire a strong sense of guilt about *any* self-initiated activities. One risk of early formal instruction, then, is that it may encourage a sense of guilt at the expense of a sense of initiative.

Let me recount an anecdote to make this risk concrete. Several years ago I met a renowned psychiatrist who told me the following story. In the 1930s, psychologist Myrtle McGraw carried out what has become a classic study of the contributions of nature and nurture to motor development.[12] McGraw's study involved twin boys, Johnny and Jimmy. In her study, McGraw trained one of the twins, Johnny, in a variety of motor tasks, such as riding a tricycle and climbing. Jimmy was not trained. Johnny soon surpassed Jimmy in the skills in which he had been trained. On the other hand, after the training was discontinued, Jimmy quickly caught up with his brother, so that, by the end of the year in which the training was initiated, there was no difference in the motor skills of the twins. In motor learning, maturation appeared to be at least as important as training.

What the psychiatrist told me, however, was that he had seen the twins several years after the investigation had been completed. When he examined the boys, he found a striking difference in their personalities and, particularly, in their approach to learning. Johnny, the twin who had been trained, was difficult and insecure. He seemed always to be looking for adult direction and approval of his activities. Jimmy, the untrained twin, was quite the opposite. Self-confident and self-assured, he undertook activities on his own without looking to adults for guidance and direction. Though this example is anecdotal, it does illustrate the potential risk of too much adult intervention in the self-directed learning of young children.

Early formal instruction also puts the child at intellectual risk. Jean Piaget emphasized the importance of what he called "reflective abstraction" for the mental ability of the child.[13] A child who is engaging in self-directed learning can reflectively abstract from those activities. That reflective abstraction encourages the growth of new mental abilities. Piaget cited the example of a child who is rearranging 10 pebbles. First, the child makes them into a square, then into a circle, and next into a triangle. What the child discovers, as a result of that activity, is that no matter how he or she arranges the pebbles they still remain 10 in number. In effect, the child has learned the difference between perception and reason. Perceptually, it appears as if there are more pebbles in one configuration than in another. Reason tells the child that they are the same.

When adults intrude on a child's learning, they also interfere with the process of reflective abstraction. Formal instruction presents the child with some content to be learned. Flash cards present the child with a visual configuration that the child must first discriminate and then memorize. Teaching young children phonics is another example of presenting the child with an association that he or she must learn without much active intervention or exploration. Rote learning and memorization, the stuff of much formal education, provide little opportunity for reflective abstraction. Such reflective abstraction, however, is essential for the full realization of a child's cognitive abilities.

Introducing formal instruction too early also puts the child at social risk. One aspect of formal instruction—thankfully absent in sound early childhood education—is the introduction of the notions of "correct" and "incorrect." These notions not only orient the child's thinking but also introduce social comparison. One child gets an answer right, and another gets it wrong. Therefore, one child is smarter, somehow better than the other.

Such social comparisons are harmful enough among school-age children, but they are truly damaging among preschoolers.

This damage can occur because the focus on right and wrong turns the child away from self-directed and self-reinforcing sources of self-esteem. Instead, it directs children to look primarily to adults for approval and to social comparison for self-appraisal. This works against the formation of self-esteem that a child attains from successfully completing a self-initiated and self-directed task. From the point of view of socialization, the danger of early instruction is that it can make children too dependent on others for their sense of self-worth. Sound early childhood education encourages children to feel good about themselves as a consequence of their own achievements.

To be sure, the foregoing descriptions of damage to motivation, intellectual growth, and self-esteem are potential risks that are not always realized in every child who is miseducated. But why put a child at risk in the first place? There is really no evidence that early formal instruction has any lasting or permanent benefits for children. By contrast, the risks to the child's motivation, intellectual growth, and self-esteem could well do serious damage to the child's emerging personality. It is reasonable to conclude that the early instruction of young children derives more from the needs and priorities of adults than from what we know of good pedagogy for young children.

WHAT CAN WE DO?

The miseducation of young children, so prevalent in the United States today, ignores the well-founded and noncontroversial differences between early childhood education and formal education. As educators, our first task is to reassert this difference and insist on its importance. We have to reeducate parents, administrators, and legislators regarding what is sound education for young children. And we must make it clear that it is not out-of-home care for young children that is potentially harmful—only the wrong kind of out-of-home care. Sound early childhood education is an extension of the home, not of the school.

As a profession, we have no choice but to go public. Those who are making money from the miseducation of young children are the ones about whom parents hear and read the most. We need to write for popular magazines, speak out on television forums, and encourage newspaper articles about the difference between good early childhood education and miseducation. We are in a war for the well-being of our children, and in this war the media are our most powerful weapon. It is a war we can never absolutely win, no matter how hard we fight. But, unless we fight as hard as we can, it is a war we will certainly lose.

NOTES

1. Sheldon H. White, "Some General Outlines of the Matrix of Developmental Changes Between 5 and 7 Years," *Bulletin of the Orton Society*, vol. 20, 1970, pp. 41–57.

2. See, for example, Glen Doman, *Teach Your Baby to Read* (London: Jonathan Cape, 1965); Peggy Eastman and John L. Barr, *Your Child is Smarter Than You Think* (New York: Morrow, 1985); and Sidney Ledson, *Teach Your Child to Read in 60 Days* (Toronto: Publishing Company, Ltd., 1975).

3. Sigmund Freud, "Infantile Sexuality," in A. A. Brill, ed., *The Basic Writings of Sigmund Freud* (New York: Random House, 1938).

4. Jerome Bruner, *The Process of Education* (Cambridge, Mass.: Harvard University Press, 1960).

5. Benjamin S. Bloom, *Stability and Change in Human Characteristics* (New York: Wiley, 1964).

6. James McV. Hunt, *Intelligence and Experience* (New York: Ronald Press, 1961).

7. Seymour Papert, *Mindstorms* (New York: Basic Books, 1980).

8. David Elkind, *The Miseducation of Children: Superkids at Risk* (New York: A. A. Knopf, 1986).

9. David Elkind, *All Grown Up and No Place to Go: Teenagers in Crisis* (Reading, Mass.: Addison-Wesley, 1984).

10. T. Berry Brazelton, quoted in E. J. Kahn, "Stressed for Success," *Boston Magazine*, December 1985, pp. 178–82, 255–57.

11. Erik H. Erikson, *Childhood and Society* (New York: Norton, 1950).

12. Myrtle B. McGraw, *A Study of Johnny and Jimmy* (New York: Appleton-Century-Crofts, 1935).

13. Jean Piaget, *The Psychology of Intelligence* (London: Routledge & Kegan Paul, 1950).

POSTSCRIPT

Should Preschoolers Receive Academic Instruction?

Resolution of this particular controversy resides in the production of evidence supporting one side or the other. While you might have obvious prejudices regarding one basic stance or the other, you should remain open to convincing evidence regarding the effects of variable types of intervention or, indeed, of no particular intervention at all.

Research and expert opinions abound. Among the more interesting and instructive are these: Judith S. Glazer, "Kindergarten and Early Education: Issues and Problems," *Childhood Education* (September/October 1985); Alice Sterling Honig, "Reflections on Infant Intervention Programs: What Have We Learned?" *Journal of Children in Contemporary Society* (Fall 1984); Peter E. Haiman, "Viewpoint: There is More to Early Childhood Education Than Cognitive Development," *Young Children* (November 1984); and Paula Jorde, "Early Childhood Education: Issues and Trends," *Educational Forum* (Winter 1986).

Two particularly interesting studies have some bearing on the issue at hand. They are Sally Lubeck's *Sandbox Society: Early Education in Black and White America* (1985), an ethnographic comparison that examines the effects of early schooling experiences on young children, and *Changed Lives: The Effects of the Perry Preschool Program on Youths through Age 19* (1984), a longitudinal study that concluded that the type of early intervention involved was a worthwhile investment in terms of school failure prevention and crime reduction.

The November 1986 issue of *Educational Leadership* addresses the theme of "The Young Child at School," with some 25 articles on various aspects of the basic problem. The important issue of readiness for academic learning is addressed specifically in the article by Shepard and Smith, "Synthesis of Research on School Readiness and Kindergarten Retention."

Additionally, the book *Summer Children: Ready or Not for School* (1986), by James K. Uphoff, June E. Gilmore, and Rosemarie Huber, explores the proposition that the bright are not necessarily ready for school. "Policy Options for Preschool Programs," an exploration of alternatives for preschoolers, by Lawrence J. Schweinhart, Jeffrey J. Koshel, and Anne Bridgman, can be found in the March 1987 *Phi Delta Kappan*. Theoretical considerations are presented by Evelyn Weber in her 1984 book, *Ideas Influencing Early Childhood Education*. David Elkind has extended his ideas in another book, *Miseducation: Preschoolers at Risk* (1987).

ISSUE 13

Should Whole-Language Replace Basal Readers?

YES: Zelene Lovitt, from "Rethinking My Roots as a Teacher," *Educational Leadership* (March 1990)

NO: Richard D. McCallum, from "Don't Throw the Basals Out With the Bath Water," *The Reading Teacher* (December 1988)

ISSUE SUMMARY

YES: Zelene Lovitt, a reading recovery teacher, explains how conversion to the whole-language approach altered her basic assumptions about teaching.
NO: Richard D. McCallum, a specialist in teaching reading, warns of the dangers of rejecting research-based basal readers.

Recent decades have witnessed a growing anxiety in America over the teaching of reading and the level of literacy attained by the citizens of this country. Rudolph Flesch's *Why Johnny Can't Read* (1966) and Jonathan Kozol's *Illiterate America* (1985), among other books, have stirred public concern. School boards and teachers have been buffeted by recommendations from zealous advocates of basal readers, of "real literature" approaches, of phonics, of "look-say" methodologies, and, most recently, of "whole-language" approaches.

Among professionals in the field of reading instruction, two books have provided the basic fuel for what *Newsweek* magazine calls "The Reading Wars"—Jeanne Chall's *Learning to Read: The Great Debate,* published in 1967 and updated in 1983, and Ken Goodman's *What's Whole in Whole Language?* (1986). Chall, an advocate of the phonics approach, thinks that whole language works against children who do not come from homes that are reading-supportive. Poor people, immigrants, and the learning-disabled, she contends, all need more structure than whole language provides. The fatal flaw that she sees in the methodology of whole language is that it treats beginning reading and later reading as essentially the same.

Goodman holds that all children learn best when taught in a way that make sense to them and when what is learned has a direct function in their lives. He says that this is the objective of whole language and that the phonics approach of breaking words down into syllables works against that aim and defeats the joy of learning to read.

The whole-language approach emphasizes natural communication, the achievement of meaning as a primary aim, and the use of "real" books as opposed to "artificially constructed" readers. It includes a limited use of phonics. On the other hand, the phonics approach employs research-based basal readers at the beginning stages of reading instruction and places emphasis on code-interpretation skills and letter-sound correspondences.

While the debate between the two groups continues, there are those who contend that the real enemies are Nintendo video game systems and Saturday morning television cartoons. Some others, among them reading expert Dorothy Strickland, see the conflict as a power struggle over the control of reading instruction in this country, which works against a compromise that would most likely benefit the students. A recently released book on the issue, *Beginning to Read: Thinking and Learning About Print*, by Marilyn Jager Adams, a major study conducted under the auspices of the Center for the Study of Reading at the University of Illinois and sponsored by the U.S. Department of Education, concludes that what is indeed needed is a balance between phonics activities and the reading-for-meaning context provided by whole-language techniques. Each is declared to be an essential component in the development of effective reading programs.

Rather than going to the theories of Chall and Goodman, we have selected two writers from the front lines for our pairing on this issue. Zelene Lovitt is an elementary school teacher of reading and Richard D. McCallum works with reading teachers. Lovitt relates her experiences with whole-language methodologies to her total philosophical grounding as a teacher. McCallum reports that his experience with beginning teachers leads him to conclude that the use of basal readers is not only justified as an essential component in learning how to read but also serves as an effective training mechanism for the teachers themselves.

YES

RETHINKING MY ROOTS AS A TEACHER

When I began working with a student teacher last fall, I was forced to conceptualize and verbalize for her the ideas and philosophies that are the underpinnings of my classroom functioning. What had 15 years of classroom teaching taught me? What made me a whole-language teacher?

MY SEARCH FOR ANSWERS

These questions set me in search of answers upon which my student teacher might build. When I finally pared away various strategies, approaches, tricks, and theories, I was left with a single thought: *If a whole-language class is student-centered and therefore teacher responsive, then the teacher must have few of the preconceived notions and assumptions typically found in the classroom.*

One of the strengths of a whole-language approach is the impact its philosophy has on teacher professionalism, which in turn advances student development. In order for the approach to succeed, however, teachers must relinquish a number of commonly held assumptions.

False Assumption 1: Children perform at a specific level of functioning.
On the contrary, children perform at multiple levels of functioning concurrently. For that reason, I constantly regroup my students based on interest, ability, self-selection of materials, and the topic being addressed. In other words, there are no "Bluebirds," "Redbirds," or "Buzzards" in my class. Trying to pigeonhole students and narrowly stratify their specific levels at a given point in time severely restricts and limits the realization of their potential. Statically leveled groups by necessity force teachers to address only parts of the child and parts of the child's learning.

Therefore, we should recognize that children develop in different areas at different rates and should program appropriately to meet the various needs of each student.

False Assumption 2: Children's abilities develop in predictable ways that can be addressed by a stringently sequenced curriculum.
On the contrary, children and their various abilities appear to mature in a continuous lurch-forward-scramble-backward manner in multiple areas

From Zelene Lovitt, "Rethinking My Roots as a Teacher," *Educational Leadership*, vol. 47, no. 6 (March 1990), pp. 43–46. Copyright © 1990 by the Association for Supervision and Curriculum Development. Reprinted by permission. All rights reserved.

simultaneously. Because of this inconsistent developmental rate, a prescribed curriculum cannot precisely match where the children are when the scope and sequence says they should be there. We should view education as a puzzle—the order in which the pieces are placed in the puzzle is irrelevant as long as successful completion occurs.

Therefore, within the curriculum objectives required by state and district mandates, we should develop our own programs, to match our students' needs, abilities, and strengths.

False Assumption 3: Educationally, basal publishers know my students better than I do.

How could they? They've never met my class. They don't know the differences among my students in terms of abilities, interests, and development. Further, my students are never the same two days in a row. Publishers cannot know the "teachable moment" I have just "seized" nor the learning mosaic my classroom paints. How could someone thousands of miles away, who wrote the material months, perhaps years ago, be sensitive to what is happening in my class today?

Therefore, we should have confidence in our own professional judgment about the appropriate teaching of what is relevant and useful. Further, we should inundate our students with primary sources rather than diluted material. We should be responsive to the immediacy of the teaching situation and assume the position of authority and knowledge inherent in our role.

False Assumption 4: Assessment should take place at regular intervals and can be accomplished with tests that accompany the basals.

Because the teacher must constantly respond to the student, assessment must be ongoing, constant, formative and summative. Preconceived measures limit responsiveness to evaluating the meaningful learning that takes place within the unevenly developing student. The true measure of assessment is the ability of the student to apply information and skills in a realistic, meaningful fashion and to transfer knowledge to enhance functioning.

Therefore, assessment must take place while the students are in action and must be based on criteria relevant to the task at hand. To validly assess learning, we should increase our focus on process and not rely largely on product measures.

False Assumption 5: Children need to be programmed so that learning can take place.

Wrong. Children need to be *inspired* to actively take hold of a learning situation and explore the opportunities that the teacher provides for investigation. The trick is not to have a multitude of tasks for students to do but to know how to "read" students so that we can motivate them to embrace the learning situation. Then, in order to match the situation to students' abilities, we must provide appropriate experiences, materials, and opportunities.

Therefore, we should so involve students in learning that they develop a sense of ownership in their day-to-day education. When students have an investment in what they are doing, they are motivated, involved, and dedicated. That is when learning takes place.

False Assumption 6: Teachers are the source of all significant learning.

Although teachers do not have all answers to all questions, we have acquired considerable knowledge, and we can help our students connect with the knowledge they want or need. We can ensure that they know how to acquire knowledge for themselves after they've left school and teach them how to share their knowledge with others. When appropriately guided, students are quite capable of teaching each other skills, concepts, and attitudes. In particular, the group/cooperative learning activities common in whole-language classrooms help students learn the valuable social skills that will enable them to learn from each other and to function together successfully in the work world.

Therefore, teachers should not function as if we are the core of all significant learning but, rather, should give students frequent opportunities for direct intellectual involvement with ideas, concepts, and learning.

False Assumption 7: Teachers are to maintain order and control at all times.

Teachers must define for ourselves (and for our supervisors) the meaning of the words *control* and *discipline*. For me, they mean ensuring that students are pursuing learning in an active manner that doesn't interfere with the pursuit of learning in which others are engaged. My active students are on-task and deeply involved in the business of learning, and the goals of their activities dictate the type of tasks in which they are involved. Students who primarily stay in their seats and quietly work on papers do not necessarily accomplish meaningful learning. As long as I am able to involve and direct the behaviors of the children positively, I am in control.

Therefore, we should measure our control of our students and their behaviors not by the activity level of the classroom but, rather, by the productive manner in which they function while involved in academic pursuits.

False Assumption 8: For learning to take place efficiently, teachers must be the planners.

It is my role to ensure that my students are mastering the objectives and moving successfully toward the goals of the curriculum. However, students are capable of varying degrees of collaborating on and assuming joint responsibility for unit planning and for the direction learning explorations take. How better to make learning relevant for students than for it to be on their own agendas?

Therefore, teachers should share our practical life skills and knowledge and prepare our students so that they develop the important skills needed to formulate and execute plans. Further, we should ensure that, throughout their lives, our students can take and apply this knowledge.

False Assumption 9: Content areas must be addressed discretely.

I have found it effective and efficient to teach integrated language arts in the content areas. For addressing process learning in the lower elementary grades, integrated learning broadens the areas for relevance and interest of those skills being taught. In the upper elementary grades, integrated learning is expedient and relevant: it addresses the goal of extrapolating information in content area materials. The reading expectations for content materials differ from those involving the acquisition of how to decode and comprehend; they need to be addressed by employing the material that is used as a part of real-life demands.

Therefore, to strengthen the transfer of skills and knowledge from one area to another, we should integrate language arts and the content areas. We should teach what children need to know, both content and process, in a manner that mirrors life—interwoven, inter-related, and compacted.

False Assumption 10: If whole language is so good, everybody would be doing it already.

Not so. For many years we teachers have allowed ourselves to be dependent upon others for direction regarding how and what we teach. Principals and administrators are often perceived as having their own fixed agenda of how we should function. To a certain extent, this perception may be accurate. I believe, however, that teachers have a lot of "wiggle room" and that principals will support impassioned teachers who are committed to student learning and will work diligently to prove the validity of their beliefs.

Therefore, we should take ultimate responsibility for our students' learning, teach, lead and learn from other teachers, and experiment and trust ourselves and our students. We must test the reality of our supposed limits because teacher empowerment can come only from, within, and by our own efforts.

Freedom to Act

As I sat with my student teacher, I pondered these weighty ideas and their importance. Each assumption, when translated into behaviors, has far-reaching consequences for successful student learning. I hope my examination of common assumptions and recommendations for action will serve as a springboard for other professionals to scrutinize their own beliefs and behaviors. Deciding to let go of these common assumptions removes (inappropriate) restrictions; it frees us to function in a manner that ensures achieving our own and our students' potential.

Therefore, we need to develop a strong knowledge base for classroom decision making. We should develop a cycle of educating ourselves and of assessing our needs as educators—planners, implementors, and evaluators of instruction. We should think carefully . . . and then act.

NO

Richard D. McCallum

DON'T THROW THE BASALS OUT WITH THE BATH WATER

Basal bashing is in. Critics' attacks have increased and they have spread like a wave of religious fundamentalism.

Let me make it clear that I have never been nor am I currently employed by publishers of basal series. Further, I do not believe that basals in and of themselves will solve all the problems associated with developing a nation of readers. But we must be careful not to discard practices or materials which have been shown to produce results. We must be honest with ourselves when evaluating the usefulness of basals.

Basals do have limitations, but these stem from our ever changing understanding of the reading process and the application of that understanding to teacher training and classroom practice.

Three key points are introduced in this article. First, basal series play a critical role in reading instruction in part because of the difficulties associated with translating research findings and theory into practices which are sensitive to the pressures that teachers face. Second, basals have changed over time in light of public and pedagogical pressure, and in so doing have acted to translate research into practice. And third, in effect, basals have provided on the job training for reading teachers.

THE TAR PIT OF EDUCATION

It is unreasonable to insist that basal series reflect all current understanding of the reading process, for a gap exists between theory and practice. This gap, which Venezky calls the "La Brea tar pit of education," is sticky enough to "mire many well intentioned people" (1979, p. 279). Researchers generate ideas and plans, but often little comes from them (Singer, 1970). As Clifford has pointed out, research results "rarely changed educational practice directly, [and] when they have, generally several decades have passed" (cited in Venezky, 1986, p. 151).

The difficulty associated with translating research into practice is partially a result of the myriad of forces that are at work in schools. Schooling is a complex process that defies easy solutions. Discussing instructional change, Anderson, Evertson, and Brophy (1979, p. 220) note:

> Every day teachers must orchestrate a vast array of behavior meeting many different objectives within a formidable set of constraints imposed by the building, the clock and other human beings in the school environment. Teachers should not be expected to seize on advice that will cause additional demands on their time and energy unless they are given specific assistance in implementing it and a rationale that convinces them it's worth the trouble.

Basal series partially fill the gap between research and practice by translating research findings into instructional practices which meet the constraints under which teachers operate. Given the traditional gap between theory and practice, this is no small feat.

Basal series play a key role in reading instruction today, with an estimated 98% of U.S. teachers using such series (Flood and Lapp, 1986). Their popularity and importance can be attributed, in part, to the fact that such series come as a package designed to address a wide range of reading related skills from diagnosis to decoding and literary appreciation. Not only are instructional practices suggested, but opportunities are provided for guided practice within the text, as well as in workbooks and "skillpacs," supplementary materials Osborn (1984) views as essential for many readers.

Further, basal systems provide a management system for coordinating reading instruction. A scope and sequence of skills to be introduced is provided, and evaluation and diagnosis are facilitated via criterion referenced tests. The importance of this management function

cannot be overlooked. As Anderson, Evertson, and Brophy (1979) point out, good teachers are good managers of both the classroom and the reading lesson.

The majority of reading teachers do not have the time, energy, or expertise to develop the types of materials and activities required to meet the goals set by parents and legislators. Basal readers are a necessary tool for most teachers. As we will see in the next section, basals as a package act to translate research into practice.

HISTORICAL PERSPECTIVE

Basal series have to a large extent kept abreast, within a reasonable time frame, with changes in our understanding of reading and demands from the public and from educators. There is ample evidence that the content and instructional practices associated with reading materials have changed over time to accommodate prevailing views.

The religious content of such early U.S. texts as hornbooks and the *New England Primer* gave way to the more nationalistic and humanistic content of 19th century texts. "As church government gave way to civil government, and old country patterns of family and society changed, morality and good character gained equal footing with religion in reading texts" (Venezky, 1986, p. 136).

Content has continued to change during the 20th century. "Good literature" arrived on the scene in the early decades and as Venezky states, "this literary emphasis continues up to the present day, when real life and fantasy account for the majority of reading selections" (1986, p. 144). Content changes have continued with the inclusion of minorities, women, and the handicapped in reading selections.

Instructional practices have also changed over time under public and pedagogical pressure. An emphasis on rote memorization and oral reading gave way to trends toward silent reading in the 1920s. Programs in how "to break the code" have evolved into the skill management systems of today.

The same holds true in comprehension instruction. As late as the 1950s, research on comprehension processes was "so sparse that even the phrase 'reading comprehension' was seldom found" (Venezky, 1984, p. 13). But the last 20 years have seen an intense focus on the role of comprehension, which has spawned new and more effective comprehension techniques.

This historical development seems natural enough: Reading materials and techniques have changed as our understanding of the reading process has changed. In the best of all possible worlds, reading materials would incorporate current knowledge of the reading process. But to insist that basal series encompass *all* current conceptions of the reading process ignores the realities of the classroom and the ever changing state of understanding of the reading process.

Basal series over the years have moved to incorporate successful instructional techniques. The "model" lesson as presented in most basal series is one example. According to Beck and Block (1979), a typical basal lesson in the Ginn 720 series consists of 4 steps: (1) preparation for reading; (2) reading and discussing the lesson; (3) interrelated activities; and (4) developing reading skills. This includes the introduction of new sight words and setting a purpose for reading in step (1), teacher direction of student interaction in step (2), teacher presentation of decoding lessons and comprehension exercises in step (3), and independent work in step (4).

This model lesson has found support in the literature on comprehension, particularly in the area of prereading, or what Beck and Block call "preparation for reading." In a recent review of comprehension research, Tierney and Cunningham (1984, p. 610) tie basal lessons directly to effective techniques:

> Most reading lessons include a prereading activity which provides a bridge of sorts between a reader's knowledge base and the text. Most lessons used in conjunction with basal and content area textbooks consider this step a preparatory one in which purpose setting and concept development are primary goals.

Current understanding of the reading process has found its way into the comprehension instruction offered in basal series. Such changes reflect the symbiotic relationship between theory and practice and the role that basal series play in the process.

The implementation of successful instructional techniques into basal reading series also can be seen in the area of decoding. The early code emphasis in basals has found support in the literature. After reviewing existing studies of initial reading, Chall (1967, p. 83) concluded:

> Early stress on code learning . . . not only produces better word recognition and spelling, but also makes it easier for the child to eventually read with understanding—at least up to the fourth grade.

Ten years and many studies later Chall's position remained unchanged. In "The Great Debate Revisited" (1979, p. 33), she reinforced her initial position·

"Would my conclusion regarding the benefits of code emphasis be the same today—after ten years of research? I would tend to say yes, since I don't see any viable data to disconfirm it."

The importance of systematic instruction in decoding skills has also been stated quite empirically by Resnick (1979, p. 329):

> As a matter of routine practice, we need to include systematic code-oriented instruction in the primary grades, no matter what else is done. This is the only place in which we have any clear evidence for any particular practice. We cannot afford to ignore that evidence or the several instructional programs already in existence that do a good job teaching the code.

We must be very careful, particularly in the area of initial reading instruction, not to throw the baby out with the bath water when discussing the merits of basal series. Knowledge of the code is a critical feature of reading ability, and burning our basals may do more harm than good.

BASALS AND TEACHER TRAINING

But why, one may ask, are basal series so popular? It is my contention that basals serve an important function, one that is directly related to the scope of the management systems discussed above. Basal programs provide on the job training for teachers. Such programs are source books for reading instruction.

The popularity of such programs is in part due to our failure to provide adequate preservice training for teachers. As stated earlier, classroom management is a skill critical to teachers' success, but many teacher training programs, such as those in California, require only one read-

ing methods course. To expect teachers in training to develop the competencies necessary to direct growth in reading in one semester is overly optimistic. In the absence of adequate training, teachers will turn to where they can get the kind of help they need: basals.

Research by Bacharach and Alexander (1986) suggests that it is not the text which fails in instruction, but rather an inappropriate application of the texts. Bacharach and Alexander surveyed and observed 31 classroom teachers. Only half of them employed the basal's prereading questions and none employed the background knowledge information suggestions in the teacher's manual. Sound instructional activities are suggested but not employed. Why?

Take the plight of the first year teacher. I can tell you from experience that when faced with a seemingly endless supply of planning, assessment, and management issues, I opted for a system that, in effect, trained me to be a reading teacher. I stuck to the basal. There is truth to Osborn's comment that reading teachers' behavior "has been more affected by basal reading programs than by their professors" (1984, p. 53).

The state of preservice and inservice training is directly related to our current understanding of the reading process as well as our understanding of the broader context in which these skills develop. Basal series must be understood in this light. Realization of the realities of the classroom and an understanding of the ever changing nature of our conceptions of the reading process must be considered before criticizing basal reading series.

In conclusion, the calls for continued revisions of basal series are well founded. And, as history has suggested, basal series will change over time under public and pedagogical pressure. But, if we as a profession are concerned with the effective application of basal series, if we honestly desire to break the often irrational grip of basals over teachers, then we need to take a long hard look at teacher training. After reviewing the situation I must remain conservative: Don't throw the basals out with the bath water.

REFERENCES

Anderson, Linda M., Carolyn M. Evertson, and Jere E. Brophy. "An Experimental Study of Effective Teaching in First-Grade Reading Groups." *Elementary School Journal*, vol. 79, no. 4 (1979), pp. 193–223.

Bacharach, Nancy, and Patricia Alexander. "Basal Reading Manuals: What Do Teachers Think of Them and How Do They Use Them? *Reading Psychology*, vol. 7, no. 3 (1986), pp. 163–72.

Beck, Isabel L., and Karen K. Block. "An Analysis of Two Beginning Reading Programs: Some Facts and Opinions." In *Theory and Practice of Early Reading, Volume I*, edited by Lauren B. Resnick and Phyllis Weaver. Hillsdale, NJ: Lawrence Erlbaum, 1979.

Chall, Jeanne. *Learning to Read: The Great Debate.* New York, NY: McGraw-Hill, 1967.

Chall, Jeanne. "The Great Debate: Ten Years Later, with a Modest Proposal for Reading Stages." In *Theory and Practice of Early Reading, Volume I*, edited by Lauren B. Resnick and Phyllis Weaver. Hillsdale, NJ: Lawrence Erlbaum, 1979.

Flood, James, and Diane Lapp. "Types of Texts: The Match between What Students Read in Basals and What They Encounter in Tests." *Reading Research Quarterly*, vol. 21, no. 3 (1986), pp. 284–97.

Osborn, Jean. "The Purposes, Uses, and Contents of Workbooks and Some Guidelines for Publishers." In *Learning to Read in American Schools*, edited by Richard Anderson, Jean Osborn, and Robert J. Tierney. Hillsdale, NJ: Lawrence Erlbaum, 1984.

Resnick, Lauren B. "Theories and Prescriptions for Early Reading Instruction." In *Theory and Practice of Early Reading, Volume II*, edited by Lauren B. Resnick and Phyllis Weaver. Hillsdale, NJ: Lawrence Erlbaum, 1979.

Singer, Harry. "Research That Should Have Made a Difference." *Elementary English*, vol. 47 (January 1970), pp. 27–34.

Tierney, Robert J., and James Cunningham. "Research on Teaching Reading Comprehension." In *Handbook of Reading Research*, edited by P. David Pearson. New York, NY: Longman, 1984.

Venezky, Richard L. "Harmony and Cacophony from a Theory-Practice Relationship." In *Theory and Practice of Early Reading, Volume II*, edited by Lauren B. Resnick and Phyllis Weaver. Hillsdale, NJ: Lawrence Erlbaum, 1979.

Venezky, Richard L. "The History of Reading Research." In *Handbook of Reading Research*, edited by P. David Pearson. New York, NY: Longman, 1984.

Venezky, Richard L. "Steps Toward a Modern History of American Reading Instruction." In *Review of Research in Education*, edited by Ernst Rothkoph. Washington, DC: American Educational Research Association, 1986.

POSTSCRIPT

Should Whole-Language Replace Basal Readers?

While the arguments among the experts and professionals go on, many suggestions have emerged that provide guidance to parents regarding the encouragement of good reading habits and attitudes. These include reading to children at a very early age, attending story hours at local libraries, giving books as gifts, having quiet reading times for the whole family, subscribing to children's magazines, continuing the practice of reading to children after they have become proficient readers, and, at that point, allowing them to read to their parents. Such suggestions would seem to hold true regardless of the specific methodologies used in the schools.

The person studying this crucial issue will want to get a sampling of views on the matter. The March 1990 issue of *Educational Leadership* offers a variety of articles on the subject, including "On Teaching Reading: A Conversation with Ethna Reid," by Ron Brandt; "Implementing Whole Language: Bridging Children and Books," by Patricia A. Robbins; "Redefining Reading Comprehension," by Robert J. Tierney; and "Creating the Condition to Encourage Literate Thinking," by Gordon Wells. Another theme issue of *Educational Leadership* (March 1989) contains "Filling the Hole in Whole Language," by Carla R. Heymsfeld, and "Transforming Literacy Instruction," by Nancy Leavitt Shanklin and Lynn K. Rhodes, among others.

Other recommended sources are "Real Books for Real Readers for Real Purposes," by Jean Hudson, *Reading* (July 1988), and "Reading Achievement in the First Grade Classroom: A Comparison of Basal and Whole Language Approaches," by Kathy Holland and Lee Ellis Hall, *Reading Improvement* (Winter 1989). *Education Week* has also provided some interesting treatments of the issue recently in "From a 'Great Debate' to a Full-Scale War: Dispute Over Teaching Reading Heats Up," by Robert Rothman, in the March 21, 1990, edition, and "Weighing Claims of 'Phonics First' Advocates," by Connie Weaver, in the March 28, 1990, edition.

ISSUE 14

Should Literacy Be Based on Traditional Culture?

YES: E. D. Hirsch, Jr., from "Restoring Cultural Literacy in the Early Grades," *Educational Leadership* (December 1987/January 1988)

NO: Stephen Tchudi, from "Slogans Indeed: A Reply to Hirsch," *Educational Leadership* (December 1987/January 1988)

ISSUE SUMMARY

YES: Professor of English E. D. Hirsch, Jr., argues that educators need to re-examine slogans that undermine the teaching of traditional knowledge to young children.
NO: Stephen Tchudi, director of the Center for Literacy and Learning at Michigan State University, contends that cultural literacy cannot be prescribed, since it evolves from the complexities of children's experiences.

The recent focus on the lack of cultural literacy in the United States, as defined by E. D. Hirsch, Jr., in his book *Cultural Literacy* and by Allan Bloom in his popular book *The Closing of the American Mind* (1987), has renewed the blaze of controversy over the role a student's social experiences should play in shaping schools. Can there be a specific designation of the knowledge essential to the attainment of cultural understanding in a given society? When that society is multicultural, should so-called literacy be drawn exclusively from the dominant cultural source within that society? While Dewey (see Issue 1) advocated a flexible curriculum geared to personal interests and social problems, Hutchins identified the Great Books (of the Western world) as the key to cultural understanding and social functioning.

The subtitle of Allan Bloom's 1987 book is *How Higher Education Has Failed Democracy and Impoverished the Souls of Today's Students,* and it stirred fears in a manner similar to the earlier "Nation at Risk" document. Mortimer Adler's *Paideia Proposal,* William Bennett's *To Reclaim a Legacy,* Lynne Cheney's *American Memory,* Diane Ravitch and Chester Finn, Jr.'s *What Do Our 17-Year-Olds Know?* and Bennett's "James Madison" curricula are all 1980s documents that sounded alarms about the state of education in the United States and offered fairly consistent methods for redirecting educational efforts.

The pattern enunciated in these works centers on the internalization of cultural knowledge and on the study of original works drawn primarily from the United States' European heritage. Early and consistent exposure to the chronological development of that heritage through the public schools as well as the larger community are seen as vital elements in the "recovery" process.

A number of critics, however, are concerned about the almost total emphasis on a Eurocentric perspective. Molefi Kete Asante, for example, has written forcefully on his advocacy of "multicultural literacy," and Ira Shor's book *Culture Wars: School and Society in the Conservative Restoration, 1969–1984* (1987) claims that the underlying motivation of the movement is "to restore conservative themes and 'right words' that establish raw authority at the top while discrediting the [liberal] 1960s."

In the articles presented here, E. D. Hirsch, Jr., observes that the teaching of traditional knowledge through good literature has been severely undermined. He contends that the uniformity of literature textbooks that prevailed in decades past has evaporated under the influence of erroneous doctrines and slogans, which have come to dominate educational decisions. Everyone, he contends, must be able to participate in the national culture—the disadvantaged as well as the advantaged—and this requires uniform exposure to a common body of materials. In rebuttal, Stephen Tchudi warns that the *background* for cultural literacy of the sort Hirsch advocates is acquired variously and in complex ways by the young. Enculturation does not happen automatically, he feels, and it cannot be reduced to "the presentation of selected bits of 'traditional literate culture' in some prescribed order."

YES

E. D. Hirsch, Jr.

RESTORING CULTURAL LITERACY

In recent decades we have assumed that the early curriculum should be "child-centered" and "skill-centered." Yet there is a growing consensus among reading researchers that adequate literacy depends upon the specific information called "cultural literacy," and we should therefore begin to impart traditional literate culture to children at the earliest possible age.[1]

The need to begin such instruction early is based on technical as well as social considerations. From a purely technical standpoint, our children need traditional background information early to make sense of significant reading materials, and thus gain further information that enables them to make further progress in reading and learning. From a social standpoint, the need to start as early as possible is even more urgent. Young children from the middle class sometimes receive necessary literate information outside the school, but disadvantaged children rarely have access to literate background information outside the school.[2] Therefore, to change the cycle of illiteracy that debars disadvantaged children from high literacy, we need to impart enough literate information from preschool through third grade to ensure continued progress in literacy on the part of all our children.

EXAMINING THE EDUCATIONAL SLOGANS

Now that these basic truths are becoming widely known, it is time to question and qualify some educational slogans inconsistent with those truths that have actively hindered the teaching of literate information to young children. I do not suggest that the three slogans I shall examine constitute all the intellectual barriers to curriculum reform in the early grades (sheer inertia must never be underestimated). But the harmful slogans are powerful and widely spread. Calling them into doubt might help foster the urgently needed reform of giving young children early instruction in our traditional literate culture.

From E. D. Hirsch, Jr., "Restoring Cultural Literacy in the Early Grades," *Educational Leadership*, vol. 45, no. 4 (December 1987/January 1988). Copyright © 1987 by E. D. Hirsch, Jr. Reprinted by permission of the author.

1. *The home is more decisive for literacy than the school.* No one with common sense would doubt that a child whose parents actively encourage conscientious performance in school will do better, all things equal, than a child whose parents discourage academic performance. We know that many children are all too heavily influenced by the anti-academic values (usually defensive reactions) of their parents and peers. Every conscientious teacher, principal, and supervisor tries to counteract the anti-school ethic that is especially powerful and self-defeating among just those disadvantaged children who are most in need of a pro-school ethic. Although few of us in education have the time or opportunity to abolish the anti-school ethic in all its defensive manifestations, one good sign of the times is that we are getting help. Parents and the public at large have identified the problem, and are trying to help the schools combat it.

But quite apart from lamenting the negative influences of anti-academic attitudes, some educators have held a rather defeatist view about the possibility of breaking the illiteracy cycle. They accept as axiomatic the slogan that the educational and economic level of the home is more decisive for high literacy than the school can ever be, no matter how supportive the attitudes of the home. This defeatist attitude dates, of course, from the first Coleman report of 1966. Since that time, the slogan that the socioeconomic status of the home is inherently decisive for academic achievement has been part of the received wisdom of many specialists in education.[3]

The slogan is, of course, true as a description of educational outcomes under our current educational arrangements. Children from middle-class homes per-

form better on the whole than children from poor homes, no matter what schools they attend or what moral support they receive in the home. Viewed in broad, statistical terms, a child's socioeconomic status is at present the decisive factor in academic performance. But two inferences from the first Coleman report are open to serious criticism: first, the inference that the state of affairs described by the report is inherent and inevitable, and, second (a corollary of the first), that any attempt to reverse the sociological finding by specific school policies would be futile. These doleful inferences are used to support the claim that we can at best try to change the attitudes and actions of parents, but that nothing of consequence regarding the cycle of illiteracy will be accomplished by changing the policies of our already-beleaguered schools.

We must, of course, acknowledge that all attempts to reinforce children's education within the home are welcome. Parental help is useful not only for motivating students, but also for increasing their time-on-task and attitude to learning. My aim in criticizing the slogan of the decisiveness of the home is not to discourage vigorous appeals to parents to help, supervise and encourage their children's learning. My purpose, rather, is to insist that, despite the importance of the home, our schools can do a much better job of teaching literacy to all students, even without effective reinforcement from the home.

There is positive evidence, not considered by the first Coleman report, that under a different curriculum our schools can make children acceptably literate even when they come from illiterate homes. The positive evidence is just as compelling as the negative evidence cited in the report. In fact, the positive evidence is more compelling, because it takes into account a larger number of instances and a greater amount of experimental data. I mean by this the historical record.

In the later nineteenth and early twentieth century, American schools succeeded in creating a literate middle class by teaching children of illiterate parents. One factor in their success, lacking in our schools today, was the use of a traditional literate curriculum. Ruth Elson has demonstrated the uniformity of American textbooks in the 19th century, and to her study may now be added Kathryn Neeley's examination of school readers between the 1840s and the 1940s.[4] Both studies find a consistent tendency in earlier schoolbooks to teach common, traditional materials. The commonalty of our elementary curriculum in the early twentieth century gave students from literate and illiterate families alike a common foundation in the literate culture, which, as I show in *Cultural Literacy*, is a prerequisite to mature literacy.

Looking outside the United States and taking a still broader historical view of home influence produces evidence that is even more decisive. In the eighteenth century, the established of wide-scale national literacy in Britain, France, and Germany (and every other literate country) was first accomplished through the school, not through the home.[5] In Perpignan, for example, literacy in the French language was achieved by schools that taught children who heard and spoke no French in their homes. Indeed, their Catalan-speaking parents were not literate in any language, and were in fact *opposed* to their children's learning French in school.

The only way national literacy could have been achieved in such large multilinguistic nations as France and Great Britain was through the deliberate agency of a national school system that conveyed a common core of literate culture. Parents in Wales, for example, did not always approve of or cooperate with schools that taught English to their children. Nonetheless, Welsh schools graduated pupils who were literate in English language and culture. The cooperation of parents was certainly not available in the schools of Brittany, where Breton-speaking parents opposed the teaching of French. But that did not prevent the schools of Brittany from producing pupils who were literate in French language and culture. In short, the schools can impart high literacy even under severe handicaps, if they do so by teaching not only the mechanical skills of decoding but also the literate national culture. Ernest Gellner has pointed out that all literate national cultures in the modern world have been school-transmitted cultures rather than home-transmitted cultures, and has explained in detail why the pattern has necessarily been followed in every modern nation.[6]

Why, then, did we accept the slogan that the socioeconomic status of the home is more decisive than the policies of the school in achieving mature literacy? What lies behind the well-documented findings of the first Coleman report?

The best explanation I can devise is this: Up to about 1945 in many schools (give or take a decade to allow for the slowness of curricular change), literacy *had* been effectively taught to disadvantaged students under a largely traditional curriculum. It was not until the 1940s that older generations of teachers and administrators had retired in large numbers and were replaced by disciples of Dewey and Kilpatrick who imposed the latest child- and skill-centered textbooks. Up to the 1940s or so, many of our schools were still able to graduate highly literate students who had come from illiterate homes. They effected this transformation through a traditional curriculum both for native black children as well as for children from immigrant European families.

But by the 1940s, with the newer theories ever more dominant in teachers, administrators, and textbooks, our public schools were turning slowly and overwhelmingly to less traditional, more up-to-date, child-centered materials that gradually ceased to transmit our traditional literate culture. This curricular change constituted a particularly catastrophic turn for the early grades. The effects of the change were not immediately noticed, because the earlier curriculum had already created a large number of literate homes that continued to supply their children with the traditional literate information that had disappeared from the schools.

Thus the new curriculum was not at first disabling for those children who were lucky enough to come from highly literate homes, where they received traditional (originally school-transmitted) literate culture. But the new curriculum did cease to supply literate background information to children from illiterate homes, and consequently those unfortunates did not receive the needed information from any source. This hypothesis probably explains why the Coleman report of 1966 turned out to be inconsistent with the larger historical record. Unhappily, this hypothesis about the effects of the new curriculum may also explain why our schools in the past four decades have done little to improve the educational and economic status of children from illiterate homes.

The practical implication of these historical observations, when coupled with the data from reading research, is to suggest that we should once again teach all of our children the elements of our traditional literate culture, starting at an early age. That means, for instance, teaching Mother Goose at school, instead of assuming that Mother Goose rhymes might bore children who have already heard them. The argument about boredom has an easy answer; if parents don't want their children to be bored, and if they know that our schools are going to teach Mother Goose, they can read their kids *Pat the Bunny* or *The Cat in the Hat* or whatever else they choose, with full confidence that "Jack and Jill" are on the way.

In sum, we cannot validly generalize the findings of the Coleman report of 1966. We cannot justifiably continue to repeat the easy slogan that the home is the fundamental determinant of literacy. Our children are not trapped in a cycle of sociological determinism. As late as the 1930s and 1940s our schools were our chief, and at times our only conveyors of our literate traditions. History and common sense suggest that our schools can successfully resume that primary responsibility with better results than ever before. The home should, of course, foster a pro-school ethic, and should, where possible, enhance, enlarge, and encourage the teaching of our literate traditions. But it is our schools which must make sure that our literate traditions are successfully conveyed to every child from every sort of home.

2. *Schools should stress general skills and broad understanding, not mere facts.* Along with the new child- and skill-centered curriculum went an antipathy to "mere facts." The phrases "rote-learning" and "piling up of facts" are still used today as scapegoat terms against a traditional education that has not in fact existed in our public schools for several decades. In the 1920s such terms of abuse radiated from lectures at Teachers College, Columbia, and slowly spread to schools of education throughout the nation.[7] You will immediately recognize that these scapegoat terms still function as banner slogans, even though the education they attack has long since vanished from the scene. On the other hand, the typical terms of approval in educational writing since the '20s continue to be such phrases as "relevant materials" that are "meaningful to the child," and that inculcate "higher-order skills."

Since we now know that, in order to become literate, young children must gain a store of traditional information at an early age, it is time to reconsider the pejorative use of phrases like "memorization," (better to say "learning by heart") and "piling up of facts" as though they were insult terms. Many "higher-order skills" of literacy are gained *only* by piling up information. No study of language acquisition, for instance, has challenged the commonsense observation that children learn the names of objects by repeatedly being told those names until they remember them.[8] Thus, at the very roots of language acquisition we find memorization and the piling up of facts. Later on, in earliest training, children must learn the alphabet by heart. I cannot conceive how a child could acquire the alphabet other than by memorization and the piling up of facts. The

same applies to the multiplication table, the days of the week, and the months of the year. There's no other way of acquiring those skills.

Of course everybody knows these things. I do not wish to make the shibboleths of modern educational theory seem totally without merit. My point is subtler and gentler. Only recently have we come to understand that "Jack and Jill" and "George Washington" belong to an alphabet that must be learned by heart, and which is no less essential to higher-order literacy skills than the alphabet itself. Certain linguistically based concepts (researchers call them "schemata") belong to the very ABCs of literacy.[9] The methods by which children learn these higher-order ABCs can be exciting and fun, or they can be deadening and painful. Good teachers always try to choose the pleasant over the painful, if only because the pleasant is more effective. But learning the higher-order ABCs, like learning the alphabet itself, does require learning by heart and piling up information.

The negative connotations of terms like "mere facts" and "memorization" arise from the theory that acquiring facts is inferior to "meaningful" learning experiences that cause children to take interest in and understand the significance of what they are being taught. It is assumed that the piling up of information cannot be meaningful, or interesting, or motivational to children. Given such alternatives, who would choose to be meaningless and dull? To reinforce this anti-fact, anti-memorization view, psychology since the time of Herbart has instructed us that the only materials that are meaningful to children are those that resonate with their own imaginations and experiences. Hence, the humane principle of meaningful, nonrote instruction has been reinforced by the scientific principle that curricular materials should connect directly with the experiences of young children.

But expert teaching and well-conceived texts, not modernity of content, are the bridges of relevance that connect reading materials with a child's experience. The life experiences of children who enter American classrooms are much too varied to form a definite content basis for child-centered materials. Moreover, most of the literate culture that children will need for later life consists of traditional, intergenerational materials. Consequently, their literacy is more effectively enhanced when they are successfully taught durable, traditional subjects like Ulysses and the Cyclops than when they are taught ephemera like Dick and Jane at the Supermarket.

It's quite doubtful that "mere facts" are really meaningless to young children, any more than they are to adults. We should unblinkingly face the truth that many of the facts we adults know are not perfectly interconnected in our minds. Meaningfulness does not require complete clarity and coherence, or even powerful emotion. E. B. White once said that he learned how to write just as he learned how to drive, without understanding what went on under the hood. How many adults can explain coherently what happens when they switch on a TV set? Most of us just know the less-than-coherent facts about TV: the picture comes on when we punch the power switch, it changes when we change the channel switch, and it goes off when we punch the power switch again. In the technological era, many of us still live in the "magic years"; things happen for us as they happen for children in ways that we do not fully understand and cannot accurately explain.

Take another example. The names that we give to objects and concepts rarely have any coherent logic to them. It is the nature of language to be arbitrary. *Dog* has no more inherent rightness or logical aptness than *chien* or *Hund*. We have just gotten used to the words. This is as true for adults as for children. In short, the world of adults, like that of children, is at least partly incoherent and arbitrary. The child's world is less coherent and certainly less accurate than our own, but the differences are of degree, not kind. Perhaps many differences between children and adults have been, as Mark Twain said of reports of his death, greatly exaggerated.

Much of the essential information that we adults need can be gained only by being "piled up" as schemata in our memories. If parents and teachers waited until children could adequately understand the alphabet, they would wait until the first year of a doctoral program in linguistics. If they waited until children could adequately understand the first line of "My country, 'tis of thee," they would wait until tenth grade before divulging the words of the song. (Does anyone know an elementary school child who can explain the linguistic meaning of the words "My country, 'tis of thee"? For that matter, does anyone believe that a first-grader can understand "The Star-Spangled Banner," whose readability score probably ranks at the eleventh- or twelfth-grade level? Shall we therefore defer teaching "The Star-Spangled Banner" until twelfth grade?)

Even the most ardent proponents of "meaningful" instruction and "higher-order skills acquisition" must accept such inconsistencies when slogans about developmental learning readiness are applied to the early grades. I don't know anyone who is so opposed to learning by heart as to deplore the teaching of the alphabet, or "The Star-Spangled Banner," or "America." But if we acquiesce in accepting *those* incompletely understood elements into the curriculum, why should we exclude other "mere facts" that are equally useful to literacy? Answer: We should *not* exclude those traditional facts, but recognize that young children need many, many items of traditional information that are no less necessary to literacy than the alphabet and "The Star-Spangled Banner."

Another grave weakness in the theory that children are interested only in immediately meaningful, child-centered materials is that young children take great joy in learning vaguely understood information that will only later be fully meaningful to them. Although many of the facts that children need to learn are meaningless to them in a linguistic sense, they are nonetheless highly meaningful to them in a social sense. Children give their own context to such items, and correctly believe them to belong to the fabric of the adult community they wish to join. Children thrive only as members of a community. From the cradle, they take to language and culture like ducks to water. They come into the world with an appetite for acculturation. It is impractical, indeed absurd, to thwart that *natural* appetite for culture on the basis of an abstract theory about learning readiness. Nothing better expresses the absurdity than Dewey's deploring the "facility" with which young children absorb the cultural facts we pile upon them, or his approval of Rousseau's fatuous remark that "the apparent ease with which children learn is their ruin."

3. *The optimal contents of a language arts curriculum can be determined on scientific principles.* This doctrine about the early curriculum is less a slogan than an unexamined assumption. Science is a neutral servant of our educational purposes. Science represents the reality principle in education. It does not set our goals; it serves them. It helps define their inherent limits, and indicates the best avenues for us to follow in order to achieve them. Any more substantial claim for the role of science in education is a misleading claim.

Suppose, for example, that our primary goal is to achieve high literacy for all children. How can science guide us in choosing the *specific* materials to reach that goal? One currently used, so-called "scientific" approach is to use a quantitatively determined first-grade vocabulary for first grade, a second-grade vocabulary for second grade, and so on. And how does science yield up these graded vocabularies? By word frequency studies. The most frequent words should be taught first, the next frequent next, and so on.

There are serious difficulties hidden under this apparently neutral, apparently scientific approach. Assuming that makers of children's texts use common sense, as McGuffey did long before there were any word frequency studies, they wouldn't have to take special measures to supply young children with the most frequent words of English. They could assume that children would encounter those primary words with approximately the standard frequency in *any* reasonably chosen reading materials. They could rely on the fact that any diverse sampling of texts in a language will produce a similar list of its most frequent words. For instance, the Francis-Kucera frequency list, taken from the huge Brown University corpus consisting of several million words, puts the word *from* in position 26.[10] The Carroll-Davies-Richman (CDR) frequency list, taken from a corpus of elementary and secondary school materials, puts the word *from* in position 23.[11] It is safe to assume that *any* intelligently chosen materials for the early grades will provide automatic reinforcement of the most frequent words of the English language.

An even stronger reason for not depending on word frequencies to determine suitable elementary reading materials is that after a certain point—somewhere after the top few thousand words—word frequencies depend entirely on the particular corpus of texts chosen to determine them. But what is the right corpus for the early grades? No one can answer that question on neutral scientific grounds. There is no purely objective, scientific way of choosing the right corpus for determining the correct grade-level of words. Consider, for example, some implications for choosing proper names in texts for early grades by means of the Carroll-Davies-Richman frequency list. On the basis of the most frequent words from 1 to 10,000, the corpus tells us that early texts should contain:

- The Alamo *but not* The Iliad
- Jack and Jill *but not* Cinderella
- Blake *but not* Milton
- Helen Keller *but not* Joan of Arc
- Moss *but not* Jesus
- Galileo *but not* Copernicus
- John Glenn *but not* Charles Lindbergh
- Louis Pasteur *but not* Marie Curie
- Scrooge *but not* Dickens
- Edison *but not* Locke
- Einstein *but not* Socrates
- Hitler *but not* Churchill

This list on its face suggests the inappropriateness of using word frequency as a "scientific" basis for the content of the language arts curriculum. In fact, such a use of word frequency is quite *unscientific* when we simply take the existing word frequencies that are found in current school materials as "objective" guides for determining the proper frequencies for new school materials.

Understanding this, suppose we did agree upon an appropriate corpus for determining grade-by-grade vocabulary according to word frequency. One characteristic of such a corpus would be that it must be constantly revised to reflect changes in the literate culture. Otherwise, the frequency analysis might become quite misleading. Consider this example. The biggest analyzed corpus of English that we have is the one at Brown University, compiled by Francis and Kucera. This corpus not only takes materials from a deliberately indiscriminate sampling of genres, it also remains stuck in the year 1961. Thus, according to the frequencies of the Brown corpus, the first surname that our children should learn after Washington is Khrushchev.

What inference should we draw from this interesting fact? Not, of course, that first-graders should be taught about Nikita Khrushchev before they are taught about Abraham Lincoln. Rather, we should draw the inference that it is all too easy to misapply scientific data. Consider, by contrast, the *scientific* virtues of simply asking a group of literate adults to choose the words and concepts that are most important for children to know to become literate adults. These people will do a much better job than either the Brown or the CDR frequency lists, in part because the corpus of texts they have read will be many, many times bigger than even the huge Brown corpus, and in part because their sense of the most appropriate words will be constantly adjusting itself to significant cultural change. Consequently, their judgments will be far less likely to exhibit the Khrushchev effect. This advantage alone will make their judgments more, not less, scientific than the current word frequency approach. Of course, these observations imply no criticism of the valuable work of Carroll, Davies, and Richman, Francis, and Kucera, but are directed toward the unsound, uncritical use of quantitative research.

Other examples of pseudoscience in education could teach us the same moral: there can be no substitute for informed judgments by educated adults regarding the most important contents to be taught to children. If we as a nation decide that we want our children to possess mature literacy, there is no substitute for asking literate persons collectively to decide upon the contents required for mature literacy. After we make that determination, we need to develop an effective sequence of those core contents and effectively present them during the 13 years of schooling. Science can surely help us accomplish those jobs, but science alone is not in a position to tell us which words, concepts, and facts we need to teach.

CHANGING A LOSING GAME

In criticizing certain slogans and assumptions that are current among some educators, my purpose has, of course, been a constructive one. I take no pleasure in showing prized educational doctrines to be half-truths. Rather, I have tried to focus on just those doctrines,

slogans, and assumptions that have actively impeded the teaching of traditional literate information to young children. Only by imparting that information early can we achieve higher literacy and greater social justice. Any half-truth or slogan, no matter how dearly held, that stands in the way of that aim should be ruthlessly cast aside. Our children are more important than our theories.

We have given our theories a reasonable chance during the past four decades, and in light of the current ignorance explosion among young people, our results do not tend to confirm our theories. Even those educators who do not agree with my specific proposals for higher national literacy may nonetheless readily agree with the great tennis player Bill Tilden, whose immortal strategic advice holds for educational policy just as well as for tennis matches: "Always change a losing game."

NOTES

1. R. C. Anderson, *Becoming a Nation of Readers* (Washington, D.C.: U.S. Department of Education, 1985).
2. E. D. Hirsch, Jr., *Cultural Literacy: What Every American Needs to Know* (Boston: Houghton Mifflin, 1987).
3. James S. Coleman et al., *Equality in Educational Opportunity* (Washington, D.C.: Government Printing Office, 1966).
4. Ruth Miller Elsen, *Guardians of Tradition: American Schoolbooks of the Nineteenth Century* (Lincoln: University of Nebraska Press, 1964). Kathryn Neeley, "From Tradition to Fragmentation: American College Readers from 1840 to 1980" (unpublished paper).
5. François Furet and Jacques Ozouf, *Reading and Writing: Literacy in France from Calvin to Jules Ferry* (Cambridge: Cambridge University Press, 1982).
6. Ernest Gellner, *Nations and Nationalism* (Ithaca, N.Y.: Cornell University Press, 1983).
7. L. A. Cremin, *The Transformation of the School: Progressivism in American Education, 1876-1957* (New York: Knopf, 1964).

8. Roger Brown, *A First Language: The Early States* (Cambridge: Harvard University Press, 1973).

9. See, for example, Rand J. Spiro, "Constructive Processes in Prose Comprehension and Recall," in Rand J. Spiro et al., *Theoretical Issues in Reading Comprehension* (Hillsdale, N.J.: Erlbaum Associates, 1980).

10. W. N. Francis and Henry Kucera, *Frequency Analysis of English Usage: Lexicon and Grammar* (Boston: Houghton Mifflin, 1982).

11. John B. Carroll, Peter Davies, and Barry Richman, *Word Frequency Book* (Boston: Houghton Mifflin, 1971).

NO

Stephen Tchudi

SLOGANS INDEED

Professor Hirsch aroused my suspicions in the opening line of his article by employing that all-inclusive pronoun *we* to assert " . . . we have assumed that the early curriculum should be 'child centered' and 'skill centered.' " Although I am a firm believer in children and skills, I don't like to be taken for granted as a reader and included in propositions without my assent. Thus I looked closely at the pattern of argument Professor Hirsch used to attack the ways in which "we" are alleged to have accepted three slogans and with apparent thoughtlessness implemented them in "our" schools.

Professor Hirsch's rhetoric consists of stating three "slogans"; attributing them broadly to a variety of educators, most of them said to be "disciples" of Dewey and Kilpatrick; then arguing that the slogans are half-truths that need to be overturned. The slogans were phrased in his own language in the first place, in the rhetorical strategy of the "straw man," an argument created for the very purpose of being knocked down. I found his slogans to be half-truths in quite another sense: they are exaggerations and distortions based on a selective presentation of educational history and research. Having knocked the stuffings out of them, Professor Hirsch then describes his own concept of "cultural literacy" and argues for its centrality in the future of education.

I quite agree with Professor Hirsch that "any half-truth or slogan, no matter how dearly held, that stands in the way of [achieving higher literacy and greater social justice] should be ruthlessly cast aside." However, I must include some of Professor Hirsch's statements about cultural literacy among those which need to be cast aside, or at least carefully rethought.

I don't want to dismiss his essay as "mere rhetoric." But neither am I prepared to argue for the validity of the three slogans, particularly since they are coinings of Professor Hirsch's realm and reality, not necessarily "ours." Thus, I will identify some key issues in teaching culture and literacy that I hope the reader will find more fully dimensional than his view of cultural literacy, which seems to me a form of cultural indoctrination rather than genuine education.

From Stephen Tchudi, "Slogans Indeed: A Reply to Hirsch," *Educational Leadership*, vol. 45, no. 4 (December 1987/January 1988). Copyright © 1987 by the Association for Supervision and Curriculum Development. Reprinted by permission. All rights reserved.

BACKGROUND FOR LITERACY

On the matter of home versus school learning, for example, he alludes to a "recent consensus among reading researchers that adequate literacy depends upon the specific information called 'cultural literacy.' " This assertion simply is not accurate. To the extent that a consensus exists among reading researchers, it does *not* include a mandate to "impart traditional literate culture to children at the earliest possible age." A considerable amount of reading research *does* emphasize the informational background of the reader, but "background" includes not only factual information, but also the experiences, attitudes, and values the reader brings to a text.[1]

Reading is much more than simply comprehending words on a page; it is an active process of "meaning making," of synthesizing diverse ideas and experiences and meshing them with a decodable text. Although what Professor Hirsch calls "traditional literate culture" may be a part of that background, it is by no means the most critical aspect of it. Home values and home learning have a powerful effect on literacy, as do experiences inside and outside the school. Most critically, the stream of reading research he cites states emphatically that background information is *not* something that should be force-fed to inexperienced readers. Such a conclusion is not "defeatist"; it simply recognizes that background for literacy is acquired in complex ways.

NO GOLDEN AGE OF LITERACY

Professor Hirsch uses the example of history to support his argument that school matters; but his reading of history is highly selective, once again leading him to declare a mandate for obligatory cultural literacy where none exists. He presents the image of a golden era of schooling in the late nineteenth and early twentieth centuries, when youngsters studied textbooks with common content and supposedly mastered a common literate culture. Yet Professor Hirsch seems to take the existence of texts themselves as evidence that youngsters actually *learned* the material in them (an error few present-day teachers and administrators are likely to make). Further, he ignores historical studies that show there was at least as much criticism then as now that students don't know the materials of "traditional literate culture."[2]

For example, the push toward college entrance examinations in the late nineteenth century was based on the fears of college professors that, despite the textbooks commonly used in schools, from the McGuffeys on up, children were not receiving "traditional literate culture." In other words, although the textbooks had some common elements (they were, on the whole, less unified than Professor Hirsch implies), there is little concrete evidence that children were absorbing the prescribed culture.

When one compares the differences between democratic education in the 1980s with that of the 1890s or 1920s, particularly with differences in student bodies, retention rates, and the sociopolitical purposes of education, it becomes increasingly clear that there never was a golden age of literacy. Further, there is little reason to believe that a prescribed curriculum of cultural nuggets will bring about that ideal.[3] One can accuse the children of being obstinate, boneheaded, and illiterate, but a more sensible approach might be to ask why cultural indoctrination has so consistently failed over the years.

THE ROLE OF CONTEXT

A partial answer may be found in the reading research Professor Hirsch cites so selectively. Many researchers recognize that facts and information are required as background to read successfully, but they are also aware of the role of *context* in learning. Information is retained only when the child can, implicitly or explicitly, see some purpose to it and place it in a context of previous learning and experience.

Such a view is not mindlessly "child centered" and should not be equated with the false notion of "relevance," which means "anything that sells or has facile, temporary appeal." Nor does it require discarding the classics in favor of TV culture or pop literature. However, schooling needs to be much more than "piling on of facts." A sensitive "piling on" of *experiences*, challenging children's powers of imagination and inquiry, may well be in order, for it is through assimilated, evaluated experience (as John Dewey observed) that facts as well as concepts, values, and even critical thinking skills are mastered.

Professor Hirsch is correct when he argues that "children thrive only as members of a community. From the cradle, they take to language and culture like ducks to water. They come into the world with an appetite for acculturation." Yet he seems to ignore the significance of this assertion. Youngsters with an appetite for learning don't need to be force-fed "traditional literate culture." Mother Goose will survive because she speaks to perennial childhood (and adult) concerns through engaging, enjoyable yarns, not because she is an obligatory part of the curriculum.

EXPERIENCE VERSUS INDOCTRINATION

How, then, are books to be selected? Professor Hirsch argues against "scientific principles" in curriculum design, but he also trivializes his discussion by reducing it to the word lists used in the preparation of basals. He's right to question the pseudoscience of the basals,[4] but his scheme of "asking literate persons collectively to decide upon the contents that are required for mature literacy" presents no real solution and drifts perilously close to pseudoscience itself. In the first place, an honest scientific sampling of what literate adults know and read would largely duplicate the present culture, not lead back to "traditional literate background." I suppose if one fudged the definition of "literate" to exclude certain elements of mass culture, one could get closer to that tradition. Still, even that is beside the point: over the years we've had plenty of committees prescribing curriculums, including cultural contents, and children have simply not learned from these curriculums to anyone's great satisfaction.[5]

Language and acculturation don't happen automatically, but *naturally*, through extensive reading, writing, speaking, listening, thinking, and experiencing. Knowledgeable, concerned adults at home and school can consciously broaden the range of youngsters' experiences with culture and language, but they must not reduce enculturation to the presentation of selected bits of "traditional literate culture" in prescribed order.

MOVING BEYOND SLOGANS

I agree that it's a good idea to change a losing game. However, Professor Hirsch doesn't offer us a new game; he simply argues for a variation of the old one, a game that has never been played successfully. To design a new game, educators, and the public will need to move beyond slogans and straw men. They will need to acknowledge that cultural literacy extends far beyond what "literate persons collectively" declare it to be. Cultural literacy is a process of participating fully and actively in society, a product of home and schooling, and above all of living in society. It is not something that will ever be mastered by "piling up facts" independently of the child's need to participate in that culture.

NOTES

1. Two recent comprehensive reviews of this research are Anne M. Bussis, "Burn It At the Casket: Research, Reading Instruction, and Children's Learning of the First R," *Phi Delta Kappan* (December 1982): 237–241; and Wayne Sawyer, "Literature and Literacy: A Review of Research," *Language Arts* 64 (January 1987): 33–39.

2. See Arthur Applebee, *Tradition and Reform in the Teaching of English* (Urbana, Ill.: National Council of Teachers of English, 1974); and David England and Stephen Judy, eds., "An Historical Primer on the Teaching of English," *The English Journal* 68 (April 1979).

3. For a detailed examination of the myth of a golden age of literacy, see Harvey Daniels, *Famous Last Words* (Carbondale, Ill.: Southern Illinois University Press, 1983) or my *ABCs of Literacy* (New York: Oxford University Press, 1980). Lawrence Cremin's *The Transformation of the Schools: Progressivism in American Education*, cited by Professor Hirsch, also clearly documents the failures of traditional nineteenth-century education, particularly when directed toward children who were not members of the middle classes.

4. A particularly strong discussion of the flaws in basal readers can be found in Kenneth S. Goodman (for the Reading Commission of the National Council of Teachers of English), "Basal Readers: A Call for Action," *Language Arts* 63 (April 1986): 358–363.

5. I discuss the dangers of what I call the "adult standards approach," which presents mature adult knowledge as the model for the in-process acquisition of thinking, knowledge, and language by young people, in *Explorations in the Teaching of English*, Chapter 2, "Language, Experience, and the Teaching of English" (New York: Harper and Row, 1980).

POSTSCRIPT

Should Literacy Be Based on Traditional Culture?

In the *Educational Leadership* issue from which the selections for this debate were taken, the dialogue continues with further commentary from the authors and reactions from other writers. The central point that Hirsch makes in the continuation is that the conservative curriculum content, which he and other like-minded individuals espouse, is actually socially progressive. This is a crucial point to consider. Just as Mortimer Adler contends that democracy depends on our ability to bring traditional content and the ways of thinking needed to understand that content to *all* of the people, so Hirsch and Bennett and others stress the egalitarian nature of the common curriculum.

The issue is complex and difficult to resolve. For further exploration, you may want to consult the following sources: the December 1987 issue of *Language Arts*; Margaret Bedrosian's "Multi-Ethnic Literature: Mining the Diversity," *Journal of Ethnic Studies* (Fall 1987); Hirsch's more detailed examination of concrete proposals for change in "Cultural Literacy: Let's Get Specific," *NEA Today* (January 1988); and Janet K. Swaffar's "Reading and Cultural Literacy," *Journal of General Education* (vol. 38, no. 2, 1986).

A recent yearbook of the National Society for the Study of Education (NSSE), edited by Ian Westbury and Alan C. Purves, is entitled *Cultural Literacy and the Idea of General Education* (1988). It is related to an earlier NSSE effort edited by Benjamin Ladner, *The Humanities in Precollegiate Education* (1984), which contains excellent articles by John J. McDermott ("Cultural Literacy: Time for a New Curriculum") and Benjamin DeMott ("The Humanities and the Summoning Reader"). While both volumes contain constructive thinking on the possibilities of improvement, the 1988 collection ends on a pessimistic note. In the concluding article, "The Fortress Monastery: The Future of the Common Core," Mark Holmes states: "Perhaps the public school system will be held together by some ramshackle coalition of interests—of educators, of government, of the ABCs. Perhaps it will be gradually replaced by private and semi-private (for example, religious) alternatives. Either way a universal, common core much beyond the ABCs seems unlikely."

In 1989 Lynne Cheney, head of the National Endowment for the Humanities, kept the controversy alive in *50 Hours: A Core Curriculum for College Students.* Also, the March 1989 issue of *The Clearing House* was devoted to the topic of cultural literacy.

ISSUE 15

Is Measurement-Driven Instruction Desirable?

YES: W. James Popham, from "The Merits of Measurement-Driven Instruction," *Phi Delta Kappan* (May 1987)

NO: Gerald W. Bracey, from "Measurement-Driven Instruction: Catchy Phrase, Dangerous Practice," *Phi Delta Kappan* (May 1987)

ISSUE SUMMARY

YES: Professor of education W. James Popham portrays measurement-driven instruction as the most cost-effective way to improve the quality of public education.

NO: Gerald W. Bracey, director of research and evaluation for public schools in Cherry Creek, Colorado, sees fragmentation, trivialization, and curricular narrowing as the true costs of this methodological approach.

Permeating almost all segments of the school curriculum in the 1990s is an emphasis on measurable objectives and the standardized testing of achievement, particularly in the assessment of so-called minimum competencies. Reliance on test results to chart learner progress has always been part of the process of schooling, but many teachers and parents feel that the current "mania" is having negative effects.

Mental measurement and scientifically grounded assessment instruments date back to the beginnings of the twentieth century as part of a general movement to devise a "science of education." John Dewey, for one, was skeptical about the claims of measurement advocates, chiding them with a remembrance of pig-weighing on his grandfather's Vermont farm, wherein a pig and a pile of rocks were perfectly balanced at opposite ends of a board, after which grandpa would guess the weight of the rocks. Somewhat similarly, the current dispute concerns whether the art of teaching and the art of learning can be fairly assessed by the science of testing.

W. James Popham, an advocate of testing in general and measurement-driven instruction in particular, contends that high-quality testing programs are essential to the survival of public schooling. The taxpaying public has exerted great pressure for more concrete and reliable evidence of school performance in light of what is seen as a decline in standards and an increase in functional illiteracy.

Opponents raise questions about the quality and fairness of tests and about the effects of test result competition on both students and teachers. Banesh Hoffman's 1962 book *The Tyranny of Testing* posed some of these issues, and they are still under discussion today. Andrew J. Strenio, in his book *The Testing Trap* (1981), attacked the meritocratic competitiveness of most testing programs, the perpetuation of the threat of failure, the curricular manipulation open to the test-construction business, the unfairness of total-school evaluation on the basis of student test performance, the distortion of the teaching process, and, worst of all, the resultant "branding" of children.

On the current scene, state legislatures and state education authorities are wielding increased power to bring about improvements by mandating standardized achievement tests and curricular and methodological changes geared to bolstering scores. Former school superintendent Larry Cuban contends that these strategies *will* bring about higher test scores and *will* affect the way teachers teach, but that they will also cause teachers to be torn between meeting bureaucratic requirements and meeting the diverse needs of their students.

The latest manifestations of the testing controversy are discussed in the following selections. W. James Popham presents the case for effective instruction geared to well-constructed criterion-referenced tests and deals with predominant points of criticism. Gerald W. Bracey counters that rising test scores are not an adequate index of the efficacy of measurement-driven instruction and are not worth the tribulations visited upon teachers and students in the name of efficiency and accountability.

YES

W. James Popham

THE MERITS OF
MEASUREMENT-DRIVEN INSTRUCTION

If properly conceived and implemented, measurement-driven instruction currently constitutes the most cost-effective way of improving the quality of public education in the United States. That's a pretty hefty claim. Let's see if the evidence supports it.

Of course, other effective ways of boosting the quality of public schooling exist. For example, if we were able to replace mediocre instructional materials with more potent, empirically proven alternatives, then pupils would surely benefit. Similarily, if we were to infuse into our current teaching force a host of well-paid, highly skilled teachers, we could surely expect major educational dividends.

But such strategies, though they are surely *effective,* are very costly. Because measurement-driven instruction (MDI) is an effective improvement strategy that is markedly less expensive, it is a far more cost-effective strategy for improving the quality of public schooling. It is a strategy for instructional improvement that American educators should consider seriously.

MDI DEFINED

Before I consider the arguments and evidence in favor of measurement-driven instruction, let me define some terms and set the stage. Starting with definitions, *measurement-driven instruction* occurs when a high-stakes test of educational achievement, because of the important contingencies associated with the student's performance, influences the instructional program that prepares students for the test. There are two major types of high-stakes tests. One category consists of examinations that are associated with important consequences for examinees. Tests of this sort include those that qualify students for promotion to the next grade or for receipt of a high school diploma. The second type of high-stakes test consists of examinations whose scores are seen as reflections of instructional quality. Such tests include the many statewide achievement tests whose results are reported by local newspapers on a school-by-school or district-by-district basis.

Few educators would dispute the claim that these sorts of high-stakes tests markedly influence the nature of instructional programs. Whether they are concerned about their own self-esteem or their students' well-being, teachers clearly want students to perform well on such tests. Accordingly, teachers tend to focus a significant portion of their instructional activities on the knowledge and skills assessed by such tests. A high-stakes test of educational achievement, then, serves as a powerful *curricular magnet*. Those who deny the instructional influence of high-stakes tests have not spent much time in public school classrooms recently.

Although with less fanfare than during the late Seventies, when many states instituted high school graduation tests, high-stakes educational tests continue to be introduced. Every month or so we hear of another high-stakes test being established. Some of the most recently established high-stakes tests are examinations that prospective teachers must pass in order to be certified. Student assessment programs in Texas and California are being expanded to include more grade levels, and in more and more states—South Carolina and Texas, for example—tests are being used as requirements for high school graduation.

DIMENSIONS OF QUALITY

As I said above, MDI can be a potent force for educational improvement if *properly conceived and implemented*. What are the attributes of good measurement-driven instruction? Although there are surely other elements that might be incorporated into an effective MDI program, meeting the following five criteria will almost certainly guarantee that a program of measurement-driven instruction will have a beneficial effect.

Criterion-referenced tests. The chief virtue of MDI stems from the clarity with which instructional targets—that is, the skills and knowledge being tested—are described. Even skillful teachers cannot target their instruction if they are unaware of what the assessment targets are. Thus criterion-referenced tests, rather than norm-referenced tests, must be employed in a program of measurement-driven instruction because the descriptive clarity of well-constructed criterion-referenced tests gives teachers comprehensible descriptions of what is being tested. Norm-referenced tests, while useful for other important educational functions, lack the descriptive clarity required for purposes of instructional design. Although teachers have a general idea of what will be tested by norm-referenced examinations, there is too much descriptive ambiguity in such tests to encourage on-target teaching.

Defensible content. If measurement-driven instruction is to enhance the quality of schooling, its tests must assess genuinely defensible skills and knowledge. Why drive instruction toward trivial destinations? Sadly, a number of the minimum competency tests adopted in the late 1970s could have been more accurately labeled "most minimum imaginable" competency tests. The content of high-stakes educational tests should be subjected to intense scrutiny by all concerned clienteles, so that the tests measure truly worthwhile content. Because of the clarity with which the content of a criterion-referenced test can be defined, rigorous judgments can be rendered about whether or not that content is defensible. It is time for U.S. educators to pursue loftier curricular aspirations—aspirations that can be embodied in a high-stakes test.

A manageable number of targets. Too many instructional targets turn out to be no targets at all. Well-crafted high-stakes tests should not be used to assess a multitude of skills or objectives. Rather, in order for teachers to give meaningful attention to promoting the content to be tested, the number of assessment targets covered by the test should be in the neighborhood of five or 10. We learned an important lesson during the heyday of behavioral objectives. Teachers who are inundated with endless litanies of miniscule instructional targets will pay heed to none. A high-stakes test must focus on only a reasonable number of important skills or knowledge targets—targets sufficiently general to subsume enabling skills and content. A number of high-stakes tests in reading, for instance, assess only five or six truly essential skills, such as finding the "main idea" and drawing the correct "inference."

Instructional illumination. Although it is not widely recognized by the education community, criterion-referenced tests can be constructed in such a way that they actually encourage teachers to design effective instructional sequences. For example, a skill that requires examinees to make sophisticated discriminations can be assessed via multiple-choice items constructed according to carefully designed, *instructionally relevant* rules. Suppose that the correct answer to a multiple-choice test item must explicitly satisfy all of three positive criteria while violating none of four negative criteria. Because teachers who are informed of these criteria will recognize the importance of students' mastering them, it is likely that the seven criteria will be emphasized instructionally. Those who develop high-stakes tests for measurement-driven instruction must conceptualize the skills or knowledge to be tested in such a way that teachers can use the targeted skills and knowledge to design effective instructional sequences. In this way, well-made tests will function as catalysts to improved instruction.

Instructional support. Appropriately crafted high-stakes tests are a necessary, but not sufficient, condition for effective programs of measurement-driven instruction. Ample instructional support must also be provided to educators so that they can make the best use of MDI. During 1986, for example, Texas officials provided the state's educators with guides that outlined instructional strategies for all subjects tested statewide at grades 1, 3, 5, 7, 9, and 11. For each skill to be tested, the guides contain 1) a description of the skill, 2) an illustrative test item, 3) an analysis of how the skill might be taught, and 4) potentially useful instructional activities and exercises. Such materials to support instruction are needed if measurement-driven instruction is to work most effectively.

Historically, testing has been something that teachers have thought about only after instruction was over. Tests have been employed to determine how much students have learned, so that teachers could use this information to assign grades. For most teachers, test-making has been an end-of-instruction endeavor.

But with the advent of high-stakes testing, such traditional conceptions of measurement must be jettisoned. No longer can we view test development as an afterthought. Instead, educators must reconceive the relationship between measurement and instruction, so that tests are employed as vehicles of *instruc-*

tional clarification. Because high-stakes tests will surely function as instructional magnets, the challenge is to fashion those tests so that they become a potent force for educational improvement.

IS MDI NEEDED?

There's really little need to employ an improvement strategy, such as measurment-driven instruction, if all is well in American education. Those who believe that the quality of public schooling in the U.S. today is acceptable also believe that—despite isolated instances of instructional ineptitude—teachers are generally doing a decent job, students are spontaneous and creative, and most curricula embody a meaningful number of high-level goals. If I shared this belief, I would have little need to try to enhance the quality of education through the use of measurement-driven instruction or any other tactic.

I believe, however, that the quality of schooling in the U.S. is far from acceptable. Although there are pockets of pedagogical brilliance, far too many classrooms can be found in which teaching is intolerably weak—classrooms choked with irrelevant, time-filling activities that leave hordes of students bored, unmotivated, and lacking mastery of even the most basic skills.

Whatever the causes of such ineffectiveness, its consequences are visible whenever a high-stakes test is initially installed. Far too many students know far too little. In confirming such a perception, Chester Finn, assistant secretary for research and improvement in the U.S. Department of Education, recently characterized the performance of American students as "scandalously low."[1]

Critics of measurement-driven instruction often contrast its possible ill effects with a benign depiction of the success of public schools that simply doesn't square with reality. The merits of MDI must be honestly contrasted with what currently exists in the nation's classrooms. And what currently exists in the public schools needs improvement, not applause.

RESPONSIBLE CRITICISM

Those who would have U.S. educators reject measurement-driven instruction as a strategy to improve schooling must do more than simply trot out a horror story or two about its negative consequences. Of course, any effective tool can always be misused. A scalpel that can save lives when used by a skilled neurosurgeon can become a murder weapon in the wrong hands. That possibility, however, should not incline us to outlaw scalpels.

Critics of measurement-driven instruction must demonstrate, via argument and evidence, that this improvement strategy is so fundamentally flawed that it is either *certain* or *far more likely* to have negative rather than positive consequences. Proponents of MDI, on the other hand, must show that it stands a reasonably good chance of succeeding.

Let us briefly consider some of the more commonly voiced criticisms leveled at measurement-driven instruction. For the most part, these are specious attacks, lacking both analytic rigor and empirical support.

Curricular reductionism. It is alleged that measurement-driven instruction will necessarily lead to the pursuit of trivial, indefensible goals. Of course, this is not necessarily so. Why should we believe that public school educators—who, in their typical activities, pursue high-level goals—would suddenly, when creating a high-stakes test, aim exclusively for low-level goals? Basic skills are being measured in many student assessment programs because students do not possess such skills—not because they are the only skills that could be measured. High-stakes tests need not be directed only toward basic skills. In Pennsylvania and California, for example, new statewide "honors" tests have been established that deal with genuinely higher-order skills.

Curricular stagnation. Critics claim that the use of high-stakes tests will lock educators into an unalterable pursuit of the content being assessed by the tests. But such inflexibility is not necessary. Already a number of states—New Jersey and Connecticut, for example—have meaningfully refurbished their student assessment programs in order to assess more demanding skills.

Constrained teacher creativity. Critics contend that the pressures of instructional assessment will constrain teachers' spontaneity in the classroom. Yet for every teacher the critics can find whose creativity has been stifled by high-stakes tests, I'll produce many more who, because of those tests, waste far less of their student's time with irrelevancy and busywork. Creative teachers can *efficiently* promote mastery of content-to-be-tested and then get on with other classroom pursuits.

Lowered student aspirations. Some critics of measurement-driven instruction argue that the aspirations of students will be diminished because they will pursue only the skills and knowledge being tested. Tell that to a chemistry teacher whose students don't need to know chemistry for a statewide basic skills test. Would such a teacher be likely to implore

students to "take it easy" because there's no chemistry content on the statewide test? Of course not. There's obviously more to school than what's covered on a high-stakes test. Teachers know this; students know this. And if the critics of MDI don't know it, they ought to.

Inappropriate role of tests. Some critics of measurement-driven instruction have argued that tests should follow, not lead, the curriculum. These critics contend that considering testing before determining curriculum is putting the cart before the horse.[2] It can be empirically demonstrated that a carrot-laden cart will provide a powerful incentive if placed in the path of an underfed pony. As I suggested above, educators need to abandon outmoded notions that testing must follow teaching. Properly conceptualized tests can provide the requisite clarity to make instruction more effective.

EVIDENCE OF SUCCESS

Happily, the case for measurement-driven instruction need not depend on rhetoric. During recent years a number of states and school districts have installed high-stakes educational tests in an effort to enhance the quality of local instruction. Table 1 [next page] presents improvements in the test performance of students in six states and one urban school district.[3]

Table 1 shows us that substantial improvements in student mastery of basic skills have been seen during the past half-dozen years. These percentage improvements represent the increased proportions of students who have displayed mastery of established standards—for example, a passing standard of 70% correct on a basic skills test. It is impossible to consider the evidence reported from these seven settings without concluding that, in situations in which measurement-driven instruction has been properly installed, improved student performance on high-stakes tests follows.

How would critics of measurement-driven instruction attempt to discount the sort of evidence presented in Table 1? For one thing, they would probably suggest that the skills measured by the tests aren't all that important; hence the reported gains aren't all that meaningful. But let us recall that these are *basic skills* and that improvements occur only when students display such skills who previously could not. In effect, no matter how the level of the skills measured before the installation of measurement-driven instruction, students had not mastered them. After the advent of MDI, far more students can attain such fundamental skills.

It is particularly gratifying that measurement-driven instruction is apparently reducing the performance gap between majority and minority students. For example, between 1980 and 1984 in Texas, a disparity between the reading and mathematics skills of ninth-grade black students and white students was cut nearly in half. During a similar period, dramatic reductions in the difference between the performance of black students and that of white students have been observed in South Carolina. Connecticut officials report that the greatest improvements have been seen for minority and economically disadvantaged students in urban settings. Clearly, effective assessment systems can go a long way toward reducing differences between majority and minority students in the mastery of skills.

Properly conceived and implemented, measurement-driven instruction can constitute a potent force for educational improvement. Obviously, the installation of an effective program of measurement-driven instruction is not fool's play. Care

Table 1

Improvements in Student Achievement Associated with Measurement-Driven Instruction

Locale	Subjects	Grade(s)	Period	Improvement (%)*
Ala.	3 R's	3, 6, 9	1981–86	1–13
	3 R's	11	1983–85	4–8
Conn.	3 R's	9	1980–84	6–16
Detroit	3 R's	12	1981–86	19
Md.	3 R's	9	1980–86	13–25
	Citizenship	9	1983–86	23
N.J.	Reading and Math	9	1977–85	16–19
	Reading and Math	10	1982–85	8–11
S.C.	Readiness	1	1979–85	14
	Reading and Math	1, 2, 3, 6, 8	1981–86	12–20
Tex.	Reading and Math	3, 5, 9	1980–85	7–14

*Figures for improvement represent the increased percentage of students who have mastered standards of quality during the period in question. (For Alabama, in grades 3, 6, and 9, the percentage of improvement reflects test-score percentage improvements rather than improvements in mastery of standards.)

must be taken to create an assessment system that does not produce the negative outcomes feared by critics.

Remember, truly ineffectual interventions usually give but small cause for alarm. Only when an intervention is sufficiently powerful to bring about changes, possibly the "wrong" changes, does it provoke resistance. In measurement-driven instruction we have a potent and cost-effective intervention that can substantially boost the quality of schooling in our nation. It's time to use it.

NOTES

1. Finn's remarks were made during the Education Commission of the States/Colorado Department of Education Conference on Large-Scale Assessment, Boulder, Colo., June 1986.

2. Robert Calfee, "Establishing Instructional Validity for Minimum Competency Programs," in George F. Madaus, ed., *The Courts, Validity, and Minimum Competency Testing* (Hingham, Mass.: Kluwer-Nijhoff, 1983).

3. I am grateful to the following individuals for the information presented in Table 1: Anne C. Hess, Alabama; Douglas A. Rindone, Connecticut; Sharon Johnson-Lewis and Stuart C. Rankin, Detroit; Ann E. Chafin, Maryland; Stephen Koffler, New Jersey; Paul D. Sandifer, South Carolina; and Keith L. Cruse, Texas.

NO

Gerald W. Bracey

DANGEROUS PRACTICE

The various reform efforts of recent years have given those who make education policy many new uses for tests: tests for certification and recertification of teachers, tests as graduation requirements, and so on. James Popham has coined the phrase "measurement-driven instruction," and he and some others concerned with testing contend that allowing testing to drive instruction is a useful technique for education reform. In the May 1985 *Kappan*, Popham and his colleagues put forth—perhaps—the concept of measurement-driven instruction (MDI) and presented four exemplary programs.[1]

I say "perhaps" in the preceding sentence because considerable question exists about whether the proponents of MDI have actually proposed a new concept or simply delivered a catchy phrase that collapses under close scrutiny. In addition to describing testing as a driving force, the supporters of MDI have also referred to it as a "catalyst" and as a "magnet"[2]—terms that imply quite different functions. In other forums, the advocates of MDI have used such phrases as "measurement-clarified instruction, measurement-enhanced instruction, and measurement-enabled instruction."[3]

Given the plethora of fuzzy definitions and foggy analogies used to define MDI, we might expect the concept to cause considerable confusion in the minds of others. We are left with a significant problem of definition that must be resolved before we can proceed. Not being the author of the phrase, I feel uncomfortable offering such a definition, but I can provide the following general considerations.

In the normal order of things, we decide what needs to be learned, how to facilitate such learning, and how such learning might be assessed. Then we develop instructional materials and strategies, staff development programs (where needed), and assessment strategies (which may or may not be traditional tests). We are dealing with MDI whenever a concern with measurement interrupts this cycle of events.

We are also dealing with MDI whenever mandates require testing without clearly specifying what, if anything, is to be tested. Most minimum competency testing programs would come under this heading. MDI would also include such programs as the "literacy passport" testing program recently proposed for the state of Virginia by Gov. Gerald Baliles' Commission on Excellence in Education.

We are dealing with MDI whenever concern for the technical considerations of the test becomes more important than other considerations. This would incorporate most writing assessments. In the 1985 *Kappan* article by Popham and his colleagues, this aspect of MDI can be seen in the section by Paul Williams, who writes, "The most important developmental activity was the production of test specifications."

I contend that MDI, as described above, has many interrelated and pernicious effects on curriculum and instruction—and on learning. With regard to the curriculum, MDI fragments it, narrows it, deflects it, trivializes it, and causes it to stagnate. With regard to instruction and learning, MDI has similar effects; in addition, MDI exacerbates the problems of the teacher-centered classroom, in which 70% of instructional time is taken up by teacher talk. I concede that there is nothing *in principle* that requires MDI to produce such negative outcomes, but they invariably occur in practice wherever MDI is found. Because these negative outcomes are so widespread, MDI advocates need, at the very least, to examine why they occur.

FRAGMENTATION AND NARROWING

MDI continues the long and unhappy tendency of American psychology to break learning into discrete pieces and then treat the pieces in isolation. From James Mill's "mental mechanics," through Edward Titchener's structuralism, to behavioral objectives and some "componential analysis" in current cognitive psychology, U.S. educators have acted as if the whole were never more than the sum of its parts, as if a house were no more than the nails and lumber and glass that went into it, as if education were no more than the average number of discrete objectives mastered. We readily see that this is ridiculous in the case of a house, but we seem less able to recognize its absurdity in the case of education. MDI reinforces this unfortunate tendency toward absurd conclusions.

There is a great deal of fragmentation in U.S. education already. Examples abound. In one study, Richard Richardson and his colleagues at the University of Arizona referred to the typical processes of education at a community college as "bitting."[4] Richardson found students copying bits of information from chalkboards and skimming textbooks to find other bits of information that would answer questions in study guides. The study guides themselves prepared students to answer bits-of-information (multiple choice) tests. MDI would only extend the domain of bitting.

John Goodlad has also pointed out the bitting that is present in U.S. elementary and secondary classrooms:

> Children listened; they responded when called on to do so; they read short sections of textbooks; they wrote short responses to questions or chose from alternative responses on quizzes. But they rarely planned or initiated anything of length or created their own projects. . . . Writing even short essays is conducive to organization of thought

and learning. Students were not doing much of this.[5]

To reduce the level of fragmentation in U.S. classrooms we should not employ MDI, which will only exacerbate the problem. Rather we need a multi-pronged program to increase coherence. Ernest Boyer and Howard Gardner, among others, have already suggested sound approaches to providing coherence that are quite different from the MDI approach. Boyer put it this way:

> The single most important way to measure student progress is to ask them to write a serious essay on a consequential topic. And that, more than any single measure, indicates whether they can take knowledge from across disciplines, put it together in a coherent way, and develop persuasively an independent idea of their own.[6]

Gardner endorses "a shift away from reliance on standard, timed, short-answer tests" and calls for "an emphasis instead on student involvement in projects. A project is an activity which takes place over a nontrivial amount of time and mobilizes several of an individual's propensities."[7] I should note that, if we follow Boyer's (and probably Gardner's) advice, we must give up the narrow concept of instructional validity, which is widely used today. The integration of material into one's own idea, into one's own project, precludes instructional validity, narrowly construed.

DEFLECTION AND NARROWING

MDI has probably been deflecting curricula from their intended purposes ever since tests began to be used to evaluate teachers and/or schools. The more extreme the sanction attached to poor test performance, the more extreme such de-flection is likely to be. A few years ago I referred to an instance of such deflection in a *Kappan* article, but it is worth repeating here.[8] In order to graduate from high school, students in Virginia must be able to recognize parallel lines. They need not be able to recognize perpendicular lines. However, on one form of the minimum competency tests that all students must pass to become eligible for a diploma, some items pertaining to perpendicular lines were inadvertently included. The performance on the two types of items was widely different, and one school system threatened to sue the state for including them at all.

When a test drives instruction, parts of subject areas that are important tend to be ignored. For example, to graduate from Virginia schools, students are required to learn how to multiply fractions, the denominators of which can be no larger than 5. Virginia students are not required to learn how to add, subtract, or divide fractions. Are the advocates of MDI willing to argue that multiplication of fractions is a more basic or more important operation than adding, subtracting, or dividing fractions? I doubt it. But these other operations are typically more difficult to master. Including such operations on a minimum competency test might produce a politically unacceptable number of failures. When measurement drives instruction, it drives some instruction right out of the classroom.

I hasten to add that Virginia is not alone among the states in skewing its curriculum to meet the demands of testing programs. Virginia's minimum competency reading test and supporting materials were purchased from the Instructional Objectives Exchange, owned by MDI's leading enthusiast, James Popham. And they are nearly identical in content and format to the reading materials developed in sites touted as having MDI programs.

Moreover, in the Cherry Creek (Colorado) Schools, where I work, students score well above the national norm on any test you throw at them. When the results of the first-ever statewide testing program came in last year, we discovered that children in the lower grades were weakest in mathematics computation, though still above the national norm.

Some teachers and administrators *immediately* began to think that we should devote more effort to teaching computation. That scores in problem solving and mathematics concepts were well above the scores in computation seemed not to count. That the National Council of Teachers of Mathematics has recommended for years that students be given calculators for computation—a recommendation supported by overwhelming evidence—seemed not to count. That the computation scores may have been low *because* "back-to-basics" programs around the nation had stressed computation (and hence the norming sample would tend to score higher, thereby effectively raising the norm) seemed not to count. That problem solving and mathematics concepts might suffer if more time were devoted to computation seemed not to count. What counted was that the box score showed computation to be lower than anything else. *That* is how MDI operates.

By targeting instruction on unconnected skills, measurement-driven deflection of instruction has still another pernicious effect: it discourages people from teaching for transfer. Eva Baker and Joan Herman argue that, in constructing a test for one purpose, we *should* specify the range of behaviors and other tasks to which we expect the behaviors to generalize.[9] Their arguments have been echoed and amplified by virtually everyone working in the higher-order thinking skills. To my knowledge, such specification almost never occurs—perhaps never at all.

Why not? If we were using either Robert Glaser's original definition of criterion-referenced tests or the somewhat different but commonly accepted definition, such specifications could be readily accomplished. But we cannot specify the range of generalization or transfer, because we are not using any meaningful definition of "criterion-referenced," because the tests' objectives sit in splendid isolation from one another and from any general theory of cognitive processing or cognitive development.

The problem of deflection extends well beyond school-taught skills. In 1974 Leo Munday and Jean Davis summed up many of the problems of test-induced deflection in a wider context:

> One of the undesirable by-products of testing practice has been the emphasis on academic talent, with its accompanying indifference to other kinds of talent. Tests have fostered a narrow conception of ability and restricted the diversity of talent which might be brought to the attention of young people considering various professions. It is small wonder that some people have mistakenly interpreted test scores as measures of personal worth and have mistakenly assumed talent in school is related in a major way to later adult accomplishments.[10]

TRIVIALIZATION

MDI can lead to trivialization in several ways. First, as I have already indicated, there is a tendency to choose trivial objectives for assessment. More commonly, however, trivialization occurs when one goes from an unassailably desirable objective to the operational test items.

A classic example often occurs when objectives have to do with the "main idea." Thus the *Parent Guide* to the Detroit High School Proficiency Exam advises that one objective is that "the student can determine the main point of a short article from a newspaper, or magazine, or a general interest book." Who can argue with that? A parent might hope that the teachers would also teach children how to judge the *credibility* of the paper, magazine, or book. But, as far as it goes, it is an objective that ranks right up there with respecting Mom and the flag. What the *Parent Guide* does not say is that the children of Detroit will be certified as having met this objective on the basis of passages that will be 125 to 200 words long. The test specifications (the "most important developmental activity") don't allow anything longer.

Similarly, who would argue that students should not learn how to "understand official documents"—another Detroit competency? But the excerpts from these documents can be no longer than 200 words, and those given as examples appear to be simplified versions of what students will encounter in the real world.

I do not mean to pick on Detroit. Detroit has simply done what must be done with all such MDI programs: it has designed a program stringent enough to satisfy those who called for it in the first place—yet lenient enough not to overwhelm the schools with failures.

When measurement drives instruction, the assessment techniques must be convenient. This almost invariably means that the format of the assessment will be multiple choice. There is considerable question about the usefulness of multiple-choice questions in assessing nontrivial outcomes in all subject areas, but the limitations are more apparent in some areas than in others. Our school district is currently combing the country for items that measure "science as process." Almost all of those we have found to date have been in multiple-choice format, and almost all those multiple-choice questions sample simple recall. It is difficult to present science as an ongoing process of discovery, as a detective story, when test items converge on the recall of a single right answer.

Popham has written, "If the competencies [covered by the test] are significant, rather than trivial, they will have a decidedly salutary effect on the instructional program."[11] Perhaps. But aside from tiny writing samples, MDI programs have used multiple-choice examinations, and considerable doubt exists about how significant an objective can be and still be measured by multiple-choice questions. David Wiley raised this issue some years back:

[T]hen there is the dilemma of multiple choice technology: can we really evaluate its costs and benefits without having a conception of validity which allows us to ask scientifically answerable questions concerning the magnitude of measurement distortion induced by multiple choice formats? These are important questions which we are ill prepared to ask precisely, let alone answer.[12]

Judging by those testing programs described as being MDI, test builders have been content not to even try to ask the questions.

WRAP-UP

During the Clarification Hearings on Minimum Competency Testing, sponsored by the National Institute of Education, the position advanced by the advocates of the tests was that rising test scores were sufficient to prove the efficacy of such programs, most of which would fall under the rubric of MDI. That they expressed such satisfaction was due in no small part to the dearth of corroborating evidence from these programs that the level of achievement underlying the test scores was increasing. In any case, rising test scores are not an adequate index of the efficacy of MDI. A number of years ago, Lee Cronbach put it this way:

The demand that tests be closely matched to the aims of a course reflects awareness that examinations of the usual sort "determine what is taught." If questions are known in advance, students give more attention to learning their answers than to learning other aspects of the course. This is not necessarily detrimental. Whenever it is critically important to master certain content, the knowledge that it will be tested produces a desirable concentration of effort. On the other hand, learning the answer to a set of questions is by no means the same as acquiring *understanding* of whatever topic the question represents.[13]

Beyond this, students are often told that they must pass a test in order to graduate. Or teachers are told, as they have been in St. Louis, that their jobs are contingent on their students' performance on tests. Or principals and superintendents tell teachers to bring up the test scores so they'll look good in the newspaper. This is the way MDI operates in practice. And under such circumstances, it is something less than miraculous to find that test scores rise. It is also something less than proof that MDI is useful.

Kappan editor Robert Cole recently reported a conversation with Ernest Boyer, in which Boyer expressed concern that "[t]esting and assessment may become the most consequential matter of the entire education reform movement." Proponents of MDI would cheer this development, but Boyer was concerned. The testing and assessment we're entering into don't flow from a predetermined picture of what we're trying to accomplish, Boyer told Cole, and thus the entire reform movement could "freeze around measurable objectives."[14]

Precisely. And MDI would be the natural refrigerant to ice everything up.

NOTES

1. W. James Popham, Keith L. Cruse, Stuart C. Rankin, Paul D. Sandifer, and Paul L. Williams, "Measurement-Driven Instruction: It's on the Road," *Phi Delta Kappan*, May 1985, pp. 628–34.
2. W. James Popham, "Measurement as an Instructional Catalyst," in Ruth B. Ekstrom, *Measurement, Technology, and Individuality in Education* (San Francisco: Jossey-Bass, 1983).
3. W. James Popham, "Measurement-Driven Instruction: Halcyon Highway," paper presented at the annual Education Commission of the States/Colorado Department of Education Conference on Large-Scale Assessment, Boulder, Colo., June 1986.
4. Richard C. Richardson, "How Are Students Learning?" *Change*, June 1985, pp. 43–49.
5. Quotation compiled from John I. Goodlad, "A Study of Schooling," *Phi Delta Kappan*, March 1983 and April 1983.
6. Ernest L. Boyer, quoted in Jim Bencivenga, Tightening the Agenda for U.S. Schools," *Christian Science Monitor*, 12 April 1985, p. 24.
7. Howard Gardner, "Notes on Some Educational Implications of the Theory of Multiple Intelligences," in *Measures in the College Admissions Process* (New York: College Board, 1986), pp. 130–33.

8. Gerald W. Bracey, "On the Compelling Need to Go Beyond Minimum Competency," *Phi Delta Kappan*, June 1983, pp. 717–21.

9. Eva Baker and Joan Herman, "Beyond Linkage: Task Structure Design," *Journal of Educational Measurement*, Summer 1983, pp. 149–64.

10. Leo Munday and Jean Davis, *Varieties of Accomplishment: Perspectives on the Meaning of Academic Talent* (Ames, Ia.: American College Testing Program, Technical Report No. 62, 1974).

11. Popham et al., p. 629.

12. David Wiley, *The Vicious and the Virtuous: ETS and College Admissions* (Evanston, Ill.: Studies of Educative Processes, Report No. 16, Northwestern University, March 1981).

13. Lee J. Cronbach, "Course Improvements Through Evaluation," *Teachers College Record*, vol. 64, 1963.

14. Robert W. Cole, Jr., "A Matter of Balance," *Phi Delta Kappan*, November 1986, p. 186.

POSTSCRIPT

Is Measurement-Driven Instruction Desirable?

In formal education, tests have historically been deemed necessary to assess qualifications, to indicate aptitudes, to chart intellectual development, and to select and sort for the purpose of rewards. Grading, testing, and "correcting" seem to be inextricably woven into the fabric of schooling—so much so that any meaningful alteration may require a complete change in fabric. The progressive education of the John Dewey era and the humanistic education movement of the late 1960s certainly attempted to find other ways of motivating students and of measuring and reporting their progress. But the inherent imprecision of these alternatives does not seem to sit well in the current era.

One negative aspect of standardized testing, according to Daniel Koretz in "The New National Assessment: What It Can and Cannot Do," *NEA Today* (January 1989), is the role that it has assumed. Achievement tests were originally designed to measure students' educational progress and to evaluate curricula. During the last two decades, though, the purposes of achievement tests became generalized and are now used to assess the effectivity of entire educational systems, not just the performance of individuals. In addition, the value placed on test scores has risen to the point where students, teachers, and principals alike are affected by test results. Koretz describes how some communities even pressure educators into falsely raising test scores to positively reflect the local school or to promote better school funding, which is also linked to test performance. As a result, many educators tend to teach specifically for tests, de-emphasizing items that, while still important, would not be mentioned on the standardized tests.

Perhaps some grounds for compromise will emerge. In search of such grounds, one could turn to sources such as the following: *The Reign of ETS: The Corporation That Makes Up Minds* (1980), by Allan Navin and associates (a Ralph Nader report); *Goodbye to Excellence: A Critical Look at Minimum Competency Testing* (1981), by Mitchell Lazarus; *The Development, Use, and Abuse of Educational Tests* (1979), by Edward Burns; "Some Reservations About Minimum Competency Testing," by Gerald W. Bracey, *Phi Delta Kappan* (April 1978); and "The Case for Minimum Competency Testing," by W. James Popham, *Phi Delta Kappan* (October 1981).

Of more recent vintage are these: Larry Cuban's "State-Powered Curricular Reform, Measurement-Driven Instruction," *National Forum: The Phi Kappa Phi Journal* (Summer 1987); "A Cognitive and Motivational Agenda for Reading Instruction," by Peter Winograd and Scott G. Paris, *Educational Leadership* (December 1988/January 1989); and "Are We Evaluating What We Value?" by Jane A. Stallings, *Action in Teacher Education* (Fall 1987).

A group of articles on the standardized testing controversy are included in the May 1989 issue of *Phi Delta Kappan*, and Kenneth H. Ashworth's "Standardized Testing. A Defense," *The College Board Review* (Winter 1989–1990) deserves attention.

In an op-ed piece in the *New York Times* (October 11, 1988), the venerable Jacques Barzun portrays multiple-choice questions as inappropriate educational devices because they test nothing but passive-recognition knowledge. Barzun suggests that "instead of forcing—and coaching—young minds in form-filling exercises, telling them 'choose and take a chance,' schools would be well advised to return to Ralph Waldo Emerson's 'Tell us what you know.' "

ISSUE 16

Are Packaged Discipline Programs Harmful?

YES: Richard L. Curwin and Allen N. Mendler, from "Packaged Discipline Programs: Let the Buyer Beware," *Educational Leadership* (October 1988)

NO: Lee Canter, from "Let the Educator Beware: A Response to Curwin and Mendler," *Educational Leadership* (October 1988)

ISSUE SUMMARY

YES: Assistant professor of education Richard L. Curwin and psycho-educational consultant Allen N. Mendler argue that packaged discipline approaches obtain quick results at the expense of developing student understanding of responsibility.
NO: Lee Canter, president of Lee Canter & Associates, contends that his program and others like it give teachers effective strategies that lead to positive learning experiences.

Discipline has always been a central problem in formal education. In centuries past the problem was handled by corporal punishment, threats, and other repressive measures. In the twentieth century a number of factors—the emergence of psychology as a dominant influence on schooling, the legal granting of broader rights to the young, the formation of a "youth culture" influenced greatly by the mass media, and the erosion of traditional authority patterns in home, school, and community—have brought new complexities to the concept of discipline.

In the past three decades, the implementation of Skinnerian behaviorism in the instructional and disciplinary procedures of public education has led to the "packaging" of techniques and strategies aimed at the improvement of classroom control, the enhancement of motivation, and the routinization of desirable patterns of student behavior. Just as Carl R. Rogers attacked B. F. Skinner's stimulus-response-reinforcement approach to motivation and self-control as being too "external" and merely expedient (see Issue 6), so have some of today's theorists contended that we must look "inside" the behaving person in order to ground our approach to discipline.

The various contending theories of discipline on the current scene can be placed along a continuum that stretches from "noninterventionists" to "interventionists," with "interactionists" taking up the middle ground position. Noninterventionists (Harris's "I'm O.K. You're O.K." and Gordon's "teacher effectiveness training") rely mainly on observation, questioning, and nondirective statements in an effort to understand the inner workings of student behavior. Interactionists (Dreikurs's "discipline without tears" and Glasser's "schools without failure") also probe with questions, but add directive statements and engage in the subtle molding of student behavior. Interventionists (Axelrod's "behavior modification" and Canter's "assertive discipline") mold behavior more directly, emphasize positive reinforcement, and sometimes employ threats and physical intervention strategies.

A full portrait of these and other current theories of discipline can be found in *Innovative School Discipline* (1985), by John Martin Rich, and in *Building Classroom Discipline: From Models to Practice* (1980), by C. M. Charles.

In William Glasser's *Control Theory in the Classroom* (1986), an extension of his 1985 work *Control Theory*, Glasser claims that educators fail to understand that students will not work in classes that do not satisfy their needs. He identifies these needs as love (belonging), power, freedom to make choices, and fun. He sees power as the key factor and suggests cooperative learning environments for the fulfillment of that need. (Detailed examples can be found in the May 1987 *Phi Delta Kappan* interview of Glasser.)

In the pairing presented here, Richard L. Curwin and Allen N. Mendler, reflecting some of the sentiments of Glasser and Rogers, offer a critique of discipline "packages" and the theories behind them. Lee Canter, creator and distributor of one of the programs that has gained wide acceptance among teachers and administrators, rises to the defense.

YES

Richard L. Curwin
and Allen N. Mendler

PACKAGED DISCIPLINE PROGRAMS. LET THE BUYER BEWARE

Educators consistently feel the need to accomplish miracles. Given far too few hours and resources to accomplish all that is expected of them, many buy packaged curriculum and training programs. While short training programs and packaged materials can save precious time, such programs can also yield negative effects upon certain efforts, such as school and classroom discipline. It is easy to understand the appeal of packaged discipline programs that are advertised as easy to learn and quick to implement. But it is folly to believe that a process as complex as managing student behavior can be understood in a brief inservice at the beginning of school or in a two-hour session on conference day.

ABOUT DISCIPLINE PROGRAMS

Every discipline program, prepackaged or not, has in one form or another goals, principles, rules, enforcement or intervention procedures, and an implicit or explicit evaluation process (fig. 1). Each model also sets the stage for incidental or secondary learning by students, who additionally learn about their self-worth, about their ability to handle responsibility, how to solve problems, how much control they have over their lives and how to use that control, and whether or not they can affect the consequences of their behavior.

Most educators agree that secondary or incidental learnings must be carefully considered when assessing the impact of a discipline program. For example, claims such as "Program X yields an 80 percent reduction in referrals for discipline" are often misleading. If teachers do not refer students because they equate discipline referrals with poor teaching, then the program's apparent success might be the result of teacher fear. If Richard shapes up after the third check mark on the chalkboard because the fourth means a phone call home to an abusive parent, did the program improve his self-control, or did it simply transfer the inner turmoil of a child caught in a dysfunctional family? If Susan is seen by her classmates as responsible for their losing out on a coveted marble in a jar, who assesses the subsequent communications between Susan and her classmates on the playground, on the bus, or in the cafeteria?

Rules are central to all discipline programs, but they can be highly overemphasized, for conceptual and practical reasons. Both *consequences* and *principles* are more influential for achieving long-term behavior change. Rules work best when they are behavioral and are expressed in black-and-white terms. Thus, students and teacher should easily see whether a specific behavior violates a rule. Examples of rules are: When you want to speak, raise your hand; Bring your books and materials to class; Be in your seat when the bell rings. When rules are vague, students have difficulty making the connection between their behavior and the consequences that follow.

Because principles, unlike rules, cannot be enforced, they are overlooked or ignored by packaged programs. Principles define attitudes and expectations for long-term behavioral growth. Examples of principles are: be respectful, care about others, be prepared. If the teacher attempts to enforce principles, students may blame the teacher or make excuses by looking for "gray area" loopholes to justify their behavior. When rules are not developed naturally from principles, students learn, for example, to be in their seats when the bell rings without understanding the importance of responsible work habits. Effective discipline programs enforce rules without sacrificing the opportunity for the higher levels of learning that principles provide.

OBEDIENCE MODELS

Packaged programs are by design simple to learn, easy to implement, and quick with results. Their greatest attraction, though, is paradoxically their greatest weakness. To achieve their lofty claims, packaged programs must resort to power-based methods. They rely on an obedience model of discipline (see fig. 2) because "telling students what to do" requires the least amount of work or change on the teacher's part. Obedience models have as their goals (1) minimal or no rule violations and (2) students' following orders. Punishment is the main intervention or enforcement procedure. The results, if the model is successful, are fewer rule violations and *less* self-discipline; that is, students obey orders but learn little about responsibility.

Unfortunately, both the goals and the results of "obedience" type programs are in direct conflict with one of the main goals of schooling—to teach students responsibility—and one of the main goals of discipline models—to emphasize principles and rules equally.

Another problem common to many packaged programs is that they provide limited opportunity for teacher discretion. Some programs offer only one alternative intervention for teachers when a rule is violated. Others have a lockstep approach that requires a specific intervention for violation number one, another for violation two, and so forth. Either system removes teacher judgment from the process. The result cripples the ability of the teacher to examine rule violations in their broader context. There are a number of factors to consider when choosing an appropriate intervention; yet, when left with only an either-or choice, teachers often have no alternative but to look the other way. This is the only way they can factor in special circumstances that don't fit "the program." Thus, in time, built-in inconsistency dooms the program. Even worse, teachers themselves develop an external locus of control since the major decisions are prescribed by the program designers. Under these conditions, teachers either redesign the program or resent using it.

RESPONSIBILITY MODELS

Teaching students responsibility is harder to package and requires more effort than teaching them to be obedient. Sometimes progress seems slow because students are in the process of learning. Because teachers desire more than a quick end to disruptions, the results are not always immediately apparent. Teachers have the opportunity to see how they contribute to creating situations that foster discipline problems, for example, by developing lessons that stimulate little motivation, offering students little or no hope for behavioral or academic success, forcing students to back down in front of their peers, providing students with few choices or none at all, and/or denying students acceptable opportunities to express their feelings.

Misbehavior is often the only way a student can cope with living in an adverse environment. It keeps students sane and maintains their integrity. Discipline models based on punishment do not usually provide students a voice in determining classroom structure, nor do they examine discipline problems from the viewpoint of students. Obedience models are directed far more toward keeping students in line than toward maintaining their dignity.

Models based on teaching responsibility (see fig. 3), therefore, not only take longer to develop and implement, but invite more risk-taking on the part of the teacher. In the long run, however, these models are more effective because they encourage improved teaching as well as improved learning.

Fig. 1.

Generic Discipline Model

Goals: What the program will accomplish.

Principles: What general attitude and behavioral guidelines teachers model and students are exposed to and encouraged to learn while in class.

Rules: What are enforced every time they are broken.

Enforcement or intervention: What happens when a rule is broken.

Student (incidental) learning: What the student learns as a result of the enforcement or intervention.

Evaluation: How well the program goals are being met.

"If you want true power, you must give some of it away." The key word in this adage is *some*. For many years, we gave away too much control to students. Now we must be careful not to overreact and try to take *all* of it back. Students cannot learn responsibility without choices and without opportunities to make mistakes and learn from them

The responsibility model is far more consistent with the current classroom emphasis on critical thinking and decision making. What do students learn when the curriculum says, "Make decisions based upon critical thinking skills," while they are simultaneously told, "Do what I say, or else you'll have your name written on the blackboard for all to see"?

THE 80–15–5 PRINCIPLE

The responsibility model is also more consistent with the makeup of most classrooms. Generally, there are three groups of students in a typical classroom. (The percentages may vary from classroom to classroom, but there is consistency in the group structure.)

1. *80 percent.* These students rarely, if ever, break rules or violate principles. They come to school motivated to learn, prepared to work, and accepting of classroom restrictions. By and large, these students have been successful by both formal and informal standards and have every reason to expect success in the future. Most discipline plans are either unnecessary or intrusive to them.

2. *15 percent.* These students break rules on a somewhat regular basis. They do not blindly accept the classroom principles, and they fight restrictions. Their motivation ranges from completely "on" to completely "off," depending on what happened at home that morning, how they perceive the daily classroom activities, and possibly the shape of the moon. Their achievement can range from high to low, depending on the teacher, the class, or their expectations for success. These students need a clear set of expectations and consequences. If they are not given enough structure, they can disrupt learning for the other students.

3. *5 percent.* These students are chronic rule breakers and out of control most of the time. Nothing seems to work for them. They have typically experienced

failure in school from an early age and maintain no hope for success in the future. They believe they have no reason to try to behave or to learn. They have severe learning or emotional problems and may come from troubled homes.

The trick of a good discipline plan is to control the 15 percent without alienating or overly regulating the 80 percent and without backing the 5 percent into a corner. Plans that are heavily punitive tend to control the 15 percent, thus giving the illusion that they are successful. However, the seeds are sown for the out-of-control students to explode or for some of the 80 percent to lose interest in learning. Teachers often feel trapped between their desire for consistency and the conflicting fear of coming down too hard on the rare rule violation of the naturally motivated student. Teachers also know that they need to give out-of-control students hope and a little "space" and to make school as positive an experience for them as possible.

Fig. 2.

Obedience Discipline Model

Principle: Do what I (the teacher or administrator) want.

When a student misbehaves (breaks a rule):

   Punishment is the primary intervention:
   1. *External* locus of control.
   2. Done *to* student.

Examples:

   1. Threats.
   2. Scoldings.
   3. Writing "I will not _____ " 500 times.
   4. Detentions.
   5. Writing student's name on chalkboard.

Student learns:

   1. Don't get caught.
   2. It's not my responsibility.

QUESTIONS TO POSE BEFORE YOU CHOOSE

Whether or not discipline programs based on the punishment model work is the subject of a lively debate. However, whether or not they do, *working* is not enough. A reduction in the number of rule violations does not justify the resultant loss of dignity, dislike for school, desire "to finish rather than learn lessons,"[1] or reduction in developing responsibility on the part of students.

Administrators in the market for a discipline program must carefully examine more than immediate results. Here are 10 questions to ask about any discipline program before implementing it in your school:

1. What happens to students who break rules? Punishments or consequences?

2. Is it realistically possible to reinforce this program consistently?

3. What do students learn as a result of the enforcement?

4. Are the principles of behavior as visible and as important as the rules?

5. Do students have a say in what happens to them?

6. Do teachers have discretion in implementing consequences?

7. Is adequate time given for professional development of teachers and administrators? Is the training completed in only a day or two? Is there continuous follow-up and administrative support?

8. Does the plan account for the special relationship between teaching and discipline style, or does it focus exclusively on student behavior? Does it encourage teachers to examine their potential contributions to discipline problems?

9. Is the dignity of students preserved? Are students protected from embarrassment?

10. Is the program consistent with the stated goals of your school?

Fig. 3.

Responsibility Discipline Model

Main Goal: To teach students to make responsible choices.

Principle: To learn from the outcomes of decisions.

When a student misbehaves (breaks a rule):

Consequences:
1. *Internal* locus of control.
2. Done *by* student.
3. Logical or natural.

Examples:
1. Developing a plan describing how you will behave without breaking the rule when you are in a similar situation.
2. Practicing appropriate behavior in a private meeting with the teacher.

Student learns:
1. I cause my own outcomes.
2. I have more than one alternative behavior in any situation.
3. I have the power to choose the best alternative.

FROM THE HEART OF THE TEACHER TOWARD SELF-DISCIPLINE

What most students learn about their behavior affects them as profoundly, if not more so, than what they learn about their subjects. When teachers devote as much energy and enthusiasm to behavior as they do to "content," and perceive misbehavior as an opportunity to affect students' lives positively, good things happen. Students recognize that teachers genuinely care, and teachers feel less like police. Cynicism is replaced by hope for teachers and students.

Effective discipline, then, does not come from the quick mastery of techniques nor the use of a packaged method. Effective discipline comes from the heart and soul of the teacher. It comes from the belief that teaching students to take responsibility for their behavior is as much the job of the teacher as is teaching history or math. It comes from the belief that most students do the best they can in what many feel is an adverse environment. It comes from the belief that all students need hope. And it comes from the positive energy of the teacher. Only within the framework of the teacher's internal strength and the development of a caring classroom environment can a discipline plan yield responsible and self-disciplined school citizens.

NOTE

1. We wish to thank Raymond Wlodkowski of the University of Wisconsin at Milwaukee for sharing this insight.

NO   Lee Canter

LET THE EDUCATOR BEWARE: A RESPONSE TO CURWIN AND MENDLER

I was asked to respond to Curwin and Mendler's article because I was told it criticized the Assertive Discipline approach to classroom management. In reading their article, however, I find it difficult to see exactly where they refer to Assertive Discipline and exactly what they object to. The majority of their points are vague and theoretical. Assertive Discipline, on the other hand, is based on experience and research. Therefore, in responding to Curwin and Mendler, I will address those parts of their article to which I feel I can respond in a concrete manner. Opinions are easy to come by; facts are hard to dispute.

AN EFFECTIVE CLASSROOM MANAGEMENT STRATEGY

First, I would like to address the theme of the article. Curwin and Mendler seem to be warning educators about discipline programs that are not only ineffective but can have negative effects. If they are referring to Assertive Discipline, I suggest they consider the following facts.

In 1983, Mandlebaum and her colleagues at Bowling Green University examined the results of implementing the Assertive Discipline approach in a 3rd grade classroom in a midwestern metropolitan school district. They found that teachers were able to reduce inappropriate behavior as a result of using Assertive Discipline and concluded that the program "is an effective and practical behavior management strategy" (Mandlebaum et al. 1983).

Mandelbaum's conclusions are supported by other researchers, teachers, and administrators who report substantial reductions of discipline problems and improvements in pupil behavior after Assertive Discipline was implemented (Becker 1980, Moffett et al. 1982, Ward 1983, Webb 1983). These findings are supported by school district observation reports in California, Arizona, and Minnesota (Loss 1981, Lubow 1979). Additionally, follow-up surveys indicate that observable pupil behavior continued to improve two to five years after introduction of Assertive Discipline (Crawley 1982, Bauer 1982).

Curwin and Mendler also warn against discipline programs that are "lockstep" and have a limited potential for application. I agree that finding an effective classroom management system that has broad application is a formidable task. How does Assertive Discipline measure up to that challenge? McCormack (1985) concluded in her study of 36 3rd grade classrooms that "Assertive Discipline works to reduce off-task behavior of students of varying reading levels, socioeconomic status, ethnicity, sex, and parental influence. Further, Assertive Discipline works for teachers who have varying qualifications, experience, and knowledge of the subject" (69-70).

IMPROVED SELF-CONCEPT
OF STUDENTS, TEACHERS

Curwin and Mendler criticize discipline programs that adversely affect students' "dignity." If they are referring to Assertive Discipline, they must have overlooked the following studies.

Ersavas surveyed four elementary schools in which Assertive Discipline was not used and then introduced the program to the staffs of those schools, where the teachers subsequently implemented it. In addition to finding improved self-concept of teachers and pupils at the four schools, Ersavas (1980) validated the program's effectiveness in improving classroom behavior.

Other studies have also found improvement in teacher and pupil self-concept (Bauer 1982, Henderson 1982, and Parker 1985). In addition, Swanson (1984) reported positive self-concept findings in the Compton Unified School District in California (approximately 1,300 teachers)

after Assertive Discipline was implemented in the entire district.

POSITIVE REINFORCEMENT,
PROVEN AND POWERFUL

Curwin and Mendler advocate a "responsibility" model for behavior management but offer no validation of its effectiveness. I believe I can help them there. Assertive Discipline is based on presenting students with choices (Canter and Canter 1976, 119), and it is through choice that students learn about responsibility (Dreikurs 1957). For students to choose to behave, they must know the rules, the positive reinforcement they will receive if they choose to follow the rules, and the negative consequences that will result if they choose not to follow the rules.

Curwin and Mendler completely overlook the importance of positive reinforcement, a proven and powerful tool in behavior management (Weber et al. 1958). From the beginning, Assertive Discipline has been based on a balance of positive reinforcement and negative consequences (Canter and Canter 1976, 118). Negative consequences can stop unwanted behavior, but the way to encourage continued good behavior is to recognize and reward it (Madsen and Madsen 1981).

Assertive Discipline trains teachers to use positive reinforcement consistently to focus students' attention on desired behavior and to encourage them to continue that behavior because of the recognition they receive. Any classroom management program not based on positive reinforcement ignores the behavior of those students who regularly choose to behave appropriately.

A POSITIVE LEARNING EXPERIENCE

Curwin and Mendler also question discipline approaches that deal with 5 to 15 percent of disruptive students at the expense of the majority of the class. I agree with their premise but not with their numbers. All it requires is 1 student to take 29 other students off task. For an approach to discipline to be effective, it must stop the disruptive student(s) but improve learning and make education a more positive experience for all students.

Can Assertive Discipline improve learning? In her study, McCormack stated that classrooms using Assertive Discipline had 5 percent more on-task time than classrooms not using the program (1985, 79, 80). That's 15 minutes per day, 75 minutes per week, 5 hours per month more time teachers have to teach and *all* students have to learn.

A SYSTEMATIC APPROACH TO DISCIPLINE

Curwin and Mendler seem to prefer discipline programs that are not systematic and take a long time to develop and implement. But what is the classroom teacher to do while this development process is taking place? When Johnny decides to hit Billy because it is his only way of "coping with living in an adverse environment"? When that "5 percent" of students are disrupting because they haven't yet developed their "internal locus of control"?

A vital point Curwin and Mendler fail to address is what happens when teachers do not have a systematic way of responding to discipline problems. Too many times, teachers who are overwhelmed by constant disruptions react in ways that are emotionally or physically harmful to students. If you think we are dealing with a theoretical problem, what do you say to the 1,099,731 children who received physical punishment (paddling) for misbehaving in class in 1985-86 (U.S. Department of Education 1988)?

Assertive Discipline not only prevents teachers from responding emotionally, but the approach is also replacing corporal punishment in some districts; for example, Clear Creek in Texas (Snooks 1988) and Williams Valley in Pennsylvania ("Sparing the Rod," 1988). The program is working because it is fair, it is proven, and it does not hurt children.

THE TRUE TEST

I could cite other studies that support the effectiveness of Assertive Discipline, but the real test of any educational approach is its use by teachers, in classrooms, with students. Assertive Discipline undergoes that testing in tens of thousands of classrooms every day.

Theories such as those of Curwin and Mendler make interesting reading, but teachers don't need more educational literature. They need answers, and they need them now. And to those who are concerned about protecting teachers from ineffective systems and approaches, I say, "Don't worry." Teachers and the process of educational natural selection are taking care of that.

REFERENCES

Bauer, R. "A Quasi-Experimental Study of the Effects of Assertive Discipline." *Dissertation Abstracts International* 43: 25A. Miami University, 1982. (University Microfilms No. 82-14316).

Becker, R., ed. *The Troy Reporter.* Troy, Ohio: Troy Schools, March 1980.

Canter, L., and M. Canter. *Assertive Discipline—A Take Charge Approach for Today's Educator.* Santa

Monica, Calif.: Canter and Associates, Inc., 1976.

Crawley, K. "Teacher and Student Perceptions with Regard to Classroom Conditions, Procedures, and Student Behavior in Classes of Teachers Trained in Assertive Discipline Methods." *Dissertation Abstracts International* 43: 2840A. Miami University, 1982. (University Microfilms No. 82-01140).

Dreikurs, R. *Psychology in the Classroom.* Evanston, Ill.: Harper and Row, 1957.

Ersavas, C. M. "A Study of the Effect of Assertive Discipline at Four Elementary Schools." Doctoral diss., United States International University, 1980.

Henderson, C. "An Analysis of Assertive Discipline Training and Implementation on Inservice Elementary Teachers' Self-Concept, Locus of Control, Pupil Control Ideology and Assertive Personality Characteristics." *Dissertation Abstracts* 42: 4797A. Indiana University, 1982. (University Microfilms No. 82-09893).

Loss, J. "Assertive Discipline: A New Tool But Not a Plug-In Module." *Minnesota Elementary School Principal* (Fall 1981): 17.

Lubow, A. "How to Get Tough." *Newsweek*, July 10, 1979, 69.

Madsen, C., and C. Madsen. *Teaching Discipline: A Positive Approach for Educational Development.* Boston: Allyn and Bacon, 1981.

Mandlebaum, Linda, et al. "Assertive Discipline: An Effective Behavior Management Program." *Behavioral Disorders Journal* 8, 4 (1983): 258–264.

McCormack, S. "Students' Off-Task Behavior and Assertive Discipline." Doctoral diss., University of Oregon, 1985.

Moffett, K., et al. "Assertive Discipline." *California School Board* (June/July/August 1982): 24–27.

Parker, P. "Effects of Secondary-Level Assertive Discipline in a Central Texas School District and Guidelines to Successful Assertion and Reward Strategies." Texas A&M University, 1985. In *Dissertation Abstracts* 45,3504A.

Snooks, M.K. "How We Banned Paddling." *People Opposed to Paddling Students Newsletter* (Spring 1988): 9.

"Sparing the Rod." *Republican.* Pottsville, Pennsylvania, April 9, 1988.

Swanson, M. *Assessment of the Assertive Discipline Program.* Compton, Calif.: Compton Unified School District, 1984.

U.S. Department of Education. *The Condition of Education*, 1987 edition. Washington, DC: United States Printing Office, 1988.

Ward, L. "The Effectiveness of Assertive Discipline as a Means to Reduce Classroom Disruptions." Doctoral diss., Texas Technical University, 1983. In *Dissertation Abstracts* 44, 2140–2141A.

Webb, M. "An Evaluation of Assertive Discipline and Its Degree of Effectiveness as Perceived by the Professional Staff in Selected School Corporations." Doctoral diss., Indiana University, 1983. In *Dissertation Abstracts* 43, 25A.

Weber, W., et al. *Classroom Management: Reviews of the Teacher Education and Research Literature.* Princeton, NJ: Stanford University Press, 1958.

POSTSCRIPT

Are Packaged Discipline Programs Harmful?

"If we continue to follow the dead end of stimulus-response psychology and focus on the symptom rather than the cause," William Glasser contends, "our schools will never be significantly better or more 'disciplined' than they are now." If this is true, then those who hold the position must achieve the theoretical and practical precision that has been a hallmark of behaviorism and assertive discipline programs.

While the focus of discussion on this issue has been primarily on theoretical aspects, there is a wealth of material available that attempts to translate theory into practical, situational terms. Among the more provocative works are these: *Violence in Schools* (1977), by James McPartland and Edward McDill; R. C. Newell's "Learning to Survive in the Classroom," *American Teacher* (February 1981); "Good, Old-Fashioned Discipline: The Politics of Punitiveness," by Irwin A. Hyman and John D'Alessandro in *Phi Delta Kappan* (September 1984); and "Effective Teacher Techniques: Implications for Better Discipline," by Elizabeth M. Reis in the April 1988 issue of *Clearing House*.

In "Discipline Alternatives That Work," *The Humanist* (November/December 1988), Marilyn Gootman outlines eight characteristics of an alternative discipline program that is rooted in Glasser's theories, along with the reasons why her system is successful.

The Summer 1987 issue of *Pointer* contains articles on a variety of discipline approaches, as does the January 1988 issue of the *National Association of Secondary School Principals Bulletin*. A recent piece by Lee Canter, "Assertive Discipline and the Search for the Perfect Classroom," appears in the January 1988 issue of *Young Children*. Positive results of Canter's program are reported by Elden R. Barrett and K. Fred Curtis in "The Effects of Assertive Discipline Training on Student Teachers," *Teacher Education and Practice* (Spring–Summer 1986).

Other articles of interest are Thomas R. McDaniel's "Practicing Positive Reinforcement: Ten Behavioral Management Techniques," *Clearing House* (May 1987); "This 'Step System' of Discipline Helps Kids Improve Their Behavior," by Steve Black and John J. Welsh, *The American School Board Journal* (December 1985); and Larry Bartlett's "Academic Evaluation and Student Discipline Don't Mix: A Critical Review," *Journal of Law and Education* (Spring 1987).

The March 1989 issue of *Educational Leadership* offers a special feature on the topic of discipline. Of particular interest is an article on "What Research Really Shows About Assertive Discipline." David Hill's "Order in the Classroom," *Teacher Magazine* (April 1990) draws a provocative portrait of the Canter system.

ISSUE 17

Is Mainstreaming Beneficial to All?

YES: Dean C. Corrigan, from "Political and Moral Contexts That Produced Public Law 94–142," *Journal of Teacher Education* (November/December 1978)

NO: W. N. Bender, from "The Case Against Mainstreaming: Empirical Support for the Political Backlash," *Education* (Spring 1985)

ISSUE SUMMARY

YES: Dean of education Dean C. Corrigan traces the political and moral roots of Public Law 94–142 and concludes that mainstreaming handicapped children can restore a sense of social purpose to the education system.
NO: Professor W. N. Bender reviews research evidence that shows mainstreaming has negative effects on nonhandicapped students and disrupts the classroom ecology.

The Education for All Handicapped Children Act of 1975 (Public Law 94–142) is an excellent example of federal influence in translating social policy into practical alterations of public school procedures at the local level. The general social policy of equalizing educational opportunity and the specific social policy of assuring that young people with various physical, mental, and emotional disabilities are constructively served by tax dollars have come together in a law designed to bring the handicapped closer to the public norm.

Legislation of such delicate matters does not ensure success, however. While most people applaud the intentions of the act, there are those who find the expense involved ill-proportioned and those who feel the federal mandate is unnecessary and heavy-handed.

A staunch supporter of the law, Senator Edward M. Kennedy, has stated that "P.L. 94–142 is designed and intended to protect the rights of all—the child, the parents, and the school. . . . Children are being educated who were formerly at home or in state institutions. It is not easy, but it is gratifying" (*Journal of Teacher Education*, November/December 1978). One reason that it is not easy is that most of the regular classroom teachers receiving mainstreamed students are ill-prepared for the task. In-service and preservice programs to correct this deficiency are slowly being incorporated.

As Ann A. Abbott points out, in "Durkheim's Theory of Education: A Case for Mainstreaming," *Peabody Journal of Education* (July 1981), French sociologist Emile Durkheim felt that attachment and belonging were essential to human development. If this is the case, the integration of young people with handicaps into regular classroom settings and into other areas of social intercourse, when possible, is highly desirable. Public Law 94–142 prompts a closer identification of handicapped individuals in order to assure proper placement in appropriate learning environments. It further requires individualized planning and consultation with parents and experts to ensure the efficacy of the placement.

But practical consequences of the law sometimes result in questions about its desirability. In a period of economic restrictions, how much money can society afford to spend on the special needs of certain students? The 1982 U.S. Supreme Court decision in the *Rowley* case, which denied continuous sign language interpretation for a deaf student in a public school, seems to have drawn some limits. Justice Rehnquist, in stating the majority position, contended that the schools are not obliged to provide services "sufficient to maximize each child's potential."

The value of the legislation is still in question. In the following articles, Dean C. Corrigan, an advocate of the law, details the history of P.L. 94–142 and explains how its full implementation could improve the overall institution of education. W. N. Bender claims that the effects of mainstreaming on a classroom would compromise the quality of education for all students.

YES

Dean C. Corrigan

POLITICAL AND MORAL CONTEXTS THAT PRODUCED PUBLIC LAW 94-142

The Education for All Handicapped Children Act, Public Law 94-142, received a clear mandate in the U.S. Congress. Passed by votes of 404-7 in the House of Representatives and 87-7 in the Senate, this Act is the most important piece of educational legislation in this country's history.

ROOTS OF P.L. 94-142

Basically, this Act is Civil Rights as well as educational legislation, and can be fully understood only from that perspective. Congressional testimony on P.L. 94-142 indicates the basic rationale in support of providing access to equal educational opportunity for persons with handicaps is that they are *human beings* living in America and therefore have a right to *access* to equal educational opportunity, *even if it costs more to provide it*.

As we implement the educational concepts in P.L. 94-142, we must remember that this Act calls for social, political, and economic reforms as well as educational reforms, or our strategies for change will not succeed.

P.L. 94-142 has its roots in the 1960s Civil Rights movement. The same rationale behind the 1954 Supreme Court decision, *Brown v. Board of Education*, influenced advocates for the handicapped. That is, segregation has harmful effects on both the person who is segregated and the person who does the segregating (Friedman, 1969). Blatt and Kaplan's *Christmas in Purgatory* (1966) vividly described the inhumane treatment of the handicapped in isolated settings. This book and Blatt's later books (1970a, 1970b, 1976) pricked America's conscience by revealing the plight of the handicapped for all to see.

Spurred by the struggle for civil rights in the larger context, parents of handicapped children joined with civil rights lawyers to attack segregated settings for the handicapped on many of the same grounds that other

From Dean C. Corrigan, "Political and Moral Contexts That Produced Public Law 94-142," *Journal of Teacher Education* (November/December 1978). Copyright © 1978 by the American Association of Colleges for Teacher Education. Reprinted by permission.

advocates were attacking segration based on race. The stigma placed on their children by a school system patterned on "regular or general" education for the so-called "normal" and another quite separate system for the so-called "abnormal" came under sharp attack by groups from all segments of the population.

Another emerging factor—financing educational programs—disturbed many parents, and not just the parents of handicapped children. As state and federal financial support for special education grew, it became profitable for school systems to set up "special classes," often away from "regular" school settings. Too often these classes became dumping grounds for "behavior problems," and a place to segregate ethnic or racial minorities (Sarason & Doris, 1978). There was a dramatic increase in classes for the mentally retarded after the 1954 Brown decision, but the disproportionate number of children from ethnic or racial minorities placed in special classes did not go unnoticed by civil rights advocates or the parents of the segragated children.

As educational critics examined schools for other concerns—discrimination in testing, due process in suspensions, confidentiality of records, and racial bias—the ways that handicapped children were identified, evaluated, and placed came under scrutiny.

The advocates' hard work for the handicapped paid off in 1972 when the landmark court case in Pennsylvania ordered zero reject education, that is, access to free public schools for retarded children. Of the 15,000 previously out-of-school children admitted to public schools because of that decree, the greater proportion, some 52%, were only mildly retarded (Gilhool, 1976). The Peter Mill case in

Washington, D.C., extended the zero-reject imperative to *all* handicaps. Parents' rights to due process hearings, as well as the integration imperative, were recognized in these and other cases (Weintraub, Abeson, Bullard, & Lavor).

While the court battles continued, state legislatures began to pass legislation in response to pressure from citizens groups representing the handicapped. Vermont passed its education for the handicapped act in 1972 and Massachusetts in 1974. State legislation included most of the concepts and requirements that appeared later in Congressional legislation. Today, all states except New Mexico have enabling legislation that complements P.L. 94-142.

At the national level, provisions to insure that handicapped children would get "appropriate" education in the so-called "regular education environments" was framed in the Mathias Amendment, P.L. 380, U.S. Code Section 1413. This amendment, fashioned after the model statute developed by the Council for Exceptional Children (CEC), enjoined that handicapped children be educated with children who were not handicapped, but that their education be differentiated by special needs and appropriate service.

As the right to equal access to education in "least restrictive environments" moved down the legal constitutional road, CEC became an active advocate. Its 1972 Policy Statement and the CEC model statute in establishing the changed facts before the Court required that special educators loudly and clearly say that they had changed (Gilhool, 1966). Other professional groups have taken somewhat longer to take a position in support of free "appropriate" education for the handicapped in the mainstream of education.

(The American Association of Colleges for Teacher Education recently stated its position in *Beyond the Mandate, . . .*)

With these court cases and events as a foundation for legislative action, a strong coalition of parents, lawyers, and legislators, supported by the Education Commission of the States, brought P.L. 94-142 through the Congress. This powerful mandate to all educators, a law that Maynard Reynolds calls an educational Magna Carta for all handicapped children, was signed into law on Nov. 29, 1975.

P.L. 94-142 became fully effective on Oct. 1, 1977 (Fiscal Year 1978). To insure that the law's requirements are carried out in every school district in a State, "State plans" are submitted to the U.S. Office of Education Bureau of Education for the Handicapped (BEH).

Throughout the struggle to pass P.L. 94-142, BEH responded with skill, knowledge, commitment, and political savvy. The educational philosophy that guided the Bureau's action was expressed by Edwin Martin, BEH chief and Associate Commissioner of Education. To improve education for *all* children, he believes that the dichotomous constructs existing at all levels of the educational system and in society, in general, must be eliminated. To make human rights a reality in America, the notion that handicapped, black, or any children are different and should be set apart must be rejected. All children are more alike than different in their basic human nature (Martin, 1974). Under Martin's leadership, BEH shifted its concern from children's handicaps to their learning needs, and changed the educational setting from segregated classrooms and institutions to "appropriate" education in the "least restrictive environment."

IMPLICATIONS FOR SCHOOLS

The Education for All Handicapped Children Act identifies the regular classroom as the "least restrictive environment," unless another setting is prescribed as more appropriate to meet a child's special needs. If other settings are used, they must be justifed.

The implications of using regular classrooms are enormous, not the least of which is that all educators—teachers, counselors, administrators, and other support personnel—must be educationally prepared to work with handicapped persons. This calls for a change in roles of all education personnel, particularly special educators who will join and share their expertise with instructional teams as well as students.

The beneficiaries of this act are approximately 12% of the human beings in the United States between the ages of 3 and 21 who have a handicap, as defined in P.L. 94-142.[1] By school year 1978, a "child find" should have been completed and services extended to include persons aged 3 through 21. Some states have gone beyond this age group in their enabling legislation, and have started the "child find" of children age 1, and extended services beyond age 21. Because many agencies work with these age groups, school personnel must view themselves as part of a human service delivery system rather than a school system. New means of linking with these agencies and new systems of pre- and in-service training must be developed to bring about better collaboration.

Another goal discussed for years by educators is parent involvement. This act requires the child's parent, guardian, or surrogate to sign-off on the individualized plan and consultation at each step of identification, evaluation, and placement into an appropriate setting.[2] How these child-parent-teacher relationships are developed, starting with the "child find," will be critical in achieving the act's goals.

P.L. 94-142 requires individually designed education.[3] If not provided, due process procedures offer parents legal alternatives to insure an individualized education for their children. It is critical to note that the legislation addresses individualized *programs* and individualized *instruction*. Even though it is not stipulated, this legislation views the total school and classroom setting, as well as individual interaction between teachers and students, as being educative. School milieu affects the attitudes of students and educators, such as developing an understanding and respect for individual differences of persons with handicaps, and accepting responsibility in the community for protecting the human rights of other persons. Therefore, the plan for mainstreaming includes consideration of the total learning environment.

American schools must be based now on the principle of "no rejects"; every human being has a right to an education and the right to be treated as a person— not an object, or a symbol on a chart, or a category in a student grouping stucture. The labeling and classification of children, and the social stigma that this labeling produces, must be eliminated. . . .

New evaluation systems should include criterion or domain-referenced evaluation practices in which the concepts of expectancy and capacity are related more to access to competent teaching in educational settings than inherent individual learner traits. The current over-reliance on normative testing, and the misinterpretation and misuse of intelligence,

achievement, and aptitude tests must be corrected. Also, under P.L. 94-142, parents must be notified that the evaluation instruments will not discriminate in any way against a child on the basis of race or culture.

To develop the kind of individualized-personalized relationships between teachers and students called for by P.L. 94-142, we must eliminate overcrowding and the resulting class loads, easy anonymity, and shallow teacher-pupil contacts. The basic classroom configuration must change.

The educational setting must be organized so that students know what they can do to achieve *success*. The methods used to differentiate instruction should be neither exclusively behavioristic nor cognitive, child centered nor discipline centered. They should be purposefully eclectic. Curricular tracking that fosters a caste system, and the grade level lockstep that ignores what we know about the ways unique selves develop, must be eliminated. The school must develop ways to use the individual's rhythm, learning speed and style, and exceptionality.

IMPLICATIONS FOR TEACHER EDUCATION

Until educators get rid of the special education-regular education dualism in teacher education institutions, public schools will continue to mirror the same dualism. *All* teachers must be prepared to implement P.L. 94-142. Hence, we must reform *all* aspects of teacher education, not just special education departments. . . .

A major shakeup is needed in the form and substance of teacher education from the first introduction through the teacher's entire career. Financial and personal resources must be directed toward strategies that link schools seeking to change with teacher education institutions seeking to break out of established patterns.

CONCLUSIONS

The Education for All Handicapped Children Act calls on educators to reaffirm some fundamental premises of American education. It implies that all children have a right to an educational environment that helps them to become all they are capable of becoming.

P.L. 94-142 calls on educators to eliminate isolation of the handicapped, the prejudice and discrimination that isolation breeds, and the mockery that it makes of the fundamental right of access to equal educational opportunity.

If the individualization plan, the zero reject principle, the due process requirement, the parent involvement directive, and the integration imperative of P.L. 94-142 are implemented for handicapped children, in the end they will be extended to all children. Thus special education will become general education and general education, special.

The teaching profession controls, for better or worse, the environment within which handicapped children will live intellectual-personal lives. We can destroy it and them, or we can give them hope and happiness by giving them a framework of educational ideas and values.

The most severe shortcoming of teaching and teacher education is that we have concentrated on means rather than ends. Too often we have maintained the "illusion of neutrality," but there is no such thing as "value-free" education. There is only the choice to be conscious of and

positive about our values or to conceal and confuse them.

What is needed most from our profession is a moral stance on the issues raised by P.L. 94-142. How far should the majority go in accommodating the needs of the minority? Are the schools and teacher education responsible for teaching this generation of children and parents how to take responsibility to assure the human rights of others? If educators and education are to become effective instruments for social progress, we must restore a sense of social purpose to all levels of the educational system.

NOTES

1. In the law, the term handicapped includes nine categories of handicapping conditions. Schools must have programs for children who are: (1) deaf; (2) hard of hearing; (3) mentally retarded; (4) orthopedically impaired; (5) other health impaired; (6) seriously emotionally disturbed; (7) specific learning disability; (8) speech impaired; and (9) visually handicapped.

2. Parents have the right to obtain an impartial due process hearing with regards to these various steps (identification, evaluation, placement). They must first be notified of the time and place of the hearing that they request and of all their procedural rights. Parents may be accompanied and advised by counsel and by individuals with special knowledge or training with respect to handicapped children. Parents have the right to present evidence at the hearing and to confront, cross examine, and compel the attendance of witnesses. They must be supplied with a record of the hearing, including the written findings of fact and a clear written statement of what the decision is and the basis for reaching it. Finally, they have the right to appeal the hearing.

3. The Individualized Education Program (IEP) is defined in Section 602 (19) of Public Law 94-142, Education for All Handicapped Children Act of 1975, as "a written statement for each handicapped child developed in any meeting by a representative of the local education agency or an intermediate educational unit who shall be qualified to provide, or supervise the provision of, specially designed instruction to meet the unique needs of handicapped children; the teacher; the parents or guardian of such child; and, whenever appropriate, such child.

The statement shall include: (1) a statement of the present levels of educational performance; (2) a statement of annual goals, including short-term instructional objectives; (3) a statement of the specific educational services to be provided to such child, and the extent to which such child will be able to participate in regular educational programs; (4) the projected dates for initiation and anticipated duration of services; (5) appropriate objective criteria and evaluation procedures and schedules for determining, on at least an annual basis, whether instructional objectives are being achieved.

REFERENCES

Blatt, B. *Exodus from pandemonium.* Boston: Allyn and Bacon, 1970. (a)

Blatt, B. *The revolt of the idiots.* Glenn Ridge, N.J.: Exeptional Press, 1976.

Blatt, B. *Souls in extremis.* Boston: Allyn and Bacon, 1970. (b)

Blatt, B., & Kaplan, F. *Christmas in purgatory.* Boston: Allyn and Bacon, 1966.

Friedman, L. (Ed.). *Argument: The oral argument before the Supreme Court in Brown vs. Board of Education of Topeka, 1952–55.* New York: Chelsea House, 1969.

Gilhool, T.K. Changing public policies: Roots and forces. In *Mainstreaming: Origins and Implications.* University of Minnesota, Minneapolis. Minnesota Education, Vol. 2, Number 2, Spring, 1976. p. 9.

Howsam, R.B., Corrigan, D.C., Denemark, G.W., & Nash, R.J. *Educating a profession.* Washington, D.C.: American Association of Colleges for Teacher Education, 1976.

Martin, E.W. An end to dichotomous constructs: A reconceptualization of teacher education. *Journal of Teacher Education,* Fall 1974, 25, 219.

Sarason, S., & Doris, J. Mainstreaming: Dilemmas, opposition, opportunities. In M.C. Reynolds (Ed.), *Futures of education for exceptional students: Emerging structures.* University of Minnesota, Minneapolis: National Systems Project, 1978.

Weintraub, F., Abeson, A., Bullard, J., & Lavor, M.L. (Eds.). *Public policy and the education of exceptional children.* Reston, VA.: Council for Exceptional Children, 1976.

NO

W. N. Bender

THE CASE AGAINST MAINSTREAMING

The social and educational imperative to integrate the handicapped into the least restrictive environment commensurate with their needs, was incorporated into law in 1975, resulting in the placement of most mildly handicapped children in the mainstream (Abeson, 1977). With this legal mandate in place, arguments against mainstreaming became as outdated and irrelevant as arguments that women and blacks—two other groups originally denied educational rights, be excluded from public education.

Nevertheless, with the anticipated national monetary cutbacks and the oftmentioned parental and educational backlash against mainstreaming (Stedman, 1980), special educators must take a rigorously honest look at mainstream classes. One concern, representing the arena from which a great deal of the political backlash will come, is the question regarding effects of mainstreaming on non-handicapped learners in the class (Ringlaben and Price, 1981). Also, this may be one of the most important questions for parents of the non-handicapped, yet in some respects it has largely been ignored by researchers interested in mainstreaming. Areas of concern include teacher attitudes, teachers' use of time, potential effects of negative role models, and the general ecology of the classroom.

While most special educators would probably argue mainstreaming is morally right, this does not eliminate the possibility of certain negative effects. The best defense against these negative consequences and the political backlash they engender is probably an offensive tactic of demonstrating problem areas and suggesting research, and where possible, educational programming options to minimize these problems.

THE TEACHER'S ATTITUDE

One of the initial pieces of evidence available indicating problems with mainstreaming practice is the literature which suggests that many mainstream teachers are opposed to mainstreaming (Abramson, 1980; Baker and

From W. N. Bender, "The Case Against Mainstreaming: Empirical Support for the Political Backlash," *Education* (Spring 1985). Copyright © 1985 by Project Innovation, Chula Vista, California. Reprinted by permission.

Gottlieb, 1980; Glickling and Theobald, 1975; Larrivee and Cook, 1979; Stevens and Braun, 1980). For example, Stevens and Braun (1980) used a questionnaire format distributed to 1,034 elementary teachers in twenty school districts. The response rate of 83.6% indicates the validity of these data. A full 39% of these respondents indicated an unwillingness to integrate handicapped children in mainstream classes. The data also indicate that primary and middle grade teachers were more willing to integrate handicapped children than teachers in grades seven and eight. Results in a similar study by Larrivee and Cook (1979) also suggested that mainstream teachers in upper grades have less positive attitudes about mainstreaming than earlier grade teachers.

Researchers have recently focused on the reasons for the negative attitude regarding mainstreaming (Baker and Gottlieb, 1980; Frith and Edwards, 1982; Larrivee and Cook, 1979; Ringlaben and Price, 1981). For example, Ringlaben and Price (1981) sent questionnaires to 250 elementary and secondary teachers. The low response rate of 47% suggests concern over the validity of the results. Nevertheless, an interesting analysis of the data was performed. The researcher employed a principal components analysis of the 22 items to identify two distinct factors. The educational-social philosophy, comprised of factors such as agreement with philosophy of mainstreaming and effects of mainstreaming on mainstreamed students accounted for 36% of the variance in responses. The second factor, education-academic content, was comprised of course work in mainstreaming, preparation, and law knowledge concerning mainstreaming. This accounted for 10% of the variance. Apparently, few of the teachers in this study

felt adequately prepared to deal with mainstream children.

Other research suggests that negative attitudes may be associated with anticipated time requirements for mainstream children. Frith and Edwards (1982) administered questionnaires to 46 regular class teachers who had no prior experience with physically handicapped children. Of that group, 59% expressed concern of the disproportionate amount of time required by handicapped students.

Interventions for Teacher Attitudes

The first intervention usually recommended is the requirement of course and/or in-service training with handicapped children (Crisci, 1981; Frith and Edwards, 1982; Stephens and Braun, 1980). For example, Stephens and Braun (1980) present evidence to suggest that mainstream teachers' willingness to integrate handicapped children increases as the number of special educational classes increases. Preservice teacher training should include competencies and observational exposure to handicapped students for all preservice educators (Crisci, 1981), and the new Standards for the Accreditation of Teacher Education (NCATE, 1982) include statements to this effect. A number of in-service opportunities could be made available to school personnel now teaching along these same lines.

Some research has indicated that the attitude of teachers can be changed through exposure to handicapped children in addition to increased knowledge on how to deal with these students (Clark, 1976; Frith and Edwards, 1982; Horasymiro and Horne, 1975; Higgs, 1975). The suggestion has been made that exposure to handicapped learners without increased course work in this area will improve attitudes (Clark, 1976). This form of intervention, if replicated by other research, offers the advantage of being an "in-house" intervention which school systems may implement on their own with no involvement from teacher training institutions.

THE MAINSTREAMING TEACHER'S TIME

Teachers' concern that handicapped children take more time in planning and in class seems plausible, based on limited research (Barton, Barton, Brulle and Wharton, 1983; Chow, Thomas, Thum and Phillips, 1980; Decker and Decker, 1977; Forness, Guthrie and MacMillan, 1981; Raber and Weisz, 1981; Bender, 1984). For example, Bender (1984) used an observational methodology to compare individualized instructional time of third, sixth and ninth grade LD and non-handicapped students (N = 45 LD and 45 non-handicapped). This is the only study available which identifies the overall percentage of time in which individualized instruction (either direct teacher/aide tutoring or individualized instructional activities) is concerned. The results indicated that the third and sixth grade LD children received individualized instruction roughly 10% of the time, compared to less than 2% for their non-LD peers. The adolescent LD group received 2% individualized instruction, comparable to the comparison non-LD groups at that grade level.

A second indicator that handicapped students require more time is research which suggested that handicapped learners engage in more verbal interactions with the teacher than non-handicapped students (Chapman, Larsen and Parker, 1979; Dorval, McKinney and Feagans, 1982; Parker, Larsen and Roberts, 1981; Raber and Weisz, 1981). For example, Dorval, et al. (1982) coded the dialogues of 12 LD normally achieving classmates. The comparison children were matched on race and sex with the LD children. Results indicated that teachers initiated conversations more frequently with LD students. Over 42% of teacher initiated dialogues directed at individuals were directed at LD children, compared to 13% directed at the comparison sample.

Methodological Concerns

Critics of current mainstreaming practice will find the limited support for their fears discussed above, though several problems exist with this logic. First of all, none of the studies attempted to discuss competitive time allocations. While the excess of teacher attention to handicapped students is documented to a limited extent, none of the studies suggested that this excess time was taken away from the time which would ordinarily be spent with non-handicapped learners. The extra time used for planning, instruction and verbal initiations with handicapped children may have been time "borrowed" from non-instructional activities, which therefore would not directly result in compromising the education of non-handicapped children in the class.

A second concern related to the methodological question of comparison peer selection. Most of the studies used average achievers as the comparison group (Chow, et al., 1980; Dorval, McKinney and Feagans, 1982; Bender, 1984). It is therefore difficult to argue that the teacher should spend equal time and attention with each group, since the handicapped children demonstrate lower achievement anyway.

Nevertheless, the research does tentatively suggest that handicapped learners require more teacher time and attention than non-handicapped learners. This is problematic for special educators, given the fact that the number of handicapped students mainstreamed into a class is not routinely documented. For example, whereas one handicapped learner in a mainstream class of twenty will make some excess demands for teacher attention, this would probably not disrupt teacher instruction to other class members a great deal. However, the mainstreaming of seven children into that class may very well increase the likelihood of compromising the education of non-handicapped class members. For example, Bradfield, Brown, Kaplan, Rickert and Stannard (1973) indicated that when a class of 22 non-handicapped youngsters was given a complement of six handicapped students, the overall academic level of non-handicapped learners in the class went down compared to a control class which did not receive any mainstream children.

Future Research on Teacher Time

Research in the mainstream classes must be conducted initially to identify the educational environment for mainstreamed exceptional students. Research should focus on the number of handicapped children and the anticipated demands on teacher time. Dependent variables should include percentage of individualized instructional time, tutoring time, out-of-class planning time, verbal interactions, and the quality of these interactions for both handicapped and non-handicapped students. This research must document the effect of increased teacher instructional time spent with handicapped students on the achievement of both handicapped and non-handicapped students in the class.

Second, the administrative procedures which decide the mainstream class placement must be documented. For example, the administrative placement committee may decide on mainstreaming a fourth grade LD child, but the principal usually decides which of the three fourth grade teachers receive that child. Research must specify the mechanisms by which administrators should make this decision in order to insure that effective teachers who can handle wide variance in classroom behavior are not overloaded with handicapped children, while less effective teachers escape responsibility for special students.

Finally, researchers must begin to identify an appropriate ratio of handicapped to non-handicapped to provide some empirical basis for class placement decisions. For example, Chow, et al. (1980), found from one to eight handicapped students in a class (the mean being 3.2). Because that study included only LD students, one may assume that additional exceptional students (educable, physically impaired, gifted) may also have been present. The amount of variance in behavior and achievement which a single class can stand without compromising the education of non-handicapped members must be documented. Researchers must indicate an appropriate ratio of handicapped to non-handicapped—taking into consideration the level of severity of the handicap. This ratio must be based on consideration of the needs of all students in the mainstream.

Intervention for Teacher Time

Interventions on teacher use of time may involve several facets, including placing an aide, grandparent tutor, or peer tutor in mainstream classes. This could lighten the teacher's time requirements for non-instructional activities, thus permitting more instruction. For example, Hiatt (1979) demonstrated that teachers with aides spend 25% less time managing disruptive behavior, with the majority of this time savings devoted to instruction.

Another option is the use of special material and equipment, such as teaching machines which may be integrated into the mainstream class in order to meet the needs of the handicapped without requiring the teacher's in-class time. A cautionary note must be made: the teacher must still plan for the successful use of these options so planning time outside of class is still required.

Finally, in addition to providing aides, tutors, and equipment in the mainstream, pre-service and in-service training should be made available to teachers in order to instruct them on professional time management skills. Often, teachers do not fully realize the maximum benefit from the use of aides, tutors, and other personnel. Little net benefit will be realized by providing aides or tutors to mainstream classes where teachers have not been instructed in effective use of such personnel.

PEER ATTITUDES

The social relationships of handicapped individuals suggest some concern relative to the overall effectiveness of mainstreaming. For example, research throughout the years has consistently demonstrated that mildly handicapped children who are mainstreamed are socially rejected by their non-handicapped peers (Bryan, 1974, 1976; Bender, Bailey, Wyne and Stuck, 1984; Goodman, Gottlieb and Harrison, 1976; Gottlieb and Budoff, 1973; Gottlieb and Davis, 1973). Because the focus of this research has been social acceptance of the handicapped, little research has been done to determine the effects of these negative attitudes among the non-handicapped on the non-handicapped students themselves. There is no research to date which assesses the impact of negative attitudes toward the handicapped on other children's attitudes toward school work, class field trips, or school in general. One could well argue that, even if negative attitudes towards the handicapped lead to less participation in field trips among the non-handicapped, this would not be an indictment of mainstreaming but rather a result of prejudice. Nevertheless, in documenting the effects of mainstreaming, this issue must be addressed.

Intervention for Social Acceptance

Research has suggested several interventions to improve the social acceptance of handicapped learners (Allen, 1980; Gottlieb, 1980; Guralnick, 1976; Hoben, 1980; Johnson and Johnson, 1980; Jones, Sowell, Jones and Butler, 1981). For example, Gottlieb (1980) recommended group discussion of handicapping conditions as a method to facilitate integration. Custer and Osguthorpe (1983), in one of the more innovative approaches to integration, used 15 mildly retarded elementary school children to tutor non-handicapped children individually in sign language with some success.

However, one problem with techniques is the time loss, the time devoted to such activities which must come out of instructional time, and the research on teaching has amply demonstrated the critical necessity to maximize instructional time in basic skills (Walberg, Schiller and Haertel, 1979).

An intervention which can be structured to not usurp instructional time is the use of cooperative learning situations in the classroom (Hoben, 1980; Johnson and Johnson, 1980). Johnson and Johnson (1980) have recommended the use of cooperative learning situations to increase integration in the mainstream. Presumably, the cooperative learning situation can incorporate basic skills work and thus not take time allocated to basic skills for handicapped and non-handicapped class members.

EFFECTS OF CLASSROOM BEHAVIOR

The classroom behavioral research completed within mainstream classes has documented the fact that both learning disabled and educable children behave differently than non-handicapped children (Bender, in press; Bender, Bailey, Wyne and Stuck, 1984; Bryan, 1974; Forman and McKinney, 1975; Forness and Esveldt, 1975; Kuveke, 1978; Krupski, 1979; McKinney, McClure and Feagans, 1982; Richey and McKinney, 1978). This issue of classroom behavior became a critical concern of proponents of mainstreaming in several ways.

Peer Imitation

One major concern, largely unaddressed by research, is negative imitation, or the degree to which non-handicapped learners are likely to imitate the inappropriate behavior of handicapped learners (Allen, 1980; Cooke, Apolloni and Cooke, 1972; Peterson, Peterson and Scriven, 1977). In the only data based study available, Peterson, et al. (1977), used an observational strategy in a non-classroom learning task. Fourteen handicapped and fifteen non-handicapped children were observed

in a situation in which each student observed a ten step task sequence and then modeled the sequence. Results indicated that both handicapped and non-handicapped students were likely to imitate non-handicapped models. This suggests that negative imitation is unlikely. Nevertheless, given the data which suggests that handicapped learners receive more teacher attention (Dorval, et al., 1982), the question remains, will non-handicapped children interpret this teacher attention in the classroom as reinforcement and therefore imitate inappropriate behaviors?

Classroom Ecology

The first issue under general classroom ecology concerns the type of off-task behaviors demonstrated by handicapped students. Behaviors which are disruptive to other students in the class such as acting out or hyperactivity, would provide a rationale for arguing that mainstreaming compromises the education of non-handicapped learners, whereas more passive forms of off-task behavior would not, since this type of off-task behavior is not as disruptive.

Both teacher rating and observational methodologies have indicated that learning disabled and educable students emit socially undesirable behaviors in the mainstream (Bender, in press; Kuveke, 1978; Krupski, 1979; McKinney, McClure and Feagans, 1982; Richey and McKinney, 1978). Teacher rating studies with disabled populations indicate a presence of a range of disruptive behavior including hyperactivity, aggressiveness, and lack of task orientation (Bender, in press; Forman and McKinney, 1975). However, observational studies with LD populations usually indicate that the handicapped students are more often off-task in passive ways which do not have as much of a tendency to disrupt other students (Bender, in press; McKinney, McClure and Feagans, 1982; Richey and McKinney, 1978). For example, Richey and McKinney (1978) compared 15 LD and 15 matched peers in the mainstream class on an observational scale including 12 categories of task oriented, social, and affective behavior. Only the difference in distractibility favoring the non-LD children differentiated the two groups.

The observational results of mentally retarded students generally suggest higher levels of disruptive behavior (Forness, Guthrie and MacMillan, 1981; Kuveke, 1978; Krupski, 1979). For example, observational studies report that educable students emit more socially undesirable behavior (Kuveke, 1978) and out-of-seat behavior (Krupski, 1979) than non-handicapped. This type of behavior would certainly be distracting to non-handicapped students in the class.

While more distractible and disruptive behavior demonstrated by handicapped children could cause lower task orientation by non-handicapped children, these disruptive behaviors seem certain to cause recriminations by the teacher. Measures of punitiveness which may result from increases in disruptive behavior represent the second ecological concern. Research on teacher interactions has suggested that teachers do interact more negatively with handicapped learners (Chapman, et al., 1979; Dorval, et al., 1982; Raber and Weitz, 1981). In the Dorval, et al. (1982), study, behavior management statements were much more likely to be directed at a mainstreamed LD child than a non-handicapped child. Further, these handicapped statements were three times more likely to deal with rule infraction rather than routine class management. A

sharp increase in disciplinary statements would compromise the ecology of any classroom.

Research on Behavior and Classroom Ecology

The critical aspects regarding classroom ecology seem to be the type of handicapped child being mainstreamed, the number of mainstream children and the level of severity. If educable students demonstrate more behaviors which are disruptive than do LD students, the classroom environment could accept fewer educable students without becoming unduly punitive. Likewise, research must specify the level of severity appropriate for mainstream settings and the ratio of mainstreamed children to non-handicapped children.

Also, assessment devices which incorporate measures of classroom behavior should be developed for use in mainstreaming decisions (Bender, in press; McKinney, McClure and Feagans, 1982). Wilkes, Bailey and Schultz (1974) note that this consideration is already being made in certain situations.

CONCLUSIONS

The critics of current mainstreaming practice can marshall some evidence to suggest that mainstreaming may compromise the education of non-handicapped learners. These include negative teacher and peer attitudes regarding mainstreaming; increased demands of the handicapped children on teacher instructional time; the possibility of negative imitation; and the possibility of a less constructive classroom ecology. Interventions were recommended for the first three of these because research has to a degree established the validity of these concerns.

Future research must begin to look at mainstreaming processes in the classroom, and in the larger organizational concerns of the entire school. An appropriate ratio of handicapped to non-handicapped learners must be identified based on the findings relative to teacher time, negative imitation, and the possibility of a less constructive classroom ecology. The appropriate procedures for mainstreaming must then be broadened to include recommendations on which specific class a child should be placed in and the criteria for placement.

While arguments against mainstreaming became irrelevant in 1975, many concerns about effective mainstreaming do linger on, particularly issues concerning the education of the non-handicapped. The myopic perspective of studying only the effects of mainstreaming on handicapped children will not well serve the interests of the handicapped, either in the long run or in the political backlash budget battles on the immediate horizon.

REFERENCES

Abeson, A. The educational least restrictive alternative. *Amicus*, 1977, 2, (4) 23–26.

Abramson, M. Implications of mainstreaming: a challenge for special education. In L. Mann and D. A. Sabitino (Eds.) *Fourth Review of Special Education*, New York: Grune and Stratton, 1980.

Allen, K. E. Mainstreaming: What have we learned? *Young Children*, 1980, 35, (5), 54–63.

Baker, J. L., and Gottlieb, J. Attitudes of teachers toward mainstreaming retarded children. In J. Gottlieb (Ed.) *Educating Mentally Retarded Persons in the Mainstream*. Baltimore, Maryland: University Park Press, 1980.

Barton, C. L., Barton, L. E., Brulle, A. R., and Wharton, D. L. A comparison of teacher time spent with physically handicapped and able-bodied students. *Exceptional Children*, 1983, 49, 543–545.

Bender, W. N. Differences in temperament and behavior between learning disabled and non-learning disabled children. *Learning Disabilities Quarterly*, in press.

———. *Instructional Groupings and Individualization for Mainstream Learning Disabled Children and Adolescents*. Manuscript submitted for publication, Bluefield State and Concord College, Athens, West Virginia, 1984.

———, Bailey, D. P., Wyne, M., and Stuck, G. (1984). Relative peer status of learning disabled, educable mentally handicapped, low achieving and normally achieving students. *Child Study Journal*, 1984, 13, 209–216.

Bradfield, R. H., Brown, J., Kaplan, P., Rickert, E., and Stannard, R. The special child in the regular classroom. *Exceptional Children*, 1973, 39, 384–392.

Bryan, J. H. An observational analysis of classroom behavior of children with learning disabilities. *Journal of Learning Disabilities*, 1974, 7, 35–43.

Bryan, T. H. Peer popularity of learning disabled children: A replication. *Journal of Learning Disabilities*, 1979, 9, 307–311.

Chapman, R. B., Larsen, S. C., and Parker, R. M. Interactions of first grade teachers with learning disordered children. *Journal of Learning Disabilities*, 1979, 12, 225–230.

Chow, S. H. L., Thomas, C. F., Thom, S. R. and Phillips, M. L. *A Study of Academic Learning Time of Mainstream Handicapped Students*. Final Report: Far West Laboratory for Research and Development, San Francisco, 1980.

Clark, E. A. Teacher attitude toward integration of children with handicaps. *Education and Training of the Mentally Retarded*, 1976, 11, 333–335.

Cooke, T. P., Apolloni, T., and Cooke, S. A. Normal preschool children as behavioral models for retarded peers. *Exceptional Children*, 1977, 43, 531–535.

Crisci, P. E. Competencies for mainstreaming: problems and issues. *Educational Training of the Retarded*, 1981, 16, 175–181.

Custer, J. D., and Osguthorpe, R. T. Improving social acceptance by training handicapped students to tutor their non-handicapped peers. *Exceptional Children*, 1983, 50, 173–174.

Decker, R. J., and Decker, L. A. Mainstreaming the L. D. child: a cautionary note. *Academic Therapy*, 1977, 12, 253–256.

Dorval, B., McKinney, J. D., and Feagans, L. Teacher interaction with learning disabled children and average achievers. *Journal of Pediatric Psychology*, 1982, 17, 317–330.

Forman, B. P., and McKinney, J. D. Teacher perceptions of the classroom behavior of learning disabled and non-learning disabled children. *Proceedings of the National Association of School Psychologists*, 1975, 2, 285–286.

Forness, S. R., and Esveldt, K. C. Classroom observation of children with learning and behavior problems. *Journal of Learning Disabilities*, 1975, 8, 382–385.

_____, Guthrie, P., and MacMillan, D. L. Classroom behavior of mentally retarded children across different classroom settings. *The Journal of Special Education*, 1981, 15, 497–509.

_____, Guthrie, D., and MacMillan, D. L. Classroom environments as they relate to mentally retarded children's observable behavior. *American Journal of Mental Deficiency*, 1982, 87, 259–265.

Frith, G. H., and Edwards, R. Misconceptions of regular classroom teachers about physically handicapped students. *Exceptional Children*, 1982, 48, 182–184.

Glickling, E. E., and Theobald, J. T. Mainstreaming: affect or effect. *The Journal of Special Education*, 1975, 9, 317–328.

Goodman, H., Gottlieb, J., and Harrison, R. H. Social acceptance of EMRs integrated into a non graded elementary school. *American Journal of Mental Deficiency*, 1972, 76, 412–417.

Gottlieb, J. Improving attitudes toward retarded children by using group discussion. *Exceptional Children*, 1980, 47, 106–113.

_____, and Budoff, M. Social acceptability of retarded children in non-grade schools differing in architecture. *American Journal of Mental Deficiency*, 1973, 78, 15–19.

_____, and Davis, J. E. Social acceptance of EMR's during overt behavioral interaction. *American Journal of Mental Deficiency*, 1973, 78, 141–143.

Guralnick, M. J. The value of integrating handicapped and non-handicapped preschool children. *American Journal of Orthopsychiatry*, 1976, 46, 236–245.

Hiatt, D. B. Time allocation in the classroom: Is instruction being shortchanged? *Phi Delta Kappan*, 1979, 61, 289–290.

Higgs, R. W. Attitude formation—contact or information? *Exceptional Children*, 1975, 41, 496–497.

Hoben, M. Toward integration in the mainstream. *Exceptional Children*, 1980, 47, 100–105.

Horasymiro, W. J., and Horne, M. D. Integration of handicapped children: Its effect on teacher attitude. *Education*, 1975, 96, 153–158.

Johnson, D. W., and Johnson, R. T. Integrating handicapped students into the mainstream. *Exceptional Children*, 1980, 47, 90–99.

Jones, T. W., Sowell, V. M., Jones, D. K., and Butler, L. G. Changing children's perceptions of handicapped people. *Exceptional Children*, 1981, 47, 365–368.

Keveke, S. H. *School Behaviors of Educable Mentally Retarded Children*. Doctoral Dissertation. Heshira University, 1978.

Krupski, A. Are retarded children more distractible? Observational analysis of retarded and nonretarded children's classroom behavior. *American Journal of Mental Deficiency*, 1979, 84, 1–10.

Larrivee, B., and Cook, L. Mainstreaming: A study of the variables affecting teacher attitude. *The Journal of Special Education*, 1979, 13, 313–324.

McKinney, J. D., McClure, J., and Feagans, L. Classroom behavior of learning disabled children. *Learning Disability Quarterly*, 1982, 5, 45–52.

National Council for Accreditation of Teacher Education, *Standards for the Accreditation of Teacher Education*, Washington, D.C., 1982.

Parker, R., Larsen, S., Roberts, T. Teacher-Child interactions of first grade students who have learning problems. *The Elementary School Journal*, 1981, 81, 163–171.

Peterson, C., Peterson, J., Scriven, G. Peer imitations by nonhandicapped and handicapped preschoolers. *Exceptional Children*, 1977, 43, 223–224.

Raber, S. M., and Weisz, J. R. Teacher feedback to mentally retarded and nonretarded children. *American Journal of Mental Deficiency*, 1981, 86, 148–156.

Richey, D. D., and McKinney, J. D. Classroom behavioral styles of learning disabled boys. *Journal of Learning Disabilities*, 1978, 11, 297–302.

Ringlaben, R. P., and Price, J. R. Regular classroom teacher's perception of mainstreaming effects. *Exceptional Children*, 1981, 47, 302–304.

Stedman, D. J. Possible effects of public law 94-142 on the future of teacher education: in M.C. Reynolds (Ed.) *A Common Body of Practice for Teachers: The Challenge of Public Law 94-142 to Teacher Education*. National Support Systems Project: American Association of Colleges of Teacher Education, 1980.

Stephens, T. M., and Braun, B. L. Measures of regular classroom teachers attitudes toward handicapped children. *Exceptional Children*, 1980, 46, 292–294.

Walberg, H. J., Schiller, D., and Haertel, D. The quiet revolution in educational research. *Phi Delta Kappan*, 1979, 61, 197–183.

Wilkes, H. H., Bailey, M. K., and Schultz, J. J. Criteria for mainstreaming the learning disabled child into the regular classroom. *Journal of Learning Disabilities*, 1979, 12, 251–256.

POSTSCRIPT

Is Mainstreaming Beneficial to All?

One wit has claimed that P.L. 94–142 is really a "full employment act for lawyers." Indeed, much litigation regarding the identification, classification, placement, and specialized treatment of children with handicaps has been initiated. The parental involvement aspect of the law invites cooperation but can lead to conflict. Also some parents of "normal" children are beginning to wonder if their offspring might not be entitled to greater specialized services as well.

These problems and many others associated with the full implementation of this landmark legislation are treated in a number of publications. Focusing on the larger aspects, such as social and ethical issues, research, and legal matters, are *Shared Responsibility for Handicapped Students: Advocacy and Programming* (1976), edited by Philip H. Mann; Catherine Morsink's "Implementing P.L. 94–142: Challenge of the 1980s," *Education Unlimited* (October 1979); *Special Education in Transition* (1980), edited by Dean C. Corrigan and Kenneth R. Howey; *P.L. 94–142: A Guide for the Education of All Handicapped Children Act* (1979), by Clarence J. Jones and Ted F. Rabold; *Educating the Handicapped: Where We've Been, Where We're Going* (1980), by Mitchell Lazarus; *Educational Handicap, Public Policy, and Social History* (1979), by Seymour B. Sarason and John Doris; and *Foundations of Teacher Preparation: Responses to Public Law 94–142* (1982), edited by Maynard C. Reynolds.

Among works directed specifically at regular classroom teachers are: *Mainstreaming Handicapped Students: A Guide for the Classroom Teacher* (1979), by Ann P. Turnbull and Jane B. Schulz; *Mainstreaming Students with Learning and Behavior Problems* (1981), by Coleen Blankenship and M. Stephen Lilly; and *Teaching Handicapped Students in the Mainstream: Coming Back . . . or Never Leaving*, 2d ed (1981), by Anne L. Pasanella and Cara B. Volkmor.

Recent research studies include Martin Diebold's "A School-level Investigation of Predictions of Attitudes About Mainstreaming," *Journal of Special Education* (Fall 1986) and "Willingness of Regular and Special Educators to Teach Students with Handicaps," *Exceptional Children* (October 1987), by Karen Derk Gans. Some thought-provoking observations are offered by Susan Ohanian in "P.L. 94–142: Mainstream or Quicksand?" *Phi Delta Kappan* (November 1990).

Mainstreaming presents both moral and practical issues. As Seymour Sarason tells us: "It raises age-old questions: How do we want to live with each other? On what basis should we give priority to one value over another? How far does the majority want to go in accommodating the needs of the minority?"

ISSUE 18

Does Tracking Create Educational Inequality?

YES: Jeannie Oakes, from "Keeping Track, Part 1: The Policy and Practice of Curriculum Inequality," *Phi Delta Kappan* (September 1986)

NO: Charles Nevi, from "In Defense of Tracking," *Educational Leadership* (March 1987)

ISSUE SUMMARY

YES: Social scientist Jeannie Oakes argues that tracking exaggerates initial differences among students and contributes to mediocre schooling for many who are placed in middle or lower tracks.
NO: Charles Nevi, director of Curriculum and Instruction for the Puyallup School District in Washington, feels that tracking accommodates individual differences while making "high-status knowledge" available to all.

One of John Franklin Bobbitt's scientific management principles, designed for application to public schooling early in this century, was this: Work up the raw material into that finished product for which it is best adapted. During the first four decades of the century, public school officials became more and more captivated by the "efficiency" movement, and, according to Edward Stevens and George H. Wood, in *Justice, Ideology, and Education* (1987), "the ideal of a unified curriculum gave way to the ideal of differentiating students for predetermined places in the work force." The application of these principles of management resulted in a tracking system in schools that tended to reproduce the divisions of the social class system.

Books such as Willard Waller's *The Sociology of Teaching* (1967), Paulo Freire's *The Pedagogy of the Oppressed* (1973), and *Schooling in Capitalist America* (1976), by Samuel Bowles and Herbert Gintis, mounted a pungent criticism of this prevailing practice. In more recent times, during which a conscious effort has been made to "equalize" opportunities for all students regardless of their backgrounds, the race is still rigged. According to Stevens and Wood: "The very structure of the school, particularly its tracking and sorting function, is designed to assure the success of some at the expense of others."

Many people now realize the importance of reducing the social and racial homogeneity of the school environment. As presently structured, the schools seem unable to overcome initial differences based on social and cultural disadvantages whether or not tracking and grouping are employed. The National Association for the Advancement of Colored People (NAACP) has officially called for the elimination of tracking and homogeneous grouping, the utilization of multimethod assessments of ability and achievement, and the assurance that high expectations will be held for all students.

In her 1985 book *Keeping Track*, Jeannie Oakes presents the results of her analysis of a wide selection of tracking studies. She found that there is little evidence that grouping improves the achievement levels of *any* group. She also found that students from disadvantaged backgrounds are given a less demanding and less rewarding set of curricular experiences and that children in the lower tracks suffer losses of self-esteem and develop negative self-concepts.

In the following articles, Jeannie Oakes defines tracking, examines its underlying assumptions, and summarizes what she judges to be the disappointing effects of the practice. She contends that even as they voice commitment to equality and excellence, schools organize and deliver educational experiences in ways that advance neither. Charles Nevi counters with the argument that while students are obviously equal under the law they are not equal in ability. Tracking and grouping provide for these individual differences, he contends, whereas treating all students the same is not a formula for equity or excellence.

YES   Jeannie Oakes

KEEPING TRACK

The idea of educational equality has fallen from favor. In the 1980s policy makers, school practitioners, and the public have turned their attention instead to what many consider a competing goal: excellence. Attempts to "equalize" schooling in the Sixties and Seventies have been judged extravagant and naive. Worse, critics imply that those well-meant efforts to correct inequality may have compromised the central mission of the schools: teaching academics well. And current critics warn that, given the precarious position of the United States in the global competition for economic, technological, and military superiority, we can no longer sacrifice the quality of our schools to social goals. This view promotes the judicious spending of limited educational resources in ways that will produce the greatest return on "human capital." Phrased in these economic terms, special provisions for underachieving poor and minority students become a bad investment. In short, equality is out; academic excellence is in.

On the other hand, many people still argue vociferously that the distinction between promoting excellence and providing equality is false, that one cannot be achieved without the other. Unfortunately, whether "tight-fisted" conservatives or "fuzzy-headed" liberals are in the ascendancy, the heat of the rhetoric surrounding the argument largely obscures a more serious problem: the possibility that the unquestioned *assumptions* that drive school practice and the *basic features of schools* may themselves lock schools into patterns that make it difficult to achieve *either* excellence *or* equality.

The practice of tracking in secondary schools illustrates this possibility and provides evidence of how schools, even as they voice commitment to equality and excellence, organize and deliver curriculum in ways that advance neither. Nearly all schools track students. Because tracking enables schools to provide educational treatments matched to particular groups of students, it is believed to promote higher achievement for all students under conditions of equal educational opportunity. However, rather than promoting higher achievement, tracking contributes to mediocre schooling for *most* secondary students. And because it places the greatest obstacles to achievement in the path of those children least advantaged in American society—poor and minority children—tracking forces schools to play an active role in perpetuating school and economic inequalities as well. Evidence about the influence of tracking on student outcomes and analyses of how tracking affects the day-to-day school experiences of young people support the argument that such basic elements of schooling can *prevent* rather than *promote* educational goals.

WHAT IS TRACKING?

Tracking is the practice of dividing students into separate classes for high-, average-, and low-achievers; it lays out different curriculum paths for students headed for college and for those who are bound directly for the workplace. In most senior high schools, students are assigned to one or another *curriculum track* that lays out sequences of courses for college-preparatory, vocational, or general track students. Junior and senior high schools also make use of *ability grouping*—that is, they divide academic subjects (typically English, mathematics, science, and social studies) into classes geared to different "levels" for students of different abilities. In many high schools these two systems overlap, as schools provide college-preparatory, general, and vocational sequences of courses and also practice ability grouping in academic subjects. More likely than not, the student in the vocational curriculum track will be in one of the lower ability groups. Because similar overlapping exists for college-bound students, the distinction between the two types of tracking is sometimes difficult to assess.

But tracking does not proceed as neatly as the description above implies. Both curriculum tracking and ability grouping vary from school to school in the number of subjects that are tracked, in the number of levels provided, and in the ways in which students are placed. Moreover, tracking is confounded by the inflexibilities and idiosyncrasies of "master schedules," which can create unplanned tracking, generate further variations among tracking systems, and affect the courses taken by individual students as well. Elective subjects, such as art and home economics, sometimes become low-track classes because college-preparatory students rarely have time in their schedules to take them; required classes, such as drivers' training, health, or physical education, though they are intended to be heterogeneous, become tracked when the requirements of other courses that *are* tracked keep students together for large portions of the day.

Despite these variations, tracking has common and predictable characteristics:

• The intellectual performance of students is judged, and these judgments determine placement with particular groups.

• Classes and tracks are labeled according to the performance levels of the students in them (e.g., advanced, average, remedial) or according to students' postsecondary destinations (e.g., college-preparatory, vocational).

• The curriculum and instruction in various tracks are tailored to the perceived needs and abilities of the students assigned to them.

• The groups that are formed are not merely a collection of different but equally-valued instructional groups. They form a hierarchy, with the most advanced tracks (and the students in them) seen as being on top.

• Students in various tracks and ability levels experience school in very different ways.

UNDERLYING ASSUMPTIONS

First, and clearly most important, teachers and administrators generally assume that tracking promotes overall student achievement—that is, that the academic needs of all students will be better met when they learn in groups with similar capabilities or prior levels of achievement. Given the inevitable diversity of student populations, tracking is seen as the best way to address individual needs and to cope with individual differences. This assumption stems from a view of human capabilities that includes the belief that students' capacities to master schoolwork are so disparate that they require different and separate schooling experiences. The extreme position contends that some students cannot learn at all.

A second assumption that underlies tracking is that less-capable students will suffer emotional as well as educational damage from daily classroom contact and competition with their brighter peers. Lowered self-concepts and negative attitudes toward learning are widely considered to be consequences of mixed-ability grouping for slower learners. It is also widely assumed that students can be placed in tracks and groups both accurately and fairly. And finally, most teachers and administrators contend that tracking greatly eases the teaching task and is, perhaps, the *only* way to manage student differences.

THE RECORD OF TRACKING

Students clearly differ when they enter secondary schools, and these differences just as clearly influence learning. But separating students to better accommodate these differences appears to be neither necessary, effective, nor appropriate.

Does tracking work? At the risk of oversimplifying a complex body of research literature, it is safe to conclude that *there is little evidence to support any of the assumptions about tracking.* The effects of tracking on student outcomes have been widely investigated, and the bulk of this work *does not* support commonly-held beliefs that tracking increases student learning. Nor does the evidence support tracking as a way to improve students' attitudes about themselves or about schooling.[1] Although existing tracking systems *appear* to provide advantages for students who are placed in the top tracks, the literature suggests that students at all ability levels can achieve at least as well in heterogeneous classrooms.

Students who are *not* in top tracks—a group that includes about 60% of senior high school students—suffer clear and consistent disadvantages from tracking. Among students identified as average or slow, tracking often appears to retard academic progress. Indeed, one study documented the fact that the lowered I.Q. scores of senior high school students followed their placement in low tracks.[2] Students who are placed in vocational tracks do not even seem to reap any benefits in the job market. Indeed, graduates of vocational programs may be less employable and, when they do find jobs, may earn lower wages than other high school graduates.[3]

Most tracking research does not support the assumption that slow students suffer emotional strains when enrolled in mixed-ability classes. Often the opposite result has been found. Rather than helping students feel more comfortable about themselves, tracking can reduce self-esteem, lower aspirations, and foster negative attitudes toward school. Some studies have also concluded that tracking leads low-track students to misbehave and eventually to drop out altogether.[4]

The net effect of tracking is to exaggerate the initial differences among students rather than to provide the means to better accommodate them. For example, studies show that senior high school students who are initially similar in background and prior achievement become *increasingly* different in achievement and future aspirations when they are placed in different tracks.[5] Moreover, this effect is likely to be cumulative over most of the students' school careers, since track placements tend to remain fixed. Students placed in low-ability groups in elementary school are likely to continue in these groups in middle school or junior high school; in senior high school these students are typically placed in non-college-preparatory tracks. Studies that have documented increased gaps between initially comparable high school students placed in different tracks probably capture only a fraction of this effect.

Is tracking fair? Compounding the lack of empirical evidence to support tracking as a way to enhance student outcomes are compelling arguments that favor exposing all students to a common curriculum, *even if differences among them prevent all students from benefiting equally.* These arguments counter both the assumption that tracking can be carried out "fairly" and the view that tracking is a legitimate means to ease the task of teaching.

Central to the issue of fairness is the well-established link between track placements and student background characteristics. Poor and minority youngsters (principally black and Hispanic) are disproportionately placed in tracks for low-ability or non-college-bound students. By the same token, minority students are consistently underrepresented in programs for the gifted and talented. In addition, differentiation by race and class occurs within vocational tracks, with blacks and Hispanics more frequently enrolled in programs that train students for the lowest-level occupations (e.g., building maintenance, commercial sewing, and institutional care). These differences in placement by race and social class appear regardless of whether test scores, counselor and teacher recommendations, or student and parent choices are used as the basis for placement.[6]

Even if these track placements are ostensibly based on merit—that is, determined by prior school achievement rather than by race, class, or student choice—they usually come to signify judgments about supposedly fixed abilities. We might find appropriate the disproportionate placements of poor and minority students in low-track classes if these youngsters were, in fact, known to be innately less capable of learning than middle- and upper-middle-class whites. But this is not the case. Or we might think of these track placements as appropriate *if* they served to remediate the obvious educational deficiencies that many poor and minority students exhibit. If being in a low track prepared disadvantaged students for success in higher tracks and opened future educational opportunities to them, we would not question the need for tracking. However, this rarely happens.

The assumption that tracking makes teaching easier pales in importance when held up against the abundant evidence of the general ineffectiveness of tracking and the disproportionate harm it works on poor and minority students. But even if this were not the case, the assumption that tracking makes teaching easier would stand up *only if* the tracks were made up of truly homogeneous groups. In fact, they are not. Even within tracks, the variability of students' learning speed, cognitive style, interest, effort, and aptitude for various tasks is often considerable. Tracking simply masks the fact that instruction for any group of 20 to 35 people requires considerable variety in instructional strategies, tasks, materials, feedback, and guidance. It also requires multiple criteria for success and a variety of rewards. Unfortunately, for many schools and teachers, tracking deflects attention from these instructional realities. When instruction fails, the problem is too often attributed to the child or perhaps to a "wrong placement." The fact that tracking *may* make teaching easier for some teachers should not cloud our judgment about whether that teaching is best for any group of students—whatever their abilities.

Finally, a profound ethical concern emerges from all the above. In the words of educational philosopher Gary Fenstermacher, "[U]sing individual differences in aptitude, ability or interest as the basis for curricular variation denies students equal access to the knowledge and understanding available to mankind." He continues, "[I]t is possible that some students may not benefit equally from unrestricted access to knowledge, but this fact does not entitle us to control access in ways that effectively prohibit all students from encountering what Dewey called the 'funded capital of civilization.' "[7] Surely educators do not intend any such unfairness when by tracking they seek to accommodate differences among students.

WHY SUCH DISAPPPOINTING EFFECTS?

As those of us who were working with John Goodlad on A Study of Schooling began to analyze the extensive set of data we had gathered about 38 schools across the U.S., we wanted to find out more about tracking.[8] We wanted to gather specific information about the knowledge and skills that students were taught in tracked classes, about the learning activities they experienced, about the way in which teachers managed instruction, about the classroom relationships, and about how involved students were in their learning. By studying tracked classes directly and asking over and over whether such classes differed, we hoped to begin to understand why the effects of tracking have been so disappointing for so many students. We wanted to be able to raise some reasonable hypotheses about the ways in which good intentions of practitioners seem to go wrong.

We selected a representative group of 300 English and mathematics classes. We chose these subjects because they are most often tracked and because nearly all secondary students take them. Our sample included relatively equal numbers of high-, average-, low-, and mixed-ability groups. We had a great deal of information about these classes because teachers and students had completed extensive questionnaires, teachers had been interviewed, and teachers had put together packages of materials about their classes, including lists of the topics and skills they taught, the textbooks they used, and the ways in which they evaluated student learning. Many teachers also gave us sample lesson plans, worksheets, and tests. Trained observers recorded what students and teachers were doing and documented their interactions.

The data gathered on these classes provided some clear and consistent insights. In the three areas we studied—curriculum content, instruction quality, and classroom climate—we found remarkable and disturbing differences between classes in different tracks. These included important discrepancies in student access to knowledge, in their classroom instructional opportunities, and in their classroom learning environments.

Access to knowledge. In both English and math classes, we found that students had access to considerably different types of knowledge and had opportunities to develop quite different intellectual skills. For example, students in high-track English classes were exposed to content that can be called "high-status knowledge." This included topics and skills that are required for college. High-track students studied both classic and modern fiction. They learned the characteristics of literary genres and analyzed the elements of good narrative writing. These students were expected to write thematic essays and reports of library research, and they learned vocabulary that would boost their scores on college entrance exams. It was the high-track students in our sample who had the most opportunities to think critically or to solve interesting problems.

Low-track English classes, on the other hand, rarely, if ever, encountered similar types of knowledge. Nor were they expected to learn the same skills. Instruction in basic reading skills held a prominent place in low-track classes, and these skills were taught mostly through workbooks, kits, and "young adult" fiction. Students wrote simple paragraphs, completed worksheets on English usage, and practiced filling out applications for jobs and other kinds of forms. Their learning tasks were largely restricted to memorization or low-level comprehension.

The differences in mathematics content followed much the same pattern. High-track classes focused primarily on mathematical concepts; low-track classes stressed basic computational skills and math facts.

These differences are not merely curricular adaptations to individual needs, though they are certainly thought of as such. Differences in access to knowledge have important long-term social and educational consequences as well. For example, low-track students are probably prevented from *ever* encountering at school the knowledge our society values most. Much of the curriculum of low-track classes was likely to lock students into a continuing series of such bottom-level placements because important concepts and skills were neglected. Thus these students were denied the knowledge that would enable them to move successfully into higher-track classes.

Opportunities to learn. We also looked at two classroom conditions known to influence how much students will learn: instructional time and teaching quality. The marked differences we found in our data consistently showed that students in higher tracks had better classroom opportunities. For example, all our data on classroom time pointed to the same conclusion: students in high tracks get more; students in low tracks get less. Teachers of high-track classes set aside more class time for learning, and our observers found that more actual class time was spent on learning activities. High-track students were also expected to spend more time doing homework, fewer high-track students were observed to be off-task during class activities, and more of them told us that learning took up most of their class time, rather than discipline problems, socializing, or class routines.

Instruction in high-track classes more often included a whole range of teacher behaviors likely to enhance learning. High-track teachers were more enthusiastic, and their instruction was clearer. They used strong criticism or ridicule less frequently than did teachers of low-track classes. Classroom tasks were more various and more highly organized in high-track classes, and grades were more relevant to student learning.

These differences in learning opportunities portray a fundamental irony of schooling: those students who need more time to learn appear to be getting less; those students who have the most difficulty learning are being exposed least to the sort of teaching that best facilitates learning.

Classroom climate. We were interested in studying classroom climates in various tracks because we were convinced that supportive relationships and positive feelings in class are more than just nice accompaniments to learning. When teachers and students trust one another, classroom time and energy are freed for teaching and learning. Without this trust, students spend a great deal of time and energy establishing less productive relationships with others and interfering with the teacher's instructional agenda; teachers spend their time and energy trying to maintain control. In such classes, less learning is more likely to occur.

The data from A Study of Schooling permitted us to investigate three impor-
tant aspects of classroom environments: relationships between teachers and students, relationships among the students, and the intensity of student involvement in learning. Once again, we discovered a distressing pattern of advantages for high-track classes and disadvantages for low-track classes. In high-track classes students thought that their teachers were more concerned about them and less punitive. Teachers in high-track classes spent less time on student behavior, and they more often encouraged their students to become independent, questioning, critical thinkers. In low-track classes teachers were seen as less concerned and more punitive. Teachers in low-track classes emphasized matters of discipline and behavior, and they often listed such things as "following directions," "respecting my position," "punctuality," and "learning to take a direct order" as among the five most important things they wanted their class to learn during the year.

We found similar differences in the relationship that students established with one another in class. Students in low-track classes agreed far more often that "students in this class are unfriendly to me" or that "I often feel left out of class activities." They said that their classes were interrupted by problems and by arguing in class. Generally, they seemed to like each other less. Not surprisingly, given these differences in relationships, students in high-track classes appeared to be much more involved in their classwork. Students in low-track classes were more apathetic and indicated more often that they didn't care about what went on or that failing didn't bother most of their classmates.

In these data, we found once again a pattern of classroom experience that seems to enhance the possibilities of learning for those students already disposed to do well—that is, those in high-track classes. We saw even more clearly a pattern of classroom experience likely to inhibit the learning of those in the bottom tracks. As with access to knowledge and opportunities to learn, we found that those who most needed support from a positive, nurturing environment got the least.

Although these data do show clear instructional advantages for high-achieving students and clear disadvantages for their low-achieving peers, other data from our work suggest that the quality of the experience of *average* students falls somewhere between these two extremes. Average students, too, were deprived of the best circumstances schools have to offer, though their classes were typically more like those of high-track students. Taken together, these findings begin to suggest *why* students who are not in the top tracks are likely to suffer because of their placements: their education is of considerably lower quality.

It would be a serious mistake to interpret these data as the "inevitable" outcome of the differences in the students who populate the various tracks. Many of the mixed-ability classes in our study showed that high-quality experiences are very possible in classes that include all types of students. But neither should we attribute these differences to consciously mean-spirited or blatantly discriminatory actions by schoolpeople. Obviously, the content teachers decide to teach and the ways in which they teach it are greatly influenced by the students with whom they interact. And it is unlikely that students are passive participants in tracking processes. It seems more likely that students' achievements, attitudes,

interests, perceptions of themselves, and behaviors (growing increasingly disparate over time) help produce some of the effects of tracking. Thus groups of students who, by conventional wisdom, seem less able and less eager to learn are very likely to affect teacher's ability or even willingness to provide the best possible learning opportunities. The obvious conclusion about the effects of these track-specific differences on the ability of the schools to achieve academic excellence is that students who are exposed to less content and lower-quality teaching are unlikely to get the full benefit out of their schooling. Yet this less-fruitful experience seems to be the norm when average- and low-achieving students are grouped together for instruction.

I believe that these data reveal frightening patterns of curricular inequality. Although these patterns would be disturbing under any circumstances (and though many white, suburban schools consign a good number of their students to mediocre experiences in low-ability and general-track classes), they become particularly distressing in light of the prevailing pattern of placing disproportionate numbers of poor and minority students in the lowest-track classes. A self-fulfilling prophecy can be seen to work at the institutional level to prevent schools from providing equal educational opportunity. Tracking appears to teach and reinforce the notion that those not defined as the best are *expected* to do less well. Few students and teachers can defy those expectations.

TRACKING, EQUALITY, AND EXCELLENCE

Tracking is assumed to promote educational excellence because it enables schools to provide students with the curriculum and instruction they need to maximize their potential and achieve excellence on their own terms. But the evidence about tracking suggests the contrary. Certainly students bring differences with them to school, but, by tracking, schools help to widen rather than narrow these differences. Students who are judged to be different from one another are separated into different classes and then provided knowledge, opportunities to learn, and classroom environments that are vastly different. Many of the students in top tracks (only about 40% of high-schoolers) do benefit from the advantages they receive in their classes. But, in their quest for higher standards and superior academic performance, schools seem to have locked themselves into a structure that may *unnecessarily* buy the achievement of a few at the expense of many. Such a structure provides but a shaky foundation for excellence.

At the same time, the evidence about tracking calls into question the widely held view that schools provide students who have the "right stuff" with a neutral environment in which they can rise to the top (with "special" classes providing an extra boost to those who might need it). Everywhere we turn we find that the differentiated structure of schools throws up barriers to achievement for poor and minority students. Measures of talent clearly seem to work against them, which leads to their disproportionate placement in groups identified as slow. Once there, their achievement seems to be further inhibited by the type of knowledge they are taught and by the quality of the learning opportunities they are afforded. Moreover, the social and psychological dimensions of classes at the bottom of the hierarchy of schooling seem to restrict their chances for school success even further.

Good intentions, including those of advocates of "excellence" and of "equity," characterize the rhetoric of schooling. Tracking, because it is usually taken to be a neutral practice and a part of the mechanics of schooling, has escaped the attention of those who mean well. But by failing to scrutinize the effects of tracking, schools unwittingly subvert their well-meant efforts to promote academic excellence and to provide conditions that will enable all students to achieve it.

NOTES

1. Some recent reviews of studies on the effects of tracking include: Robert C. Calfee and Roger Brown, "Grouping Students for Instruction," in *Classroom Management* (Chicago: 78th Yearbook of the National Society for the Study of Education, University of Chicago Press, 1979); Dominick Esposito, "Homogeneous and Heterogeneous Ability Grouping: Principal Findings and Implications for Evaluating and Designing More Effective Educational Environments," *Review of Educational Research*, vol. 43, 1973, pp. 163-79; Jeannie Oakes, "Tracking: A Contextual Perspective on How Schools Structure Differences," *Educational Psychologist*, in press; Caroline J. Persell, *Education and Inequality: The Roots and Results of Stratification in America's Schools* (New York: Free Press, 1977); and James E. Rosenbaum, "The Social Implications of Educational Grouping," in David C. Berliner, ed., *Review of Research in Education, Vol. 8* (Washington, D.C.: American Educational Research Association, 1980), pp. 361-01.

2. James E. Rosenbaum, *Making Inequality: The Hidden Curriculum of High School Tracking* (New York: Wiley, 1976).

3. See, for example, David Stern et al., *One Million Hours a Day: Vocational Education in California Public Secondary Schools* (Berkeley: Report to the California Policy Seminar, University of California School of Education, 1985).

4. Rosenbaum, "The Social Implications . . ."; and William E. Shafer and Carol Olexa, *Tracking and Opportunity* (Scranton, Pa.: Chandler, 1971).

5. Karl A. Alexander and Edward L. McDill, "Selection and Allocation Within Schools: Some Causes and Consequences of Curriculum Place-

ment." *American Sociological Review*, vol. 41, 1976, pp. 969–80; Karl A. Alexander, Martha Cook, and Edward L. McDill, "Curriculum Tracking and Educational Stratification: Some Further Evidence," *American Sociological Review*, vol. 43, 1978, pp. 47–66; and Donald A. Rock et al., *Study of Excellence in High School Education: Longitudinal Study, 1980–82* (Princeton, N.J.: Educational Testing Service, Final Report, 1985).

6. Persell, *Education and Inequality . . . ;* and Jeannie Oakes, *Keeping Track: How Schools Struc-*ture Inequality (New Haven, Conn.: Yale University Press, 1985).

7. Gary D. Fenstermacher, "Introduction," in Gary D. Fenstermacher and John I. Goodlad, eds., *Individual Differences and the Common Curriculum* (Chicago: 82nd Yearbook of the National Society for the Study of Education, University of Chicago Press, 1983), p. 3.

8. John I. Goodlad, *A Place Called School* (New York: McGraw-Hill, 1984).

NO

Charles Nevi

IN DEFENSE OF TRACKING

In his book, *A Place Called School*, John Goodlad presents a dire picture of low-level tracked classes. These classes, he says, are characterized by unmotivated teachers teaching uninspired students; the material has little significant content or relevance. The picture he presents is enough to embarrass any educator who has ever been associated with tracking in any way, other than to rail against it.[1]

In *Keeping Track* Jeannie Oakes takes the same data that were available to Goodlad for *A Place Called School* and adds even more dire information. In addition to considerably more verbiage, Oakes adds a historical perspective and develops the possibility that tracking is a conscious, deliberate conspiracy on the part of the capitalistic bourgeois elements in society. Oakes claims these groups seek to protect their privileges and property by providing low-level educational programs for the less advantaged to keep them content with their menial roles in society.[2]

Goodlad and Oakes muster enough data and emotion so that it is difficult to dispute them. But with a little reflection, something seems amiss in the pictures of tracking that they present. Somehow, one is reminded of a poem by Issa that goes something like this:

The world is a drop of dew,
And yet—and yet . . .

They are stating the obvious, and one hesitates to dispute them, and yet there still seems to be more to the issue.

Despite the criticism of tracking, ability-grouping is a common, even universal characteristic of public education. Others who have studied the issue indicate that it was being practiced at least as early as the turn of the century and that today it is established in "thousands of American schools."[3] Some observers even say that the history of education is the history of tracking. Tracking was born the first time an enterprising young teacher in a one-room schoolhouse in the 1800s divided his or her class into those who knew how to read and those who didn't. Certainly it began when teachers

From Charles Nevi, "In Defense of Tracking," *Educational Leadership*, vol. 44, no. 8 (March 1987), pp. 24–26. Copyright © 1987 by the Association for Supervision and Curriculum Development. Reprinted by permission. All rights reserved.

286

started organizing their students into grade- and age-level groups, a clear indication that some students were going to cover different content or the same content at a different rate.

REASONS FOR TRACKING

As education has become more complex, content more broad, and students more heterogeneous, tracking has increased. In recent years guidelines for certain federal funds—special and gifted education, Chapter 1—require that students be grouped for the purpose of different specialized instruction.

Oakes argues that tradition is one of the main reasons for the existence of tracking. And certainly this historical sorting of students into groups was done for one of the reasons that Oakes gives for tracking today: homogeneous groups are easier to teach.

A variety of additional reasons explain why tracking has become a tradition. It is one method of trying to improve the instructional setting for selected students, or what one researcher refers to as a "search for a better match between learner and instructional environment."[4] Tracking becomes a very common way of attempting to provide for individual differences. Unless everyone is going to be taught everything simultaneously, grouping is necessary. It may be as simple and obvious as putting some students in grade four, or some students into a primer and others into a novel.

Tracking is not an attempt to create differences, but to accommodate them. Not all differences are created by the schools; most differences are inherited. In reading Goodlad, and particularly Oakes, one can get the impression that all students come to school with exactly the same kinds of abilities, aptitudes, and interests. The reality, of course, is that students vary widely. Socioeconomic status does account for differences in students. Learning disabilities may make some students less able to learn than others, and even though educators seldom deal publicly with the fact, some students are more able learners than others. Some students, for whatever reasons, are just plain smarter than others. Other students come to school with a broader and deeper range of experiences, with attitudes that foster learning, and with a positive orientation to school, rather than a neutral or a negative one. The schools did not create these differences, but the schools must accommodate them, and one way is through grouping students according to their needs and abilities. Even Oakes seems to recognize this.

Schools must concentrate on equalizing the day-to-day educational experiences for all students. This implies altering the structures and contents of schools that seem to accord greater benefits to some groups of students than to others.[5]

EQUALIZING EDUCATIONAL OPPORTUNITY

But how are educational experiences made equal? It is easy to argue that putting all students in the same classes is not going to equalize their expectations. In fact, an approach that treats all students the same and ignores the real differences among them can guarantee unequal experiences for all. Treating all students the same is not a formula for equity or excellence.

Indeed, research supports tracking. A meta-analysis of 52 studies of secondary tracking programs found "only trivial effects on the achievement of average and below average students." The researchers added that "this finding . . . does not support the view of other recent reviewers who claim that grouping has unfavorable effects on the achievement of low-aptitude students. The effect is near zero on the achievement of average and below-average students; it is not negative."[6]

Despite the zero effect on achievement of average and below-average students, these studies did show some benefits for tracking.

> The controlled studies that we examined gave a very different picture of the effects of grouping on student attitudes. Students seemed to like their school subjects more when they studied them with peers of similar ability, and some students in grouped classes even developed more positive attitudes about themselves and about school.[7]

Tracking is more than a tradition. In a balanced view of tracking, the issue becomes not whether tracking is good or bad, but whether any particular example of tracking accomplishes the goal of matching the learner to the instructional environment.

APPROPRIATE TRACKING

If there is such a thing as good and bad tracking, how does one tell the difference? Can we establish objective criteria? Obviously no magic formulas exist, but *Keeping Track* provides a basis for distinguishing between good and bad tracking.

Oakes cites the decision in the court case of Hobson v. Hansen, and calls it "the best known and probably still the most important rule on tracking."[8] The

court's decision stated that tracking is inappropriate and unlawful when it limits educational opportunities for certain students "on the assumption that they are capable of no more." The court also provided a definition of appropriate tracking.

> Any system of ability grouping which, through a failure to include and implement the concept of compensatory education for the disadvantaged child or otherwise fails in fact to bring the great majority of children into the mainstream of public education denies the children excluded equal opportunity and thus encounters the constitutional bar.[9]

This decision suggests the characteristics of appropriate tracking. One obvious consideration is content. Oakes uses the term "high-status knowledge" which she defines initially as "a commodity whose distribution is limited" to enhance its value. But it is also defined as the knowledge that "provides access to the university."[10] For the purposes of this discussion, high-status knowledge can be thought of as the combination of skills, experiences, attitudes, and academic content needed to create an informed and productive member of society. At the risk of using a cliche: it is the idea that knowledge is power, and that the primary function of the schools is to empower students.

Goodlad and Oakes express legitimate concern that students in the lower tracks are denied access to high-status knowledge, increasing the gap between lower- and higher-tracked (or nontracked) students. Tracking is not appropriate when the intent is to provide the lower-track student with an alternative curriculum that does not lead to the high-status knowledge. An appropriate program of tracking has the same expectations for all students and uses low-level tracking only to provide remediation and to upgrade selected students.

Another consideration, not directly addressed by the court but implicit in the decision, relates to the quality of instruction. Goodlad and Oakes apparently never observed good instruction in a lower-level tracked class, and they seem to assume that quality instruction in a lower track is not possible.

It is true that the attitudes, behaviors, and abilities of the students make lower-track classes more difficult to teach. But these conditions do not magically improve when the students are scattered among untracked classes. They only become hidden from view and easier to ignore. Appropriate tracking is an attempt to structure situations in which the students' special needs and abilities can be recognized and considered. It enables students in lower-level tracks to move toward the worthwhile goal of achieving high-status knowledge.

Appropriate tracking, then, can provide the best possible match between the learner and the instructional environment. Teachers using it can build a good instructional climate and motivate students toward attaining high-status knowledge.

Inappropriate tracking assumes that low-track students are not capable of acquiring high-status knowledge, and they must be given something less.

Oakes points out that the judge in the Hobson v. Hansen decision felt he was making an educational decision that would have been better left to educators. The court's decision concluded, "It is regrettable, of course, that in deciding this case, the court must act in an area so alien to its expertise."[11] But alien or not, the court's decision against limiting educational opportunities for some provides the essential basis for distinguishing between appropriate and inappropriate tracking.

NOTES

1. John I. Goodlad, *A Place Called School* (New York: McGraw-Hill, 1983), see esp. pp. 155–57.

2. Jeannie Oakes, *Keeping Track, How Schools Structure Inequality* (New Haven: Yale University Press, 1985), see esp. pp. 191–213.

3. Chen-Lin C. Kulik and James A. Kulik, "Effects of Ability Grouping on Secondary School Students. A Meta-Analysis of Evaluation Findings." *American Educational Research Journal* (Fall 1982): 416.

4. Deborah Burnett Strather, "Adopting Instruction to Individual Needs. An Eclectic Approach." *Phi Delta Kappan* (December 1985): 309.

5. Oakes, p. 205.

5. Oakes, p. 205.

6. Kulik, p. 426.

7. Kulik, p. 426.

8. Oakes, p. 184.

9. Oakes, p. 184.

10. Oakes, pp. 199–200.

11. Oakes, p. 190.

POSTSCRIPT

Does Tracking Create Educational Inequality?

In his *Paideia Proposal*, Mortimer J. Adler argues that all students in the public schools, regardless of ability level, must be given access to the same basic curriculum. For some, the pace will be slower than for others, and in some cases the depth and extent of study in a given area of the curriculum will vary, but there will be no separation into vocational or business or "basic" tracks. The goal of the proposal is to move toward a true democratization of education.

Should the schools end the practice of ability grouping and tracking in the name of democracy and equity? The January 1989 issue of *Update*, a publication of the Association for Supervision and Curriculum Development, contains commentary by prominent educators on this basic question. Robert Slavin feels that a decision to assign a child to an ability group or track at one point in that child's school experience will greatly influence later grouping decisions; therefore, the practice should be used only when there is a clear educational justification and an absence of other alternatives. Ralph Scott contends that fair and equal opportunities should consist of *appropriate* schooling experiences for individual students; therefore, ability grouping is an essential means for effective education. Don Hindman claims that research has made it clear that homogeneous grouping has a detrimental effect on achievement and social development for students in the low and intermediate tracks; for students in the higher group, achievement effects are negligible.

Some helpful articles to consider are Ray C. Rist, "Student Social Class and Teacher Expectations: The Self-Fulfilling Prophecy in Ghetto Education," *Harvard Educational Review* (August 1970); Walter C. Parker, "The Urban Curriculum and the Allocating Function of Schools," *The Educational Forum* (Summer 1985); Jean Anyon, "Social Class and the Hidden Curriculum of Work," *Journal of Education* (Winter 1980); Kenneth A. Sirotnik, "What You See Is What You Get: Consistency, Persistency, and Mediocrity in Classrooms," *Harvard Educational Review* (vol. 53, no. 1, 1983); and "We Must Offer Equal Access to Knowledge," by John I. Goodlad and Jeannie Oakes, *Educational Leadership* (February 1988). The specific issue of separate classes for the gifted and talented is addressed by Arthur R. King, Jr., and Mary Anne Raywid in *Educational Perspectives* (vol. 26, 1989).

ISSUE 19

Do Group Rewards Undermine Cooperative Learning?

YES: Alfie Kohn, from "Group Grade Grubbing versus Cooperative *Learning,*" *Educational Leadership* (February 1991)

NO: Robert E. Slavin, from "Group Rewards Make Groupwork Work," *Educational Leadership* (February 1991)

ISSUE SUMMARY

YES: Alfie Kohn, an author and lecturer, argues that group rewards decrease individual motivation and performance.
NO: Research professor Robert E. Slavin counters that a system of rewards encourages subject matter mastery.

One of the central suggestions that John Dewey, the influential philosopher and educator, made for the improvement of schooling involved the necessity of moving away from competitiveness among students and toward cooperative activities. The classroom was to be a "miniature society" in which student groups addressed problems through participation in cooperative inquiry within the context of the subject matter at hand. These activities were linked to the overall social interaction goals of the school (see Issue 1).

This fundamental suggestion has found its way into the present discourse about educational aims and instructional methods in the form of various approaches to cooperative learning. The movement is being well received by theoreticians and practitioners alike, but a good deal of controversy rages among its advocates. Robert E. Slavin, whose 1983 book *Cooperative Learning* brought the movement to a position of wide attention, recommends a curriculum-specific approach that employs the motivational force of group rewards. The version of cooperative learning developed by David and Roger Johnson at the University of Minnesota emphasizes social skill building without particular reference to specific curriculum content. Spencer Kagan, director of Resources for Teachers in California, espouses a "structural" approach, while Alfie Kohn, author of *No Contest: The Case Against Competition* (1986), argues for a methodology which does not rely on a system of external rewards at all.

All of the variations focus on experiential situations, group problem-solving techniques, personal academic and social outcomes, and improvement of broader social relations. Groups are formed with diversity in mind, with members representing different levels of academic achievement, socio-economic status, racial and ethnic background, etc. Heterogeneity is the theme.

A number of specific programs have been developed, such as team-assisted individualization in mathematics, cooperative integrated reading and composition, student teams achievement divisions, group investigation, and jigsaws. The programs have a sound research base, are widely adopted by school systems, and have met with a high level of teacher enthusiasm. Nevertheless, Slavin and others warn that there are dangers that the movement is becoming too faddish, that the techniques are not being integrated into the total school program, that many users of the approach are undertrained and often minimize elements essential to the program's success, and, in some cases, that there is a lack of administrative support for the effort.

In the first of the articles offered here for consideration, Alfie Kohn points to the perils of using rewards to bribe students to engage in cooperative activities. He is particularly disturbed by Slavin's insistence on making rewards the "linchpin of cooperation." Kohn, drawing on research in social psychology, explains that reliance on extrinsic motivators leads to a disintegration of natural intrinsic motivation. This, he warns, is the hidden cost of group rewards. Robert E. Slavin, who has done extensive research on all aspects of cooperative learning, stands by his assertion that group rewards are an essential element in bringing about the student effort needed to achieve subject matter mastery.

YES

Alfie Kohn

GROUP GRADE GRUBBING VERSUS COOPERATIVE *LEARNING*

Even before the recent surge of interest in cooperative learning (CL), researchers and practitioners were already staking out positions on precisely what the term denotes and how the idea should be implemented. Constructive controversies (or, less charitably, factional disputes) have arisen with respect to almost every aspect of CL theory and practice. Everyone in the field agrees that students benefit when they can help each other learn instead of having to work against each other or apart from each other; beyond this, unanimity is in short supply.

What should be one of the central areas of discussion, however, has not yet received the attention it deserves. I refer to the prominent role assigned to grades, awards, certificates, and other rewards in many of the CL models now being offered to teachers. While some approaches incorporate these rewards without calling attention to that fact, others assert that rewards are the linchpin of cooperation. Some writers even go so far as to use the phrases "cooperative goals" and "cooperative reward structures" interchangeably.

Most researchers would agree, I think, that effective CL depends on helping students to develop what the social psychologist Morton Deutsch (1949) called "promotive interdependence," in which the goals of group members are positively linked and their interactions are characterized by mutual facilitation. (Counterbalancing this in most versions of CL is some feature to assure individual accountability so that each student is held responsible to an external source for participating in the process and for learning.) But the assumption that interdependence is best achieved—or even, as some would have it, that it can *only* be achieved—by the use of rewards is a claim that demands critical examination. An impressive body of research in social psychology has shown that rewards are not only surprisingly limited in their effectiveness but also tend to undermine interest in the task. Over the long run, they may actually reduce the quality of many kinds of performance.

From Alfie Kohn, "Group Grade Grubbing versus Cooperative *Learning*," *Educational Leadership*, vol. 48, no. 5 (February 1991), pp. 83–87. Copyright © 1991 by Alfie Kohn. Reprinted by permission.

HIDDEN COSTS OF REWARDS

In terms of motivational power, no artificial inducement can match the strength of intrinsic interest in a task. Think of someone whom you regard as extraordinarily good at what he or she does for a living; then ask yourself whether this individual is concerned primarily with collecting a paycheck. Most people who reach for excellence truly enjoy what they do. The same is true of students in the classroom.

But the "hidden costs of rewards" (Lepper and Greene 1978) have to do not only with their relative lack of efficacy but with their corrosive effects on both attitude and performance. The psychologist Robert J. Sternberg (1990) recently summarized what a growing number of motivation researchers now concede: "Nothing tends to undermine creativity quite like extrinsic motivators do. They also undermine intrinsic motivation: when you give extrinsic rewards for certain kinds of behavior, you tend to reduce children's interest in performing those behaviors for their own sake" (p. 144). More succinctly, rewards have been described as the "enemies of exploration" (Condry 1977).

Despite the continuing influence of Skinnerian psychology on education and on lay thinking, this phenomenon is not entirely counterintuitive. The following three-step sequence of events will sound all too familiar to many of us: (1) we engage in some activity simply because it is pleasurable, (2) we get paid for doing it, and (3) we suddenly find ourselves unwilling to do it unless we are paid. We have come to see ourselves as working in order to receive the reward—in this case, money—with the result that our interest in the activity has mysteriously evaporated along the way.

This effect has been documented repeatedly, beginning in the early 1970s with the research of Mark Lepper at Stanford University (for an early summary, see Lepper and Greene 1975), Edward Deci at the University of Rochester (Deci and Ryan 1985), and their respective students. Since then, other researchers replicating and clarifying the phenomenon include John Nicholls (1989), Judith M. Harackiewicz and associates (1984), Mark Morgan in Ireland (1983, 1984), and Ruth Butler in Israel (Butler and Nisan 1986; Butler 1987, 1988, 1989). Their experiments have shown, *inter alia*, that:

• preschoolers who are told they will receive an award for drawing with felt-tip markers subsequently show less interest in using them (Greene and Lepper 1974);

• college students competing to solve a puzzle are less likely to continue working on such puzzles than are those who had not competed (Deci et al. 1981);

• merely watching someone else get rewarded for doing a task is enough to reduce one's own motivation to do it (Morgan 1983);

• the expectation of being evaluated distracts one from the task at hand and interferes with involvement and interest in it (Harackiewicz et al. 1984);

• not only grades but even some kinds of praise (as opposed to purely informational feedback) can undermine interest in an activity (Ryan 1982, Butler 1987).

In addition to these studies, whose dependent variable is motivation, Teresa Amabile at Brandeis University and other researchers have shown that rewards often lead to lower performance, particularly at creative tasks. For example,

• Students promised a reward if they were effective at tutoring younger children took longer to communicate ideas, got frustrated more easily, and ended up with pupils who didn't understand as well as a group of children whose tutors were promised no reward (Garbarino 1975);

• Children and undergraduates who expected to receive a prize for making collages or telling stories proved to be less imaginative at both tasks than those who received nothing (Amabile et al. 1986);

• When creative writers were asked to spend a few minutes reflecting on extrinsic reasons for writing—making money, impressing teachers, and so forth—their poetry dropped in quality and also was judged to be worse than the poems written by people who weren't thinking about these things (Amabile 1985);

• Teenagers offered a reward for remembering details about a newspaper story they had recently read had poorer recall than those who received nothing for their efforts; moreover, they also scored lower on two measures of creativity (Kruglanski et al. 1971).

All of these studies have direct implications for classroom learning, but other research has shown that the destructive effects of rewards extend to other spheres: They are counterproductive for promoting generosity and other prosocial behavior (see a review in Kohn 1990), for eliciting love toward one's romantic partner (Seligman et al. 1980), and for motivating employees to use seat belts (Geller et al. 1987). In short, the conclusion offered for one experiment seems an apt summary of an entire body of research: "The more salient the reward, the more undermining of performance [is] observed" (Condry 1977, p. 464).

Several explanations have been proposed to account for these remarkably consistent findings. First, people who think of themselves as working for a reward feel controlled by it, and this lack of self-determination interferes with creativity (Deci and Ryan 1985). Second, rewards encourage "ego involvement" to the exclusion of "task involvement," and the latter is more predictive of achievement (Nicholls 1989). Third, the promise of a reward is "tantamount to declaring that the activity is not worth doing for its own sake" (A. S. Neill, quoted in Morgan 1984); indeed, anything construed as a prerequisite to some other goal will likely be devalued as a result (Lepper et al. 1982).

TAKING AWAY WHAT'S BEEN GIVEN

All of these explanations account for reduced performance on the basis of how rewards reduce interest in the given task. But the decline of interest and the decline in performance are distinct phenomena, each significant in itself. The reduction in motivation also has undesirable effects on "self-esteem, perceived cognitive competence, and sense of control" (Ryan et al. 1985, p. 45); it is undesirable apart from its achievement effects. Conversely, extrinsic inducements may also reduce creativity for a reason having nothing to do with intrinsic motivation: they encourage students to work as quickly as possible, take few risks, and focus narrowly on a task. A reward-driven child (or adult) is after the goodie, and this mental set is hardly conducive to the playful encounter with words or numbers or ideas that characterizes true creativity (Amabile 1983).

It should not be surprising, then, that students for whom rewards are salient—even high-achieving students—will choose the easiest possible tasks (Harter 1978, Greene and Lepper 1974). Commenting on "Book It!," a program sponsored by the Pizza Hut restaurant chain that dangles free pizza before children to induce them to read, John Nicholls says the likely long-term consequence is "a lot of fat kids who don't like to read" (personal communication, 1989). Children are likely to pick books that are short and simple, the aim being to plow through them fast rather than coming to appreciate the pleasures of reading. The same is true with respect to inedible extrinsics as well. Thus, if the question is *Do rewards motivate students?*, the answer is *Absolutely—they motivate students to get rewarded.* Unfortunately, such motivation is often at the expense of interest in, or excellence at, whatever it is they are doing.

All of this prompts several disconcerting questions for anyone committed to CL. If bribing individuals to learn is so demonstrably ineffective and disadvantageous, what makes us think that bribing groups to learn is productive and benign? Why, in other words, should CL be exempt from the principle that emerges from this research—namely, the less salient grades and other rewards are for students, the better? Might it not be naive, in light of the corrosive effect of extrinsics, to assume that we can simply remove the rewards "as soon as the intrinsic motivation inherent in cooperative learning groups becomes apparent" (Johnson et al. 1986, p. 63)?

Alternatively, we could frame the challenge this way: many of us were drawn to CL because of the manifest failure of competition as a pedagogical tool. One of the reasons for competition's failure is precisely its status as an extrinsic motivator (Deci and Ryan 1985, Kohn 1986, Nicholls 1989). So could it not be said that the use of grades and other rewards to ensure cooperation takes away with one hand what has been given with the other?

To answer these questions definitively, we first need to consider the evidence offered in support of reward-driven CL by such careful researchers as Robert Slavin. His review of the data has persuaded him that "cooperative learning methods that use specific group rewards based on group members' individual learning consistently increase achievement more than control methods" (1983, p. 53). I believe, however, that the force and relevance of this conclusion is sharply limited by several factors.

First, many, if not most, of the measures in the studies to which Slavin refers are tasks that require only the straightforward application of a known principle (that is, algorithmic or convergent tasks), and these are less vulnerable to the destructive effects of extrinsics than are more open-ended (heuristic or divergent) tasks. Teachers who care about stimulating creativity and curiosity will not take much comfort from the fact that the promise of a certificate may prompt students to memorize more facts. That striving for a reward may enhance performance on a boring task may be less important than the finding that rewards, from a student's perspective, turn interesting tasks into boring ones.

Second, while Slavin's notion of methodological adequacy turns in part on whether an experiment lasted for several weeks or several days, we also need to attend to the very long term. It is true that the toxicity of rewards typically manifests itself with alarming rapidity: in many of the studies cited above, a single trial—that is, one presentation of an extrinsic reward—was sufficient to undermine performance and interest. But how do children who are repeatedly bribed to learn come to view the process of learning months or years later? Specifically, how do they view a given subject when no one is around to reward them? A temporary performance gain on routine classroom assignments may mask a chronic shift in students' attitude that will have long-term negative effects on learning. We already know that "children" become increasingly more extrinsically oriented over the school years" (Harter, paraphrased in Barrett and Boggiano 1988; see also Ryan et al. 1985)—an occurrence that Slavin presumably finds as troubling as I. It appears likely that the widespread use of extrinsics (mostly by people who have never even heard of cooperative learning) has something to do with this. Continuing to use extrinsics at the level of the group would seem to be ill-advised.

Third, we need to ask what exactly is being contrasted with reward-driven CL in the studies that find a performance advantage. My impression is that the control condition typically consists of either (a) a "traditional" classroom, which, as I have just noted, is also characterized by reward-based motivation, or (b) some loose, unstructured arrangement ("Why don't you four work together on this ditto sheet?") that scarcely qualifies as CL. The first comparison tells us nothing about the effects of rewards *per se*—only about rewarding individuals versus groups. The second comparison does nothing to discredit the possibility of carefully structured, non-reward-based approaches to CL.

A PROPOSAL FOR SUCCESS

When Slavin says, as he did in this journal ("Cooperative Learning and Student Achievement," October 1988), that "the cooperating groups must have a group goal that is important to them," I heartily agree. The problem is that he goes on in the very next sentence to operationalize the concept of group goals in terms of "working to earn certificates or other recognition, to receive a few minutes extra of recess, or to earn bonus points on their grades."

Those of us who are both persuaded and disturbed by all the evidence indicating that such rewards are counterproductive will want to turn to (or create) models of CL that can claim all the familiar advantages—but without relying on extrinsics. I would propose three key components of successful CL: curriculum, autonomy, and relationship.

Curriculum obviously matters in many respects, but the point to be emphasized here is that the perceived need to bribe children often tells us more about what they are being asked to learn (namely, that it lacks any intrinsic appeal) than about how learning per se takes place. While some proponents have proudly described CL as a method that can be used to teach anything—which implies that teachers who adopt it need not ask difficult questions about the value of what they are requiring students to do—others have challenged the value of "using cooperative techniques to have students cover the same boring, inconsequential, or biased material or to have them 'get through' worksheets with more efficiency" (Sapon-Shevin and Schniedewind 1989/1990, p. 64). I sympathize with the latter point of view.

Autonomy is vital for producing intrinsic motivation because people are more likely to find a task interesting when they have had a role in deciding what they are to do and how they are to do it (Nicholls 1989, Deci and Ryan 1985, Amabile and Gitomer 1984). Rewards are destructive, in the view of Deci and others, primarily because they restrict autonomy. But teachers should not only minimize extrinsic motivators, they should affirmatively help students to become responsible for their own education. A child who can make (teacher-guided) choices about what happens in his or her classroom is a child who will be less likely to require artificial inducements to learn.

Relationship refers to the specific trainable social skills that already play a part in some models of CL (for example, Johnson et al. 1986) as well as to a broader emphasis on caring for others. Explicit attention to the value (and intrinsic appeal) of prosocial behavior may encourage students to view others in their group as collaborators rather than as obstacles to their own success. By contrast, a certain cynicism inheres in the assumption that students will work together only on the basis of self-interest (Kohn 1990)—that is, that no classroom environment could possibly develop norms leading to cooperation without the use of rewards.

Several models of CL already emphasize these things. First, "if the task is challenging and interesting, and if students are sufficiently prepared for skills in group process, students will experience the process of groupwork itself as highly rewarding," as Cohen (1986, p. 69) has written. Similarly, the scores of lessons and activities offered in Schniedewind and Davidson's (1987) introduction to CL are based on the idea that *what* gets taught not only matters as much as *how* it is taught but actually can be the central impetus for learning. Second, autonomy is key to the Group Investigation approach: Achievement comes chiefly from giving "students more control over their learning" (Sharan and Sharan 1989/1990,

p. 20), not from waving a gradebook at them.

Finally, relationship, and specifically the idea of creating a community within the classroom, is the primary feature of the program developed by the Child Development Project in San Ramon, California. For that matter, the project also places special emphasis on the quality of the curriculum and on helping students to take responsibility for their learning—all of which have moved the project developers away from relying on punishments or rewards (Solomon et al. 1990).

In sum, my hypothesis is that a carefully structured cooperative environment that offers challenging learning tasks, that allows students to make key decisions about how they perform those tasks, and that emphasizes the value (and skills) of helping each other to learn constitutes an alternative to extrinsic motivators, an alternative both more effective over the long haul and more consistent with the ideals of educators.

But even if we lack certainty about how to make CL work—even if subsequent research modifies this preliminary three-part formulation—it is time to abandon the project of trying to fine-tune a system of grades and other extrinsic motivators and instead to set about trying to maximize the benefits of CL in the absence of rewards.

REFERENCES

Amabile, T. M. (1983). *The Social Psychology of Creativity.* New York: Springer-Verlag.
Amabile, T. M. (1985). "Motivation and Creativity: Effects of Motivational Orientation on Creative Writers." *Journal of Personality and Social Psychology* 48: 393–399.
Amabile, T. M., and J. Gitomer. (1984). "Children's Artistic Creativity: Effects of Choice in Task Materials." *Personality and Social Psychology Bulletin* 10: 209–215.

Amabile, T. M., B. A. Hennessey, and B. S. Grossman. (1986). "Social Influences on Creativity: The Effects of Contracted-for-Reward." *Journal of Personality and Social Psychology* 50: 14–23.

Barrett, M., and A. K. Boggiano. (1988). "Fostering Extrinsic Orientations: Use of Reward Strategies to Motivate Children." *Journal of Social and Clinical Psychology* 6: 293–309.

Butler, R. (1987). "Task-Involving and Ego-Involving Properties of Evaluation: Effects of Different Feedback Conditions on Motivational Perceptions, Interest, and Performance." *Journal of Educational Psychology* 79: 474–482.

Butler, R. (1988). "Enhancing and Undermining Intrinsic Motivation: The Effects of Task-Involving and Ego-Involving Evaluation on Interest and Performance." *British Journal of Educational Psychology* 58: 1–14.

Butler, R. (1989). "Interest in the Task and Interest in Peers' Work in Competitive and Noncompetitive Conditions: A Developmental Study." *Child Development* 60: 562–570.

Butler, R., and M. Nisan. (1986). "Effects of No Feedback, Task-Related Comments, and Grades on Intrinsic Motivation and Performance." *Journal of Educational Psychology* 78: 210–216.

Cohen, E. G. (1986). *Designing Group-work: Strategies for the Heterogeneous Classroom.* New York: Teachers College Press.

Condry, J. (1977). "Enemies of Exploration: Self-Initiated Versus Other-Initiated Learning." *Journal of Personality and Social Psychology* 35: 459–477.

Deci, E. L., G. Betley, J. Kahle, L. Abrams, and J. Porac. (1981). "When Trying to Win: Competition and Intrinsic Motivation." *Personality and Social Psychology Bulletin* 7: 79–83.

Deci, E. L., and R. M. Ryan. (1985). *Intrinsic Motivation and Self-Determination in Human Behavior.* New York: Plenum Press.

Deutsch, M. (1949). "A Theory of Cooperation and Competition." *Human Relations* 2: 129–152.

Garbarino, J. (1975). "The Impact of Anticipated Reward Upon Cross-Age Tutoring." *Journal of Personality and Social Psychology* 32: 421–28.

Geller, E. S., J. R. Rudd, M. J. Kalsher, F. M. Streff, and G. R. Lehman. (1987). "Employer-Based Programs to Motivate Safety Belt Use: A Review of Short-Term and Long-Term Effects." *Journal of Safety Research* 18: 1–17.

Greene, D., and M. R. Lepper. (1974). "Effects of Extrinsic Rewards on Children's Subsequent Intrinsic Interest." *Child Development* 45: 1141–1145.

Harackiewicz, J. M., G. Manderlink, and C. Sansone. (1984). "Rewarding Pinball Wizardry: Effects of Evaluation and Cue Value on Intrinsic Interest." *Journal of Personality and Social Psychology* 47: 287–300.

Harter, S. (1978). "Pleasure Derived from Challenge and the Effects of Receiving Grades on Children's Difficulty Level Choices." *Child Development* 49: 788–799.

Johnson, D. W., R. T. Johnson, and E. J. Holubec. (1986). *Circles of Learning: Cooperation in the Classroom,* rev. ed. Edina, Minn.: Interaction Book Co.

Kohn, A. (1986). *No Contest: The Case Against Competition.* Boston: Houghton Mifflin.

Kohn, A. (1990). *The Brighter Side of Human Nature: Altruism and Empathy in Everyday Life.* New York: Basic Books.

Kruglanski, A. W., I. Freidman, and G. Zeevi. (1971). "The Effects of Extrinsic Incentive on Some Qualitative Aspects of Task Performance." *Journal of Personality* 39: 606–617.

Lepper, M. R., and D. Greene (April 1975). "When Two Rewards Are Worse Than One: Effects of Extrinsic Rewards on Intrinsic Motivation." *Phi Delta Kappan:* 565–566.

Lepper, M., and D. Greene, eds. (1978). *The Hidden Costs of Reward.* Hillsdale, N.J.: Lawrence Erlbaum Associates.

Lepper, M. R., G. Sagotsky, J. L. Dafoe, and D. Greene. (1982). "Consequences of Superfluous Social Constraints: Effects on Young Children's Social Inferences and Subsequent Intrinsic Interest." *Journal of Personality and Social Psychology* 42: 51–65.

Morgan, M. (1983). "Decrements in Intrinsic Motivation Among Rewarded and Observer Subjects." *Child Development* 54: 636–644.

Morgan, M. (1984). "Reward-Induced Decrements and Increments in Intrinsic Motivation." *Review of Educational Research* 54: 5–30.

Nicholls, J. G. (1989). *The Competitive Ethos and Democratic Education.* Cambridge, Mass.: Harvard University Press.

Ryan, R. M. (1982). "Control and Information in the Intrapersonal Sphere: An Extension of Cognitive Evaluation Theory." *Journal of Personality and Social Psychology* 43: 450–461.

Ryan, R. M., J. P. Connell, and E. L. Deci. (1985). "A Motivational Analysis of Self-Determination and Self-Regulation in Education." In *Research on Motivation in Education, vol. 2, The Classroom Milieu,* edited by C. Ames and R. Ames. Orlando, Fla.: Academic Press.

Sapon-Shevin, M., and N. Schniedewind. (December 1989/January 1990). "Selling Cooperative Learning Without Selling It Short." *Educational Leadership* 47, 4: 63–65.

Schniedewind, N., and E. Davidson. (1987). *Cooperative Learning, Cooperative Lives: A Sourcebook of Learning Activities for Building a Peaceful World.* Dubuque, Iowa: William C. Brown Co.

Seligman, C., R. H. Fazio, and M. P. Zanna. (1980). "Effects of Salience of Extrinsic Rewards on Liking and Loving." *Journal of Personality and Social Psychology* 38: 453–460.

Sharan, Y., and S. Sharan. (December 1989/January 1990). "Group Investigation Expands Cooperative Learning." *Educational Leadership* 47, 4: 17–21.

Slavin, R. E. (1983). *Cooperative Learning*. New York: Longman.

Slavin, R. E. (October 1988). "Cooperative Learning and Student Achievement." *Educational Leadership* 46, 2: 31–33.

Solomon, D., M. Watson, E. Schaps, V. Battistich, and J. Solomon. (1990). "Cooperative Learning as Part of a Comprehensive Classroom Program Designed to Promote Prosocial Development." In *Cooperative Learning: Theory and Research*, edited by S. Sharan. New York: Praeger.

Sternberg, R. J. (1990). "Prototypes of Competence and Incompetence." In *Competence Considered*, edited by R. J. Sternberg and J. Kolligian, Jr. New Haven: Yale University Press.

Authors note: I wish to thank Eric Schaps and Marilyn Watson for their helpful comments on an earlier draft of this article.

THE ARTICLE YOU HAVE JUST READ BY ALFIE KOHN, "Group Grade Grubbing versus Cooperative Learning," originally appeared in the February 1991 issue of *Educational Leadership*. Professor Robert E. Slavin, whose work on cooperative learning is considered important and very influential, replied to Kohn with a commentary of his own, which was entitled, "Group Rewards Make Groupwork Work." That commentary appears in this volume as the NO reading. See pp. 303–306. But Kohn wrote a follow-up response to the Slavin piece, and here is that response:

DON'T SPOIL THE PROMISE OF COOPERATIVE LEARNING: RESPONSE TO SLAVIN

If bribing students with rewards undermines their interest in learning and, in the long run, reduces the quality of their work, then, yes, we would have to conclude it *is* "so terrible"—even though this is hardly the result that Slavin (or teachers) intend. The question is whether extrinsic motivators really do have this effect.

If students are unmotivated to begin with—perhaps because they have been assigned mind-numbing worksheets and drills—then Slavin is quite right to suggest that rewards may "have no effect on continuing motivation." After all, their motivation can't drop any lower. But where are the studies he alludes to that ostensibly refute the work of Deci, Lepper, Amabile, Nicholls, and others by showing that motivation is *enhanced* by rewards—and that it stays high even after there is no teacher to hand out an *A* or a gold star for doing the task? I can't find them.

Reward or Penalty?

A closer look at the research Slavin does cite raises more doubts about his argument than it allays. Because my space is limited here, I will mention only four examples. First, and most telling, his opening paragraph cites the work of David Johnson and Roger Johnson, and Neil Davidson in support of the idea that cooperative learning boosts achievement only if group rewards are used. But in fact, David Johnson (1990) says, "For achievement gains to occur, positive *goal* interdependence has to be present. Group rewards are optional." And Davidson (1990) says, "Several recent studies suggest that rewards are not always necessary to increase student achievement on problem-solving and reasoning tasks."

Second, Slavin invokes the names of Deci and Ryan (1985) to support his claim that social (as opposed to tangible) rewards can boost intrinsic motivation. But in fact, their research suggests that positive feedback will have precisely the same motivation-killing effects as money or grades if it is experienced as controlling. Indeed, Butler (1987, p. 481) found that "subsequent performance declined after both grades and praise" and that "praise did not yield higher subsequent intrinsic motivation than grades."

Third, Slavin dismisses the Child Development Project's (1990) experience with non-reward-based cooperative learning on the grounds that these students did not outperform their peers. But in fact, when 6th graders were given an essay exam to measure higher-order reading comprehension, children in the program did significantly better than the carefully matched comparison students (effect size .34). (Slavin may have been unaware of these very recent findings from the project.)

Fourth, the only evidence Slavin cites on the question of cooperative learning and intrinsic motivation is an unpublished paper by Harry Hom and his colleagues (1990). This study, however, merely compared individual rewards with group rewards; it tells us nothing about non-extrinsic cooperative learning. Moreover, reward-driven cooperative learning failed to produce higher intrinsic motivation on one of the two behavioral measures that Hom used *or* on the self-report measure.

Chasing Trophies

Slavin may be correct that few non-reward-based classrooms now exist in the U.S., but this hardly demonstrates that the best, let alone the only, alternative to bribing individuals is to bribe groups. And if the only studies he can cite simply compare these two versions of education-by-extrinsics, then he has failed to demonstrate his central thesis: that cooperative learning won't work unless it is shot through with artificial incentives. When presented with a success story for cooperative learning without extrinsics, such as the Group Investigation method, he mysteriously tries to claim it as fur-

ther substantiation for his behaviorist approach.

If we offer children rewards for eating an unfamiliar food, they will probably like that food *less* as a result (Birch et al. 1984). If we offer children rewards for learning, they will like learning less. Let's not spoil the promise of cooperative learning by turning it into yet another exercise in chasing rewards.

References

Birch, L. L., D. W. Marlin, and J. Rotter. (1984). "Eating as the 'Means' Activity in a Contingency." *Child Development* 55:431–439.

Butler, R. (1987). "Task-Involving and Ego-Involving Properties of Evaluation." *Journal of Educational Psychology* 79:474–482.

Davidson, N. (1990). Personal communication.

Deci, E. L., and R. M. Ryan. (1985). *Intrinsic Motivation and Self-Determination in Human Behavior.* New York: Plenum.

Developmental Studies Center. (April 1990). "Evaluation of the Child Development Project: Summary of Findings to Date." Unpublished manuscript. San Ramone, Calif: DSC.

Hom, H. L., M. Berger, M. Duncan, A. Miller, and A. Blevin. (1990). *The Influence of Cooperative Reward Structures on Intrinsic Motivation.* Springfield, Mo.: Southwestern Missouri State University.

Johnson, D. (1990). Personal communication.

NO

Robert E. Slavin

GROUP REWARDS MAKE
GROUPWORK WORK

One of the poignant ironies of the cooperative learning movement is that the educators and researchers most often drawn to such a humanistic, prosocial form of instruction are the very people most likely to be ideologically opposed to the use of rewards for learning. Yet classroom research over two decades has consistently found that in elementary and secondary schools, the positive effects of cooperative learning on student achievement depend on the use of group rewards based on the individual learning of group members (see Slavin 1988, 1989/90, 1990; Newmann and Thompson 1987; Davidson 1985; Johnson and Johnson 1989). There are a few exceptions, but almost every study of cooperative learning in which the cooperative classes achieved more than traditional control groups used some sort of group reward.

For example, in our own research this reward usually consists of certificates for teams whose average performance on individual assessments exceeds a pre-established standard of excellence (Slavin 1986). The methods of Spencer Kagan (1989) employ similar rewards. David and Roger Johnson (1987) often recommend giving grades on the basis of group performance (a practice I oppose on ethical grounds, but that's another story). Shlomo Sharan and his colleagues (Sharan and Shachar 1988) evaluate group projects to determine which group members contributed unique elements—an appraisal that can be seen as a type of reward.

NINTENDO VERSUS SHAKESPEARE

In this issue Alfie Kohn makes a case against the use of cooperative rewards. This case rests on two major arguments. The first is that extrinsic rewards undermine intrinsic interest and that this effect is likely to apply to cooperative learning. The second is that there are effective alternatives to the use of group rewards; thus, they are unnecessary.

Kohn's reading of research on the "undermining" effect of rewards is extremely narrow and therefore misleading. He is correct in saying there are many studies that demonstrate this undermining effect, but he fails to note there are at least as many studies that demonstrate this undermining effect, but he fails to note there are at least as many studies that show just the opposite: that rewards *enhance* continuing motivation or that they have no effect on continuing motivation.

In the classic experiment in this area, preschoolers who freely selected drawing with felt-tipped markers from among a choice of activities were rewarded for drawing with the markers. Afterwards, these students were less likely to choose a drawing activity than were similar students who were never rewarded (Lepper et al. 1973). This experiment, which has been replicated many times, does show that rewards can undermine intrinsic interest. However, the experiment involves a very short time period (usually about an hour), preschool children, an artificial setting, and a task unlike most school tasks. Does the undermining effect apply in situations more like typical elementary and secondary classrooms? Scores of studies have been done to test the limits of this finding, and the results certainly do not support the simplistic view that rewards are bad. Perhaps the most important counterevidence is the consistent finding that rewards *increase* motivation when the task involved is one that students would not do on their own without rewards (Bates 1979, Morgan 1984, Lepper and Greene 1978).

I don't know many students who would put away their Nintendo games to do complex math problems, to write reports on the economy of Brazil, to write essays comparing Shakespeare and Molière, or to learn to use the subjunctive case in French. Students will productively fool around with science equipment or learn

from visits to museums, and there is no reason to reward such intrinsically motivating activities. There is also a need for teachers to try to make everything they teach as intrinsically interesting as possible. But students are unlikely to exert the sustained, systematic effort needed to truly master a subject without some kind of reward, such as praise, grades, or recognition. Besides, try to imagine a highly motivated scientist who has not been rewarded for doing science, a singer who has not been rewarded for singing, an inventor who has not been rewarded for inventing. Outstanding achievement always produces extrinsic rewards of some kind; how else, then, do outstanding achievers maintain their motivation?

Many other aspects of the undermining effect show how little it is likely to apply to real school situations. One is the finding that rewards given over a period of days or weeks do not diminish intrinsic motivation (for example, see Vasta et al. 1978). Other studies find that rewards enhance intrinsic motivation if they convey information on performance relative to others (e.g., Boggiano et al. 1982) or if they are social rather than tangible (Lepper and Greene 1978, Deci and Ryan 1985).

It is clear, then, that the undermining effect of rewards on continuing motivation exists, but it is equally clear that it operates in a narrow set of circumstances; it applies only to activities students would engage in without rewards, to short-term reward situations, and to concrete rather than social rewards. No study has ever shown an undermining effect of rewards in a cooperative learning context. At least one study (Hom et al. 1990) found that cooperative learning enhanced intrinsic motivation. There is no reason to expect that cooperative learning would undermine intrinsic interest.

ENSURING SUCCESS

Can cooperative learning be successful without rewards? The research cited earlier suggests that this is unlikely, although Kohn mentions the Child Development Project in San Ramon, California, as an example of how cooperative learning can work without cooperative rewards. This study has indeed fastidiously avoided the use of group rewards. Studies of the program have shown that after five years of cooperative learning (from kindergarten through 4th grade), students performed academically no better than did students in traditionally organized schools (Solomon et al. 1990). This contrasts with the results of 35 studies of cooperative methods that used group rewards and individual accountability, in which cooperative classes achieved a median of 32 percent of a standard deviation more than traditional classes on achievement measures (see Slavin 1990). Overall, the median difference in achievement between forms of cooperative learning that used neither group goals nor individual accountability and traditional methods was a trivial 5 percent of a standard deviation. Cooperative methods without group rewards have been successful in enhancing outcomes other than achievement, but the need for rewards in increasing achievement is clear.

Why are group rewards necessary in cooperative learning? Evidence points to several factors. First, a key explanation for the effects of cooperative learning on achievement is that it creates peer norms favoring achievement (see Slavin 1983). That is, students in cooperative learning say that their groupmates' achievement is important to them. Without group rewards, why should a groupmate's achievement be important? Cooperative learning

works (for achievement) only when students are actively explaining ideas to each other, not simply giving each other answers (Webb 1985). An altruistic student is likely to "help" a partner by giving answers, but to do the much tougher (and less friendly) job of *teaching*, the partner's learning must be important to his or her teammate. Without group rewards based on the learning of all group members, cooperative learning can degenerate into answer-sharing. At the same time, many students are reluctant to ask a fellow student for help (Newman and Goldin 1990). The fact that all students are striving toward a common goal helps students overcome this reluctance, since the student asking for help knows it is in the interests of the student giving help to do so.

The idea that group rewards are alternatives to no rewards is, of course, absurd. With the possible exception of Summerhill, just about every school in the world uses grades, praise, recognition, and other rewards to maintain student motivation. Cooperative learning simply focuses the classroom reward system on helping others learn (as well as on one's own learning).

CELEBRATING GOOD WORK

Perhaps someday someone will come up with a form of cooperative learning that will work without cooperative rewards. Sharan and Shachar (1988) have a successful program that deemphasizes group rewards and solves the answer-sharing problem by giving each student a unique task in a group investigation, but this program has been used successfully only for social studies projects (and only in Israel). For the bulk of the elementary and secondary curriculum, however, the idea that cooperative rewards can be dispensed with in cooperative learning is wishful thinking, and the idea that such rewards will undermine intrinsic interest or continuing motivation is unproven and unlikely.

Remember, the rewards we're talking about are generally paper certificates (current street value: $.02). Kohn (and others) would oppose rewards on ideological grounds, regardless of their achievement effects. But to me it just doesn't seem excessive to give kids a fancy certificate if they've done a good job as a team. All it does is make tangible the teachers' pride and satisfaction with their cooperative efforts. Is that so terrible?

REFERENCES

Bates, J. A. (1979). "Extrinsic Reward and Intrinsic Motivation: A Review With Implications for the Classroom." *Review of Educational Research* 19: 577–576.

Boggiano, A. K., D. N. Ruble, and T. S. Pittman. (1982). "The Mastery Hypothesis and the Overjustification Effect." *Social Cognition* 1: 38–49.

Davidson, N. (1985). "Small-Group Learning and Teaching in Mathematics: A Selective Review of the Research." In *Learning to Cooperate, Cooperating to Learn*, edited by R. E. Slavin, S. Sharan, S. Kagan, R. Hertz-Lazarowitz, C. Webb, and R. Schmuck. pp. 221–230. New York: Plenum.

Deci, E. L., and R. M. Ryan. (1985). *Intrinsic Motivation and Self-Determination in Human Behavior.* New York: Plenum.

Hom, H. L., M. Berger, M. Duncan, A. Miller, and A. Blevin. (1990). *The Influence of Cooperative Reward Structures on Intrinsic Motivation.* Springfield, Mo.: Southwestern Missouri State University.

Johnson, D. W., and R. T. Johnson. (1987). *Learning Together and Alone.* Englewood Cliffs, N.J.: Prentice-Hall.

Johnson, D. W., and R. T. Johnson. (1989). *Cooperation and Competition: Theory and Research.* Edina, Minn.: Interaction Book Co.

Kagan, S. (1989). *Cooperative Learning Resources for Teachers.* San Juan Capistrano, Calif.: Resources for Teachers.

Lepper, M. R., and D. Greene. (1978). *The Hidden Costs of Reward.* Hillsdale, N.J.: Erlbaum.

Lepper, M. R., D. Greene, and R. E. Nisbett. (1973). "Undermining Children's Intrinsic Interest With Extrinsic Rewards: A Test of the Overjustification Hypothesis." *Journal of Personality and Social Psychology* 28: 129–137.

Morgan, M. (1984). "Reward-Induced Decrements and Increments in Intrinsic Motivation." *Review of Educational Research* 54: 5–30.

Newman, R. S., and L. Goldin. (1990). "Children's Reluctance to Seek Help With Schoolwork." *Journal of Educational Psychology* 82: 92–100.

Newmann, F. M., and J. Thompson. (1987). *Effects of Cooperative Learning on Achievement in Secondary Schools: A Summary of Research.* Madison, Wis.: University of Wisconsin, National Center on Effective Secondary Schools.

Sharan, S., and C. Shachar. (1988). *Language and Learning in the Cooperative Classroom.* New York: Springer.

Slavin, R. E. (1983). *Cooperative Learning.* New York: Longman.

Slavin, R. E. (1986). *Using Student Team Learning.* Baltimore: Center for Research on Elementary and Middle Schools, The Johns Hopkins University.

Slavin, R. E. (October 1988). "Cooperative Learning and Student Achievement." *Educational Leadership* 46, 2: 31–33.

Slavin, R. E. (1989/90). "Research on Cooperative Learning: Consensus and Controversy." *Educational Leadership* 47, 4: 52–54.

Slavin, R. E. (1990). *Cooperative Learning: Theory, Research, and Practice.* Englewood, N.J.: Prentice-Hall.

Solomon, D., M. Watson, E. Schaps, V. Battistich, and J. Solomon. (1990). "Cooperative Learning as Part of a Comprehensive Classroom Program Designed to Promote Prosocial Development." In *Recent Research on Cooperative Learning*, edited by S. Sharan. New York: Praeger.

Vasta, R., D. E. Andrews, A. M. McLaughlin, L. A. Stirpe, and C. Comfort. (1978). "Reinforcement Effects on Intrinsic Interest: A Classroom Analog." *Journal of School Psychology* 16: 161–166.

Webb, N. (1985). "Student Interaction and Learning in Small Groups: A Research Summary." In *Learning to Cooperate, Cooperating to Learn*, edited by R. E. Slavin, S. Sharan, S. Kagan, R. Hertz-Lazarowitz, C. Webb, and R. Schmuck. pp. 147–172. New York: Plenum.

Author's note: This article was written under funding from the Office of Educational Research and Improvement, U.S. Department of Education (Grant No. OERI-R117-R90002). However, any opinions expressed do not necessarily represent the positions or policies of OERI.

POSTSCRIPT

Do Group Rewards Undermine Cooperative Learning?

The intrinsic rewards versus extrinsic rewards argument has its philosophical roots in phenomenology and behaviorism, as was discussed in Issue 6 by B. F. Skinner and Carl Rogers. This basic issue pervades much of the pedagogical discourse in recent years and is often related to the sense of overall purpose which the disputants have in mind. Does one necessarily work against the other or is there room for both in the process of education?

A good deal of research on the philosophical and psychological aspects of human motivation has been conducted, and included in this corpus is a vast array of studies of cooperative learning as a motivational tool. Slavin has assembled much of this research in two articles, "Cooperative Learning: Where Behavioral and Humanistic Approaches to Classroom Motivation Meet," *The Elementary School Journal* (September 1987) and "Synthesis of Research on Cooperative Learning," *Educational Leadership* (February 1991), and in his recent book *Cooperative Learning: Theory, Research, and Practice* (1990).

Some frontline reports of the use of group learning strategies can also be informative. Among the best are these: "A Teacher's Views on Cooperative Learning," by Roy A. Smith, *Phi Delta Kappan* (May 1987); "Collaborative Learning: Teacher's Game or Students' Game?" by Michael F. McClure, *English Journal* (February 1990); and "Children Working in Groups? It Doesn't Work!" by Selma Wassermann, *Childhood Education* (Summer 1989). A number of articles on the theory and practice of cooperative learning may be found in the October 1988 and December 1989/January 1990 issues of *Educational Leadership*.

For more detailed descriptions of specific methodological variations, the reader is directed to *Learning to Cooperate, Cooperating to Learn* (1985), edited by Robert E. Slavin; *Learning Together and Alone: Cooperation, Competition, and Individualization* (1975), by David and Roger Johnson; *Cooperative Learning in the Classroom: Research in Desegregated Schools* (1984), by Schlomo Sharan et al.; and *The Jigsaw Classroom* (1978), by Elliott Aronson et al.

ISSUE 20

Is Bilingual Education Justifiable as a Policy?

YES: Alberto M. Ochoa and Yvonne Caballero-Allen, from "Beyond the Rhetoric of Federal Reports: Examining the Conditions Necessary for Effective Bilingual Programs," *Equity and Excellence* (Summer 1988)

NO: Diane Ravitch, from "Politicization and the Schools: The Case of Bilingual Education," *Proceedings of the American Philosophical Society* (June 1985)

ISSUE SUMMARY

YES: Alberto M. Ochoa, director of the Southern California National Origin Desegregation Center, and Yvonne Caballero-Allen, personnel employee for the San Diego school district, examine the fallacies in recent attacks on bilingual education efforts.
NO: Professor of history and education Diane Ravitch feels that research on bilingual education is inconclusive and is often misinterpreted by zealots.

Within the context of the fundamental problems of acculturation, assimilation, and cultural pluralism (see Issue 3), the specific issue of accommodating non-English-speaking immigrants by means of a bilingual education program has been controversial since the late 1960s. Events of the past decades have brought about one of the largest influxes of immigrants to the United States in the nation's history. This has brought the condition of linguistic disadvantage that members of various ethnic groups have suffered under during formal schooling into more visible relief.

Efforts to modify this type of social and developmental disadvantage have appeared in bilingual education programs initiated at the local level and supported by federal funding. Approaches implemented include direct academic instruction in the primary language and the provision of language tutors under the English for Speakers of the Other Languages (ESOL) program. Research evaluation of these efforts has produced varied results and has given rise to controversy over the efficacy of the programs themselves and the social and political intentions served by them.

The federal government eventually curtailed its demands for uniform application of bilingual education standards, allowing local school districts more flexibility in choosing how to teach English to nonnative children, including the English immersion approach. As a result, bilingual education programs that "mainstreamed" students into English-language classes as quickly as possible were more likely to receive federal funding in the mid-1980s.

A political movement at the national and state levels to establish English as the official language of the United States has gained support in recent years. Supporters of this movement feel that the bilingual approach will lead to the kind of linguistic division that has torn Canada apart.

Perhaps sharing some of the concerns of the "official English" advocates, increasing numbers of educators seem to be tilting in the direction of the immersion approach. In a recent book, *Forked Tongue: The Politics of Bilingual Education* (1990), Rosalie Pedalineo Porter, a teacher and researcher in the field of bilingual education for over 15 years, issues an indictment of the policies and programs which have been prevalent. One of her central recommendations is that "limited-English children must be placed with specially trained teachers in a program in which these students will be immersed in the English language, in which they have as much contact as possible with English speakers, and in which school subjects, not just social conversations, are the focus of the English-language lessons from kindergarten through twelfth grade."

In the following articles, Alberto M. Ochoa and his collaborator Yvonne Caballero-Allen closely examine the various types of criticism that have been aimed at bilingual education programs from several different quarters, particularly the federal government, whose support launched such programs some 25 years ago. From their analysis they compile a number of recommendations for meeting the goal of providing a quality education for language-minority students. Educational historian Diane Ravitch finds the campaign for bilingual education to be over-politicized, contending that the program "exemplifies a campaign on behalf of social and political goals that are only tangentially related to education." She claims that "the aim is to use the public schools to promote the maintenance of distinct ethnic communities, each with its own cultural heritage and language.

YES

Alberto M. Ochoa and
Yvonne Caballero-Allen

BEYOND THE RHETORIC OF
FEDERAL REPORTS

In the last two decades, bilingual programs have evolved to address the linguistic and academic needs of language minority students. The development of bilingual programs is a response to social reform that provides equal access for all students in public school. Their development has also been a source of misunderstanding and debate.[1] The debate has focused on many issues, such as the responsibility of public institutions to serve Limited English Proficient (LEP) students (*Lau v. Nichols*, 1974), the management of bilingual education (Epstein 1977), teaching strategies and approaches (AIR Evaluation Report of 1977), the quality of instruction and program effectiveness (*Rios v. Read*, 1977), and program policy requirements (*Castaneda v. Packard*, 1981).

Most of the criticism of bilingual programs is based on the impression that such instruction is not very effective, leading critics to conclude that the concept itself, as opposed to its implementation, is unsound (Ochoa, 1983). Furthermore, evaluations and studies of bilingual programs are typically deficient because they are based on fallacious assumptions. Below, we shall place evaluations of bilingual education in the context of a global economy, provide an overview of three federal reports critical of bilingual education, and then examine seven fallacies that have shaped and therefore decreased the validity of most of the studies conducted to date.

BILINGUALISM IN A GLOBAL ECONOMY

The United States is meeting increasing economic competition in the global economy from Japan, West Germany, Russia, China, Saudi Arabia, Korea, etc.[2] Yet in its 1979 report, the President's Commission on Foreign Language and International Studies stated that, "America's incompetence in foreign languages is nothing short of scandalous, and it is becoming worse." The

Commission further suggested that the ability to speak more than one language is imperative for successful interaction in and competition with the business, professional, and technological world.

Thus, while societal transformation points to the need for bilingualism and pluralistic values, United States language policy promotes a transitional approach that yields linguistic and cultural assimilation. Embedded in this transitional policy is the goal of assimilating children of foreign language backgrounds into the English-speaking mainstream as quickly as possible.[3]

BILINGUAL EDUCATION AND LANGUAGE MINORITY STUDENTS

Initial federal attention to the educational needs of language minority students is found under Title VI of the Civil Rights Act of 1964, which contains provisions forbidding discrimination on the basis of national origin, and the Equal Protection clause of the 14th Amendment to the Constitution. This legislation led to the passage of Title VII of the Elementary and Secondary Act of 1965, which established federal support for bilingual education. Its major purpose was to prevent LEP language minority students from dropping out of school. Another objective of this legislation was to provide LEP students with meaningful instruction in the primary language until they acquired English language proficiency. Then in 1970, school districts were notified by the U.S. Office for Civil Rights that they were obligated to provide "affirmative steps" to rectify the language deficiencies of LEP students. In 1974, the *Lau v. Nichols* Supreme Court Decision and the Equal Educational Opportunity Act both affirmed

the responsibility of state educational agencies and school districts to provide meaningful educational services for language minority students.

However since 1965, federal and state support for bilingual education has been almost exclusively a means of correcting students' English language deficiencies. The rationale for this support has been to enable LEP students to make the transition from the native tongue to English in order to assimilate quickly into mainstream education. Thus, bilingual education in the United States is seen primarily as a compensatory program, not as an approach to foster cognitive and cross-cultural competence in two or more languages in order to enable students to compete in a global economy.[4]

FEDERAL REPORTS CRITICAL OF BILINGUAL EDUCATION

As a viable approach for addressing the conceptual and linguistic needs of language minority students throughout the country, bilingual education is less than twelve years old. Yet, three reports critical of bilingual programs have received national attention—the AIR Evaluation Report (1977), the de Kanter and Baker Report (1981), and the Twentieth Century Task Force Report (1983).

The AIR Evaluation Report on the Impact of ESEA Title VII Spanish/English Bilingual Education Programs funded by the U.S. Office of Education was critical of the effectiveness and quality of bilingual programs. While attempting to determine the effects of bilingual education, this study failed to examine and analyze the problems in implementing bilingual programs. Educational researchers commenting on the report said that it was

> unfortunate, and perhaps, irresponsible for the U.S. Office of Education to release and give wide dissemination to findings of such questionable validity just prior to the 1977 congressional deliberations on the refunding of the Bilingual Education Act.

Overall, the report was found to have "inadequacies in methodology, sampling, instrumentation, and implementation."[5]

The 1981 de Kanter and Baker report—"The Effectiveness of Bilingual Education: A Review of the Literature"—was written for the Department of Education's Assistant Secretary of Planning and Budget, and was also disseminated nationally. The report claimed that "there exists insufficient evidence to prove that bilingual education is the most effective approach for language minority children." Furthermore, it called for English immersion as the solution to the "language problem." Once again, researchers critiqued the report and concluded it "reflects a trend of prostituting educational research for possible political and economic expediency." The report was found to have "one of the poorest and biased research approaches to a review of literature."[6]

The Report of the Twentieth Century Fund Task Force on Federal Elementary and Secondary Education (1983) also received national attention by reporting that the "nation's public schools are in trouble." A section of the report addressed the issue of "the primacy of English." Newspapers quickly quoted the report as stating that "the federal government's most important objective of elementary and secondary education in the United States is the development of literacy in the English language" and suggested that bilingual education should not be a function of the school. However, the news media did not mention other parts of the report supporting the need "to speak and read a second language [as] a valuable resource for both the individual and the nation . . . an advantage in a business or professional career." The Task Force further emphasized its position on proficiency in a second language by recommending that "every American public school student . . . [should] have the opportunity to acquire proficiency in a second language."

The political climate and policy considerations surrounding bilingual education have often been influenced by the conclusions of these reports, despite the fact that many researchers have pointed out their conceptual and methodological shortcomings. In the 1986–87 school year, U.S. Secretary of Education William J. Bennett, citing the de Kanter and Baker Report, advocated allowing school districts more flexibility in using English as the sole language of instruction. Willig's (1985) "meta-analysis" of the same evaluation research literature that de Kanter and Baker reviewed employed statistical procedures to control for methodological inadequacies. Their analysis supported bilingual education. Furthermore, a new congressional report has charged the Department of Education with inappropriately using bilingual education research and statistics to erroneously conclude that there is little value in teaching in the primary language of the student.

Eventually, the General Accounting Office asked ten experts to examine a series of research papers that the Department of Education had cited in its criticism of bilingual education. Their 1987 report on bilingual education concluded that the Department had misinterpreted the research and downplayed the value of teaching in languages other than English.[7] In another U.S. Department of Education study conducted by SRA Technologies Inc. (Ramirez, 1986), the preliminary findings counteract the Department's support for English immersion programs. In the first year of a four-year longitudinal study comparing "all English immersion" and bilingual education treatments for LEP Hispanic students, Department results indicate that students in bilingual education programs consistently outperformed immersion students in reading, language arts, and mathematics tests conducted in both English and Spanish.

These events and the national dissemination of the above reports suggest that the federal government is inconsistent in its support for bilingual education. There also seems to be a lack of proper judgement on the part of the federal government in funding and publishing poorly designed and implemented studies. Additionally, the mass media has frequently used these reports to present the image that bilingual education is un-American, dangerous, and ineffective. While bilingual education needs to be evaluated critically to ensure the implementation of quality programs, the assumptions made about the programs need to be identified, examined, and corrected.

A RESPONSE TO FEDERAL REPORTS

Most reports and evaluations published on bilingual education are based on fallacious assumptions; typically, they oversimplify complex educational realities. Below, seven of these assumptions are identified and discussed.[8]

Fallacy 1: All language minority students have the same educational needs.

Most evaluations and reports do not attempt to control for differences among language minority students. Some differences that are related to school performance include:

- whether the student is "native born" or an "immigrant;"
- the student's prior educational experience;
- the student's level of academic achievement;
- how long the student has been in the U.S.;
- the student's age and grade level;
- how long the student has been enrolled in a special instructional program;
- the student's access to educational materials and resources in the home or school;
- whether the student's primary language is historically written;
- the student's proficiency level in his or her primary language; and
- the student's level of English-language proficiency.

Whenever bilingual program evaluators fail to take such differences among students into account, they limit the validity of their findings.

Fallacy 2: All school districts are essentially the same.

Most evaluations and reports do not attempt to control for differences among school districts. Some differences that appear to be related to student performance are:

- whether the school district enrolls a large or small proportion of language minority students;

• whether the school district enrolls language minority students speaking the same or many different languages;

• whether the school district is large or small, prosperous or needy;

• whether the school district is located in an urban or rural area;

• whether the school district has a history of discriminating against language minority students; and

• whether the school district is located in the United States or in another country.

Whenever bilingual program evaluators fail to take such differences among school districts into account, they limit the generalizability of their findings.

Fallacy 3: Bilingual education programs are fully implemented and do not vary in resources and approach.

Most evaluations and reports do not control for differences among program characteristics. Some differences that appear to be related to student performance are:

• how long the special instructional program has been in operation;

• the qualifications of the program staff (e.g., with respect to ESL [English as a Second Language], have the teachers received professional training in this special instructional methodology, and are they certified as ESL teachers?);

• the pupil-teacher/staff ratio for the program and whether the program is fully staffed;

• the level and kind of non-instructional support provided to language minority students in the program (e.g., attendance services, social services, counseling, etc.);

• the extent to which resources such as instructional tests, materials, and equipment used in the program are available and relevant;

• the functional relationship between the curriculum of the school's regular instructional program and its special program for language minority students; and

• the allocation of instructional time according to program components (e.g., with respect to Transitional Bilingual Education, how much instruction is provided in English and how much in the student's home language; does the allocation of time change as the student's English skills are developed?).

The failure to take the above differences into account can lead to program evaluations that have no validity and policy relevancy.

Fallacy 4: The only data scientific enough to affect program design decisions for language minority students come from the few evaluation studies that meet the design criteria established for experimental research projects.

In selecting criteria for determining the effectiveness of bilingual programs, evaluations and reports often neglect potentially relevant data. Often the only data that are considered come from the few studies that meet the design criteria established for experimental research projects. Norm-referenced design studies that compare program gains with district or national norms are usually not considered even though such comparisons provide a good data base for assessing how well language minority students are achieving in comparison to English-speaking students. Other information that can assist school districts to determine how best to educate their language minority students is also frequently neglected, such as:

- the student's cognitive and linguistic proficiency in his or her first language;
- the student's previous educational level in the native language;
- the logistic problems with mixtures of languages and levels of proficiency;
- costs and staffing requirements for the different approaches;
- sociocultural/linguistic background factors; and
- special problems such as a history of discrimination or passive segregation.

While no research can validate a single educational approach as "the best" to improve instructional programs for language minority students, the best available data and information should be considered.

Fallacy 5: Parents of language minority students consider English proficiency to be the most important skill for their children to acquire.

Most evaluations and reports do not consider the opinions of language minority parents. While some parents opt not to have their children in bilingual programs, a large majority of parents want them to acquire academic skills at grade level or better. They also want their children to develop cognitive academic proficiency skills in English and in their primary language. School districts should consider community factors in designing, developing, and implementing bilingual instruction. Such factors should include:

- languages spoken and reinforced in the community;
- sociocultural characteristics of the community;
- community support as a means for developing conceptual skills in the first and second language;
- shared responsibility for the development, implementation, and monitoring of bilingual instruction;
- legal rights of parents to have bilingualism as an educational goal for every student; and
- the present and future economic value of bilingualism.

The inability of school personnel to consider community factors is likely to lead to the implementation of programs that fail to address key community goals.

Fallacy 6: Evaluations and reports on the effectiveness of bilingual education are addressing the appropriate research questions.

Just as the research on school effectiveness is inconclusive regarding what constitutes effective schools (Purkey, 1986), there are many questions that need to be answered in order to know how to deliver the best education for linguistic minority children. These include:

- What district and building policies and conditions are necessary to provide language minority students with programs that address high order cognitive skills and high student expectations?
- What standards must language minority students meet to develop cognitive and linguistic competence in order to work in a high information society?
- What are the characteristics of effective schools that have a significant number of language minority students?
- Under what conditions are programs for language minority students, such as bilingual education, likely to be academically successful?

• What are the important characteristics of schools in which such programs are successful? and

• What are the characteristics of a system of accountability that promote effective schools and successful language minority student outcomes?

Answering these questions will enable committed educators to promote effective educational programs for language minority students.

Fallacy 7: bilingual education programs are designed to be a panacea for preventing student underachievement and "at risk" dropout students.

The State of California is generally considered to have the strongest bilingual legislation promoting bilingual services of LEP students. Yet, the following conditions prevail:[9]

• of the 567,630 students eligible to receive bilingual instruction in 1986–87, fewer than 40 percent were in bilingual programs;

• of the 40 percent of the students receiving bilingual instruction, fewer than half of these students are being taught by credentialed bilingual teachers; and

• 80 percent of ethnolinguistic students who are fluent in English are already underachieving in reading and math by the third grade.

It is imperative that we move away from the all too common practice of blaming the victim—the language minority student—and focus on conditions that create the existing underachievement. For many ethnolinguistic students, being labelled "at risk" is simply an institutional expectation.

In reference to the cognitive development of language minority students, little attention has been given to the research that focuses on language acquisition and its relationship to conceptual development and cognitive abilities. Research suggests that achievement in English literacy skills is strongly related to the extent of development in primary language literacy skills. Thus, there is a pedagogical need for language minority students to be given sufficient time in a bilingual program to develop high levels of biliteracy (Tikunoff, 1981; Carter, 1982).

THE CHALLENGE AHEAD

Bilingual education is only a means of achieving quality education for language minority students. In evaluating bilingual education, the initial focus should be to assure that such programs are receiving the necessary policy, fiscal, administrative, curriculum, staff, and community support. Secondly, the programs should be evaluated with respect to the academic and linguistic development of the student in his/her first and second language.

The goal of quality education and excellence for the language minority students must include:

• bilingual proficiency in English and the native tongue;

• cognitive academic proficiency skills at grade level or better;

• an understanding of other nations' cultures, their languages, and contributions to the global community;

• a strong sense of self-concept and knowledge of personal strengths and abilities;

• an opportunity to develop higher order skills for the world of work;

• an understanding of the global diversity of our world with respect to cross-cultural differences and social justice;

- skills to diagnose and solve academic, social, and personal problems.

The attainment of quality education for language minority students is a challenging and demanding task. Accountability is a shared responsibility for the school, the home, and the student. Evaluation reports that find it politically expedient to promote the assimilation of language minority students into the English-speaking mainstream are irresponsible. Such reports must focus on the necessary goals, support systems, staff, and implementation conditions of bilingual programs.

If our youth is to compete in our world's global economy, educational institutions must nurture their cognitive and multilingual skills.

NOTES

1. Confusion as to what constitutes bilingual education is illustrated in the following sources: "In plain English," October 10, 1981, Editorial: *New York Times;* "Bilingual education and federal duty," February 4, 1981, Editorial: *New York Times;* Noel Epstein, (1977), *Language, ethnicity and the schools,* Washington, D.C.: Institute for Educational Leadership.

2. Discussion of national economic shifts is discussed in Shirley McCune, "Achieving educational improvement through the use of technology," in *McREL's Resource Publication* (1982, Winter), pp. 11–13.

3. Overview of value positions on bilingual education is found in Alan Pifer, (1979), *Bilingual education and the Hispanic challenge,* Annual Report, Carnegie Corporation of New York.

4. Read Kenji Hakuta (1986), *Mirror of language: The debate on bilingualism,* New York: Basic Books, Inc. Pub.

5. The AIR Report is analyzed in Jose A. Cardenas (1977), *IDRA response to the AIR evaluation,* San Antonio: IDRA.

6. The AIR Report is critiqued in Stanley S. Seidne (1981), "Political expedience or educational research: An analysis of Baker and de Kanter's review of the literature of bilingual edu-

cation," published by The National Clearinghouse for Bilingual Education.

7. See *Education Week,* January 14, 1987, article "Finn criticizes handling of bilingual study," p. 23.

8. Five of the seven fallacies discussed were documented by the U.S. Office of Education, Legal Standards and Policy Branch of the Office for Civil Rights, in a memorandum dated October 29, 1981 by Jim M. Littlejohn.

9. Statistical overview and analysis of bilingual education in California is found in the Assembly Office of Research report, (1986, June), *Bilingual education: Learning English in California,* Sacramento, California.

REFERENCES

Castenada v. Packard (1981), 648 F. 2nd 989.

Carter, T. & Maestas, L. (1982). *Bilingual education that works: Effective school for Spanish-speaking children.* California State Department of Education, Office of Bilingual Education.

Epstein, N. (1977). *Language, ethnicity and the schools.* Washington, D.C. Institute for Educational Leadership.

Hakuta, K. (1986). *Mirror of language: The debate on bilingualism.* New York: Basic Books, Inc. Pub.

Lau v. Nichols (1974), 414 U.S. 563.

Ochoa, A. (1983). The effectiveness of programs for language minority students: A response to federal reports, in *Grants Magazine.*

Purkey, S. & Smith, M. (1983). Effective schools: A review. *Elementary School Journal,* 427–452.

Rios v. Read (1977), 73 F.R.D. 589 595 (E.D.N.Y.)

Ramirez, J. (1986). Comparing structured English immersion and bilingual education. *American Journal of Education,* 95, 1, 122–148.

Tikunoff, W., Fisher, C., & Ward, B et al. (1981). *Preliminary analysis of the data for part I of the SBIF study.* San Francisco: Far West Laboratory for Educational Research and Development.

Willig, A. (1985, Fall). A meta-analysis of selected studies on the effectiveness of bilingual education. *Review of Educational Research,* 55, 3, 269–317.

NO

Diane Ravitch

POLITICIZATION
AND BILINGUAL EDUCATION

There has always been a politics of schools, and no doubt there always will be. Like any other organization populated by human beings, schools have their internal politics; for as long as there have been public schools, there have been political battles over their budget, their personnel policies, their curricula, and their purposes. Anyone who believes that there was once a time in which schools were untouched by political controversy is uninformed about the history of education. The decision-making processes that determine who will be chosen as principal or how the school board will be selected or whether to pass a school bond issue are simply political facts of life that are part and parcel of the administration, financing, and governance of schools. There is also a politics of the curriculum and of the profession, in which contending forces argue about programs and policies. It is hard to imagine a school, a school system, a university, a state board of education, or a national department of education in which these kinds of political conflicts do not exist. They are an intrinsic aspect of complex organizations in which people disagree about how to achieve their goals and about which goals to pursue; to the extent that we operate in a democratic manner, conflict over important and even unimportant issues is inevitable.

There is another kind of politics, however, in which educational institutions become entangled in crusades marked by passionate advocacy, intolerance of criticism, and unyielding dogmatism, and in which the education of children is a secondary rather than a primary consideration. Such crusades go beyond politics-as-usual; they represent the politicization of education. Schools and universities become targets for politicization for several reasons: First, they offer a large captive audience of presumably impressionable minds; second, they are expected to shape the opinions, knowledge, and values of the rising generation, which makes them attractive to those who want to influence the future; and third, since Americans have

From Diane Ravitch, "Politicization and the Schools: The Case of Bilingual Education," *Proceedings of the American Philosophical Society*, vol. 129, no. 2 (June 1985). Copyright © 1985 by the American Philosophical Society. Reprinted by permission.

no strong educational philosophy or educational tradition, almost any claim—properly clothed in rhetorical appeals about the needs of children or of American society—can make its way into the course catalogue or the educational agenda.

Ever since Americans created public schools, financed by tax dollars and controlled by boards of laymen, the schools have been at the center of intermittent struggles over the values that they represent. The founders of the common school, and in particular Horace Mann, believed that the schools could be kept aloof from the religious and political controversies beyond their door, but it has not been easy to keep the crusaders outside the schoolhouse. In the nineteenth century, heated battles were fought over such issues as which Bible would be read in the classroom and whether public dollars might be used to subsidize religious schools. After the onset of World War I, anti-German hostility caused the German language to be routed from American schools, even though nearly a quarter of the high school population studied the language in 1915. Some of this same fervor, strengthened by zeal to hasten the process of assimilation, caused several states to outlaw parochial and private schools and to prohibit the teaching of foreign language in the first eight years of school. Such laws, obviously products of nationalism and xenophobia, were struck down as unconstitutional by the United States Supreme Court in the 1920s. The legislative efforts to abolish nonpublic schools and to bar the teaching of foreign languages were examples of politicization; their purpose was not to improve the education of any child, but to achieve certain social and political goals that the sponsors of these laws believed were of overwhelming importance.

Another example of politicization in education was the crusade to cleanse the schools of teachers and other employees who were suspected of being disloyal, subversive, or controversial. This crusade began in the years after World War I, gathered momentum during the 1930s, and came to full fruition during the loyalty investigations by state and national legislative committees in the 1950s. Fears for national security led to intrusive surveillance of the beliefs, friends, past associations, and political activities of teachers and professors. These inquiries did not improve anyone's education; they used the educational institutions as vehicles toward political goals that were extraneous to education.

A more recent example of politicization occurred on the campuses during the war in Vietnam. Those who had fought political intrusions into educational institutions during the McCarthy era did so on the ground of academic freedom. Academic freedom, they argued, protected the right of students and teachers to express their views, regardless of their content; because of academic freedom, the university served as a sanctuary for dissidents, heretics, and skeptics of all persuasions. During the war in Vietnam, those who tried to maintain the university as a privileged haven for conflicting views, an open marketplace of ideas, found themselves the object of attack by student radicals. Student (and sometimes faculty) radicals believed that opposition to the war was so important that those who did not agree with them should be harassed and even silenced.

Faced with a moral issue, the activist argued, the university could not stand above the battle, nor could it tolerate the expression of "immoral" views. In this spirit, young radicals tried to prevent those with whom they disagreed from speaking and teaching; towards this end, they heckled speakers, disrupted classes, and even planted bombs on campus. These actions were intended to politicize schools and campuses and, in some instances, they succeeded. They were advocated by sincere and zealous individuals who earnestly believed that education could not take place within a context of political neutrality. Their efforts at politicization stemmed not from any desire to improve education as such, but from the pursuit of political goals.

As significant as the student movement and the McCarthy era were as examples of the dangers of politicization, they were short-lived in comparison to the policy of racial segregation. Segregation of public school children by their race and ancestry was established by law in seventeen states and by custom in many communities beyond those states. The practice of assigning public school children and teachers on the basis of their race had no educational justification; it was not intended to improve anyone's education. It was premised on the belief in the innate inferiority of people whose skin was of dark color. Racial segregation as policy and practice politicized the schools; it used them to buttress a racist social and political order. It limited the educational opportunities available to blacks. Racial segregation was socially and politically so effective in isolating blacks from opportunity or economic advancement and educationally so devastating in retarding their learning that our society continues to pay a heavy price to redress the cumulative deficits of generations of poor education.

The United States Supreme Court's 1954 decision, *Brown v. Board of Education*, started the process of ending state-im-

posed racial segregation. In those southern states where segregation was the cornerstone of a way of life, white resistance to desegregation was prolonged and intense. The drive to disestablish racial segregation and to uproot every last vestige of its effects was unquestionably necessary. The practice of assigning children to school by their race and of segregating other public facilities by race was a national disgrace. However, the process through which desegregation came about dramatically altered the politics of schools; courts and regulatory agencies at the federal and state level became accustomed to intervening in the internal affairs of educational institutions, and the potential for politicization of the schools was significantly enlarged.

The slow pace of desegregation in the decade after the *Brown* decision, concurrent with a period of rising expectations, contributed to a dramatic buildup of frustration and rage among blacks, culminating in the protests, civil disorders, and riots of the mid-1960s. In response, Congress enacted major civil rights laws in 1964 and 1965, and the federal courts became aggressive in telling school boards what to do to remedy their constitutional violations. Initially, these orders consisted of commands to produce racially mixed schools. However, some courts went beyond questions of racial mix. In Washington, D.C., a federal district judge in 1967 directed the school administration to abandon ability grouping, which he believed discriminated against black children. This was the first time that a federal court found a common pedagogical practice to be unconstitutional.[1]

In the nearly two decades since that decision, the active intervention of the federal judiciary into school affairs has ceased to be unusual. In Ann Arbor, Michigan, a federal judge ordered the school board to train teachers in "black English," a program subsequently found to be ineffectual in improving the education of black students. In California, a federal judge barred the use of intelligence tests for placement of students in special education classes, even though reputable psychologists defend their validity. In Boston, where the school board was found guilty of intentionally segregating children by race, the federal judge assumed full control over the school system for more than a decade; even reform superintendents who were committed to carrying out the judge's program for desegregation complained of the hundreds of court orders regulating every aspect of schooling, hiring, promotion, curriculum, and financing. In 1982, in a case unrelated to desegregation, a state judge in West Virginia ordered the state education department to do "no less than completely reconstruct the entire system of education in West Virginia," and the judge started the process of reconstruction by setting down his own standards for facilities, administration, and curriculum, including what was to be taught and for how many minutes each week.[2]

Perhaps this is as good a way of bringing about school reform as any other. No doubt school officials are delighted when a judge orders the state legislature to raise taxes on behalf of the schools. But it does seem to be a repudiation of our democratic political structure when judges go beyond issues of constitutional rights, don the mantle of school superintendent, and use their authority to change promotional standards, to reconstruct the curriculum, or to impose their own pedagogical prescriptions.

Now, by the definition of politicization that I earlier offered—that is, when educational institutions become the focus of dogmatic crusaders whose purposes are primarily political and only incidentally related to children's education—these examples may not qualify as politicization, although they do suggest how thin is the line between politics and politicization. After all, the judges were doing what they thought would produce better education. The court decisions in places like Ann Arbor, Boston, California, and West Virginia may be thought of as a shift in the politics of schools, a shift that has brought the judiciary into the decision-making process as a full-fledged partner in shaping educational disputes, even those involving questions of pedagogy and curriculum.

The long struggle to desegregate American schools put them at the center of political battles for more than a generation and virtually destroyed the belief that schools could remain above politics. Having lost their apolitical shield, the schools also lost their capacity to resist efforts to politicize them. In the absence of resistance, demands by interest groups of varying ideologies escalated, each trying to impose its own agenda on the curriculum, the textbooks, the school library, or the teachers. Based on the activities of single-issue groups, any number of contemporary educational policies would serve equally well as examples of politicization. The example that I have chosen as illustrative of politicization is bilingual education. The history of this program exemplifies a campaign on behalf of social and political goals that are only tangentially related to education. I would like to sketch briefly the bilingual controversy, which provides an overview of the new politics of education and demonstrates the tendency within this new politics to use educational programs for noneducational ends.

Demands for bilingual education arose as an outgrowth of the civil rights movement. As it evolved, that movement contained complex, and occasionally contradictory, elements. One facet of the movement appealed for racial integration and assimilation, which led to court orders for busing and racial balance; but the dynamics of the movement also inspired appeals to racial solidarity, which led to demands for black studies, black control of black schools, and other race-conscious policies. Whether the plea was for integration or for separatism, advocates could always point to a body of social science as evidence for their goals.

Race consciousness became a necessary part of the remedies that courts fashioned, but its presence legitimized ethnocentrism as a force in American politics. In the late 1960s, the courts, Congress, and policymakers—having been told for years by spokesmen for the civil rights movement that all children should be treated equally without regard to their race or ancestry—frequently heard compelling testimony by political activists and social scientists about the value of ethnic particularism in the curriculum.

Congress first endorsed funding for bilingual education in 1968, at a time when ethnocentrism had become a powerful political current. In hearings on this legislation, proponents of bilingual education argued that non-English-speaking children did poorly in school because they had low self-esteem, and that this low self-esteem was caused by the absence of their native language from the classroom. They claimed that if the children were taught in their native tongue and about their native culture, they would have higher self-esteem, better attitudes toward school, and higher educational achievement. Bilingual educators also insisted that children would learn English more readily if they already knew another language.

In the congressional hearings, both advocates and congressmen seemed to agree that the purpose of bilingual education was to help non-English speakers succeed in school and in society. But the differences between them were not then obvious. The congressmen believed that bilingual education would serve as a temporary transition into the regular English language program. But the bilingual educators saw the program as an opportunity to maintain the language and culture of the non-English-speaking student, while he was learning English.[3]

What was extraordinary about the Bilingual Education Act of 1968, which has since been renewed several times, is that it was the first time that the Congress had ever legislated a given pedagogical method. In practice, bilingual education means a program in which children study the major school subjects in a language other than English. Funding of the program, although small within the context of the federal education budget, created strong constituencies for its continuation, both within the federal government and among recipient agencies. No different from other interest groups, these constituencies pressed for expansion and strengthening of their program. Just as lifelong vocational educators are unlikely to ask whether their program works, so career bilingual educators are committed to their method as a philosophy, not as a technique for language instruction. The difference is this: techniques are subject to evaluation, which may cause them to be revised or discarded; philosophies are not.

In 1974, the Supreme Court's *Lau v. Nichols* decision reinforced demands for bilingual education. The Court ruled against the San Francisco public schools for their failure to provide English language instruction for 1,800 non-English-speaking Chinese students. The Court's decision was reasonable and appropriate. The Court said, "There is no equality of treatment merely by providing students with the same facilities, textbooks, teachers, and curriculum; for students who do not understand English are effectively foreclosed from any meaningful education." The decision did not endorse any particular remedy. It said "Teaching English to the students of Chinese ancestry who do not speak the language is one choice. Giving instruction to the group in Chinese is another. There may be others."[4]

Despite the Court's prudent refusal to endorse any particular method of instruction, the bilingual educators interpreted the *Lau* decision as a mandate for bilingual programs. In the year after the decision, the United States Office of Education established a task force to fashion guidelines for the implementation of the *Lau* decision; the task force was composed of bilingual educators and representatives of language minority groups. The task force fashioned regulations that prescribed in exhaustive detail how school districts should prepare and carry out bilingual programs for non-English-speaking students. The districts were directed to identify the student's primary language, not by his proficiency in English, but by determining which language was most often spoken in the student's home, which language he had learned first, and which language he

used most often. Thus a student would be eligible for a bilingual program even if he was entirely fluent in English.[5]

Furthermore, while the Supreme Court refused to endorse any given method, the task force directed that non-English-speaking students should receive bilingual education that emphasized instruction in their native language and culture. Districts were discouraged from using the "English as a Second Language" approach, which consists of intensive, supplemental English-only instruction, or immersion techniques, in which students are instructed in English within an English-only context.

Since the establishment of the bilingual education program, many millions of dollars have been spent to support bilingual programs in more than sixty different languages. Among those receiving funding to administer and staff such programs, bilingual education is obviously popular, but there are critics who think that it is educationally unsound. Proponents of desegregation have complained that bilingual education needlessly segregates non-English speakers from others of their age. At a congressional hearing in 1977, one desegregation specialist complained that bilingual programs had been funded "without any significant proof that they would work. . . . There is nothing in the research to suggest that children can effectively learn English without continuous interaction with other children who are native English speakers."[6]

The research on bilingual education has been contradictory, and studies that favor or criticize the bilingual approach have been attacked as biased. Researchers connected to bilingual institutes claim that their programs resulted in significant gains for non-English-speaking children.

But a four-year study commissioned by the United States Office of Education concluded that students who learned bilingually did not achieve at a higher level than those in regular classes, nor were their attitudes toward school significantly different. What they seemed to learn best, the study found, was the language in which they were instructed.[7]

One of the few evidently unbiased, nonpolitical assessments of bilingual research was published in 1982 in the *Harvard Educational Review*. A survey of international findings, it concluded that "bilingual programs are neither better nor worse than other instructional methods." The author found that in the absence of compelling experimental support for this method, there was "no legal necessity or research basis for the federal government to advocate or require a specific educational approach."[8]

If the research is in fact inconclusive, then there is no justification for mandating the use of bilingual education or any other single pedagogy. The bilingual method may or may not be the best way to learn English. Language instruction programs that are generally regarded as outstanding, such as those provided for Foreign Service officers or by the nationally acclaimed center at Middlebury College, are immersion programs, in which students embark on a systematic program of intensive language learning without depending on their native tongue. Immersion programs may not be appropriate for all children, but then neither is any single pedagogical method. The method to be used should be determined by the school authorities and the professional staff, based on their resources and competence.

Despite the fact that the Supreme Court did not endorse bilingual education, the lower federal courts have tended to treat this pedagogy as a civil right, and more than a dozen states have mandated its use in their public schools. The path by which bilingual education came to be viewed as a civil right, rather than as one method of teaching language, demonstrates the politicization of the language issue in American education. The United States Commission on Civil Rights endorsed bilingual education as a civil right nearly a decade ago. Public interest lawyers and civil rights lawyers have also regarded bilingual education as a basic civil right. An article in 1983 in the *Columbia Journal of Law and Social Problems* contended that bilingual education "may be the most effective method of compensatory language instruction currently used to educate language-minority students."[9] It based this conclusion not on a review of educational research but on statements made by various political agencies.

The article states, for example, as a matter of fact rather than opinion: " . . . by offering subject matter instruction in a language understood by language-minority students, the bilingual-bicultural method maximizes achievement, and thus minimizes feelings of inferiority that might accompany a poor academic performance. By ridding the school environment of those features which may damage a language-minority child's self-image and thereby interfere with the educative process, bilingual-bicultural education creates the atmosphere most conducive to successful learning."[10]

If there were indeed conclusive evidence for these statements, then bilingual-bicultural education *should* be imposed on school districts throughout the country. However, the picture is complicated;

there are good bilingual programs, and there are ineffective bilingual programs. In and of itself, bilingualism is one pedagogical method, as subject to variation and misuse as any other single method. To date, no school district has claimed that the bilingual method succeeded in sharply decreasing the dropout rate of Hispanic children or markedly raising their achievement scores in English and other subjects. The bilingual method is not necessarily inferior to other methods; its use should not be barred. There simply is no conclusive evidence that bilingualism should be preferred to all other ways of instructing non-English-speaking students. This being the case, there are no valid reasons for courts or federal agencies to impose this method on school districts for all non-English speakers, to the exclusion of other methods of language instruction.

Bilingual education exemplifies politicization because its advocates press its adoption regardless of its educational effectiveness, and they insist that it must be made mandatory regardless of the wishes of the parents and children who are its presumed beneficiaries. It is a political program whose goals are implicit in the term "biculturalism." The aim is to use the public schools to promote the maintenance of distinct ethnic communities, each with its own cultural heritage and language. This in itself is a valid goal for a democratic nation as diverse and pluralistic as ours, but it is questionable whether this goal is appropriately pursued by the public schools, rather than by the freely chosen activities of individuals and groups.

Then there is the larger question of whether bilingual education actually promotes equality of educational opportunity. Unless it enables non-English-speaking children to learn English and to enter into the mainstream of American society, it may hinder equality of educational opportunity. The child who spends most of his instructional time learning in Croatian or Greek or Spanish is likely to learn Croatian, Greek, or Spanish. Fluency in these languages will be of little help to those who want to apply to American colleges, universities, graduate schools, or employers, unless they are also fluent in English.

Of course, our nation needs much more foreign language instruction. But we should not confuse our desire to promote foreign languages in general with the special educational needs of children who do not know how to speak and read English in an English-language society.

Will our educational institutions ever be insulated from the extremes of politicization? It seems highly unlikely, in view of the fact that our schools and colleges are deeply embedded in the social and political mainstream. What is notably different today is the vastly increased power of the federal government and the courts to intervene in educational institutions, because of the expansion of the laws and the dependence of almost all educational institutions on public funding. To avoid unwise and dangerous politicization, government agencies should strive to distinguish between their proper role as protectors of fundamental constitutional rights and inappropriate intrusion into complex issues of curriculum and pedagogy.

This kind of institutional restraint would be strongly abetted if judges and policymakers exercised caution and skepticism in their use of social science testimony. Before making social research the basis for constitutional edicts, judges and policymakers should understand that social science findings are usually divergent, limited, tentative, and partial.

We need the courts as vigilant guardians of our rights; we need federal agencies that respond promptly to any violations of those rights. But we also need educational institutions that are free to exercise their responsibilities without fear of pressure groups and political lobbies. Decisions about which textbooks to use, which theories to teach, which books to place in the school library, how to teach, and what to teach are educational issues. They should be made by appropriate lay and professional authorities on educational grounds. In a democratic society, all of us share the responsibility to protect schools, colleges, and universities against unwarranted political intrusion into educational affairs.

REFERENCES

1. *Hobson v. Hansen*, 269 F. Supp. 401 (D.D.C., 1967); Alexander Bickel, "Skelly Wright's Sweeping Decision," *New Republic*, July 8, 1967, pp. 11–12.

2. Nathan Glazer, "Black English and Reluctant Judges," *Public Interest*, vol. 62, Winter 1980, pp. 40–54; *Larry P. v. Wilson Riles*, 495 F. Supp. 1926 (N.D. Calif., 1979); Nathan Glazer, "IQ on Trial," *Commentary*, June 1981, pp. 51–59; *Morgan v. Hennigan*, 379 F. Supp. 410 (D. Mass., 1974); Robert Wood, "The Disassembling of American Education," *Daedalus*, vol. 109, no. 3, Summer 1980, pp. 99–113; *Education Week*, May 12, 1982, p. 5.

3. U.S. Congress, Senate, Committee on Labor and Public Welfare, Special Subcommittee on Bilingual Education, 90th Cong., 1st sess., 1967.

4. *Lau v. Nichols*, 414 U.S. 563 (1974).

5. U.S. Department of Health, Education, and Welfare, "Task Force Findings Specifying Remedies Available for Eliminating Past Educational Practices Ruled Unlawful under *Lau v. Nichols*" (Washington, D.C., Summer 1975).

6. U.S. Congress, House, Subcommittee on Elementary, Secondary, and Vocational Education of the Committee on Education and Labor, Bilingual Education, 95th Cong., 1st sess., 1977, pp. 335–336. The speaker was Gary Orfield.

7. Malcolm N. Danoff, "Evaluation of the Impact of ESEA Title VII Spanish/English Bilingual Education Programs" (Palo Alto, Calif.: American Institutes for Research, 1978).

8. Iris Rotberg, "Some Legal and Research Considerations in Establishing Federal Policy in Bilingual Education," *Harvard Educational Review*, vol. 52, May 1982, pp. 148–168.

9. Jonathan D. Haft, "Assuring Equal Educational Opportunity for Language-Minority Students: Bilingual Education and the Equal Educational Opportunity Act of 1974." *Columbia Journal of Law and Social Problems*, vol. 18, no. 2, 1983, pp. 209–293.

10. Ibid., p. 253.

POSTSCRIPT

Is Bilingual Education Justifiable as a Policy?

Further specification of some of the trends and viewpoints cited in the Introduction and in the articles may be found in the following sources: "Defusing the Issues in Bilingualism and Bilingual Education," by Charles R. Foster, *Phi Delta Kappan* (January 1982); "The Bilingual Education Battle," by Cynthia Gorney, *The Washington Post National Weekly Edition* (July 29, 1985); "Synthesis of Research on Bilingual Education," by Kenji Hakuta and Laurie J. Gould, *Educational Leadership* (March 1987); and "The English Language Amendment: One Nation . . . Indivisible?" by S. I. Hayakawa, *The World & I* (March 1986).

Some books to note are Jane Miller's *Many Voices: Bilingualism, Culture and Education* (1983), which includes a research review; Kenji Hakuta's *Mirror of Language: The Debate on Bilingualism* (1986); *Bilingual Education: A Sourcebook* (1985), by Alba N. Ambert and Sarah E. Melendez; and *Sink or Swim: The Politics of Bilingual Education* (1986), by Colman B. Stein, Jr.

The Fall 1985 issue of *Equity and Choice* features "Bilingual Education: An Introduction to the Issues" and includes "Viewpoints on Bilingual Education," both by Nathan Glazer and Jim Cummins. The September 1985 issue of *Educational Leadership* offers a number of views, including "A Case for Structured Immersion," by Russell Gerston and John Woodward. *The New York Times Magazine* of November 10, 1985 contains "The Politics of Bilingualism," by Larry Rohter, and "One Language or Two?" by Edward B. Fiske.

Thomas Weyr's book *Hispanic U.S.A.: Breaking the Melting Pot* (1988) presents a detailed plan of action in light of the prediction that "by the year 2000 as many people in the U.S. will be speaking Spanish as they will English." A helpful overview article is David Rosenbaum's "Bilingual Education: A Guide to the Literature" in *Education Libraries* (Winter 1987).

A number of articles may be found in the March 1989 issue of *The American School Board Journal*, the March 1988 issue of *The English Journal*, and the Summer 1988 issue of *Equity and Excellence*. Some especially provocative articles are these: "Bilingual Education: A Barrier to Achievement," by Nicholas Sanchez, *Bilingual Education* (December 1987); " 'Official English': Fear or Foresight?" by Nancy Bane, *America* (December 17, 1988); and "The Language of Power," by Yolanda T. DeMola, *America* (April 22, 1989).

Research comparing the effectiveness of the several approaches to helping linguistically disadvantaged students remains inconclusive. At the same time the effort is clouded by the political agendas of those who champion first-language instruction and those who insist on some version of the immersion strategy. Politics and emotional commitments aside, what must be placed first on the agenda are the needs of the students and the value of native language in a child's progress through school.

ISSUE 21

Are Current Sex Education Programs Lacking in Moral Guidance?

YES: Kevin Ryan, from "Sex, Morals, and Schools," *Theory into Practice* (Summer 1989)

NO: Peter Scales, from "Overcoming Future Barriers to Sexuality Education," *Theory into Practice* (Summer 1989)

ISSUE SUMMARY

YES: Professor of education Kevin Ryan argues for movement toward a firmer moral grounding of sex education programs.
NO: Peter Scales, a leading advocate of sexuality education, feels that current objections to these programs are unwarranted.

As early as the middle of the nineteenth century, English philosopher Herbert Spencer was recommending that sex education be included among the school subjects that are considered essential to the leading of a complete and satisfactory life. He saw the subject as a natural part of preparing for family life that could be grounded firmly in the newly emerging body of scientific knowledge.

There are those who, still today, oppose even narrowly scientific explanations of sexual functioning in the schools. Some people object to the information itself as having a possible corrupting influence. Others contend that clinical information alone, without religiously grounded moral guidance, is misleading. Still others resent the efforts of some educators to infuse sex instruction with values which may be ideologically slanted.

On the larger cultural level, some critics of sex education feel that the recent "sexual revolution" has left many young people adrift without moral moorings and that most of the school efforts fail to counteract this situation. Church or home guidance is deemed preferable by some of these people, while inclusion of ethical considerations in the sex education curriculum is desired by others.

Some central questions are these: Are the schools qualified to handle such subject matter competently? Is there room in the public school curriculum for such studies at a time when performance in basic academic areas is weak? If the answers to these questions are affirmative, many issues stemming from the teaching of sex education need to be addressed, such as: How early should sexuality education begin? By whom should it be taught? Should it be taught separately or as a component of health or biology classes? Is it an appropriate topic for social studies courses? Are some aspects of the topic taboo? How explicit should instructional materials be? What controls on library inclusions are needed? Should parents review or approve course materials? Should parents have the right to exclude their children from such instructional programs? How early should the topic of AIDS be addressed? Should high schools provide condoms for teenagers?

Indeed, the AIDS epidemic places new urgency on increasing the schools' efforts in the area of sexuality education. A recent Gallup poll shows that 90 percent of respondents are in favor of AIDS education, with 40 percent saying it should begin in the elementary schools. A 1988 report by the Sex Information and Educational Council of the United States, titled *State Update on Sexuality Education and AIDS Education*, shows that 13 states require sexuality education and another 22 have stipulated guidelines for teaching the subject. The range of programs is indeed wide—from full K–12 treatment of the topic to a few hours of instruction on physiological aspects alone.

While some 80 percent of parents favor sex education in the schools, many feel that values and morals must be included in the instructional program to guide young people in making sex-related decisions. Some parents express concern about the "situational ethics" tone, which some programs seem to espouse, and call for a more direct moral approach.

In the following articles, Kevin Ryan, who is the director of the Center for the Advancement of Ethics and Character at Boston University, contends that sex is not a morally neutral matter and shows how the moral dimension can be infused through the use of an experimental curriculum developed at the center. Peter Scales counters that current comprehensive programs, often run by sexuality educators and health professionals, operate from a firm base of values and ethical concerns.

YES

Kevin Ryan

SEX, MORALS, AND SCHOOLS

Sexuality is an important part of our humanity and an issue that is vital to the survival of the species. It is, therefore, a necessary part of the education we offer to the young. Yet sex has historically been an aspect of human relations shrouded in taboos and rarely talked about openly. Despite changes in this regard, parents who have tried to discuss sex with their children know that it can be an awkward topic.

Sex is controversial today because the authorities in sexual matters have changed. Until this century, many people in this country were guided in what was acceptable sexual practice and what was unacceptable by their religious leaders. Medical doctors have also been a source of advice, often being asked to give talks on sex to high school students. Today, however, authority status seems to be gained by an appearance on a TV talk show or inclusion in the reading rack at the supermarket checkout.

We have undergone a revolution in sexual attitudes and practices in a very short period of time. This change appears to be the result, in part, of our expanded individualism and in part, of easier and improved methods of birth control. Twenty years ago sex before marriage became more acceptable, as did sexual relations between people of the same sex. Many of our prohibitions and inhibitions slipped away, and more and better sex became the goal of many.

Several things have happened since then, however, to give even the most ardent of the apostles of the new sexuality pause. Our family rearing practices have been radically affected. We appear to live in a no-fault divorce climate where it is projected, for instance, that 44 percent of the marriages contracted in 1983 will end in divorce. Since 1970, marriages are down 30 percent and divorces are up 50 percent (Christensen, 1988). We have recently seen the advent of, first, herpes complex B, and now, AIDS.

More to the issue of moral education and sex education, we have the highest levels of teenage sexuality ever recorded in this country. More than one-half of our nation's young people have had sexual intercourse by the time they are 17 (Bennett, 1987, p. 134). In 1980, two professors from Johns

From Kevin Ryan, "Sex, Morals, and Schools," *Theory into Practice*, vol. 28, no. 3 (1989), pp. 217–220. Copyright © 1989 by the College of Education, The Ohio State University. Reprinted by permission.

Hopkins University reported that 49.8 percent of girls between 15 and 19 had premarital sex, compared with 30 percent when they began their study in 1971 (cited in Lickona, 1983, p. 367). Between 1940 and 1985 the rate of out-of-wedlock births to adolescents rose 621 percent (ASCD, 1988, p. 7). In this nation, the sexual landscape for children and adolescents has changed dramatically.

THE MORAL NATURE OF SEX

Teaching the young about sex raises concerns among parents due to its traditional sense of sacredness and taboo, and to the dramatic changes in sexual attitudes and practices. Schools have reacted to this social context by putting more effort and devoting more of students' time-on-task to sex (Kasun, 1979). Critics, however, are contending that our sex education programs are simply feeding the fires of sexual interest and activities among the young (Anchell, 1986; Kasun, 1979). Cuban (1986) states: "Decade after decade . . . statistics have demonstrated the ineffectiveness of such courses in reducing sexual activity, unwanted pregnancy, and venereal disease among teenagers. Before the reformers mindlessly expand school programs aimed at preventing teenage pregnancy, they ought to ask some hard questions" (p. 321). The problem seems to be that while school boards, parents, and teachers know "something is wrong" with this increase in sexual activity among adolescents, they do not approach it as the moral issue it is.

Sexual intercourse is not simply a physical value-free activity. Nor is sexual activity merely a matter of personal taste and choice, although this has been the view among many sex educators. Exemplifying this value-neutral, individualistic approach are the words of a well-known sex educator and author of a sex education curriculum guide for the state of California: 'Right' or 'wrong' in so intimate a matter as sexual behavior is as personal as one's own name and address. No textbook or classroom teacher can teach it" (cited in Cronenwett, 1982, p. 101).

By its very nature, sexual intercourse is moral. It is moral because it is social, involving another person with human dignity and rights. Sex is a mutual giving and mutual taking. It affects body and mind, a person's physical and psychological well-being.

Like all human action, sex is subject to moral judgment. Sexual activities and practices must be open to the question, "What is the right thing to do?" Because sex can have profound consequences for individuals (i.e., birth), it has traditionally been part of a society's rules of behavior, its moral code. Since sex carries the source of a community's existence, it is also natural that it is seen as part of the community's moral code.

All cultures have an overriding mission to endure. The adults in a community are committed to passing on to the young the rules they believe will enable them to endure and to live well. Schools from the time of the Greeks have been seen as one of a society's primary vehicles to pass on to its young its values and moral code (Pratte, 1988; Ryan, 1986). A culture that fails to tell its adolescents these larger facts-of-life and does not think its young have the capacity for sexual self-restraint is one that is giving up the fight.

Nevertheless, as Kasun (1979) and Bennett (1987) point out, the older generation, particularly in our schools, is hesitant to teach sex in its full moral context. A possible reason for this is that sexual morality has traditionally been intertwined with religious morality and, as Vitz (1986) has demonstrated, our public schools in recent years act as if religion is not part of our cultural life or even our history. It appears that since the moral nature of sex is of concern to many people of traditional religious beliefs, public school educators have shied away from examining the moral dimension of sex in their programs. Certainly, no major denomination in our nation's very pluralistic patchwork of churches supports sexual activity among unmarried teenagers. But neither does any responsible group of non-religious people. Most people, religious and non-religious, decry what Jesse Jackson calls, "Babies having babies" (cited in Read, 1988). What, then, keeps sex education programs from taking a strong pro-chastity, pro-abstinence stance?

Our failure to confront the young with moral arguments against engaging in sexual intercourse may be due to adults, including teachers, not wanting to be seen as old-fashioned or out-of-step with views that up until recently have been perceived as progressive and sophisticated. In our media-saturated world where sexual images are continually portrayed, attitudes valuing youth and sexual freedom are easy to acquire. Descriptions like "sexually active" connote vitality and freedom, often leaving the average monogamous married adult feeling vaguely inert and out-of-step, while chaste single adults may well perceive themselves as relics from our puritan past.

Whatever the reason for teaching sex from a biological and value-free psychological manner, it needs reconsideration. Sex is not a morally neutral matter. The dangers it holds in terms of AIDS, other diseases, and unwanted pregnancy are well known. Eunice Kennedy Shriver (1986), who for several years has been working closely with unwed teenaged mothers, has written about how teenagers want sex dealt with in a value context—values such as self-restraint, compassionate understanding of the other, and fidelity. Shriver states:

> Over the years I have discovered that teenagers would rather be given standards than contraceptives. . . . They are thirsting for someone to teach them . . . to tell them that for their own good and the good of society it is not wise for them to have sexual intercourse at 12, 13, 14, or 15 . . . that sex at this age is not necessary for a caring relationship to develop and endure. (p. 7E)

Thus, teenagers as well as adults would welcome having the morality of sex joined with the biological content.

SUGGESTIONS FOR SEX EDUCATION

Since our children will and should come to know and understand sex, it is in everyone's interest that they "get the story right." While it would be comforting to be guided in this by empirically verified procedures, how we conduct sex education must currently rely on good judgment. The following suggestions are offered in the hope that they might contribute to sound school policies in this area.

First, sex education should be taught within a moral, though not necessarily religious, context. While teachers should not be moralistic, they should join moral perspectives to the biological information. They should ensure, as Shriver (1986) and Mast (1986) have urged, that sex be a matter of reflection and moral discourse, and that the biological knowledge and issues are infused with the ethical.

Second, the teacher or the school should not be the lone arbiter of what is taught around this topic. One of a school's goals is to meet the needs of the local community. A sex education course, therefore, should reinforce what the community believes to be correct. It should not be used to separate the young from their families' values. If teachers feel unduly constrained, they should try to educate parents to their views and intentions or, if they fail, find a more accommodating school-community.

Individual parents who are uncomfortable with what their community has decided should be taught may want to find another school for their children. However, allowance has to be made for those parents who object to the school's sexual messages and mores but cannot afford to change schools. Given the many sensitivities around this issue, it is imperative that the public schools and parents find a common moral ground for the sex education programs presented in the schools.

Third, teachers should urge children to talk to their parents about the rightness and wrongness of sexual attitudes and practices. The school could also provide an important service to parents if it shared information with parents on how to talk with their children about these issues. In the same vein, while not teaching the sexual views of a particular religion, the public school could suggest to students an investigation of what their religion has to say about sexual behavior. To teach about religion as a source of knowing and guidance is not a violation of our separation of church and state.

Fourth, the schools should receive the best guidance possible about the biology and morality of sex. The secretary of education and the 50 chief state school officers ought to request a special commission composed of members of the National Academy of Science, other learned associations, and the National Council of Christians and Jews to give guidance to the public schools about what to teach and how to teach it. The state boards of education could then translate these recommendations into educational policy.

Fifth, sex education should not be the sole province of health educators. The question, "What is sex and what should we do with our sexuality?" like other great questions, such as "What is human nature?" and "What is most worth knowing?" does not yield to easy answers. The nature of human sexuality has been the subject of reflection by philosophers, theologians, poets, novelists, sociologists, biologists, and even economists, to name but a few of the groups that have given systematic attention to this topic.

In most American schools today sex education falls to health educators and sometimes physical educators. Their training tends to lean heavily on physiology and psychology. A relatively new discipline, psychology has certainly enriched our understanding of humans, and indeed, of human sexuality. However, psychology has spent much of its brief history jumping from one set of sexual verities to another, and health educators should be cautious about relying on this discipline for guidance.

If health educators continue to be given the major responsibility for sex education, they ought to be educated to draw on several disciplines in their understanding of and teaching about sex. For example, while literature has been largely ignored, much of what we as a human community have learned about sexuality is embedded in our myths, stories, and poems. In literature, sex is more than "the facts of life." It is, rather, a quality of people's lives, charged with energy and meaning, with subtleties and shadings. Literature addresses sexuality in its full complexity of love and jealousy, arousal and rejection, fulfillment and betrayal. Our poems and short stores are "case studies" of what we have learned.

Given this awareness, a group of us at Boston University constructed a literature based curriculum that tries to put the adolescent student's emerging interest in sex in a fuller context than mechanical sexual behavior. Entitled *Loving Well*, this experimental curriculum attempts to engage the student's moral imagination through old and new stories of falling in love, dating, infatuation, romantic betrayal, and the emotional roller coaster of love. Some of the stories and poems involve sexual acts, albeit the descriptions are more suggestive than clinical. However, the sexual situations are framed by lives—lives that must deal with the consequences of these acts, lives that demonstrate how these acts are permeated with ethical considerations. The purpose of the *Loving Well* curriculum, which is currently being tested in classrooms in Massachusetts and Maine, is to get students thinking about their sexuality in this larger context and to discuss the stories and their implications with other students, their teachers, and their parents. While quite preliminary, the initial reactions from students, teachers, and parents have been extremely positive. However, even if effective, we see this curriculum as only one component of a fuller, richer program of sex education.

A final suggestion is that sex education should actively promote sexual absti-nence among unmarried teenagers. Sexual abstinence should be presented to the young as an ideal, just as we present honesty as an ideal to be sought after. The self-control involved with sexual abstinence, coupled as it often is with concern for the well-being of another person (i.e., the potentially pregnant teenaged girl or the young man with a venereal disease), can be an important part of character formation for a young person.

But from where does the ideal of sexual abstinence gain its authority? Good sexual attitudes and habits should serve both the individual and the society. Most Americans, regardless of their religious or ethnic affiliation, believe that it is unwise for high school students to be sexually active. A national poll (Leo, 1986) found that two-thirds of our citizens want the schools to "urge teenagers not to have sexual intercourse" and that 76 percent of American adults old enough to have adolescent children considered it "morally wrong for (unmarried) teenagers to have sexual relations."

Thus, it seems reasonable to propose that the schools criticize promiscuity and support sexual abstinence during adolescence. Rather than a value-free approach that advances condoms, abortion, and sexual experimentation, our schools should promote a sex education that not only has the support of the community, but contributes to the development of character and moral maturity.

REFERENCES

Anchell, M. (1986, June 20). Psychoanalysis vs. sex education. *National Review*, 33–61.

Association for Supervision and Curriculum Development (ASCD). (1988). *Moral education in the life of the school*. Alexandria, VA: Author.

Bennett, W. (1987). *Sex and the education of our children*. Washington, DC: U.S. Department of Education.

Christensen, B. (1988, Spring). The costly retreat from marriage. *The Public Interest, 91,* 62.

Cronenwett, S. (1982). Response to symposium on sex and children and adolescents. In E. A. Wynne (Ed.), *Character policy: An emerging issue* (p. 101). Washington, DC: University Press of America.

Cuban, L. (1986). Sex and school reform. *Phi Delta Kappan, 68,* 319–321.

Kasun, J. (1976, Spring). Turning children into sex experts. *The Public Interest, 55,* 3–14.

Leo, J. (1986, November 24). Sex and schools. *Time,* p. 321.

Lickona, T. (1983). *Raising good children.* New York: Bantam.

Mast, C. (1986). *Sex respect.* Bradley, IL: Respect, Inc.

Pratte, R. (1988). *The civil imperative: Examining the need for civic education.* New York: Teachers College Press.

Read, E. W. (1988, March 17). Birth cycle: Teenage pregnancy becomes rite of passage in ghetto. *The Wall Street Journal,* p. 13.

Ryan, K. (1986). The new moral education. *Phi Delta Kappan, 68,* 228–233.

Shriver, E. K. (1986, July 10). Teenage pregnancy: Something can be done. *Philadelphia Inquirer,* p. 7E.

Vitz, P. C. (1986, Fall). The role of religion in public school textbooks. *Religion and Public Education, 13,* 48–56.

NO   Peter Scales

OVERCOMING FUTURE BARRIERS
TO SEXUALITY EDUCATION

In the late 1970s, the U.S. Centers for Disease Control embarked on an extensive research effort to understand and improve sexuality education. Part of that effort was funding for the Mathtech research corporation to conduct a national study of the barriers to sexuality education. Based on studying 23 communities' experiences through the 1960s and 1970s, the Mathtech study concluded that (a) administrators' fear of opposition, more than opposition itself, and (b) supporters' inadequate political skills were a central explanation for the widespread lack and/or superficiality of most sexuality education programs in the United States (Scales, 1984).

Some of those barriers have been surmounted. The '80s have seen an expansion of sexuality education, in and out of schools, and more young people seem to be participating in some type of sexuality education. However, the comprehensiveness and timing have not appeared to have changed much from the late '70s. Sonenstein and Pittman (1984) found that perhaps 15 percent of U.S. students experienced a comprehensive sexuality education course in school, as compared with the Mathtech estimate of no more than 10 percent in the late 1970s (Kirby, Alter, & Scales, 1979). This reflects an increase, but is still a distinct minority.

Most differences in when sexuality education is offered may be explained by sexual abuse prevention units in the early grades, as compared to formal sex education in the junior and senior high grades. AIDS prevention efforts do not appear to have taken hold yet below the junior high school level ("Local Districts," 1987). Also, only 10 states require sexuality education today ("Sexuality Education," 1988), as compared to 2 states in 1981 (Kirby & Scales, 1981).

The opposition to sexuality education continues to be a force, most notably in the debate over school based or school linked health clinics, and some old battles are still being fought. For instance, it took until 1987 for Tennessee to pass a law saying it is not a crime to answer relevant questions in sexuality education classes ("Highlights," 1987). However, opponents seem less likely

From Peter Scales, "Overcoming Future Barriers to Sexuality Education," *Theory into Practice*, vol. 28, no. 3 (1989), pp. 172–176. Copyright © 1989 by the College of Education, The Ohio State University. Reprinted by permission.

today to succeed in restricting sexuality education, and supporters seem to have broadened their base.

Those in support had always been the majority, at least since the first Gallup poll on the issue in 1943. The opinion polls today express a popular will to improve and expand sexuality education to a degree unthinkable a generation ago. For example, not only are the usual 80–90 percent in support of comprehensive sexuality education content in the public schools, fully two-thirds of U.S. adults say they think schools should be *required* to establish links with family planning clinics ("Teen Pregnancy," 1986).

In 1988, the theme of the annual meeting of the Society for the Scientific Study of Sex was "sexual literacy." To be sexually literate, the society's program stated, is "to possess the basic sexual information and skills to thrive in a modern world; a comprehensive knowledge of sex and sexuality; the ability to understand alternative sides of a sexual issue; tolerance for ambiguity and paradox; and understanding of the advantages and limitations of different methodologies used in the study of sex" ("Sexual Literacy," 1988). In this broad sense, few would suggest that our nation has become sexually literate.

While barriers to the offering of sexuality education have decreased, many barriers to the effectiveness of sexuality education remain or are likely to appear in the next two decades.[1] If improvement is to occur, the following barriers will have to be overcome.

BARRIER 1. TAKING A NARROW VIEW OF SEXUALITY EDUCATION

In the 1970s, sexuality educators strived to broaden understanding of the field as something more than "sex" education. The focus in many programs had been on reproductive anatomy, or what Gordon (1981) called the "relentless pursuit of the fallopian tubes" (p. 214). To counteract this approach, the term "sexuality" education was emphasized, embracing not just the physical but also the social, emotional, psychological, and spiritual aspects of being human.

Narrowness remains, however, in at least three key ways: (a) overselling the impact of school instruction alone on behavior as contrasted with the impact of broader social actions; (b) basing judgments of sexuality education only on its measurable impact; and (c) taking a "back to the basics" approach to sexuality education.

Overselling sexuality education's impact. The impact of school curriculum on teenage pregnancy and AIDS tends to be oversold, particularly in light of the small part sexuality education courses play in the everyday life of students. Teen pregnancy reduction can occur, but reaching this goal requires going beyond the school curriculum.

School based health clinics, comprehensive programs combining dropout prevention, job opportunities, recreation, and other components, and mentor programs with adults and older youth helping younger persons all have been shown to have better impact on pregnancy reduction than sexuality education alone, although sexuality education is almost always a component in these multifaceted efforts.[2] New Jersey's commissioner of human resources notes that their $6 million pilot investment in comprehensive "youth services in the schools" programs was made because the "boundaries between education and human services don't work anymore" (Sullivan, 1988, p. A23).

Sexuality education courses can make a difference, but their impact is limited. Regarding teen pregnancy prevention, for example, the impact seems to occur through promoting greater contraceptive use among those who would be having sexual intercourse anyway, rather than by reducing sexual activity rates (Kirby, 1985). Given that all of schooling takes up just 8 percent of a person's life by age 18 (Finn, 1986), and the most comprehensive sexuality education programs take up just a fraction of that, the impact of school curriculum alone should not be oversold.

The "measurement" factor. Justifying sexuality education only on the basis of its measurable "impact" instead of its intrinsic value is a second type of narrowness. This is a more subtle barrier because of the emphasis the education reform movement of the last several years has placed on "results" in the form of higher test scores, readiness of youth for the workforce, and other instrumental impacts. In contrast, sexuality education may deserve a prominent place in the curriculum because we define such knowledge as an essential part of being fully human.

A broader barrier to truly comprehensive sexuality education may be the absence of a genuinely "liberal" ethic for education, in the non-political sense of the word. Such an ethic would support education for the sake of well-roundedness, a belief that, apart from what economic purpose they serve, certain areas of human experience and knowledge must comprise the common understanding of people in our society. In the debate about what it means to be educated, we must include an answer to a new fundamental question: What place do human sexuality and gender issues have within that common understanding of "being educated"?

The "back-to-the-basics" approach. Thinking about educational excellence as "back to the basics" is a third type of narrowness, which needs to be replaced with a "forward to the basics" framework (Scales, 1987a). A new set of "basics" is required for the future demands young people will face as they deal with collisions of emerging technology, enduring values, and changing national and world politics. AIDS, surrogate parenthood, global population pressures, and myriad other issues involving sexuality and family concerns will require citizens with well-developed critical thinking skills.

These skills should include the ability to challenge one's own assumptions, set priorities, make difficult choices among competing values, negotiate differing points of view, evaluate information brought to bear on a question, and communicate clearly and effectively. All young people need these skills for the future, not only those who go on to college. Instead of toughening standards and focusing on the college bound, a genuine reconstruction of the curriculum is needed based on rethinking the basics for the future of all children.

BARRIER 2. FAILURE TO UNDERSTAND THE IMPORTANCE OF SELF-EFFICACY

For decades, sexuality educators have held that self-esteem is a key element in behavioral change, and thus must be a key goal in sexuality education curricula. Numerous curriculum guides contain exercises teachers are supposed to use to increase students' self-esteem.[3] Mostly, however, self-esteem in this context has referred to the self-worth part of the construct, rather than what researchers believe may be a more relevant component for behavioral change, the self-efficacy aspect.

Briefly, self-efficacy refers to an individual's perception that he or she is able to do or accomplish what is desired or expected. It has to do with the sense that one can make things happen. Theorists believe that a better understanding of self-efficacy can help educators promote decisions to use contraception or avoid unprotected intercourse (Lawrance & McLeroy, 1986; Rosenstock, Strecher, & Brecher, 1988).

A problem is that neither self-worth nor self-efficacy can really be *taught*, as may be inferred from the generally disappointing results of evaluations showing little increase in self-esteem from a sexuality education program (Kirby, 1985; cf. with the contrasting construct of "sexual self-concept" in Winter, 1988). Self-worth can perhaps be nurtured through self-talk and cheerleading. Years ago, I chanted "I am somebody" along with hundreds of others at a national conference for teenagers in Atlanta, led by Jesse Jackson. I have no doubt that saying "I am somebody" helps. But it doesn't instantly give people the sense that they can make things happen in the world.

Social action must be part of the equation. Perhaps the best we as educators, helpers, and policymakers can do is to maintain the conditions in which that personal sense of self-efficacy can flourish. The sense that we can make things happen doesn't come from slogans, no matter how helpful they are to self-image. It comes only from making things happen.

BARRIER 3. FAILURE TO RESOLVE THE ROLE OF PUBLIC SCHOOLS AS "SURROGATE PARENTS"

As Dryfoos and Klerman (1988) point out, the movement to use schools as "surrogate parents" is burgeoning as schools seek help with this role. Principals in Alaska use the term "second responsibility" to describe the schools' increasing responsibility for the social, physical, and emotional well-being of children. We must acknowledge, however, that all of us—not just the schools—have responsibility for the society we live in.

To expect "the schools" to miraculously solve societal problems without a thorough rethinking of the roles families and other institutions play in the development of our young, and how we invest in those families and institutions, is ludicrous. We need to move beyond this narrow view of the schools' role. To do this, we can restructure the curriculum, as discussed earlier, and improve young people's understanding of common social needs by addressing the sexism and racism that characterize much sexuality education today.

For example, Fine (1988) calls for greater attention beyond gender roles to a "discourse on desire." Fine asks whether our focus on education through fear (in this case, fear of pregnancy) is ideologically perpetuating females as "the potential victim of male sexuality." In this setting, she says, "there is little possibility" of anyone developing "a critique of gender or sexual arrangements" (p. 31). How does the absence of that critique affect our ability to lessen interpersonal violence and promote broader equality between the sexes? Does the focus and language of current sexuality education merely reinforce the victimization of females and prevent growth in self-worth and self-efficacy for many young women, especially low-income women?

This kind of discussion in sexuality education goes beyond preventing pregnancy and points toward a more fundamental examination of human rights and human potential. Perhaps the continuing need for such discussion is best illustrated by the results of a 1987 Rhode Island survey of 1,700 sixth–ninth graders. About 25 percent of the boys and 17 percent of the girls thought it was acceptable for a man to force a woman to have sex if he had spent money on her; and an astonishing 65 percent of the boys and 57 percent of the girls said such rape was acceptable if a couple had been dating for more than 6 months ("Youths in Study," 1988).

We need to call for social action as well as education. While AIDS captures our caring and our headlines, and is a life and death issue, less dramatic events consign millions of people to a slower, no less anguished death. Racism may be at the core here, for minorities are disproportionately the victims in our society, whether we talk about poverty, rates of violence, teenage parenthood, dropping out of school, or alcohol and other drug abuse (Scales, 1988).

BARRIER 4. AIDS AND THE DECLINE OF PLURALISM

Kelly (1987) notes that the anti-sexuality messages associated with AIDS prevention may already be producing, as fallout, a decline in our national acceptance of a pluralism of values that has been a fundamental tenet of modern sex education and democracy. In its extreme, this decline of pluralism can lead to (and

from some reports [Greer, 1986; Kin, 1988] has already led to) an increase in discrimination as the debate over personal liberty and public safety prompts some people to accept apparently easy answers to these complex dilemmas.

How this personal liberty versus public safety dilemma is handled will have a deep impact on many levels. The President's AIDS Commission understood this and enunciated clearly that non-discrimination is the cornerstone of any effective and ethical approach to AIDS in our democratic society. However, former President Reagan's rejection of this anti-discrimination language killed any legislative attempts to reduce AIDS discrimination in 1988 ("Presidential Rejection," 1988).

On a less noticeable level to many, but equally pernicious in its ultimate impact, the decline of pluralism will end up expressing itself in broader censorship and restrictions on freedom of speech. This danger can be expressed in subtle and sometimes not so subtle ways. For example, Sen. Alan Simpson (R-WY) was quoted as being sore at the "thousands of creative staff people" who are "cooking them [issues] up . . . all of it cranked up with special interest groups" (Lovison, 1988, p. 40). Yet, listening to that cacophony of special interest groups, not being irritated by them but welcoming them and reflecting on their messages, is part of the responsibility of governance. After all, we all belong to at least one "special interest group."

Each of us, liberal or conservative, must build honest, guiding values that are strong but still flexible enough to be open to reflection and change. If we honor this democratic process, we will find the right answers to vexing questions. This starts with a simple enough proposition; that, in a democracy, ideas, values, and people are the same. Banning an idea and discriminating against a person are just different sides of the same coin. It is only a small step from going after Anne Frank's diary to going after Anne Frank.

BARRIER 5. INADEQUATE POLITICAL SKILLS

Political savvy has improved among sexuality education advocates. Like children's advocates more generally, they are more aggressive today than 10 years ago. However, political skills still need to be developed in the following areas: (a) translating beliefs into budgets, (b) setting the right agenda, and (c) speaking for ourselves.

As former Centers for Disease Control leader Ogden (1986) wrote, the political battle is about resource allocation. On the most basic economic level, we've only just begun to translate our beliefs into budgets. Through our budgets, we express our public policy values—a different type of "values" than the sex education community has historically focused on. For example, just one Stealth bomber costs about three times as much as our entire federal family planning program (the Stealth is variously put at between $380–450 million each, while Title X stands at $138 million for fiscal year 1989 ["Appropriations," 1988]).

Seeing budgets reflect advocates' beliefs involves avoiding the wrong agenda. The wrong agenda is having just more sexuality education, or earlier, or with better trained teachers. The right agenda, on the other hand, focuses on all the issues discussed in this article, and places sexuality education into a more realistic perspective.

Such an agenda must be based on (a) a broad head start for *all* children; (b) action to lessen poverty and welfare dependence through policies that empower people; (c) greater attention to the life skills needs of the 70 percent of children who will not get a college degree; and (d) expanded opportunities for young people to become better linked with their communities through service and voluntarism, among other principles (Hamburg, 1987; Scales, 1988; Schorr & Schorr, 1988; Weckstein, 1988).

All those things achieve the goal sexuality educators have had for years: to promote healthy, capable people who have purpose, high expectations, and lots of support. These people are more likely to avoid teen pregnancy, substance abuse, suicide, and other problems.

Finally, sexuality education advocates must not allow others to say what advocates believe. To do so is to be "reactive," always being in a position of saying "no, wait a minute, what we really mean is . . ." or "no, we didn't mean that." We should not let other say what we believe in, what we stand for. We should say it ourselves. That is our first—and our final—responsibility.

NOTES

1. An update on the extent of sex education and obstacles to providing it was released just prior to publication of this article. The Alan Guttmacher Institute study of 4,200 junior and senior high teachers, superintendents of 162 of the nation's largest school districts, and all state education agencies found some improvement in the scope of sexuality education, but not dramatic improvement, so numerous inadequacies and barriers remain, including those selected for discussion here (*Risk and Responsibility*, 1989).

2. See reviews in Scales, 1987b; Scales, 1988, as well as a program example in Carrera and Dempsey, 1988, and an example of a successful community "saturation" model in Vincent, Clearie, & Schluchter, 1987).

3. Two widely used examples are "K-12 Family Life Education Curriculum" (1987) and "Family Life Education" (1980).

REFERENCES

Appropriations Fiscal 89: Labor, HHS, Education & HUD. (1988). *Youth Policy, 10*(9), 47.

Carrera, M., & Dempsey, P. (1988). Restructuring public policy priorities in teenage pregnancy. *SIECUS Report, 16*(3), 6–9.

Dryfoos, J. G., & Klerman, L. V. (1988). School-based clinics: Their role in helping students meet the 1990 objectives. *Health Education Quarterly, 15,* 71–80.

Family life education: Curriculum guide. (1980). Santa Cruz, CA: Network Publications.

Fine, M. (1988). Sexuality, schooling, and adolescent females: The missing discourse of desire. *Harvard Educational Review, 58,* 29–53.

Finn, C. (1986). Educational excellence: Eight elements. *Foundations News, 27*(2), 40–45.

Gordon, S. (1981). The case for a moral sex education in the schools. *Journal of School Health, 51,* 214–218.

Greer, W. R. (1986, November 23). Violence against homosexuals rising, groups say in seeking protections. *New York Times,* p. 15.

Hamburg, D. (1987). *Fundamental building blocks of life.* New York: Carnegie Corporation (president's annual essay).

Highlights of state-level victories for children, 1987. (1987). *Children's Defense Fund Reports, 9*(6), 3–8.

K–12 family life education curriculum (1987). Burlington, VT: Planned Parenthood of Northern New England.

Kelly, G. (1987). On being attacked by sex education foes. *Journal of Sex Education and Therapy, 13*(2), 3–4.

Kim, J. (1988, July 3). Are homosexuals facing an ever more hostile world? *New York Times,* p. E16.

Kirby, D. (1985). The effects of selected sexuality education programs: Toward a more realistic view. *Journal of School Health, 11,* 28–37.

Kirby, D., Alter, J., & Scales, P. (1979). *An analysis of U.S. sex education programs and evaluation methods.* Springfield, VA: National Technical Information Service.

Kirby, D., & Scales, P. (1981). State guidelines for sex education instruction in the public schools. *Family Relations, 30,* 229–237.

Lawrance, L., & McLeroy, K. R. (1986). Self-efficacy and health education. *Journal of School Health, 56,* 317–321.

Local districts active in AIDS education. (1987). *Family Life Educator, 5*(4), 4–12.

Lovison, D. (1988). State legislatures: The proving ground for national leadership. *State Legislatures, 14*(6), 40–44.

Ogden, H. (1986). The politics of health education: Do we constrain ourselves? *Health Education Quarterly, 13,* 1–7.

Presidential rejection of AIDS anti-bias law dashes hopes for action in 100th Congress. (1988). *The Nation's Health, 18*(9), 4.

Risk and responsibility: Teaching sex education in American schools today. (1989). New York: Alan Guttmacher Institute.

Rosenstock, I. M., Strecher, V. J., & Brecher, M. H. (1988). Social learning and the health belief model. *Health Education Quarterly, 15*(2), 175–184.

Scales, P. (1984). *The front lines of sexuality education: A guide to building and maintaining community support.* Santa Cruz, CA: Network Publications.

Scales, P. (1987a). Forward to the basics: Life skills education for today's youth. *Family Life Educator, 5*(3), 4–9.

Scales, P. (1987b). How we can prevent teenage pregnancy (and why it's not the real problem). *Journal of Sex Education and Therapy, 13*(1), 12–15.

Scales, P. (1988). An agenda for investing in children and youth. *Youth Policy, 10*(4), 3–7.

Schorr, L., & Schorr, D. (1988). *Within our reach: Breaking the cycle of disadvantage.* New York: Anchor/Doubleday.

Sexual literacy 88. (1988). Mount Vernon, IA: Society for the Scientific Study of Sex. (November 1988 annual meeting program.)

Sexuality education. (1988). New York: Planned Parenthood Federation of America Fact Sheet.

Sonenstein, F. L., & Pittman, K. J. (1984). The availability of sex education in large city school districts. *Family Planning Perspectives, 16,* 19–25.

Sullivan, J. (1988, January 10). 29 Jersey schools will offer program to aid troubled youths. *New York Times,* p. A23.

Teen pregnancy: Over one million teens become pregnant each year. (1986). *Children and Teens Today, 6*(7), 5–6.

Vincent, M. L., Clearie, A. F., & Schluchter, M. D. (1987). Reducing adolescent pregnancy through school and community-based education. *Journal of the American Medical Association, 257*(24), 3382–3386.

Weckstein, P. (1988). Youth, education and the economy. *Youth Policy, 10*(6), 4–24.

Winter, L. (1988). The role of sexual self-concept in the use of contraception. *Family Planning Perspectives, 20*(3), 123–127.

Youths in study say rape acceptable in some instances. (1988). *The Network, 3*(3), 3. (Newsletter of the North Carolina Coalition on Adolescent Pregnancy).

POSTSCRIPT

Are Current Sex Education Programs Lacking in Moral Guidance?

Protests against sex education practices in the public schools often originate through local efforts on the part of a group of parents who resent intrusions by the schools into what they consider to be very private aspects of life. The demarcation of appropriate provinces of parental and school influence has been difficult to draw—and probably always will be. As long as the schools only *offer* instruction in human sexuality without demanding that all students participate, parental protests of this sort would seem to be unjustified. When sexual topics are infused throughout the required curriculum, the problem is compounded.

Joseph Fay and Sol Gordon treat this problem in "Moral Sexuality Education and Democratic Values," *Theory into Practice* (Summer 1989), in which they explore the differences between a *moral* approach and a *moralistic* approach to human sexuality. They state that, while one cannot escape the fact that values are a major component of sexuality education, the moralistic "just say no" strategy is simplistic and ineffective in that it fails to "appreciate the complexity of sexuality and the many factors that may influence a young person's decision to become sexually active."

The Summer 1989 issue of *Theory into Practice* has additional valuable material, namely "Sexuality Education in the U.S.: What It Is, What It Is Meant To Be," by Ann Welbourne-Moglia and Ronald J. Moglia, and "AIDS and Sexuality Education," by Debra W. Haffner, the executive director of the Sex Information and Education Council of the United States (SIECUS). Questions regarding the content of AIDS instruction and the rights of HIV-infected children have been addressed recently. Some important views can be found in "AIDS: Students in Glass Houses," by Perry A. Zirkel, *Phi Delta Kappan* (April 1989); "The Legacy of Ryan White for AIDS Education," by Stephen R. Sroka, *Education Week* (May 23, 1990); and "The Social Dimensions of AIDS," by Harvey V. Fineberg, *Scientific American* (October 1988).

Serious concern about sexuality education is expressed by Jacqueline Kasun in "Turning Children into Sex Experts," *Public Interest* (Spring 1977) and "Sex Education: A New Philosophy for America?" *Family in America* (July 1989). Also see "The New Sex Education and the Sexual Revolution: A Critical View," by Lawrence and Ellen Shornack, *Family Relations* (October 1982).

In the last analysis, this issue must be resolved in the context of the purposes of education. If schooling is designed to address the needs of the "whole person," then sex education, including the problems of human sexuality, morality, and love, would seem to be of central importance.

ISSUE 22

Are Current Tests of Teacher Knowledge Fair?

YES: Gregory R. Anrig, from "Teacher Education and Teacher Testing: The Rush to Mandate," *Phi Delta Kappan* (February 1986)

NO: Linda Darling-Hammond, from "Teaching Knowledge: How Do We Test It?" *American Educator* (Fall 1986)

ISSUE SUMMARY

YES: Gregory R. Anrig, president of the Educational Testing Service, makes the case for the National Teacher Examination as a legitimate tool for measuring qualifications.
NO: Linda Darling-Hammond, director of the Education and Human Resources Program for Rand Corporation, provides examples of what she feels are serious deficiencies in this type of test.

A central part of the educational reform movement of the 1980s has been the focus on improving the quality of teachers. Criticisms of the way teachers are trained, observations on the difficulty of removing incompetent teachers from the classroom, and calls for higher standards of admission to the profession have been heard in abundance. In an effort to take some positive action, over 40 state governments have mandated the use of standardized competency tests as a precondition of teacher certification. The National Teacher Examination (NTE), a multiple-choice instrument, is the most widely used test. It is devised and administered by the Educational Testing Service of Princeton, New Jersey.

While most states have imposed the test as a certification requirement, some (notably Texas and Arkansas) have used it to determine the competencies of veteran teachers. Such action, of course, adds fuel to the basic controversy: Is this appropriate treatment of professionals? American Federation of Teachers president Albert Shanker, in an article entitled "The Making of a Profession," *American Educator* (Fall 1985), defines a professional as "a person who is an expert, and by virtue of that expertise is permitted to operate fairly independently, to make decisions, to exercise discretion, to be free of most direct supervision." If this is the case, then how do we certify this expertise, what criteria do we establish, how do we measure the fulfillment of those criteria—and who are "we"?

The "we" of the current reform movement are usually members of state legislatures or state education bureaucracies. Shanker and others feel that such external controlling forces demoralize teachers in the workforce and deter self-directed college students from choosing teaching as a career. Why should they enter an occupation in which there is little opportunity to exercise judgment or to make professional decisions?

Many contend that the "we" should be members of the profession, organized, perhaps, as independent state-level Professional Teacher Boards. Such groups of outstanding teachers would enforce self-designed standards and codes of ethics, conduct quality reviews, and hold incompetence hearings, among other things. There are many studies of the qualities good teachers possess, which would prompt one to think that some appropriate measures could be devised for entry into and development within the teaching profession.

In the articles selected for inclusion here, Gregory R. Anrig contends that there is a place for teacher tests in the American educational system. The items in the National Teacher Examination attempt to measure the *academic* knowledge of prospective teachers and must be supplemented by other measures of desirable teacher qualities. Linda Darling-Hammond states that if there are to be tests they must reflect what the members of the profession believe is the fundamental knowledge required for effective teaching. She finds that the present National Teacher Examination trivializes this knowledge base.

YES

Gregory R. Anrig

THE RUSH TO MANDATE

Some of the fastest-moving changes in these years of education reform are in the area of teacher testing. In only about five years, state-required testing for those who aspire to enter teacher preparation programs or to become certified has spread from a handful of states—mainly in the Southeast—to become a nationwide trend that now involves 38 states, with seven more currently considering teacher-testing requirements. In 1984 alone, nine states enacted teacher-testing laws or regulations.

The race to begin teacher testing is not only nationwide but across-the-board. Twenty-one states require students to pass a test before entering a teacher education program. Thirty-two states have (or, by 1988, will have) a testing requirement for certification. A smaller number of states also test at the completion of teacher training, for recertification, or for advanced certification under career ladder/merit pay plans.[1]

The teacher testing movement goes well beyond the NTE Program, administered by the Educational Testing Service (ETS). Though 25 states currently use one or another of the NTE tests, other tests used by states include the Scholastic Aptitude Test, those of the American College Testing Program, the California Achievement Test, and state-developed tests (used in Alabama, Arizona, California, Connecticut, Florida, Georgia, and Oklahoma). Teacher testing is upon us, and the issues it raises transcend any one of the tests.

WHAT TESTS CAN DO

There is a place for teacher tests on the American educational scene. National opinion surveys indicate strong public support and strong teacher support for requiring satisfactory test performance as a condition for entering the teaching profession. A 1984 Gallup poll reported that 89% of the public and almost two-thirds of the teachers polled favored state examinations for beginning teachers.[2]

Properly developed and validated, teacher tests can measure the academic knowledge of prospective teachers. Within the limits of any standardized paper-and-pencil examination, teacher tests can demonstrate that a prospective teacher has a basic knowledge of the subject (or grade level) that he or she plans to teach, has the minimum pedagogical knowledge that experienced practitioners and teacher educators deem necessary for beginning teachers, and demonstrates certain basic communication skills necessary to instruct children.

These are reasonable expectations—standards, if you will—for a prospective teacher to meet before being certified by the state. Just as lawyers, physicians, and those in scores of occupations must demonstrate basic knowledge of their fields in order to qualify for state licenses, so too it is reasonable to expect similar competence from teachers. State licenses are a means of consumer protection; schoolchildren are the primary consumers of education and are entitled to such protection.

WHAT TESTS CANNOT DO

No standardized test that I know of can accurately measure such qualities as dedication, motivation, perseverance, caring, sensitivity, or integrity. Yet, when we remember outstanding teachers from our own school days, those are among the qualities that made them excellent. We must admit the limits of tests and the restricted range of qualities that they can measure. Moreover, we should recognize that tests can present and measure only a sample of the knowledge required for teaching.

No test results guarantee that a prospective teacher will succeed and become a really good teacher in the classroom. While no teacher can succeed and be very effective without a strong knowledge of subject matter and of the skills of teaching, professional performance requires more than academic knowledge. Remember that many of the convicted Watergate defendants were lawyers who had successfully passed the bar exam. Ignorance of the law does not account for their actions.

All of this suggests that policy makers should keep teacher tests in their proper perspective. As in other fields of professional licensure and certification, tests in education are important aids for insuring that new entrants have mastered the basic knowledge relevant to the job. They can also be useful to candidates (and to those who prepare them) as ways to identify strengths and weaknesses in their preparation.

TROUBLING SIGNS

As was true in some cases with state competency testing for students in the 1970s, the rush to legislate excellence through teacher testing is raising some troubling questions and leading to some decisions that are educationally unsound.

One such decision, now law in several states, makes continued accreditation of teacher preparation programs dependent on the test performance of the prospective teachers they enroll. The Educational Testing Service has testified against using teacher tests in this way. Such use fails to recognize that from 60% to 80% of the college preparation received by prospective teachers is in academic departments, not in the college or department of education. On the NTE Core Battery, for example, more students seem to have difficulty qualifying on the Test of General Knowledge than on the Test of Professional Knowledge.

Accountability for teacher education should rest with the entire college or university, not solely with the teacher preparation unit. If significant numbers of prospective teachers graduating from a college or university are failing to meet the state's minimum standards for certification, the state certainly has a right and an obligation to question such a trend. The process of review, however, should conform to good accreditation practice, including the opportunity for institutional self-examination and external validation and the allotment of reasonable time in which to improve institutional performance. From the time an institution is placed on probation, some states allow only two years for graduating seniors to meet a predetermined standard of success on state certification tests. I believe that this practice raises some of the same questions of fairness that have been raised in court challenges of testing programs for high school graduation.

A second area of concern regarding teacher testing has arisen in Arkansas and Texas. In the course of enacting comprehensive education reform bills, the legislatures in both states included a requirement that all practicing teachers— regardless of years of service and ratings by their school supervisors—would have to pass a one-time "functional academic skills" or "literacy" test in order to retain their teaching certificates. Such a testing program is unprecedented for any other occupation requiring state licensure or certification.

Certainly no one wants illiterate or otherwise incompetent teachers in the classroom. However, just as with accreditation, there are reasonable and educationally sound procedures for addressing this problem through careful supervision and evaluation. Then, in the absence of improvement and with appropriate due process, a teacher's employment may be terminated. To put an experienced teacher's professional career on the line solely on the basis of a mandatory one-time test is both an injustice to the teacher and a misuse of the test. The Educational Testing Service and the NTE Policy Council, in an unprecedented action for test development organizations, have refused to allow the use of NTE tests for this purpose in either Texas or Arkansas.

A third area that must be of profound concern to all of us in education is the effect of the teacher testing movement on the access of minorities to the teaching profession. ETS has recently published two research reports: one on the general impact of state testing policies on the teaching profession and the general impact of state testing policies on the teaching profession and the other specifically on the impact on teacher selection of the use of the NTE tests by the states.[3] These reports present data that document the effect of current state testing policies on the access of blacks and Hispanics to the teaching profession.

To understand the dimensions of this problem, let us look at the results of teacher tests in four states. In California, passing rates on the California Basic Educational Skills Test were 76% for white test-takers, 39% for Hispanic test-takers, and 26% for black test-takers. (The California Basic Educational Skills Test is developed by ETS. The Georgia, Oklahoma, and Florida certification tests are not developed by ETS.) In Georgia, 87% of white students passed the Georgia Teacher Certification Test on the first attempt, but only 34% of black students did so. In Oklahoma, the passing rate on the state teacher certification test was 79% for white students, 58% for Hispanic students, and 48% for black students. In Florida, 83% of those who took that state's teacher certification test in 1982 passed each of its four parts. Among black test-takers, however, the pass rate was only 35%. On the Test of Communication Skills in the NTE Core Battery, using national data and the median qualifying score of states that use the test (644), the passing rates would be 94% for whites, 48% for blacks, and 70% for Hispanics.[4]

ETS research reports conclude that, by the year 2000, if there is not significant change in the current status of teacher preparation, the percentage of minorities in the teaching force in the U.S. could be cut almost in half, from its current level of approximately 12%. This decline will be taking place at the same time as the proportion of minority students enrolled in U.S. schools will be increasing dramatically. The growing mismatch between the racial and ethnic composition of the teaching force and that of the student population is a matter with serious social and educational implications for the nation and its schools.

TEST BIAS OR UNEQUAL OPPORTUNITY?

A natural and predictable reaction to these differences in the test scores of various ethnic groups is to blame them on racial or ethnic bias in the tests. Similar charges have been leveled against other national tests. Yet something encouraging is happening that counsels against such a reaction. The performance of minority students on the SAT, on the College Board Achievement Tests, on Advanced Placement tests, and on the tests

given by the National Assessment of Educational Progress has improved dramatically.[5] Similar patterns of improvement have been reported on state basic skills tests. Minority students are demonstrating that they can and will do better on standardized tests if they are provided better education opportunities.

Tests certainly can be biased. When they are not, however, they can be useful indicators (used in conjunction with other data) of the quality of education provided to minority and majority students alike. At ETS, we guard against bias in the NTE and other tests we develop. The committees that develop test items are multiracial. Before the new NTE Core Battery was inaugurated in 1982, multiracial panels of experienced classroom teachers, chosen independently by the National Education Association and by the American Federation of Teachers, examined results for every question in the field test of the new Core Battery. (Both teacher organizations are also represented on the NTE Policy Council.) In addition, all ETS test items go through a mandatory sensitivity review process, in which specially trained ETS test development experts examine each item for potential race, sex, or ethnic bias. The NTE and all other tests developed by ETS must conform to the ETS *Standards for Quality and Fairness*.[6]

Even after taking all these precautions, states are required by ETS to conduct their own validity studies before they can use NTE tests. These state validity studies provide an opportunity for an independent review of the tests for potential bias.

It is a regrettable fact that most children from financially poor families—minority or white—attend school in financially poor urban and rural school districts. Working conditions in the schools in such districts are such that the better teachers are more likely to seek employment in more affluent districts (though many able, dedicated teachers continue to serve in urban and rural districts). As someone whose entire professional career has been committed to the cause of equal educational opportunity, I believe strongly that we do not serve children well or fairly—especially educationally disadvantaged children—when we give them teachers who have not themselves mastered the basic skills that the children must learn before they graduate from high school. If those who aspire to teach can't qualify on state-mandated teacher tests, the solution isn't to do away with the tests. The solution is to improve the education being provided to aspiring teachers. This is what is needed—not permitting poorly prepared teachers, white or minority, to teach children who need and deserve better.

A CHALLENGE FOR TEACHER EDUCATION

The combination of a period of reform in education and of the growth of the teacher testing movement provides an opportunity for colleges of teacher education. Up to now the reforms have focused mainly on elementary and secondary schools, but teacher preparation should be at the forefront of reform in higher education.

Teacher preparation is higher education's *primary* responsibility to the schools. Most college and university presidents have by now identified themselves with the drive for school reform in the name of excellence. Their actions and their words, however, have concentrated on what the *schools* should do to improve. The results of teacher testing around the nation should make it abundantly clear what some *institutions of higher education* should do to improve.

Teacher preparation is a responsibility of the entire college or university, not just of the teacher education unit. The performance of aspiring teachers on the growing number of state-required teacher tests reflects on the policies and curriculum of institutions of higher education as a whole. If their performance is less than it should be, the institutions must act to improve that performance.

Some historically black colleges are taking the lead in this aspect of the reform of higher education. These colleges traditionally have prepared a large portion of America's black teachers. They are feeling the impact of the new standards reflected in the teacher testing movement, and so are their students. In collaboration with these historically black colleges, ETS held an invitational conference in December 1984 at which representatives from nine historically black colleges described how their institutions were tackling this new challenge. The approaches differ from college to college, but some common elements are evident:

• *Presidential leadership.* In each case, the college or university president is visibly involved and strongly committed to sustained improvement.

• *Institutionwide responsibility.* The improvement effort draws on and requires the involvement of all academic departments. In one college, for example, a collegewide faculty committee is taking the lead, with faculty discussions and seminars being conducted on an interdisciplinary basis. In one university, the steering committee includes the deans of education, sciences, and arts and humanities, as well as the vice chancellor for academic affairs.

• *Specified policies for student advancement or graduation.* Policies for admission to teacher preparation programs, for advancement from sophomore-level to junior-level courses, or for graduation have been reviewed, strengthened, and made more specific.

• *Student proficiency assessment.* Faculty-developed or standardized tests are being introduced for advancement of all students from sophomore-level to junior-level courses, for admission to the teacher preparation program, or for graduation. All students, not just those in teacher preparation, are now expected to demonstrate certain basic proficiencies.

• *Learning/developmental centers.* Centers are being provided for remedial study and instruction. Some institutions require attendance; in others, attendance is voluntary. One such center has an extensive instructional staff and a wide array of self-instructional materials. It is centrally located and has extended hours to encourage student use.

• *Curriculum review and modification.* Improvement efforts are focusing on curriculum and content, not just on tests. Faculty committees review the content of required tests and study their relation to the institution's strengths. But the main focus is on how each department can contribute to reaching this goal. For example, in one institution, each department will sponsor a required writing seminar for its majors.

• *Cooperative outreach and talent identification.* One college, in cooperation with a city school district, has initiated an outreach program to identify talented students who might be interested in becoming teachers. The school district and the college will provide experiences introducing such students to the teaching profession.

These actions, and others like them, are promising developments in higher education and in teacher education.

A CHALLENGE FOR TESTERS

At the same time, ETS is practicing what I am "preaching" here. We, too, must act and lead. We have and we will. In cooperation with the presidents of historically black colleges, we have jointly initiated what is called the HBC/ETS Collaboration. A series of workshops drawing on areas of ETS expertise have been conducted to address needs that the historically black colleges identified for themselves. ETS is learning a great deal from this cooperative venture that will help improve ETS services to the entire education community. Workshops have included financial aid, academic use of computers, and program evaluation. We are now planning activities related to improving student performance on teacher tests—particularly on the NTE. In a separate undertaking, ETS is cooperating with the Southern Regional Education Board to provide faculty workshops on the NTE and on faculty-developed tests.

ETS provides NTE item-summary workshops for interested colleges and universities. When an appropriate time and adequate support can be arranged, ETS staff members meet with interdisciplinary faculty committees to analyze item-by-item performance on the NTE tests by students from that institution. This helps faculty members analyze how well students in their institution perform on particular questions and allows them to compare the performance of their students with that of others across the U.S. Twenty-eight institutions of higher education have held NTE item-summary workshops over the past two years.

ETS has also acted to provide information to policy makers and teacher educators. I have already described our position on the proper use of tests in Texas and Arkansas. We have been more successful in constructively influencing public policy with regard to teacher tests in Tennessee and Florida. The two ETS research reports on the impact of state testing policies on teacher selection are yet another part of our effort to raise importance policy issues in the teacher testing movement.

Another contribution just completed is the first comprehensive job analysis of the teaching role in American elementary and secondary schools.[7] Teacher tests in the U.S. have traditionally been validated on the basis of what is taught in teacher preparation programs *before* prospective teachers enter the teaching profession. In other occupational fields, validation of licensing examinations generally depends on their relevance to duties to be performed *after* a person is actually on the job. The role of a teacher, however, was considered so complex and diverse that standard job analysis has not been thought possible until recently.

ETS will soon be publishing the results of a 16-month job analysis project for teaching. An ETS research team, led by knowledgeable program scientists in the field of job analysis, has developed a job analysis model for the teaching profession. Some 3,000 classroom teachers representing elementary, middle, and high school levels and most subject-matter fields participated in the project. We will use this job analysis model to assist in developing and validating the NTE for state certification and other purposes. We believe that the model can make a contribution not only to test construction but also to teacher education.

The strength of education reform in the 1980s lies in the fact that its dynamism has come from across the land. It has been nationwide rather than national, and that is the way it should continue. While those in the "bully pulpits" of Washington, D.C., can help by constructive exhortation, the real leadership must come from the towns, cities, and states throughout the U.S. and from educational institutions. This is especially true for the improvement of the quality and spirit of the teaching force in American public education. Higher standards must be accompanied by better preparation if we are to produce the number and variety of teachers needed in the 1990s and beyond. Teacher education ought to be in the forefront of the next stage of education reform—that which will take place in the colleges and universities.

NOTES

1. J. T. Sandefur, *Competency Assessment of Teachers: 1984 Report* (Bowling Green: Western Kentucky University, 1984).

2. Alec M. Gallup, "The Gallup Poll of Teachers' Attitudes Toward the Public Schools," *Phi Delta Kappan*, October 1984, p. 107.

3. Margaret E. Goertz, Ruth B. Ekstrom, and Richard J. Coley, *The Impact of State Policy on Entrance into the Teaching Profession* (Princeton, N.J.: Final Report to the National Institute of Education, NIE Grant No. G83–0073, Educational Testing Service, 1984); and Margaret E. Goertz and Barbara Pitcher, *The Impact of NTE Use by States on Teacher Selection* (Princeton, N.J.: Educational Testing Service, 1985).

4. Ibid.

5. For a summary of these data, see Board of Trustees, 1984 *Public Accountability Report* (Princeton, N.J.: Educational Testing Service, 1984).

6. The *ETS Standards for Quality and Fairness* meet or exceed the *Standards for Educational and Psychological Tests* (1974) of the American Educational Research Association, the American Psychological Association, and the National Council on Measurement in Education.

7. The term *job analysis* is used here in the context of the federal *Equal Employment Opportunity Commission Uniform Guidelines on Employee Selection Procedures.*

NO

Linda Darling-Hammond

TEACHING KNOWLEDGE: HOW DO WE TEST IT?

Testing teachers for certification is now the law in forty-four states. By 1990, virtually every state will require tests of basic skills, subject matter knowledge, or professional knowledge before a teacher can receive a standard license to teach. Although the tests being used make entry into teaching more selective, they do not, contrary to much of the current rhetoric, do very much to turn teaching into a profession. The tests are not developed or controlled by the profession, nor do they adequately represent what a teacher should know and be able to do.

If teacher tests are to serve the goal of professionalizing teaching, they must reflect what members of the profession believe is the fundamental knowledge required by teachers, and they must be professionally controlled. Recent proposals by teacher organizations and the Carnegie Task Force on Teaching as a Profession would lead to board certification by a professional teaching standards board, analogous to the certification awarded by the medical profession and other professional bodies. The testing involved in such certification would be voluntary, would represent a high standard of professional knowledge, and would be distinct and separate from state licensing and school district employment decisions. Teachers who decided to pursue board certification would be recognized by a body of their peers as having mastered the subject matter and professional knowledge needed for making appropriate teaching decisions.

Although such professional certification could be dismissed as overkill, given the other tests now in place, there are important reasons why board certification would improve the status and substance of teaching. These reasons, and the limitations of current approaches to teacher testing, are explored herein.

THERE ARE TWO FUNCTIONS OF PROFESSIONAL TESTS. ONE IS TO SORT AND SCREEN candidates. Many call this endeavor "raising standards." This function, which currently receives the most attention from test makers and test users, conjures up a vertical notion of standards. They go up or down; there are cut-off scores that may be raised or lowered to allow more or fewer people to pass. This function serves a symbolic purpose. It provides selectivity for entry, regardless of what the substance of the measure is. As long as a cut-off score is applied, some individuals will "pass" and others will not. The level of the standard can be changed simply by changing the pass rate on a test.

The second major function of testing—and the most important one for truly creating standards—is defining the professional knowledge base. Examinations are one means by which a profession makes an explicit statement about what is worth knowing and how it should be known and demonstrated. This statement can exert a powerful influence on training and practice independent from cut-off scores or pass rates.

When candidates prepare to take the bar examination, for example, they know they will have to study constitutional law, torts, contracts, tax law, criminal law, and so on. Regardless of the pass rate for that exam in a given year, candidates know that they will have to demonstrate their knowledge of those topics in particular ways. They will not only need to be able to identify facts about cases and legal rules, they will have to apply this knowledge in essays responding to case scenarios. The examination provides an explicit standard of knowledge that influences legal training and practice in important ways, regardless of the "vertical" standards used to determine who will be licensed.

CURRENT TEACHER TESTS BASICALLY DEFINE the knowledge needed for teaching as (1) the recognition of facts within subject areas, (2) knowledge of school law and bureaucratic procedures, and (3) recognition of the "correct" teaching behavior in a situation described in a short scenario. The tests currently used do not allow for demonstrations of teacher knowledge, judgment, and skill in the kinds of complex settings that characterize real teaching. Furthermore, they may discourage the use of such knowledge by posting a unidimensional philosophy of teaching that the test taker must consistently apply if he/she is to find the "best" answers to poorly defined questions.

My own content analysis of a sample test for one of the most frequently used tests of professional knowledge* revealed that less than 10 percent of over one hundred questions required knowledge of theory, research, or facts pertaining to teaching and learning. And most of these required only the identification of a single fact, for example, "Which of the following, if given to high school students at the beginning of a new course, is an example of an advance organizer?"

The remaining questions required knowledge about testing and assessment (10 percent), knowledge about school law and administrative procedures (25 percent), careful reading or knowledge of simple word definitions (15 percent), agreement with the test's teaching philosophy (25 percent), or agreement with the test's definition of socially or bureau-

*The sample test used for this analysis is the National Teacher Examination's Professional Knowledge Test (A Guide to the NTE Core Battery Tests. Educational Testing Service, 1984.) The items published in this sample test are quite similar to the sample questions published by other testing firms; however, no other test publisher to my knowledge publishes an entire sample test allowing a full examination of content coverage. This discussion, therefore, uses the NTE exam as an illustration of the typical range of questions used in such tests.

cratically acceptable behavior (15 percent). About 40 percent of the questions, by my reckoning, did not have a "right" answer, either because the question contained insufficient information to allow a complete evaluation of the situation or because alternative answers would be correct depending on what research one relied upon.

The questions that rely on a simplistic view of teaching are not only inadequate to assess what skilled and knowledgeable teachers know, they encourage a soft-headed approach to the preparation of teachers. In the area of educational research, consider the following question:

> In general, which of the following factors has been shown in several studies to have the strongest relationship to variation in student achievement?
> (a) Teacher experience;
> (b) School size;
> (c) Type of textbooks;
> (d) Student/teacher ratio; or
> (e) Community's average income.

Aside from the fact that many studies could be marshalled to support any one of the responses, the desired answer "e" is badly flawed, since most studies finding strong effects of income on achievement use measures of student family income, not general community income. Not surprisingly, only 19 percent of test takers chose the desired answer.

A question about statistical terms presents no right answer:

> The mean, median, and mode may be best defined as:
> (a) ranges of scores for a test;
> (b) correlations of individual test questions with the total test;
> (c) points about which scores on a test tend to cluster;
> (d) minimal acceptable scores to be obtained on a test; or

> (e) deviations of test scores from an expected value.

The desired answer, "c," is technically incorrect, since scores need not cluster about the mean or median when a normal distribution of scores does not occur. A teacher with statistical knowledge would find this question difficult to answer honestly.

Here is an example of a question intended to assess instructional knowledge:

> Use of which of the following is most important in the beginning instruction of the young, visually impaired child?
> (a) Machines with lighted screens to magnify print;
> (b) A variety of large-print books;
> (c) Extended periods of nondirected play;
> (d) Many tactile and oral activities; or
> (e) Large-print flash cards for learning sight vocabulary.

Since the question does not reveal how young the child is or how severe the visual impairment, the desired answer "d" is a safe guess, but it is not necessarily the course of action that would be appropriate for, say, teaching reading to a seven-year-old child who is at least partially sighted. Even a "correct" answer to the question does not reveal whether a teacher could design an appropriate learning experience for the child.

ALTHOUGH ONE MIGHT QUESTION WHY SO large a portion (one-quarter) of a test of teaching knowledge is devoted to knowledge about school law and administrative procedures, these questions have the virtue at least of being mostly unambiguous, e.g. "The United States Supreme Court decision against permitting prayer in the public schools was based on which of the following?" Unfortunately, knowing the answer to such questions indicates very little about whether a candidate is likely to be a good teacher.

Similarly, the most straightforward instructional questions generally require only the ability to match words with their definitions. For example:

Kinesthetic learners are likely to learn the letters of the alphabet best by doing which of the following?
(a) Singing a song about the alphabet;
(b) Playing an alphabet card game;
(c) Manipulating large plastic letters;
(d) Examining an alphabet book; or
(e) Viewing "Sesame Street" regularly.

All one needs to know to answer the question correctly is that "kinesthetic" has something to do with physical, tactile activity. Knowing this definition does not reveal whether a candidate could identify different learning styles among children or develop suitable approaches for their classroom activities.

Some questions are designed to assess whether the teacher will embarrass school officials by handling sensitive situations in noninflammatory ways:

A representative of a special interest group meets a teacher out of school and indicates that the group objects to a particular textbook being used in the teacher's classroom. Of the following, which is the best response for the teacher to give a representative in order to handle the situation in a non-threatening manner?
(a) "Such a response by parents would be appropriate, but not by groups such as yours that have no close connection with public schools."

(b) "Your group should write a letter to me and to the principal specifying the passages that the group objects to and why."
(c) "The Constitution protects a teacher's right to use any textbook that is appropriate for the purpose."
(d) "Is your interest group able to propose an appropriate but less controversial textbook?"
(e) "Since the textbook was adopted by the school board, any comments about it should be directed to the board."

The desired answer "d" keeps the burden off the principal and the school board for handling the situation, but it places the teacher squarely on a prickly professional thorn. As one teacher remarked when seeing this question, "What would I be expected to do when the group proposed a textbook that could not achieve the educational goals for the class?" Protecting the curriculum or establishing academic freedom in the schools are clearly not part of the concerns suggested by this test's conception of "professional" behavior. "Professionalism" is keeping the public quiet and avoiding conflict at all costs.

Other questions are designed to evaluate whether the teacher subscribes to the kind of liberal, highly individualized philosophy of teaching underlying the test. Even when one agrees with the answer, it is nearly always possible to cite research or conventional wisdom that support an opposing point of view. For example:

Research indicates that in classrooms where effective teaching and learning occur, the teacher is likely to be doing which of the following consistently?
(a) Gearing instruction to the typical student at a given grade level;

(b) Carefully grouping students at the beginning of the school year and making sure that these groups remain the same throughout the year;

(c) Identifying the affective behaviors that students are likely to exhibit at a given level of development;

(d) Working diligently with students to make sure that each learns all of the material planned for the class for the year; or

(e) Pacing instruction so that students can move ahead when they are able to and receive extra help when they need it.

Although many teachers, like myself, would personally endorse the desired answer "e," there is a body of research (currently labelled as part of "teaching effectiveness" research) that suggests that whole-group instruction at a common pace is to be preferred to "individualized" instruction for increasing time on task and average achievement test scores. And there is a paradigm underlying most recent educational reforms that suggests that mastery of the year's material is the most important goal of classroom activities. So, selecting the right answer is more a matter of agreement with the test's philosophy of teaching than knowledge of the "research" that the question seeks to invoke.

The problem is not that the "right" answer is not right but that the question doesn't really allow for such a straightforward response. In fact, most of the knowledge and judgment involved in good teaching is not easily boiled down to a multiple-choice question with one simple answer.

IN THE FINAL ANALYSIS, THE TEST DEFINES the professional knowledge base for teaching primarily in terms of style and adherence to a particular approach to teaching. It quizzes knowledge of educational terms and laws. It does not encompass a rigorous and comprehensive understanding of educational theory and practice. It does not require much ability to apply knowledge and judgment in unique and complex situations.

Indeed, it is hard to argue that the knowledge required for scoring well on the test is of the sort that separates good teachers from teachers who are not as good. These questions are similar to those used on other tests of professional knowledge that publish sample questions. All of the tests I have seen are limited in their measurement by the scarcity of important teaching questions answerable in multiple-choice formats; the questions with clear, correct answers are not very important or profound.

The tests are sometimes tricky, but they are rarely difficult in terms of the level of knowledge required. It is not really difficult to identify an answer that suggests that Piaget's work had something to do with stages of development, for example. That is a different level of knowledge than the task of explaining what Piaget's work indicates for the teaching of number concepts to four- or seven- or nine-year-old children who exhibit the understandings common to various stages of development. An even greater level of knowledge would be required if the task were to evaluate alternative approaches to the teaching of number concepts for children with different learning styles.

We do not have a basis in current teacher tests with any of the latter kinds of questions. We test only factual recall or the ability to choose a teaching technique in response to short scenarios that give insufficient information to make a truly reasoned judgment. Although the desired answer can be found by eliminating the ridiculous answers or those that don't fit the topic of the question, a thoughtful, honest, and knowledgeable teacher would in most cases have to answer, "It depends." It is that understanding of the base for educational decisions that comprises the real knowledge base for teaching.

One of the things that is most striking about the current conception of professional knowledge in teaching is that it primarily emphasizes techniques, with little reference to the circumstances under which they might be appropriate and why they might be useful. This is true both in teacher education and in teacher testing. This conception of teaching knowledge not only ignores the fact that any technique has limited applications, it assumes that teachers don't need to have a basis for deciding what to teach, for what purposes, and when. They only need to have a battery of tactics at their disposal for implementing a curriculum that is prescribed for them.

Indeed this assumption pretty much matches the contemporary conception of the teacher's role in education. Until teachers are expected to understand the foundations of learning, and these foundations have been spelled out in concrete terms, there will be little ammunition for arguing that teachers should have a greater role in the design of education.

IN DEFINING THE KNOWLEDGE BASE FOR teaching, it might be useful to start by thinking about the building blocks for pedagogical knowledge. In medicine, the initial part of training and the first sections of the medical board examinations focus on knowledge of anatomy, physiol-

ogy, endocrinology, pathology, and so on. It is assumed that making sound judgments about treatment depends on understanding the phenomenon one is about to treat.

In education, knowledge of how children (and adults) grow, develop, and learn is equally important for making judgments about what and how they might be taught effectively. This includes an understanding of cognitive, physical, and psychological development, as well as knowledge about how learning normally occurs and about deviations from the norm. Theories of teaching and learning posit relationships among various known attributes of learners and how they are activated in different learning situations. These theories inform judgments about the choice of techniques, suggesting alternatives and decision criteria, rather than simple choices.

Since all teachers, and even some researchers, know that effective teaching strategies vary depending on the goals of instruction, the subject being taught, the nature of the learners, and their stages of development, it is imperative that conceptions of teaching knowledge emphasize the importance of judgment in making teaching decisions in the face of uncertain and diverse situations. Although there is seldom a single right answer to a problem of teaching practice, there are bases for making a professionally appropriate judgment about how to proceed in a complex situation.

Other professions that also require the application of knowledge in complex, nonroutine situations have developed methods for testing such abilities in a variety of ways. In law and accounting, for example, essay responses to case scenarios allow for multiple "right" answers. The test is designed to assess the candidate's understanding of important considerations and the ability to apply knowledge in a professionally acceptable manner to the case at hand.

The psychiatry boards use simulated interviews with real patients to assess a candidate's ability to apply appropriate considerations to the problem of diagnosis and initial treatment. Even though the jury of peers involved in the evaluation may not agree among themselves about a diagnosis, they can apply a common standard of practice to the assessment of the process.

The medical boards also use computer simulations to test a candidate's ability to follow through a course of diagnosis and treatment, to request and use new information appropriately, and to apply knowledge in the unique case presented by an individual patient.

All of these are ways of incorporating real-world uncertainties and judgment in a performance assessment that more nearly represents the knowledge needed to be a good practitioner. What is important is that these approaches conceive professional knowledge broadly and realistically, tolerating multiple approaches and perspectives while reinforcing a standard of professionally responsible practice.

When teacher tests can reflect such a view of the professional knowledge base, and when teacher education is designed to support such a view, teaching will become a profession with a claim to authority in the decisions that shape teaching work.

POSTSCRIPT

Are Current Tests of Teacher Knowledge Fair?

The Educational Testing Service has announced that by 1992 its National Teacher Examination will be substantially altered and that it will include observation of classroom performance. While this could be a step in the right direction, a mere change in format will not obliterate the controversy that surrounds the entire process. Quality control is demanded in all professions; how to achieve it in teaching is still problematic.

The following sources are recommended for further exploration of this issue and allied concerns: Patrick Welsh's "Teachers Fight for Control of Their Own Profession," *American Educator* (Spring 1987); Gerald W. Bracey's "Pandora and Pollyanna: Some Comments on 'The Rush to Mandate' " *Phi Delta Kappan* (February 1986); Albert Shanker's "A National Teacher Examination," *Educational Measurement: Issue and Practices* (Fall 1985); and "Why Teachers Won't Teach," by Milbrey Wallin McLaughlin, R. Scott Pfeifer, Deborah Swanson-Owens, and Sylvia Yee, *Phi Delta Kappan* (February 1986). This last article contends that "in fundamental ways the U.S. educational system is structured to guarantee the failure of teachers."

Two books that get at the nature of professionalism are Gene I. Maeroff's *The Empowerment of Teachers: Overcoming the Crisis of Confidence* (1988) and Donald A. Schon's *The Reflective Practitioner* (1983). Other articles of interest are "Profile of an Effective Teacher," by Donald R. Cruickshank, *Educational Horizons* (Winter 1985), which is based on research findings; "Evaluating Teachers: The Case of Socrates," by Sophie Haroutunian-Gordon, *Teachers College Record* (Fall 1987); "The Texas Teacher Test," by Lorrie A. Shepard and Amelia E. Kreitzer, *Educational Researcher* (August/September 1987); and "Teacher Testing: A Status Report," by Harriet Tyson-Bernstein, *American Educator* (Spring 1987), which provides an overview of prevailing practices.

CONTRIBUTORS
TO THIS VOLUME

EDITOR

JAMES WM. NOLL is an associate professor at the College of Education, University of Maryland. He received his B.A. in English from the University of Wisconsin, an M.S. in Educational Administration from the University of Wisconsin, and a Ph.D. in Philosophy of Education from the University of Chicago. He is a member of the American Educational Studies Association, the National Society for the Study of Education, the Association for Supervision and Curriculum Development, and the World Future Society.

Professor Noll is the coauthor of *Foundations of Education in America,* and his articles have appeared in several education journals. He has served on the editorial boards for *Annual Editions: Education* and *Computer Studies: Computers in Education* (DPG) for many years.

STAFF

Marguerite L. Egan   Program Manager
Brenda S. Filley   Production Manager
Whit Vye   Designer
Libra Ann Cusack   Typesetting Supervisor
Juliana Arbo   Typesetter
David Brackley   Copy Editor
David Dean   Administrative Assistant
Diane Barker   Editorial Assistant
David Filley   Graphics

AUTHORS

MORTIMER J. ADLER is the director of the Institute for Philosophical Research in Chicago, Illinois, and the chairman of the board of editors for *Encyclopaedia Britannica*.

GREGORY R. ANRIG is the president of the Educational Testing Service in Princeton, New Jersey.

W. N. BENDER is a professor at both Bluefield State College in Bluefield, West Virginia, and Concord College in Athens, West Virginia.

GERALD W. BRACEY is the director of research and evaluation for the Cherry Creek School District in Englewood, Colorado.

R. FREEMAN BUTTS is the William F. Russell Professor Emeritus in the Foundation of Education at Columbia University's Teachers College and a senior fellow of the Kettering Foundation.

YVONNE CABALLERO - ALLEN is employed in the personnel office for the San Diego school district.

LEE CANTER is the president of Lee Canter & Associates in Santa Monica, California, and the developer of the Assertive Discipline program.

JOHN E. COONS is a professor of law at the University of California, Berkeley.

ROBERT L. CORD is a professor of political science at Northeastern University in Boston, Massachusetts.

DEAN C. CORRIGAN is the dean of education at Texas A&M University.

LARRY CUBAN is a professor of education at Stanford University and a member of the board of editorial consultants for *Phi Delta Kappan*.

RICHARD L. CURWIN is an assistant professor of education in the Department of Secondary Education at San Francisco State University.

LINDA DARLING-HAMMOND is the director of the RAND Corporation's Education and Human Resources Program in Washington, D.C.

JOHN DEWEY (1859–1952) was a philosopher and a leader in the field of education.

DAVID ELKIND is a professor of child study at Tufts University and a contributing editor to *Parents Magazine*.

SIEGFRIED ENGELMANN is a professor of education at the University of Oregon.

THERESE ENGELMANN holds a degree in psychology and practices law in Oregon.

DENNIS L. EVANS is the principal of Newport Harbor High School in Newport Beach, California, and an instructor of educational administration at the University of California, Irvine.

CLIFTON FADIMAN is a writer, editor, radio and television performer, and a member of the board of editors to *Encyclopaedia Britannica.*

DAVID GUTERSON teaches English at Bainbridge High School in Bainbridge Island, Washington.

E. D. HIRSCH, JR., is the Linden Kent Professor of English at the University of Virginia in Charlottesville, Virginia, and a member of the board of directors for the Foundations of Literacy Project.

JOHN HOLT (1923–1985) was an educator, a critic of public schooling, and the author of several influential books on education.

JAMES B. HUNT, JR., is a partner with the law firm of Poyner & Spriull in Raleigh, North Carolina, and is on the board of directors for the National Center for Education and the Economy.

ROBERT M. HUTCHINS (1879–1977) was the chancellor of the University of Chicago and director of the Center for the Study of Democratic Institutions.

LAWRENCE KOHLBERG (1927–1987) was a professor of education and the director of the Center for Moral Education at Harvard University.

ALFIE KOHN lectures widely on cooperative learning and other educational issues.

WILLIAM KONNERT is a professor of educational administration at Kent State University in Kent, Ohio.

ZELENE LOVITT is a reading recovery teacher at Janie Stark Elementary School in the Carrollton/Farmers Branch Independence School District of Texas.

RICHARD D. McCALLUM is a professor of education at Saint Mary's College of California.

FLORETTA DUKES McKENZIE is the former superintendent of public schools for Washington, D.C.

ALLEN N. MENDLER is a psychoeducational consultant and a school psychologist in Rochester, New York.

CHARLES NEVI is the director of curriculum and instruction for the Puyallup School District in Puyallup, Washington.

JEANNIE OAKES is an associate professor in the Graduate School of Education at the University of California, Los Angeles.

ALBERTO M. OCHOA is the chairman of the Department of Policy Studies in Language and Cross-Cultural Education at San Diego State University and the director of the Southern California National Origin Desegregation Center.

W. JAMES POPHAM is a professor in the Graduate School of Education at the University of California, Los Angeles, and the director of a Los Angeles test development agency.

DIANE RAVITCH is an adjunct professor of history and education at the Teachers College of Columbia University.

RICHARD RODRIGUEZ is an associate editor of Pacific News Service.

CARL R. ROGERS (1902–1987) was a noted psychologist and educator who taught at the University of Chicago and the University of Wisconsin, Madison.

ALBA A. ROSENMAN is an associate professor of secondary education at Ball State University.

KEVIN RYAN is a professor of education and the director of the Center for the Advancement of Ethics and Character at Boston University.

PETER SCALES is the deputy director of the Center for Early Adolescence in the School of Medicine at the University of North Carolina at Chapel Hill.

B. F. SKINNER (1904–1990), noted psychologist and influential exponent of behaviorism, was appointed to the William James Chair in psychology at Harvard University in 1947. He remained on the faculty there until his retirement.

ROBERT E. SLAVIN is the director of the Elementary School Program in the Center for Research on Effective Schooling for Disadvantaged Students at The Johns Hopkins University.

JOEL SPRING is a professor in the College of Education at the University of Cincinnati.

STEPHEN TCHUDI is a professor in the Department of English at the University of Nevada at Reno.

JOSEF WENDEL is the principal of Newbury High School and the assistant to the superintendent of schools in Newbury, Ohio.

PAUL WOODRING is the Distinguished Service Professor Emeritus of the University at Western Washington University in Bellingham, Washington.

EDWARD A. WYNNE is a professor of education at the University of Illinois, Chicago Circle.

INDEX